AF600525

PLAY AS SYMBOL OF THE WORLD

STUDIES IN CONTINENTAL THOUGHT

John Sallis, *editor*

PLAY AS SYMBOL OF THE WORLD

AND OTHER WRITINGS

Eugen Fink

Translated by Ian Alexander Moore and
Christopher Turner

Indiana University Press

Bloomington and Indianapolis

This book is a publication of

Indiana University Press
Office of Scholarly Publishing
Herman B Wells Library 350
1320 East 10th Street
Bloomington, Indiana 47405 USA

iupress.indiana.edu

Published in German as Eugen Fink, Gesamtausgabe 7: Spiel als Weltsymbol, ed. Cathrin Nielsen and Hans Rainer Sepp © 2010 Verlag Karl Alber, Freiburg im Breisgau

The paper used in this publication meets the minimum requirements of the American National Standard for Information Sciences—Permanence of Paper for Printed Library Materials, ANSI Z39.48-1992.

Manufactured in the United States of America

Cataloging information is available from the Library of Congress.

ISBN 978-0-253-02105-2 (cloth)
ISBN 978-0-253-02117-5 (ebook)

1 2 3 4 5 21 20 19 18 17 16

Contents

Appendices

PLAY AS SYMBOL OF THE WORLD

Translators' Introduction

Ian Alexander Moore and Christopher Turner

The greatest phenomenon of phenomenology for me is Fink.
Edmund Husserl[1]

TRANSLATED HERE ARE Eugen Fink's collected writings on play, published in German in 2010 as Volume 7 of the *Eugen Fink Gesamtausgabe*.[2] In addition to drafts, seminar notes, and radio lectures recorded from 1954 to 1973 on the philosophical significance of play, this text contains the first English translation of Fink's magnum opus, *Play as Symbol of the World*. Published in 1960, though first delivered as a lecture course at the University of Freiburg in 1957, it should be numbered among other great works published by former students of Martin Heidegger around this time: Hannah Arendt's *The Human Condition* (1958), Emmanuel Levinas's *Totality and Infinity* (1961), and Hans-Georg Gadamer's *Truth and Method* (1960),[3] which also devotes considerable attention to the theme of play.[4] Also included in this text is our revised translation of Fink's "Oasis of Happiness: Thoughts toward an Ontology of Play." Together, the writings collected here constitute the most intensive and comprehensive philosophical engagement with play in the twentieth century, a theme that is all too often considered to be mere idle amusement, to be valid only as a restful pause which helps us return all the more energized to what is "really" important, or to be subordinate to pedagogy as a means by which to educate the child and socialize the adult more effectively. Against these traditional views of play, Fink offers a speculative phenomenology of play that begins from the sort of play with which we are all familiar and from there attempts to reflect on play, moving from child's play all the way up to cosmic play, where the world itself is conceived as a "*game without a player*."[5] Along the way, he broaches such wide-ranging topics as embodiment, ontology, theology, sports, pedagogy, mimesis, cult practices, mythology, drama, and anthropology.

The afterword to the German volume, written by Cathrin Nielsen and Hans Rainer Sepp and also included in this translation, explains the philosophical trajectory and significance of Fink's lifelong work on the theme of play. On account of this, and since many readers of this text will be encountering Fink's independent philosophical work for the first time,[6] we thought it might prove useful to situate this material within the context of Fink's life before explaining some of our translation decisions. Because of its importance for Continental Philosophy as it is practiced above all in the Anglophone world, we will focus in particular on Fink's relation to Husserl, Heidegger, and the French reception of phenomenology.[7]

Eugen Fink's Life

Fink was born in Konstanz, Germany, on December 11, 1905, the fourth of six children. During the First World War, he and his brother Karl August Fink, later a Catholic theologian and church historian, were sent to live with an uncle who would prove to be formative for their education. Fink would accompany his uncle, a priest by calling, on his trips to minister to the sick, and his uncle tutored Fink in various subjects such as Latin. Fink was also able to avail himself of his uncle's ample library, where he discovered Kant and Nietzsche and first began to ponder the meaning of existence. By 1918, Fink was well equipped to begin secondary schooling at the prestigious humanistic Gymnasium in Konstanz (attended also by the likes of Heidegger[8]), skipping two grades and excelling with his extraordinary memory. In addition to Kant and Nietzsche, he read Hegel, Hume, and Giordano Bruno during this time, and was even an active member of the Konstanz Kant Society as a teenager. After passing the university entrance examination second in his class, he began his university studies in Münster in the summer semester of 1925. His courses were mostly in German language and literature, though one was devoted to the history of modern philosophy from Descartes to Kant.[9]

The next semester found Fink in Freiburg, where, with the exception of a semester in Berlin in 1926, he would remain until 1939. Among his classes that first semester was Husserl's "Basic Problems of Logic." Apparently, Fink would not take notes in class. Jan Patočka relates that Husserl noticed this and thought sarcastically, "That's going to produce 'great' results when he comes up for exams." Yet when Fink did come up for exams, he had everything memorized, which "he recited . . . as if reading from a book."[10] Fink would continue to impress Husserl over the next few years, attending all of Husserl's courses (except when Fink was in Berlin) until Husserl retired in 1928.[11] In February 1928, Fink submitted a prize-winning essay on the imagination. Husserl was involved in the evaluation process, at least to some extent, and Fink would have discussed the topic with Husserl as late as December 1927. It clearly must have impressed Husserl, for, in 1928, Husserl asked Fink to become his second research assistant, alongside Ludwig Landgrebe. Fink agreed, thus beginning a decade of collaboration that would see revolutions in phenomenology and politics that would profoundly shape Fink's life and thought.[12]

1928 was also the year Heidegger came to Freiburg as Husserl's successor. By this time, Heidegger was no longer merely rumored to be a "hidden king"; the publication of *Being and Time* in 1927 had established him as one of the most important living philosophers. Fink himself had already begun to wrestle with Heidegger's book in 1927.[13] Now, while working alongside Husserl, he was also able to witness Husserl's philosophical heir at work. Fink attended every one of Heidegger's courses from 1928 through 1931. He was present at Heidegger's famous debate with Ernst Cassirer in Davos, and he continued to follow Heidegger's university activities intermittently thereafter.[14] Two of these courses in particular, Heidegger's *Einleitung in die Philosophie* (Introduction to philosophy) (Winter Semester 1928–1929, Heidegger's first as Husserl's successor in Freiburg) and *The Fundamental Concepts of Metaphysics* (Winter Semester 1929–1930) were undoubtedly great catalysts for Fink's appreciation of the philosophical significance of play and the concept of world. It is in this regard that we may begin to understand Heidegger's later dedication of *The Fundamental Concepts of Metaphysics* to Fink: "*In Memory of Eugen Fink.* He listened to this lecture course with thoughtful reticence, and in so doing experienced something unthought of his own that determined his path."[15]

It was also during this time that Fink got to know Heidegger personally and to begin a philosophical dialogue with him.[16] Heidegger later recalled how Fink impressed him that first semester as "likely to achieve something."[17] This surely contributed to his decision to serve as the referee for Fink's 1929 dissertation, which built on his prize essay on the imagination and was directed by Husserl. Fink defended his dissertation on December 13, 1929; it was the only time both Husserl and Heidegger served on a dissertation committee, and perhaps even the final time they met publicly.[18]

Fink quickly became aware of the great differences between Husserl and Heidegger's thought, as his notes from 1928 to 1929 reveal.[19] Yet rather than picking sides, Fink preferred to blaze his own path, even if it was necessary for him to take Husserl and Heidegger as constant companions along the way. Husserl, for his part, did not notice these differences immediately. Only later in 1929 did he realize just how radical Heidegger's project had become, and how little it corresponded to Husserl's own phenomenological undertakings. Indeed, just one week before Fink's dissertation defense, Husserl wrote of Heidegger's work, "I must reject it entirely as to its method and in the essentials of its content."[20]

As Husserl and Heidegger grew more distant, Husserl and Fink grew closer. Fink became Husserl's only assistant in 1930,[21] and by 1931, Husserl would claim that, despite what Fink had learned from Heidegger, Fink was "the only student who remained loyal" to him.[22] Yet such loyalty by no means entailed a fawning adherence to the letter of Husserl's doctrine. Rather, Fink's loyalty to Husserl involved critical engagement, independent thinking, and a profound collaborative effort with Husserl to advance the spirit of phenomenology. It was precisely this effort that resulted in Fink's important revisions for the German edition of Husserl's *Cartesian Meditations,* as well as what would later be published as Fink's *Sixth Cartesian Meditation: The Idea of a Transcendental Theory of Method,* "one of those famous unknown works in philosophy that haunt the margins of established texts while seldom if ever coming to light themselves."[23] Fortunately, these texts have come to light, and it is thanks in large part to the exemplary scholarship of Ronald Bruzina that we can appreciate just how pivotal Fink was for the development of Husserl's phenomenology during the final decade of his life. Indeed, these texts, which, in Bruzina's words, "contributed positively and directly to the displacement of a Cartesian-based exposition of phenomenology," were so valued by Husserl that he suggested they be published under both his and Fink's name.[24] And the German edition of the *Cartesian Meditations* was, Husserl once wrote, to be "the main work of my life"![25]

According to Fink, it was not for philosophical reasons that this proposal failed to come to fruition.[26] After the Nazis seized power, Husserl was officially dismissed from the university as a "non-Aryan" in April 1933. Fink, for his part, was unable to submit his *Sixth Cartesian Meditation* as a *Habilitationsschrift* (a second dissertation required for teaching at the university level). Though he was not Jewish, his collaboration with Husserl had compromised his legitimacy in the eyes of the Nazis.[27] Rather than distance himself from Husserl, however, or try to align himself with Heidegger instead,[28] Fink went public, publishing a condensed version of the meditation, together with a foreword by Husserl, under the title "The Phenomenological Philosophy of Edmund Husserl and Contemporary Criticism."[29] At the end of the forward, Husserl writes:

> At my request, the author of the following essay has undertaken to outline a discussion with my critics which is necessary in order to clarify the principal misunderstandings of phenomenology. This is a task for which he is well qualified. I have guided his philosophical studies from the very start of his career, and since their conclusion he [h]as been my assistant for the past five years and has had almost daily contact with me. In this way, he has not only become thoroughly familiar with my philosophical intentions, but also with the principal contents of concrete unpublished investigations. I have carefully read through this essay at the request of the able editors of the *Kant-Studien,* and I am happy to be able to state that it contains no sentence which I could not completely accept as my own or openly acknowledge as my own conviction.[30]

Although such a statement could not have helped Fink politically—indeed the publication of his article was so scandalous that he was cut off by the organization from which he had been receiving funds to edit Husserl's Bernau manuscripts on time-consciousness—it is a revealing and courageous testament to their philosophical collaboration.[31]

Fink's decision to continue to co-philosophize with Husserl rather than to abandon his mentor, friend, and collaborator would result in more hardships for him in the coming years. An academic career in Germany was no longer possible under the Third Reich. Funding already awarded would be rescinded, and further funding sought in vain. Considerations of moving elsewhere with Husserl, such as to the University of California at Los Angeles, came to naught. Nonetheless, thanks to the help of various international institutions and munificent friends, Fink was able to keep working alongside Husserl in Freiburg during the final years of Husserl's life. This included organizing the entirety of Husserl's manuscript materials with Ludwig Landgrebe, editing some of this material himself, working with Husserl on such texts as would later become *The Crisis of the European Sciences and Transcendental Phenomenology,* leading private seminars and writing on Husserl's behalf, and of course developing his own ideas. Fink stayed by Husserl in the months leading up to his death in April 1938, and he delivered a moving eulogy at his cremation.[32]

Rather than abating, Fink's difficulties actually became more acute after Husserl's death. Seeing that there was little hope for Husserlian phenomenology in Germany, Fink aided Father Herman Leo Van Breda in secretly transferring Husserl's manuscripts to Leuven in 1938, where Fink himself would immigrate in March 1939. Landgrebe joined him in April, and together they proceeded to spend the next year transcribing Husserl's handwritten manuscripts, producing over 2,800 pages of material. Here, for the first time in his life, Fink was able to lecture at the university level. He was also able to deepen his friendship with Van Breda and Landgrebe, as well as to have exciting philosophical conversations with visitors such as Alphonse de Waelhens and Maurice Merleau-Ponty.[33] Yet this haven from Nazi oppression would be short-lived.

On May 10, 1940, Germany invaded Belgium, and Fink and his first wife, Martl (d. 1964), were arrested the same day as putative members of the anti-Nazi "Fifth Column." Without luggage or proper attire, they were imprisoned in Leuven, transferred to Brussels on May 15, and then crammed into cattle cars and shipped to concentration camps in France. (Fink went first to one near Orléans, then to one in St.-Cyprien; his wife to a camp near Bordeaux).[34] Some passengers were shot en route, and they barely escaped a lynch mob in Tours. Conditions in the camp at St.-Cyprien were dreadful: many starved to death, and though Fink survived, he would never fully recover his health afterward.

Ironically, it was the German occupation army that "liberated" Fink after the armistice with France. After a brief return to Belgium, Fink, formerly a Fifth Column prisoner, was now drafted into the German army and even offered an officer's position, which he refused. He was instead assigned to aerial surveillance around Freiburg, which he performed until the French took control of Freiburg in 1945. Yet rather than being imprisoned by the French army, as other German soldiers were at this time, Fink so impressed a French officer with his life story—told in fluent French—that he was allowed to go free.

Shortly after the French invasion, many previously ardent Nazis resumed their teaching activities at the University of Freiburg with only modest penalties, whereas Fink, who was never committed to the Nazi cause, now had to struggle to make ends meet. Although he had not completed his *Habilitation,* in light of the circumstances he was nonetheless granted an entry-level teaching position as a *Privatdozent* (unsalaried lecturer) on the condition that he do so. (Only in 1948 would Fink become a full professor of philosophy and pedagogy.) Fink was now faced with having to decide what to submit. Should he, for example, present more recent work, something more representative of his current interests? Or should he attempt to resuscitate Husserlian phenomenology, which had become all but forgotten in the war years? As "an act of piety," he opted for the latter. "I wanted," Fink wrote to Husserl's son Gerhart, ". . . to give expression to the fact that I was taking up the academic office of teaching in Freiburg as a resumption of a tradition that Edmund Husserl had brought into being. I could have chosen another work, one that lies on a higher level and that gave objective form to a ten-year-long intellectual development. But it is a matter here of symbolically taking up again the thinking that is Husserl's." Fink accordingly submitted the very work he had been planning on submitting over a decade earlier, his *Sixth Cartesian Meditation.* Evaluated favorably (albeit ineptly) by the psychologist Robert Heiss, who held the chair for philosophy and psychology at Freiburg, it was accepted by the philosophy faculty in early 1946. Heidegger, despite his recent mandatory retirement, had been solicited to provide an opinion on Fink's work. As Fink relates, Heidegger simply said that "as the work was fully authorized by Husserl it would need no further attestation." This unfortunately led to the false rumor that Fink had submitted his *Habilitationsschrift* under Heidegger's directorship, a rumor that would taint Fink's reputation, as well as his relation to Husserl's family and legacy, for some time. Fink's qualifying lecture was nevertheless on a topic much closer to his current and future research: "Nietzsche's Metaphysics of Play."[35]

In the years after the war, basic necessities were hard to come by, especially for an underpaid academic with two young children to provide for. Fortunately, Fink had befriended many farmers during his time as an aerial sentry in the Black Forest, and they were happy to share their crops with "the professor," as they called him. And he too was happy to help with the harvest. Americans and other friends abroad provided aid as well.

In spite of the catastrophic events of the war and the trying times that followed, Fink was able to devote himself wholeheartedly to teaching, which he saw as an opportunity "to offer [his students] new perspectives" after the war, "to provide a ground for ungrounded existence," and "to point to possible ways into the future."[36] Fink's pedagogy took many forms. In addition to always being available for students and to promoting their interests, he helped found the Freiburg community college in 1946, where, in addition to his university activities, he would teach and lecture for many years. In 1948, he was invited to spend a year as a guest professor at the New School for Social Research and at the University of Chicago, though bureaucratic difficulties prevented him from doing so. In 1950, he founded the Husserl archives in Freiburg, which he would lead until 1971. As the director of the Freiburg Studium Generale from 1954 to 1971, he fostered collaboration across disciplines. He also played a decisive role in the formulation and implementation of pedagogic reform in Germany, and organized conferences on the themes of pedagogy.

In addition to prolific publications on topics such as child pedagogy, ontology, phenomenology, poetry, anthropology, and fashion, Fink stayed busy lecturing around Europe and especially the former Yugoslavia,[37] delivering radio lectures such as "Oasis of Happiness," "Play and Celebration," and "The World-Significance of Play,"[38] and taking part in many international conferences. This led to calls to teach in Cologne (1948), Berlin (1957), and Vienna (1965), all of which Fink declined. In 1957, he was asked to take over the vacant chair of philosophy that both Heidegger and Husserl had previously occupied at the University of Freiburg. As early as 1954, Heidegger was already promoting Fink as a viable successor. Despite Heidegger's wishes and successful advocacy, when Fink was offered the position in 1957, he turned it down.[39] Not only was Fink content with the chair for philosophy and pedagogy he already held, one that he had worked so hard to build over the past decade, but after the many years of tension surrounding Heidegger's politics and personal failings—which certainly affected Fink's own life and career—Fink was also probably hesitant to be seen as publicly following in Heidegger's footsteps.

This did not, however, mean that Fink would not continue to draw on Heidegger throughout his writings. Quite the contrary. Heidegger remained an important interlocutor for Fink throughout his entire career. Nor did it mean that Fink would have nothing to do with Heidegger as a person or public figure. In fact, despite considerable resistance on the part of the university, Fink even endeavored to provide avenues for Heidegger to philosophize publicly after the denazification proceedings resulted in his forced retirement and ban from teaching in 1946 (lifted de facto in 1951[40]). In the 1950s, for example, Fink and Max Müller organized biweekly meetings in which Freiburg faculty would assemble to discuss and interpret texts from Greek antiquity. Heidegger attended several of these "Graeca" with enthusiasm.[41] Together with Fink, Heidegger also participated in various events of the Freiburg Studium Generale, organized first under Max Müller's directorship and then under Fink's. One of these, organized by Müller, Fink, and Bernhard Welte for their seminar students, took place in 1950 in Todtnauberg (the village where Heidegger's cabin was located), and was the first university-affiliated event in which Heidegger participated after his forced retirement. Heidegger availed himself of the occasion by lecturing on the "Wirklichkeit, Illusion, und Möglichkeit der Universität" (The actuality, illusion, and possibility of the university) and reading his short text "The Pathway" aloud for the first time.[42] There was also the 1952 "Colloquium über Dialektik" (Colloquium on dialectics), which was held in Muggenbrunn, not far from Heidegger's cabin in Todtnauberg. Other leading participants included Müller, Walter Biemel, and above all Eugen Fink.[43] The third noteworthy event was in 1955 and addressed the problem of the unity of the sciences. Heidegger's lecture "Science and Reflection" stood at the center of the discussion, to which Heidegger contributed by closely engaging Fink's introductory essay, "Exposition des Problems der Einheit der Wissenschaften" (Exposition of the problem of the unity of the sciences). This in turn led the participants to devote close attention to Fink's text and to bring it into dialogue with Heidegger's.[44] Finally, through the resources of the Studium Generale, Fink provided the space in which Heidegger could deliver his famous 1962 lecture "Time and Being" before a full audience at the university. Later that year, Fink participated in Heidegger's Todtnauberg seminar on this topic, which the Studium Generale sponsored as well.[45]

Fink would also frequently visit Heidegger at his home in Freiburg. During one of these visits he proposed to Heidegger that they hold a seminar together in which Fink could test out his interpretation of Heraclitus. Heidegger agreed, and even planned to conduct it with Fink over several semesters. Although it only lasted one semester (Winter 1966–1967), and would turn out to be Heidegger's final seminar at the university, this public dialogue between the two Freiburg philosophers was considered to be an extraordinary event, so much so that it was published under joint authorship a few years later to great acclaim.[46]

We should also mention Fink's particular importance for the French reception of phenomenology. This can be seen in his edition of Husserl's "Origin of Geometry," which he first published in the *Revue Internationale de Philosophie* in 1939,[47] and above all in his *Kant-Studien* article, which Leonard Lawlor notes "is mentioned almost continuously in the French interpretations of Husserl during the 1950s," such as by Paul Ricoeur, Jean-François Lyotard, and Tran Duc Thao.[48] It was also important for Jean-Paul Sartre, Emmanuel Levinas, and especially Merleau-Ponty, who wrote in the *Phenomenology of Perception*, "The best formulation of the reduction is probably given by Eugen Fink, Husserl's assistant, when he spoke [in his famous Husserl essay] of 'wonder' in the face of the world."[49] Jacques Derrida cites Fink's essay in all of his Husserl books, including his translation of and commentary on the "Origin of Geometry."[50] In a 1966 review of

Fink's *Studien zur Phänomenologie* (which contains the *Kant-Studien* piece), Derrida spoke of this book as a "remarkable monument," one that "assured Fink's thought a unique and irreducible place alongside Nietzsche's, Husserl's, and Heidegger's."[51] Indeed, Lawlor has argued that Fink's article marks "the source of Derrida's interpretation of Husserl," and even that:

> Published before Heidegger's "The Letter on Humanism," Fink's essay must be seen as the source of all contemporary anti-humanism, all contemporary philosophies of the other.[52]

It was not just Fink's work on Husserl and phenomenology that influenced twentieth-century French thinkers, however. His writings on play were also crucial for figures such as Derrida, Kostas Axelos, and Henri Lefebvre. After praising Fink's *Studien zur Phänomenologie* in the previously mentioned review, Derrida wrote that "Fink's works on Nietzsche and play are the other traces of a great thought in our epoch."[53] Derrida's various remarks on play, especially on the play of the world and the play of *différance,* may be fruitfully read alongside Fink's *Play as Symbol of the World,* which Derrida himself cites in *Of Grammatology.*[54] The same could be said for Fink's reading of Nietzsche, which endeavors to show how Nietzsche's philosophy—especially as it pertains to the theme of play—exceeds Heidegger's relegation of it to the final stage in the history of metaphysics.[55] The significance of Fink's reading was recognized by the French in various ways: Fink was invited to participate in the major colloquium on Nietzsche at Cerisy-la-Salle in 1972, alongside the likes of Sarah Kofman, Jean-Luc Nancy, Lyotard, Derrida, and Gilles Deleuze (who had also invited Fink to the 1964 Nietzsche conference at Royaumont);[56] articles on Fink's interpretation were written for important French journals;[57] and Fink's Nietzsche book was translated into French in 1965, five years after its publication in German.

Axelos, for his part, develops Fink's ideas concerning play and the world in such works as *Vers la pensée planétaire* (Toward a planetary thinking), *Le jeu du monde* (The play of the world), and *Horizons du monde* (Horizons of the world).[58] Axelos was also the editor of the book series *Arguments,* which, in addition to Fink's Nietzsche book, published French translations of Fink's *Play as Symbol of the World* and *Studien zur Phänomenologie,* as well as several works by Lefebvre, who himself develops Fink's work on these themes in creative and interesting ways, such as with respect to *mondialisation* (a kind of "becoming-worldwide" or "worldization" that is to be thought prior to what we usually mean by "globalization").[59] Fink's work, especially in its connection to Axelos and Lefebvre, has also been shown to have influenced Deleuze's notion of "planetary becoming."[60]

Another French philosopher who engages with Fink's later works is Emmanuel Levinas. Earlier, in the late 1920s, Fink and Levinas had attended Heidegger's seminars together, and they were both present at the Davos event in 1929.[61] In

God, Death, and Time, Levinas is in close dialogue with Fink's *Metaphysik und Tod* (Metaphysics and death).[62] Here, as well as in *Otherwise Than Being* and *Proper Names,* he also develops his notion of responsibility for the other by contrasting it with Fink's appreciation of the lack of responsibility that is characteristic of play.[63]

Toward the end of his life, Fink received numerous awards and honors for his accomplishments, including an honorary doctorate from Leuven in 1971[64] and induction into the Institut International de Philosophie. After a kidney operation and the onset of diabetes, Fink retired as an emeritus professor of Freiburg in 1971. On July 25, 1975, after a long period of illness, he died of a heart attack.

Yet Fink's philosophy did not disappear with his passing. Through the efforts of students and friends such as Egon Schütz and Franz-Anton Schwarz, as well as Fink's second wife, Susanne, dozens of his works were published posthumously. A major symposium was held in Freiburg in honor of the ten-year anniversary of his death,[65] and an eight-day conference on Fink's work took place in 1994 at Cerisy-la-Salle, France.[66] More recently, in 2006, the Karl Alber publishing house launched the *Eugen Fink Gesamtausgabe,* a twenty-volume edition of Fink's collected works edited by Stephan Grätzel, Cathrin Nielsen, and Hans Rainer Sepp, with the assistance of Annette Hilt and Franz-Anton Schwarz.[67] Several important volumes have also been published in German dealing with themes such as Fink's social philosophy, anthropology, cosmology, and pedagogy.[68] We hope that the present translation will help to move the Anglophone study of Fink beyond his significance as a colleague of Husserl and Heidegger and to inaugurate a greater consideration of his original contributions to twentieth- and twenty-first-century thought.

Translation Issues

In our translation, we have endeavored to stay fairly close to Fink's German. We have not, however, felt the need always to follow his syntax. The following terms present particular difficulties:

Spiel in German means both "play" and "game." We have rendered it both ways depending on context. When Fink is discussing a kind of play that we would not usually call a game in English, such as playing with a doll, we translate *ein Spiel* as "instance of play" or "kind of play," since translating it as "a play" would lead one to think of a theatrical performance or *Schauspiel,* which Fink also uses. To retain the connotation of play, we have rendered *Schauspiel,* for its part, as "dramatic play," and sometimes as "dramatic play or spectacle," when the notion of *Schau* or "spectacle" seems especially important, such as in Fink's discussion of ancient cult play, where he has in mind not merely the dramas of the Dionysia but also the pageantry of the Panathenaea, the *ludi* of the Roman circus, and in general any spectacle in which there was celebration of the gods or divine epiphany. When Fink uses the term *Darstellungsspiel* (literally, "play of portrayal"), he appears to mean more than just theatrical plays, where there are both human beings and the roles they perform on the stage. He appears to mean any instance of play in which one takes on or portrays a role, which would include games like charades.[69] We have therefore endeavored to retain the valence of role-playing in most instances of our translation of this term and its cognates. Other important *Spiel*-words without direct counterparts in English include *auf dem Spiel* (at stake), *aufs Spiel setzen* (to put on the line, to put at stake), *erspielen* (to attain, to play out), *Spielraum* (leeway, though also and more literally "play space"), *Schauspieler* (actor), *Spielzeug* (toy, though also "plaything"; literally, an "instrument of play"), and *verspielen* (squander).

Fink uses several words for the world, including *Universum* (universe), *Kosmos* (cosmos), *Weltganze* (world-whole, whole of the world), and *Weltall* and *Weltallheit* (world-totality, totality of the world). Sometimes, *das All,* which is another expression for "the universe," is rendered in English as "the All," though mostly it is rendered as "the totality." Fink also uses two different terms for beings within the world, namely, *innenweltlich* and *binnenweltlich,* translated here as "innerworldly" and "intraworldly."

Sometimes, Fink uses the German suffix *-haft* in ways that cannot be captured by familiar English suffixes. For example, while *sinnlich* means "sensuous" in Fink's text, *sinnhaft* often means "imbued, laden, or suffused with sense," where "sense" can signify both meaning and that which is sensed. While *spielerisch* means "playful" in the familiar, lighthearted sense, *spielhaft* means "playful" in the sense of "pertaining to play." While *weltlich* means "worldly," *welthaft* is often better rendered as "that which pertains to the world" or as "worlded." We have tried to retain these subtle distinctions in our translation, though this has not always been possible, especially with *spielhaft.* The reader should accordingly bear the more the literal sense of "playful" in mind when it appears throughout the translation.

There are also several words for "being" in Fink's text. In order to avoid ambiguity, *Sein* has always been translated as "Being," with a capital *B,* or as "ontological," such as when it appears in a word like *Seinsverfassung* (ontological constitution). However, its present participle, *seiend,* has sometimes been rendered as "existing," and its nominalized present participle, *Seiendes,* as "beings," "a being," or "that which is." *Wesen,* as in the syntagm *menschliches Wesen,* has also been translated as "being." Otherwise, it is rendered as "essence." We have usually translated *Mensch* as "human being," though sometimes simply as "human" when adding "being" would have been cumbersome or confusing.

Unlike Heidegger, Fink does not appear to maintain a distinction between *Dasein* and *Existenz,* even though he uses both to refer predominantly to the human being. We have therefore rendered both as "existence." We have, however, followed the lead of Heidegger translators in rendering the German adjectives *existenzial* and *existenziell* as "existential" and "existentiell," respectively.

Another important issue concerns words related to *Schein,* which we have translated as "appearance" and sometimes as "shining." When Fink speaks of the *Rückschein* of the world in play, he seems to mean not only that the world "shines back" or "is reflected" in play, but that the world offers "proof" of itself in play. (*Rückschein* is a common word for "return receipt.") We have therefore at times translated *Rückschein* as "proof of the shining back." *Anschein,* for its part, has been translated as "semblance" or sometimes also as "appearance"; *aufscheinen* as "to appear," "to come to light," or "to shine forth"; *erscheinen* as "to come to appear," "to shine forth," or just "to appear"; *Erscheinung* as "appearance" or "manifestation"; *scheinhaft* as "illusory"; and *zum Schein* as "pretend" or "in make-believe."

Schein also appears in a couple of the many words Fink uses to describe aspects and degrees of reproduction and reflection. These words have been rendered for the most part as follows: *Spiegelschein* (mirror appearance), *Widerschein* (reflection), *Abbild* (reproduction), *bildhaft* and *bildlich* (imagistic), *Kopie* (copy), *Mimesis* (mimesis), *Nachahmung* (imitation), *Nachbild* (afterimage), *nachbilden* (to copy), *nachbildlich* and *nachbildnerisch* (residual), *Reflex* (reflection), *Sinnbild* (sense-image), *Spiegelbild* (mirror-image), *Spiegelung* (mirroring, mirror-image), and *Urbild* (archetype).

Finally, some of Fink's oft-cited basic phenomena of human existence have been rendered differently depending on context: *Kampf* as either "struggle" or "battle" (whereas "warrior" and "fighter" are translations of *Kämpfer*), *Herrschaft* as "ruling" or sometimes "dominance," and *Arbeit* as "work" or "labor."

Translators' notes and interpolations in the body of the text and in the endnotes have been placed in square brackets. The pagination of the *Gesamtausgabe* volume is given in square brackets in the running heads. When applicable, numerals in roman type refer to the first German editions of Fink's texts (for further information, see appendix 1). Editorial interpolations have been placed in curly brackets. Since Fink does not use footnotes, the German editors' footnotes have been left unbracketed. The editors' notes explain the emendations and the variations in the different manuscripts, typescripts, and published versions of Fink's texts, and provide references to texts that Fink cites. We have revised these references, and added others when appropriate, for the Anglophone audience. Some of the manuscript variations and emendations are only relevant for the philologist or German reader; in such cases, they have been omitted. We have also provided notes explaining other translation issues of which it would be helpful for the English reader to be aware.

The following abbreviations are employed:

D = Printed text
MS = Manuscript
TS = Typescript

The German editors' explanations of the layout of the volume and the individual texts contained in it can be found in appendix 1, their afterword in appendix 2, our bibliography of Fink's works available in English in appendix 3, and our bibliography of secondary literature on Fink in English in appendix 4.

Acknowledgments

The translators would like to convey their sincere thanks to Ronald Bruzina, Elizabeth Rottenberg, Will McNeill, Katie Homan, and James Griffith for their help on earlier drafts of the translation and our introduction. We also thank the participants of the 2013 DePaul German reading group, who kindly agreed to spend two quarters reading Fink's writings on play with us. We are also especially grateful to the editors of the German volume, Cathrin Nielsen and Hans Rainer Sepp, not only for their admirable efforts to make Fink's works more widely known throughout the world, but also for taking the time to review and approve our translation of their afterword. In a few instances, we benefited from consulting Hans Hildenbrand and Alex Lindenberg's translation of *Play as Symbol of the World* into French. Needless to say, responsibility for any errors lies solely on us.

We gratefully acknowledge *Purlieu Journal* for allowing us to reprint material from an earlier version of "Oasis of Happiness." Ian Alexander Moore would like to express his gratitude to Dale Wilkerson, who first turned him on to Fink's writings on play. Christopher Turner would like to thank Françoise Dastur, whose seminar on Merleau-Ponty at DePaul University in 2010 spurred him to begin reading Fink soon afterward. Finally, we would like to thank Dee Mortensen at Indiana University Press for her encouragement and advocacy.

Oasis of Happiness

Thoughts toward an Ontology of Play {1957}

In our century that is plagued by the racket of machines, insight into the great significance of play within the structure[1] of human existence is on the rise for the leading intellects of cultural criticism, the pioneers of modern pedagogy, and academics of anthropological disciplines. It permeates the self-consciousness of the contemporary human being to an astounding degree, a consciousness that is reflected in literature. And it is documented in the passionate interest of the masses in play and sport. Play is affirmed and cultivated as a vital impulse of independent worth with its own status. It is thought to be a remedy for the harms of a contemporary technocratic civilization. And it is extolled as a rejuvenating, life-renewing power—like a plunge back into a morning-fresh primordiality and plastic creativity. Certainly there were times in human history that bore the mark of play more than our own, times that were more cheerful, more relaxed, more playful, times that knew more leisure and had closer contact with the heavenly Muses—but no age had more objective play-possibilities and play-opportunities, because none had at its disposal so gigantic a life-apparatus. Playgrounds and sports fields are part of urban planning. Customary games in all lands and nations are brought into international contact. Toys are manufactured through industrial mass production. But the question remains open as to whether our age has achieved a deeper and more compelling understanding of the *essence* of play, whether it has at its disposal a comprehensive perspective on the manifold manifestations of play, whether it has adequate insight into the *ontological sense* [Seinssinn] of the phenomenon of play, whether it knows philosophically what play and playing *are*. With this, we touch on the problem of an ontology of play.

In what follows, I will attempt to *reflect* [Besinnung] on the curious and peculiar ontological character of human play, to formulate its[2] structural moments conceptually, and to indicate the speculative concept of play in a preliminary manner. To some, this may appear to be a dry and abstract affair. Such people would prefer to immediately feel a breeze of the wafting lightness of playing life, of its productive fullness, its effervescent richness and its inexhaustible charm. The witty essay, which plays with the listener or reader to a certain extent, and which elicits the enchanting subtlety of words and things in surprising word-plays, appears to be the appropriate stylistic element for a treatise on play. For, to speak *seriously* about play, let alone with the grim seriousness of the word-quibbler or concept-splitter, in the end stands as a bald contradiction and a terrible corruption of play. To be sure, philosophy has, in the case of Plato,[3] for instance, ventured the light, winged course even for great thoughts and contemplated play in such a way that this thinking itself became an elevated play of the spirit. But to this belongs Attic salt.[4]

The course of our simple and sober reflection is divided into three parts: 1. the preliminary characterization of the phenomenon of play; 2. the structural analysis of play; 3. the question concerning the connection between play and Being.

I

Play is a phenomenon of life that everyone is acquainted with firsthand. Each person has already played at some point and can speak from experience about it. Thus we are not dealing with an object of research that must be first discovered and laid bare. Play is universally known. Each of us is acquainted with playing and a multitude of forms of play, indeed from the testimony of our own experience. Each was already at some point a player. Familiarity with play is more than merely individual; it is a collective, public familiarity. Play is a well-known and common fact of the social world. One lives from time to time in play; one engages in it, enacts it; one is acquainted with it as a possibility of our own activity.[5] In this way, the individual is not encapsulated or imprisoned in his solitude. In playing we are certain of our social contact with our fellow human beings in an especially[6] intense way. Every kind of play, even the stubborn play of the loneliest child, has an interpersonal horizon. That we thus live *in* play, that we do not come upon it as an extrinsic occurrence, points to the human being as the "subject" of play. Does he alone play? Doesn't the animal also play, doesn't the surge of life's exuberance arise in the heart of every living creature? Biological research offers amazing descriptions of animal behavior, behavior that resembles human play in its mode of appearance and in the motor forms of its expression. But the critical question emerges as to whether that which appears similar in external form is similar *ontologically*. I am not here contesting that a biological concept of the behavior of play can be established on good grounds, such that the human being and the animal appear related. Nevertheless, it is not yet[7] decided which mode of Being has in each case the similar-looking behavior. This problem could be plausibly resolved only when the human being's ontological constitution and the animal's way of Being are ontologically elucidated and determined beforehand. We are of the opinion that human play has its own genuine sense—only in illicit metaphors could one speak of animal play or even of the play of the ancient gods. Ultimately, it comes down to precisely *how* we use the term "play," which fullness of sense we mean by it, which contour and which conceptual transparency we are able to give to this concept.

We are asking about human play. And in so doing, we are first of all inquiring into precisely the everyday familiarity with this phenomenon. Playing does not simply occur in our life like the vegetative processes; it is always an occurrence that is luminously *suffused with sense* [sinnhaft], an enactment that is experienced. We live in the enjoyment of the act of play (which, mind you, presupposes no reflexive self-consciousness). In many cases of intense abandonment to play we are far removed from any reflection—and yet all play is maintained in an understanding self-association of human life. The everyday, accessible take on the matter, a generally accepted "interpretation" that has come to predominate as self-evident, belongs to the familiarity with play as well. According to this interpretation, play is considered to be a *marginal* phenomenon of human life, a peripheral appearance, a possibility for existence that only occasionally lights up. Clearly, the great emphases of our earthly existence lie in other dimensions. To be sure, we see how prevalent play is, the vigorous interest that human beings have in play, the intensity with which they carry it out—but we nevertheless commonly contrast play, as "rest," as "relaxation," as cheerful idleness, with the serious and responsible activity of life. One says that the life of the human being is fulfilled in rigorous struggling and striving to attain insight, in striving for virtue and competence, for reputation, dignity and honor, for power and prosperity and the like. In contrast, play has the character of an occasional interruption, of a *break*, and is related to the genuine, serious carrying out of life in a sort of analogous manner to the way in which sleep is related to wakefulness. The human being must occasionally unharness the yoke of drudgery, get loose from the pressure of incessant strivings, disencumber himself from the weight of business, release himself from the confinement of organized time into a more casual relation with time, where time becomes expendable, indeed even so ample that we drive it away again with a "pastime." In the economy of managing our lives we alternate between "tension" and "relaxation," between business and diversion; we follow the well-known prescription of "hard weeks" and "joyous feasts." Thus, in the rhythm of conducting one's life, play appears to assume a legitimate, albeit limited, role. It is valid as a "supplement," as a complementary phenomenon, as a relaxing break, as a recreational activity, as a holiday from the burdens of duties, as something that cheers us up in the severe and gloomy landscape of our life. Ordinarily, one determines what play is by contrasting it with the seriousness of life, with the obligatory ethical disposition, with work, with the sober sense of reality in general. One conceives it more or less as trifling and amusing nonsense, as an unbounded roaming in the airy realm of fantasy and empty possibilities, as a running away from the resistance of things into a dreamy, utopian realm. But precisely in order to not fall captive to the Danaidean daemon of the modern world of work, in order to not unlearn laughing as a result of ethical rigorism, in order to not fall captive to mere factuality, play is recommended to contemporary human beings by cultural diagnosticians—as a therapeutic aid for the sick soul, as it were. But "how" is the nature of play understood in the case of such well-intended advice? Does it still count as a marginal phenomenon[8]—in contrast to seriousness, genuineness, work? Do we suffer, so to speak, merely from an excess of work, from an extremely manic frenzy for work, a gloomy, unbrightened seriousness? Do we need a little of the divine sense of lightness and the joyous levity of play, in order to again come close to the "birds of the sky" and the "lilies of the field"? Should play loosen up only a mental tension from which the contemporary human being with his immense life-apparatus suffers? As long as, in such trains of thought, one still naïvely operates within the popular antitheses of "work and play," of "play and the seriousness of life," and so forth, play is *not* understood in the content and depth of its Being. It remains stuck in the contrasting shadow of the putative counter-phenomena, and is thereby obscured and distorted. It is considered to be something non-serious, non-obligatory, and in-authentic, to be caprice and idleness. In positively recommending the curative effect of play, it becomes evident that one still considers it a marginal appearance, a peripheral counterweight, a seasoning for the heavy meal of our Being, as it were.

Whether, however, even the phenomenal character of play is grasped appropriately by such a perspective is more than questionable. On the face of it, admittedly, the life of adults no longer shows much of the elated charm of playful existence; their "games" are too often techniques of passing the time that have become routine and that betray their origin in boredom. Seldom are adults able to play without inhibition. However, play in children still appears to be an intact sphere of existence. Play is considered to be an element of childhood. But soon the course of life drives out such a "sphere," shattering the intact world of childhood, and the rougher winds of unprotected life take the upper hand: duty, care, and work tie down the life-energy of the young, adolescent human being. The more obvious the seriousness of life becomes, the more obviously, too, does play disappear in regard to its scope and significance. It is extolled as an upbringing "suitable for children" when this metamorphosis from a playing to a working human being is brought about without hard and brusque ruptures, when work is brought before the child almost as play—as a sort of methodical and disciplined play—when one lets the heavy and pressing weight come to the fore slowly. In this way one wants to preserve as much of the spontaneity, the fantasy and initiative of playing as possible. One wants to achieve from child's play an uninterrupted transition to a sort of creative joy in work. Behind this well-known pedagogical experiment we find the common view that play belongs, above all during childhood, to the psychic constitution of the human being and then increasingly recedes in the course of development. Certainly, child's play more clearly reveals certain essential characteristics of human play—but it is also at the same time more harmless, less enigmatic and less concealed than the play of adults. The child still knows little about the seduction of masks. The child still plays innocently. How hidden, disguised, and secretive play is even in the so-called "serious" business of the adult world, in its honors and titles, in social conventions—what a "scene" in the encounter of the sexes! In the end it is not at all true that it is the child who predominantly plays. Perhaps the adult plays just as much, only differently, more secretly, in a more masked manner. Taking the guiding principle of our concept of play from childlike existence alone has the consequence that the uncannily enigmatic, ambiguous nature of play is misjudged. In truth, the breadth of play reaches from a little girl's puppet show [*Puppenspiel*] all the way to tragedy. Play is not a marginal manifestation in the landscape of human life, nor a contingent phenomenon only surfacing from time to time. Play belongs essentially to the ontological constitution of human existence; it is an existentiell, fundamental phenomenon. Certainly not the only one, but nevertheless a peculiar and independent one, one that cannot be derived from the other manifestations of life. Merely contrasting it with other phenomena still fails to achieve an adequate conceptual perspective. Nevertheless, on the other hand, it cannot be denied that the decisive fundamental phenomena of human existence are interwoven and entwined. They do not occur next to each other in isolation; they permeate and pervade one another. Every such fundamental phenomenon thoroughly determines the human being. Shedding light on the integration of the elementary aspects of existence—its tension, its conflict, and its backward-turning harmony—remains an open task for an anthropology that does not merely describe biological, psychological, and spiritual-intellectual facts, but rather, understanding the matter at hand, penetrates into the paradoxes of our lived life.

The human being is, in the entirety of his existence, and not merely in one domain of it, determined and marked by a death that intrudes and stands before him, a death which he encounters wherever he goes. As an embodied, sensuous being, he is just as wholly determined by his relation to opposition as to the generous boon of the earth. The same thing holds for the dimensions of power and love in his being with [*Mitsein*] his fellow human beings. The human being is essentially a mortal being, essentially a worker, essentially a fighter, essentially a lover and—essentially a player. Death, work, ruling, love, and play form the elementary structure of tension and the outline of the puzzling and polysemous character of human existence. And when Schiller says, "man only fully is when he plays,"[9] it also remains valid that he only fully is when he works, struggles, holds out against death, or loves. This is not the place or occasion to set forth the fundamental style of an interpretation of existence that inquires back into the fundamental phenomena. As an indication, however, we may observe that all the essential fundamental phenomena of human existence shimmer and appear enigmatic in an ambiguous way. This has its more profound basis in the fact that the human being is simultaneously exposed and secure. He is no longer held within the ground of nature, like the animal, and is not yet free like the incorporeal angel—he is a freedom steeped in nature. He remains bound to an obscure impulse that occupies and pervades him. He *is* not simply and naïvely; with understanding, he takes an interest in his own existence—but he cannot, on the other hand, fully define himself through the actions of his freedom. To exist as a human is, through this entanglement of exposure and security, always a tense comportment of oneself to oneself. We live in unending self-concern. Only a living being "which in its Being has this very Being as an issue" (Heidegger)[10] can die, work, struggle, love, and play. Only such a being comports itself to surrounding beings as such and to the all-encompassing whole: to the world. The threefold[11] aspect of self-relation, understanding of Being, and openness to the world is perhaps less easy to recognize in play than in the other fundamental phenomena of human existence.

The enactment-character of play is spontaneous activity, active doing, vital impulse; play is existence that is moved in itself, as it were. But the character of being moved that pertains to play does not coincide with any other movement of human life. All other activity—in everything that is done in each case, whether it be simple praxis, which has its goal in itself, or whether it be production (*poiēsis*), which has its goal in a construct of work—fundamentally points ahead toward the "ultimate goal" of the human being: felicity, *eudaimonia.* We act in order to pursue a successful existence in the proper course of life. We take life as a "task." At no moment do we have, so to speak, a peaceful abode. We know ourselves to be "under way." We are always torn away from and driven beyond each present moment by the force with which we project our life toward the proper and successful existence. We all strive for *eudaimonia*—but we are in no way agreed as to what it is. We are not only affected by the unrest of the striving that carries us along, but also by the unrest of having an "interpretation" of true happiness. It belongs to the profound paradoxes of human existence that, in incessantly chasing after *eudaimonia,* we do not reach it, and that, in the full sense of the term, no one is to be counted happy before death. As long as we breathe we are caught up in a precipitous decline of life. We are enthralled by the urge to complete and fulfill our fragmentary Being. We live in the prospect of the future. We conceive the present as a preparation, as a station along the way, as a way of passage. This remarkable "futurism" of human life is intimately connected with our fundamental trait, namely that we are not simply and plainly like plants and animals, that we are concerned with the "sense" of our existence, that we want to understand why we are here on this earth. It is an uncanny passion that drives the human being to an interpretation of his earthly life—the passion of spirit. In this passion, we have the source of our greatness and our wretchedness. The subsistence of no other living being is disturbed in such a way that it would ask about the obscure sense of its being-here. The animal cannot, and God need not, ask about itself. Every human answer to the question of the sense of life entails the positing of a "final end." For most human beings, to be sure, this does not happen explicitly, but a fundamental representation of what the "highest good" is for them always governs everything they do and leave undone. All everyday purposes are architectonically secured in aiming toward a final purpose—all particular professional purposes are united in the putative final purpose of the human being in general.

In this structure of ends, all human work bestirs itself, the serious life bestirs itself, genuineness bestirs and proves itself. The *fatal* situation of the human being, however, is revealed by the fact that he cannot become absolutely certain of his final purpose by himself, that he staggers in the dark when it comes to the most important question of his existence if no superhuman force helps him. For that reason we find among human beings an utter[12] confusion of language, as soon as it is a matter of saying what the ultimate purpose, the destiny, the true happiness of the human being is. For that reason we also find unrest, haste, and agonizing uncertainty to be characteristic features of the human being's projective manner of life.

Play does not fit into this manner of life in the way the other activities do. Play is conspicuously set apart from the whole[13] futural character of life. Play does not allow itself to be incorporated without further ado into the complex architecture of purposes. It does not happen for the sake of the "final purpose." Play is not worried and disturbed, as our acting otherwise is, by the deep uncertainty in our interpretation of happiness. In relation to the course of life and to its restless dynamic, to its obscure questionworthiness and its forward-rushing orientation toward the future, playing has the character of a pacified "present" and self-contained sense—it resembles an "oasis" of happiness arrived at in the desert of the striving for happiness and Tantalus-like seeking that is otherwise our condition. Play *carries* us *away*. When we play, we are released for a while from the hustle and bustle of life—as though transported to another planet where life seems lighter, more buoyant, easier. One often says that playing is a "purposeless" or "purpose-free" activity. Such is not the case. It is purposively determined as a comprehensive activity and in the individual steps of the course of play has in each case particular purposes that are linked together. But the *immanent* purpose of play is not, as with purposes in the rest of human activities, projected out toward the highest ultimate purpose. The activity of play has only internal purposes, not ones that transcend it. And where, for instance, we play "for the purpose" of training the body, of martial discipline or for the sake of health, play has already been distorted into an exercise for the sake of something else. In such practices play is guided by foreign goal-setting, and then clearly does not happen for its own sake. Precisely what is purely self-sufficient about play, the self-enclosed, circular sense of the activity of play, lets a possibility of human sojourn within time appear, one that does not have the character of tearing away and driving forward but rather allows one to tarry and is, as it were, a glimmer of eternity. Because it is the child who predominantly plays, this feature of time is peculiar to the child most of all, concerning which the poet declares,

> Oh hours of childhood,
> when behind each shape more than the past appeared
> and what streamed out before us was not the future.
> We felt our bodies growing and were at times
> impatient to *be* grown up, half for the sake
> of those with nothing left but their grownupness.
> Yet were, when playing by ourselves, enchanted
> with what alone endures; and we would stand there
> in the infinite blissful space between world and toy,
> at a point which, from the earliest beginning,
> had been established for a pure event.
>
> Rilke, Fourth Duino Elegy[14]

For the adult, on the other hand, play is a strange oasis, a dreamy resting point for restless wandering and continual flight. Play gives us the present. Not, to be sure, that present where we, having become still in the depths of our essence, hear the eternal breath of the world and behold the pure forms in the stream of transience. Play is activity and creativity—and yet it is near to eternal and tranquil things. Play "interrupts" the continuity and context of our course of life that is determined by an ultimate purpose. It withdraws in a peculiar manner from the other ways of directing one's life; it is at a distance from them. But while it appears to escape [ent*ziehen*] the standard flow of life, it relates [be*zieht*] to it in a manner that is particularly imbued with sense, namely, in the mode of portrayal [*Darstellung*]. If one defines play, as is usually done, only in opposition to work, actuality, seriousness, and genuineness, one merely places it, falsely, *next to* other phenomena of life. Play is a fundamental phenomenon of existence, just as primordial and independent as death, love, work and ruling, but it is *not* directed, as with the other fundamental phenomena, by a collective striving for the final purpose. It stands *over and against* them, as it were, in order to assimilate them to itself by portraying them. We play seriousness, play genuineness, play actuality, we play work and struggle, play love and death. And we even play play.

II

The play of human beings, with which we all are intimately acquainted as an often already actualized possibility of our existence, is a phenomenon of existence of an entirely enigmatic sort. It escapes from the intrusiveness of the rational concept into the polysemy of its masks. Our attempt at a conceptual structural analysis of play must reckon with such disguises. It will hardly offer itself to us as a crystal-clear structural edifice. All play is pleasurably attuned, joyfully moved in itself—it is animated. If these stimulating joys of play are extinguished, the activity of play dwindles straightaway. This pleasure in play is a strange pleasure that is difficult to grasp, one that is neither merely sensuous nor yet merely intellectual; it is a creative, formative bliss of its own kind and is in and of itself polysemous, multidimensional. It can incorporate deep sorrow and abysmal grief; it can even pleasurably engulf what is horrible.[15]

The pleasure that pervades the plot of the tragic play creates its delight and its trembling, beatifying convulsion of the human heart out of such an embrace of what is terrible.[16] In play, the face of the Gorgon, too, is transfigured. What kind of amazing pleasure is that, which is in and of itself so expansive and can merge oppositions in such a way as to encompass horror and bitter heartache[17] while at the same time still giving precedence to joy, such that we, moved to tears, can smile about the comedy and tragedy of our existence, which are brought to presence by the play? Does the pleasure of play contain sorrow and pain only in the way that a present memory, cheerfully attuned, is related to a past grief? Is it only the distance of time that makes the moments of bitterness that have since passed away easier, the pains that once were real? Not at all. In play we do not at all suffer "actual pains"—and yet the pleasure of play allows a grief to resonate in a strange way that is present and yet not actual—but seizes us, catches us, stirs us, shakes us. Sorrow [*Trauer*] is merely "played [*gespielt*]"[18] and is, nevertheless, a power that moves us in the mode of the playful.[19]

This pleasure of play[20] involves taking delight in a "sphere," in an imaginary[21] dimension; it is not merely pleasure *at* play, but also taking pleasure *in* play.

It is now necessary to single out the *sense* of play as a further aspect in the structure of play. To every instance of play as such belongs a sense-imbued element. A merely bodily movement, of a limb-loosening sort, for instance, which we rhythmically repeat, is, strictly speaking, not play. In an unclear manner of expression, one all too often calls such relaxing behavior of animals or of small children a kind of playing. Such movements do not have a "sense" for the ones moving. We can first speak of play only when a specially produced sense belongs to bodily motions. And at the same time we must still distinguish the internal play-sense of a specific instance of play, that is, the sense-context of things, acts and relations that are played—and the external sense, that is, the signification that play has for those who first decide on it, who intend to do it—or even the sense that it may eventually have for spectators who are not participating in it. Of course there are many kinds of play in which the spectators themselves belong as such within the total play-situation (for instance, kinds of play resembling the ancient circus[22] or cultic kinds of play[23])—and on the other hand there are kinds of play for which spectators are not essential.

Here a third aspect of the constitution of play can already be stated: the fellowship of play. Playing is a fundamental possibility of social existence. Playing is interplay, playing with one another, an intimate form of human community. Playing is, structurally, not an individual or isolated activity—it is open to one's fellow human beings as fellow-players. It is no objection to point out that frequently, though, the ones playing carry out their games "all alone," apart from their fellow human beings. For, in the first place, being open to possible fellow-players is already included in the sense of play, and, in the second place, such a solitary person often plays with imaginary partners. The community of play need not consist of a number of real persons. However, there must be at least *one* real, actual player, when it is a matter of actual and not merely purported play. Furthermore, another essential aspect of play concerns the rules. Playing is maintained and constituted[24] by something binding. One cannot arbitrarily do whatever one wants. Playing is not limitlessly free. One cannot play at all without something binding being determined and adopted. And yet the rules of play are not laws. What binds does not have the character of the unalterable. Even in the middle of a game we can change the rules with our fellow-players' consent; but then it is precisely the changed rule that counts and that binds the flow of the reciprocal activities. We all know the difference between traditional games, whose rules one accepts, which are publicly known and familiar possibilities of playing comportment, and improvised games, which one, so to speak, "invents"—where one first agrees on the rules in the fellowship of play. One might perhaps think that improvised games would have greater appeal, because in these games free imagination is given more room; because one can run riot in the airy realm of mere possibilities; because here one chooses what binds one; and because here invention, the unrestrained wealth of ideas, can be applied. Yet this is not unconditionally the case. For binding oneself to the already valid rules of play is often experienced pleasurably and positively. This is surprising but can be explained by the fact that in the games passed down it mostly has to do with the products of collective imagination and with what is self-binding in the soul's archetypical foundations. Some children's games that seem simple are vestiges of the most ancient magical practices.

To every game belongs also a toy or plaything [*Spielzeug*]. Each of us is familiar with playthings. But it remains difficult to say what a plaything is. It is not a matter of enumerating various types of playthings, but rather a matter of determining the nature of the plaything or rather of actually experiencing it as a genuine problem. Playthings do not delimit a self-contained region of things—as, for instance, artificially produced things do. In nature (in the broad sense of beings existing of their own accord) no artifacts are found—independently of human producers. Through his work, the human being produces artificial things for the first time. He is the technician of a human environment. He cultivates the field, domesticates wild animals, shapes natural materials into tools, forms clay into jugs, hammers iron into weapons. A tool is an artifact that has been formed by human labor. Artificial things and natural things may be distinguished, but both are things within a common and encompassing actuality.

A plaything can be an artificially produced thing; however, it need not be. Even a simple piece of wood or a broken-off branch can serve as a "doll." The hammer, which is a human meaning that has been impressed onto a piece of wood and iron, belongs, like the wood, the iron, and the human being himself, to one and the same dimension of the actual. The plaything is different. Seen, so to speak, from the outside, that is, observed from the perspective of the one who is not playing, it is obviously a part, a thing of the simply actual world. It is a thing that, for example, has the intended purpose of keeping children occupied. The doll is considered to be a product of the toy industry. It is a piece of material and wire or a mass of plastic, and can be acquired for purchase at a determined price; it is a commodity. But, seen from the perspective of a playing girl, a doll is a *child,* and the girl is its *mother.* At the same time it is in no way the case that the little girl actually believes that the doll is a living child. She does not deceive herself about this. She does not confuse something on the basis of a deceptive appearance. Rather, she simultaneously knows about the doll-figure and its significance in play. The playing child lives in two dimensions. The plaything's character of being a plaything, that is, its essence, lies in its *magical* character: it is a thing within simple actuality and at the same time has another, mysterious "reality." It is thus infinitely more than a mere instrument, more than an incidental, foreign thing that we use to manipulate other things. Human play needs playthings. Precisely in his essential, basic activities, the human being cannot remain free of things; he is dependent on them: in work on the hammer, in ruling on the sword, in love on the bed, in poetry on the lyre, in religion on the sacrificial altar—and in play on the plaything.

Each plaything is a proxy for all things in general. Playing is always a confrontation with beings. In the plaything, the whole is concentrated in a single thing. Every instance of play is an attempt on the part of life, a vital experiment, which experiences in the plaything the epitome of resistant beings in general. But human playing does not occur only as the aforementioned magical contact with the plaything. It is necessary to grasp the concept of the player more acutely and rigorously. For here there exists a very peculiar, though in no way pathological, "schizophrenia," a splitting of the human being. The one who plays, who enters into a game, performs in the actual world a certain kind of activity that is well known in its characteristic features. Within the internal context of the sense of play, however, he takes on a *role.* And now we must distinguish between the real human being who "plays" and the human role within the instance of play. The player "conceals" himself by means of his "role"; in a certain measure he vanishes into it. With an intensity of a peculiar sort he lives *in* the role—and, yet again, not like a person who is deluded, who is no longer able to distinguish between "actuality" and "appearance." The player can call himself back out of the role. In the enactment of play, there remains a knowledge, albeit strongly reduced, about his double existence. It exists in two spheres—but not from forgetfulness or from a lack of concentration. This doubling belongs to the essence of playing. All the structural aspects touched on until now come together in the fundamental concept of the *playworld.* Every sort of playing is the magical production of a playworld. *In* it lie the role of the one playing, the changing roles of the community of play, the binding nature of the rules of play, and the significance of the plaything. The playworld is an imaginary dimension, whose ontological sense poses an obscure and difficult problem. We play in the so-called actual world but we thereby attain [*erspielen*] a realm, an enigmatic field, that is not nothing and yet is nothing actual. In the playworld we move about according to our roles, but in the playworld there are imaginary figures. There is the "child," who indeed lives and breathes there—but in simple actuality is only a doll or even a piece of wood. In the projection of a playworld the one who plays conceals himself as the creator of this "world." He loses himself in his creation, plays a role, and has, within the playworld, playworldly things that surround him and playworldly fellow human beings. What is misleading about this is that we imaginatively take these playworldly things themselves to be "actual things"; indeed, in the playworld, we even repeat the difference between actuality and appearance in various ways.

Nevertheless, it is not thereby the case that the genuinely and truly actual things of our everyday environment become so concealed by the playworldly features that they would be covered up, and thus no longer recognizable. That is not the case. The playworld does not present itself like a wall or a curtain in front of the beings surrounding us; it does not obscure or veil them. The playworld does not even have, strictly speaking, a position or duration in the actual context of space and time—but it has its own inner space and its own inner time. And yet we spend actual time playing and need actual space. But the space of the playworld never uninterruptedly coincides with the space that we otherwise inhabit. The same holds for time. The noteworthy interpenetration of the dimension of actuality and the playworld cannot be elucidated by an otherwise familiar model of spatial and temporal proximity. The playworld is not suspended in a mere realm of thought; it always has a real setting, but is, however, never a real thing among real things. Yet it necessarily requires real things in order to gain a foothold in them. This means that the imaginary character of the playworld cannot be explained as a phenomenon of a merely subjective appearance, nor determined to be a delusion that exists only within the interiority of a soul but in no way is found among and between things in general. The more one attempts to reflect on play, the more enigmatic and questionworthy it seems to become.

We have specified a few fundamental features and come to draw a few distinctions. Human play is a pleasurably attuned production of an imaginary play-world. It is a wondrous joy in "appearance." Play is always also characterized by the aspect of portrayal, by its sense-imbued aspect, and it is in each case transformative: it brings about the "alleviation of life,"[25] a temporary, merely terrestrial solution, indeed almost a release from the burdens of existence. It carries us away from a factual state of affairs, from the confinement in a pressing and oppressing situation. It affords us a happiness of fantasy in the flight of possibilities, which remain without the agony of actual choice. In the enactment of play the human being manages to exist at two extremes. Play can at one time be experienced as a peak of human sovereignty; the human being then enjoys an almost unbounded creativity. He creates productively and without inhibition because he does not produce in the realm of real actuality. The player feels as if he were "master" of his imaginary[26] products. Playing becomes a distinguished—because it is scarcely restricted—possibility of human freedom. And in fact the element of freedom prevails to a high degree in play. But it remains a difficult question, whether the nature of play must be grasped fundamentally and exclusively from the power of freedom that belongs to existence—or whether completely different grounds of existence reveal themselves and are at work in play as well. And in fact we also find the opposite extreme of freedom in play. For sometimes a relief from real world-actuality can extend all the way to rapture, to enchantment, to succumbing to the daemonic character of the mask. Play can contain within itself the bright Apollonian aspect of free selfhood, but also the dark Dionysian aspect of panic-stricken self-abandonment.

The relation of the human being to the enigmatic appearance of the play-world, to the dimension of the imaginary, is *ambiguous*. Play is a phenomenon for which the appropriate categories do not easily and unambiguously present themselves. Its shimmering, inner polysemy may perhaps most readily be addressed by the cognitive resources of a dialectic that does not level out paradoxes. Great philosophy has always recognized the eminent essentiality of play, which the common understanding does not recognize, because play means to it only something that is idle, something neither serious, nor genuine, nor actual. Thus Hegel, for example, says that, in its indifference and great levity, play is the loftiest and only true seriousness. And Nietzsche puts it in *Ecce Homo* as follows: "I do not know any other way of handling great tasks than as *play*."[27]

Is it possible to shed light on play, we must now ask, if it is taken solely as an anthropological phenomenon? Must we not think beyond the human being? I do not mean by this the search for a comportment of play in another living being as well. But it is questionable whether play can be understood in its ontological constitution without determining more closely the noteworthy dimension of the imaginary. Even supposing that play is something of which only the human is capable, the question still remains whether the human being as a player stays within the human realm or at the same time necessarily comports himself to a realm *beyond* the human one [Über*menschlichen*] as well.

Originally play is a portraying symbol-activity of human existence in which the latter interprets itself. The earliest games are magical rites, the great gestures of cult, in which the archaic human being interprets his inner standing within the context of the world, where he "portrays" his fate, brings to presence the events of birth and death, of weddings, war, hunting, and work. The symbolic representation of magical games creates elements from out of the circuit of simple actuality, but it also creates from out of the nebulous realm of the imaginary. In primeval times play is not so much understood as the deeply pleasurable carrying out of life on the part of isolated individuals or groups that temporarily remove themselves from social connection and inhabit their small island of ephemeral happiness. Play is primordially the strongest *binding* power. It is community-founding—different, to be sure, from the community of the departed and the living, or from the system of rule or the elementary family. The early human community of play *embraces* all these stated forms and shapes of being together [*Miteinanderseins*] and brings the whole of existence to complete presence. It consolidates the circle of the phenomena of life as the play-community of the *festival*. The archaic festival is more than the merry-making of a people; it is the elevated actuality—the actuality that has been elevated to the magical dimension—of human life in all its relations. It is cultic dramatic play or spectacle [*Schauspiel*], where the human being feels the nearness of the gods, the heroes and the dead, and knows himself as having been placed into the presence of all the blessing and frightening powers of the world-totality. Thus primeval play also has a deep connection with religion. The community of the festival envelops the spectators, the initiates and epopts[28] of a cultic play, where the deeds and sufferings of gods and humans appear on the stage, whose boards in fact signify the *world*.

III

Our attempt up to now—to apprehend the structure of play under several conceptual forms: play-attunement, play-community, rules of play, plaything and playworld—repeatedly made use of the expression "the imaginary." One can translate this word with "appearance." But an eminent intellectual perplexity is concentrated therein. In general we understand the term "appearance," especially in specific concrete situations, in this way. But it remains troublesome and difficult to express what we actually mean by it. The greatest questions and problems of philosophy are lodged in the most ordinary words and things. The concept of appearance is as obscure and unexplored as the concept of Being—and both concepts belong together in an opaque, confusing, downright labyrinthine way, permeating one another in their interplay. The path of the thinking that engages them leads deeper and deeper into the unthinkable.

With the question of appearance, to the extent that it belongs to human playing,[29] we have touched on a philosophical problem. Play is creative bringing-forth, it is a production. The product is the playworld, a sphere of appearance, a field whose actuality is obviously not a very settled matter. And nevertheless the appearance of the playworld is not simply nothing. We move about in it while we play; we live in it—certainly sometimes lightly and airily as in a dream world, but at other times also full of ardent devotion and immersion. Such "appearance" has, from time to time, a stronger experiential reality and power of impression than the bulk of everyday things in their worn-out ordinariness. *What,* then, is the imaginary? Where is this strange appearance located; what is its status? Insight into the ontological nature of play depends, not least, on determining its position and status.

Usually we speak of appearance in multiple ways. We mean, for example, the outer semblance of the thing, the superficial aspect, the mere foreground and the like. This appearance belongs to the things themselves—as the shell to the kernel, as manifestation to essence. At another time we speak of appearance in regard to a deceptive, subjective ascertainment,[30] an erroneous view, an unclear representation. Then the appearance lies in us, in those who conceive falsely—it lies in the "subject." In addition, however, there is also a subjective appearance that is not thought of from the relation between the truth or error of the one representing and the things themselves—an appearance that legitimately dwells within our soul, precisely as a construct of the power of imagination, of fantasy. We make use of these abstract distinctions in order to formulate our question. What kind of appearance *is* the playworld? A foreground of things? A deceptive representation? A phantasm in our soul? No one would want to dispute that in every instance of play, fantasy is especially at work and runs free. But are playworlds *merely* constructs of fantasy? It would be too cheap an explanation to say that the imaginary realm of the playworld consists exclusively in human imagination, or that it is an agreement of private delusional representations or private acts of fancy with a collective delusion, with an intersubjective fantasy. Playing is always in contact with playthings. Already with regard to the plaything, one can see that playing does not occur within psychical interiority alone and without support in the objective external world. The playworld contains subjective elements of fantasy and objective, ontic elements. We are acquainted with the imagination as a faculty of the soul. We are acquainted with dreams, inner intuitions, the colorful contents of fantasy. But what is an objective or ontic appearance supposed to mean? Now, there are, in actuality, entirely remarkable things that are themselves indisputably something actual and nevertheless contain in themselves an aspect of "non-actuality." This sounds remarkable and astonishing. But everyone is acquainted with such things, yet we do not customarily characterize these things in such a roundabout and abstract way. There are simply objectively present *images*. For instance, a poplar on the lakeside casts its mirror-image on the shimmering surface of the water. Now mirrorings themselves belong to the circumstances of how actual things exist in an illuminated environment. Things in light cast shadows, trees on the shore are mirrored in the lake; on smooth, shiny metal, things in the environment find a reflection. What is the mirror-image? As an image [*Bild*] it is actual, an actual reproduction [*Abbild*] of the actual, original tree. But "in" the image a tree is portrayed. It appears on the surface of the water, and yet in such a manner that it appears there only in the medium of the mirror-appearance, not in actuality. An appearance of such a kind is an *independent* sort of being and contains as a constitutive aspect of its actuality something that is in itself specifically "non-actual"—and, furthermore, in this way rests on another, simply actual being. The image of the poplar tree does not conceal the stretch of the surface of water on which it appears in the manner of a mirror. The mirroring of the poplar is, *as* a mirroring, that is, as a determinate phenomenon of light, an actual thing [*Sache*] and contains the "non-actual" poplar of the mirror-world in itself. That may perhaps sound too stilted—and nevertheless it is not a remote matter, but rather one that is universally known, which lies before our eyes every day. The entire Platonic doctrine of Being, which in large measure has determined Western philosophy decisively, operates again and again with models of reproduction like shadows and mirroring and thereby interprets the structure of the world.

The ontic appearance (mirroring and the like) is more than just an analog of the playworld; it occurs within the playworld for the most part as a structural aspect in its own right. Playing is an actual comportment that, as it were, contains a "mirroring" in itself: the playworldly comportment according to roles. Even the possibility on the part of the human being to productively engender a playworldly appearance depends in large part on there being an actual appearance already in nature in itself. The human being cannot in general only make artifacts; he can also produce artificial things to which an aspect of *existing appearance* belongs as well. He projects imaginary playworlds. By virtue of a production imaginatively carried out, the little girl designates the material body of a doll as a "living child," and assumes the role of the "mother." Actual things always belong to the playworld—but in part they have the character of ontic appearance, and in part they are clothed with a subjective appearance stemming from the human soul.

Playing is finite creativity within the magical dimension of appearance.

It is a problem of the greatest profundity and utmost difficulty for thought to unfold precisely how actuality and non-actuality pervade one another in human play. The conceptual determination of the Being of play leads back to the cardinal questions of philosophy, to speculation about Being and nothing and appearance and becoming. Nevertheless, we cannot develop this here. But, in any case, one sees that the usual talk of the non-actuality of play remains inadequate when one does not inquire into the enigmatic dimension of the imaginary. What human and what cosmic sense does this imaginary dimension have? Does it form a demarcated[31] region within extant things? Is the strange land of the non-actual the elevated site where the *essentiality* of all things in general is invoked and brought to presence? In the magical, playworldly mirroring, the individual thing (the plaything, for instance) that is singled out by chance becomes a *symbol.* It represents. Human play is (even if we no longer know it) the symbolic activity of bringing the sense of the world and life to presence.

The ontological problems that play presents to us are not exhausted by the questions indicated previously about the *way of Being* of the playworld and about the symbolic value of the plaything or play-activity. In the history of thought one has not only sought to grasp the *Being* of play—but also ventured the tremendous reversal of determining *the sense of Being from out of play.* We call this the speculative concept of play. In brief: speculation is the characterization of the essence of Being *in the metaphor of a being.* It is a conceptual *world formula* that springs from an *innerworldly* model. Philosophers have already employed many such models: Thales water, Plato light, Hegel spirit, and so forth. But the illuminating power of such a model does not depend on the respective thinker's discretion in his selection—it depends decisively on whether in fact the whole of Being repeatedly mirrors itself, of its own accord, in a single being. Wherever the cosmos metaphorically repeats its constitution, its structure and layout in an innerworldly thing, a key philosophical phenomenon is thereby indicated, from which a speculative world formula can be developed.

Now, the phenomenon of play is a manifestation that as such is already distinguished by the fundamental feature of symbolic representation. Does play perhaps become a metaphorical dramatic play or spectacle of the whole, an illuminating, speculative metaphor for the world? This audacious, bold thought has actually been thought before. In the dawn of European thought Heraclitus poses the aphorism: "The course of the world is a playing child, moving pieces on a board—a king's power belongs to the child" (Fragment 52).[32] And after twenty-five centuries of the history of thought there is Nietzsche, who writes: "*In* this world only play, play as artists and children engage in it, exhibits coming-to-be and passing away, structuring and destroying, without any moral additive, in forever equal innocence"[33]—"The world *is* the play of Zeus . . ."[34] (*Philosophy in the Tragic Age of the Greeks*).

The profundity of such a conception—but also its danger and power of seduction—urges us on to an aesthetic interpretation of the world that cannot be unfolded here. But the strange world formula, which lets beings as a whole prevail as a game, may perhaps give rise to the notion that play is not a harmless, peripheral, or even "childish" affair—that we finite human beings, precisely in the creative power and mastery of our magical production, have "been put on the line [*aufs Spiel gesetzt*]"[35] in an abyssal sense. If the essence of the world is thought as play, it thus follows for the human being that he is the only being in the vast universe who is able to *correspond* to the prevailing whole. Only in the correspondence to what is beyond the human may the human being then attain his native essence.

To the playful openness of human existence to the playing ground of the Being of all beings, the poet thus attests:

As long as you catch self-thrown things
it's all dexterity and venial gain—;
only when you've suddenly caught that ball
which she, one of the eternal players,
has tossed toward you, your center, with
a throw precisely judged, one of those arches
that exist in God's great bridge-system:
only then is catching a proficiency,—
not yours, a world's. And if you then had
strength and courage to return the throw,
no, more wonderful: forgot strength and courage
and had *already* thrown . . . (as the year
throws the birds, those migrating bird swarms,
which an older to a younger warmth sends
catapulting across oceans—) only
in that venture would you truly join in.
No longer making the throw easy; no longer making
it hard. Out of your hands the meteor
would launch itself and flame into its spaces . . .

Rilke, *Late Poems*[36]

When thinkers and poets point in such a humanly profound way to the immense significance of play, we should also be mindful of the saying: we cannot enter into the kingdom of heaven if we do not become as children.

Play as Symbol of the World {1960}

Chapter One
Play as a Philosophical Problem

1. Play as a Possible and Worthy Topic for Philosophy

To choose *play* as the theme of a philosophical treatise may sound strange. Our commonplace understanding of philosophy finds it hard to reconcile the rigorous business of abstract thinking and its gloomy seriousness with play's carefree cheerfulness and the image-laden joy in presentation. Playing and thinking seem to belong to opposed modes of life; the naïveté of play, which delights in the senses and without qualms mixes the actual and the fantastical and is not "sicklied o'er with the pale cast of thought,"[1] is evidently far removed from every critical and careful examination of things that skeptically inquires as to whether they are, what they are, and how they are. What seems strange in our attempt to contemplate play presumably lies in the fact that a phenomenon is to be *interrogated* that in itself appears to be characterized on an elementary level as unquestionable. Is it at all possible to raise a question about what is intrinsically unquestionable? Of course, on the linguistic level it is always possible to raise a question about anything and everything. Here there is a cheap pseudo-radicality that hides behind the philosopher's cloak yet is indeed always directed toward given things and relations, in order to practice and exercise its obsessive skepticism upon them. It takes pride in being able to deny every naïve belief, to negate everything that presents itself as existing and thus to assert the empty Ego in its power to negate. Yet this Ego that thinks itself great in its power of negation continually needs the material of the world in order to be able to maintain itself in such ongoing denial and is only conveyed to itself through that which it denies. This is the fundamental position of an extreme skepticism that in its constant flight from every dogmatic commitment has indeed already fallen into the dogmatism of negation and thus displays an impotence on the part of thinking, because it can no longer immerse itself in the life of the things themselves. To doubt everything, to withdraw in the face of everything into the attitude of the Ego's refusal to believe, is no more a comprehending position of the human being toward the world than is the unthinking, naïve abandon to things in everyday life. Philosophy certainly stands in proximity to all those phenomena of life in which the immediacy of carrying on with our lives becomes unsettled; it stands in the vicinity of the uncanny experiences of existence such as angst, dread, guilt, doubt, and despair, of mistrust and suspicion, of the gnawing and agonizing question: everything that to some degree distances us from our own Being and the Being of all things also marks the experiential character of philosophy. Yet it does not stop with this "distantiality." Rather, what is decisive for philosophy is to understand and grasp, from out of the distance afforded by the question, human life *in* its unquestioned character. Our immanent stance within the Being of the world as understood, our immersion in things, our embeddedness in nature, our entire and primordial naïveté of life, which is borne by an abyssal trust in Being—this is what remains to be comprehended. Therefore, philosophy too is close to the great passions, the storms of the heart and spirit, the elemental piety that binds the living to the dead, the sensuous delights with which we feel the local and earthly. It is close to the gleam of the beautiful over all worldly things. It is itself a unique marveling amazement over the wonder that beings are, and in its amazement an admiration for the world resonates as well. From the distantiality of the question, we seek to understand the indwelling of our worlded existence. This constitutes the tension of philosophical thinking, that it must at the same time be at the furthest remove from and most intimate proximity to Being, have critical vigilance and life's elementary élan, reflection and primordiality in one. Thus considered, a philosophical interrogation of play appears to be thoroughly possible and meaningful.

But then other concerns present themselves. If play can be a *possible* topic for philosophical contemplation, if it does not, in its naïveté that is immediate to life, contradict the critical spirit of philosophy, because, indeed, the naïveté of life as such signifies the reproach of thinking—then it is to be asked whether play presents a *worthy* topic for philosophy. Play initially appears to us as a marginal phenomenon in the landscape of human life, which is determined and marked in decisive fashion by more serious phenomena. Play stands opposed to the seriousness of life, to care and work, to the concern for the salvation of one's soul—it appears as something "non-serious" and "non-binding," as the occasional relaxation of the tension of life, as a "break" or "rest," as a pastime for idle hours, as dalliance and merry mischief. At best one grants a restricted worth to play in the adult economy of life; one acknowledges it as a therapeutically effective remedy for overloads of work, worry, or seriousness. But considering it as a means of relaxation puts it precisely in the service of those phenomena of life from which it is otherwise demarcated disparagingly. Play, however, is not at all taken seriously in its own right. It is, no doubt, recognized that in the child's existence it plays an important, indeed fundamental, role and is at the center of the child's life. But one interprets the growing-up of the young human being as a process in which play is ever more displaced from the center of life and is supplanted by other phenomena of existence. Play moves on the periphery of life; it does not completely disappear but acquires the characteristic of being an occasional diversion or restful break.

Play appears to be reserved more legitimately for the small child who still lives secure in the care of the family before the beginning of serious life. In the small child, playing is manifestly the pure enactment of existence. That may signify an eminently important matter for child psychology, for pedagogy. But can play, evidently a primarily infantile affair, be a worthy topic for philosophy?

What are, in general, the worthy topics for philosophy? The systematization of philosophical questioning carried out by the Stoics divided philosophy into "Logic," "Physics," and "Ethics"; the great and worthy objects of thinking were thinking itself, insofar as human thinking coincides with the world-prevailing *logos;* then nature as the comprehensive concept [*Inbegriff*] for all things existing of their own accord; and, finally, the human being as that being which is free and determines itself in social communication. To the extent, however, that the Stoics conceived the world-logos as the "divine," their basic division of philosophy blazed a trail that has broadly determined the Western tradition and even still had a late reflection in Kant's systematization of philosophy. There, too, the great and worthy topics for philosophy are declared to be God, nature, and human freedom. These three titles delimit distinct regions of beings. Of all that is, God, nature, and human freedom are the worthiest of contemplation. The worthiness of these great topics manifestly marks them off from a general unworthiness of many insignificant and negligible things. In what—so one could now ask—is the difference between the worthy and unworthy grounded? Does philosophy already have an appraisal of innerworldly beings at hand in advance, in order to share out the favor of its interests accordingly? In pre-philosophical life the entirety of actuality is already structured for us, not merely in fields and dimensions according to the types of things; we also have at our disposal a hierarchy according to which we classify and assess manifold beings. For the most part these are mythical interpretations of the world's context. The human being interprets his position in the cosmos; from the ancient point of view, for instance, he finds himself on the back of the all-bearing earth beneath the open sky, around him land and sea, flora and fauna, with an intimation of the gods above in the constellations of the firmament. The regions of the world high in the heavens and deep below the earth, which are removed from the dwelling of mortals, are considered to be the distinctive realms of the gods. The land of human beings lies between the regions of the gods and is itself visited by the epiphanies of the heavenly ones. In the fertility of the field, in the boon of the weather, in the escape and return of Persephone, the power that divinely prevails is revealed. The human being knows of his dependence, of the futility of his plans and aspirations, knows of the superior power of the gods. From his mythical-religious disposition he acquires an evaluation of worldly things as a whole. The status of all things is measured in relation to divine power. What is most powerful is most worthy of veneration. When, however, philosophy awakens, it does not accept without question the hierarchy of the mythical interpretation of the world. Gods, land and sea, human beings, animals, plants, and human artifacts—all of them, after all, coincide in the fact that they are, that they are in each case a being. All differences of power are, after all, subtended by the one basic feature that holds equally for all. What in general is a being? The radiant god, who as Phoebus Apollo illuminates the world-totality and fills it up with gleaming sunshine, is a being—but the earthworm in the darkness of the soil is also a being. Must not this commonality in all things first of all be conceived before one commits oneself to hierarchically ordered differences? And in fact it becomes a decisive question of philosophy to ask about and to investigate beings to the extent that they are beings, beings as such, the *on hēi on*. With this question about beings as such, one at the same time also asks about *all* beings, because being a being plain and simple belongs to each and every thing that appears at all within the unity of the world. With this basic question of "metaphysics" concerning beings as such and as a whole, the hierarchical differentiation of things and with it an assessment of them according to "worthiness" and "unworthiness" appear to be eliminated. That is, however, by no means the case. To be sure, the mythic hierarchy is no longer employed uncritically, but philosophy, which develops as the question about Being, attempts in thought to determine the being a being of things according to their proper degrees: Being is, for example, understood vis-à-vis nothingness, but not in the manner of a simple and strict separation, rather more in the sense that things are grasped as an enigmatic combination of Being and nothingness, as a blending of these primal opposites. Finite things are considered to be permeated by nothingness in their Being; they have, one then says, a nugatory Being, have a lesser degree of Being, are not, to use Plato's expression, "being in the mode of being [*in seiender Weise seiend*]," are not *ontōs on*. That becomes more apparent when things are considered in regard to their temporal character, when their "Being" is interpreted from their temporality. Then that which always is and always comports itself in the same way, which does not arise and does not pass away and does not change, which is immutable, unmoved, and permanent, counts as the strongest Being. That which, though it now is, nevertheless once was not and will someday no longer be, that which is constantly subject to alterations and exhausts its power of Being in time, has a lower status of Being. Permanence or impermanence in the flow of time thus forms a basis for an evaluation of beings in their "ontological status." No longer the degree of a mythically understood "power," but rather the degree of a "strength of Being" interpreted in regards to "permanence" decides the hierarchy of all worldly things that is thought philosophically. It thereby belongs to philosophy, which does not pose questions merely to things but also to itself, that it does not have in advance an unquestionable measure for the assessment of things according to their rank of Being, but rather time and again seeks to forcefully pull back into questionworthiness the measure that guides it. The most problematic of all philosophical problems is the guiding pre-projection of the essence of Being. Without such a pre-projection philosophizing cannot begin, and in its pre-projection it cannot remain and make itself at home. That means, among other things, that philosophy must both set up a hierarchy of worldly things and also time and again destroy it; it must investigate the worthiest and highest beings and at the same time must also cast the pre-projected measure, according to which it appraises the highest rank of Being, into radical doubt. It arrives at no conclusive knowledge; the work of human wisdom resembles the activity of Sisyphus.

This character of philosophy is easily obscured where it still addresses with mythical names what for it is the being that is most of all, calling it the "divine" and bringing about a disastrous intermingling of theology and ontology. When Plato also calls the idea of ideas, the idea of the good, the *theion,* the "divine," he does not thereby understand this highest idea from the perspective of the concept of God in Greek popular belief, but rather, conversely, he wants to present philosophical knowledge of the *agathon* as the inner truth of myth. This tendency of the great thinkers to address what to them is supremely worthy of thought with the solemn names of mythical-religious language and to make use of a preformed human pathos has just as much harmed philosophy as it has religion. Philosophy is a finite possibility of the finite human being; it is the understanding of Being that is moved to question; it is the glow of twilight in which a being in the midst of all other beings, embedded in nature, seeks to understand and to grasp itself and all things in the universe and ultimately abides in its highest wisdom. We mortals never know in the manner of God; it is senseless to measure ourselves in reference to him or to determine our finitude solely on the basis of our distance to him. The words of the serpent, *eritis sicut deus,*[2] should have no further seductive power for the human spirit that takes up finitude as its fate. In religion God speaks and, through the mouth of the prophet and herald, gives a superhuman explanation of the meaning of life and of the world as a whole to be known. Philosophy is a self-interpretation of human existence and of its sojourn in the world, religion is an alien interpretation. This distinction is fundamental and irreconcilable. In no way are we thereby contesting that a religious interpretation of human life can proceed further, endlessly further beyond every immanent self-understanding of human existence. It would be rather astonishing if it did not do this. We may be as transparent as clear glass for the eyes of the gods; they may see into every hidden recess of our hearts—we are never laid bare for ourselves in a shadowless unconcealment—but the knowledge of the gods about human beings must, in order to be understandable to human beings, be "translated" into human words and human sense. As imparted revelation, the celestial light of divine truth is itself clouded by the human medium in which it is professed and promulgated. Put in terms of our problem: that which, from the perspective of myth, has the character of being worthy, venerable, and holy, does not necessarily also need to be considered what is worthy in philosophy, such that a solid and stable hierarchy would already be reliably pre-given for thought that questions.

What is worthy of question and of thought, what is question-worthy and thought-worthy, is not definitively decided in advance for philosophy but rather proves itself as such only *in* thought that questions. Nothing in the vast universe is too small for wonder to be aroused by it; and no being stands too high for human amazement and its sudden transformation into a question. Everything that *is* at all is already wonderful and enigmatic in its being a being. Socrates was able to begin a philosophical conversation with everyday things; he could set out from the banausic occupations of the saddler, weaver, or helmsman in order to discuss the essence of human activity, of good or bad activity, and to lead his interlocutor up to the question concerning the virtue of the statesman, the sage, to the question concerning virtue as such and true human felicity. He led from that which was low to that which was highest through a skillful, crafty way of posing questions. This midwifery of spirit already in antiquity enveloped this midwife's son with enchanting renown—and is cited time and again as the great, classical example for the free impartiality of philosophy vis-à-vis all things. Perhaps one should even doubt this in order to not let philosophy itself become a myth. Has Socrates ever set out (insofar as we know from the Platonic dialogues) from insignificant things or activities and from them unfolded a philosophizing question? Or, in turning to banausic activities, has he already moved in an unexpressed pre-projection of the essence of human *eudaimonia?* Were not the paltriest and most indifferent actions—in his view—also already permeated by the structure of human self-concern, thus led by the approach that in whatever we do we strive after a complete state of our life that would be at once happy and successful? *If eudaimonia* is what human life in its essential depth is about, then this is also at work down to the narrowest, most specialized subordinate activities, even when we, caught up in what we are doing, no longer see this fundamental motive. Socrates's method consisted in questioning his interlocutor to ferret out the concealed interconnected motive of all his activities, to bring him to present the sense [*Sinnvergegenwärtigung*] of the totality of life in every isolated moment of life. In truth Socrates was, for his part, already determined by a pre-projection, what to him was the highest and most worthy as an object of human contemplation, namely virtue as the state of living the true, happy, and successful life. However, he thereby initially kept up a pretense toward his interlocutor and guided him with "maieutic" questions in the direction of a reflection upon *aretē*. To be sure, he in no way asserts this pre-projection "dogmatically"; he proves it, in a certain way, through the gradual uncovering of the motive of life that is interwoven in manifold ways and united in the ultimate goal, but he also does not transcend this guiding pre-projection. In contrast, Plato surpasses the Socratic pre-projection insofar as he makes the difference, always employed there, between particular, more or less good activities and the good in itself, between virtuous activities and virtue itself, into a radical new problem and extends the difference into the universal as the difference between sensible thing and idea.

This reference to Socrates and Plato, in our present context, only has the significance of a critical and wary reserve. It is not easy to trust the philosophers when they profess to want to think about and interrogate *all* things in the same way with complete "impartiality," to attend equally to the lowest as to the highest. Are they, against their will, the secret prisoners of a pre- and extra-philosophical assessment and evaluation of beings? Certainly there is always this danger. However, the problem lies deeper. It lies in the nature of worlded things themselves, that they all coincide in a universal fundamental feature that is "indifferent" and equivalent for all, namely, that each is in each case a being, and that they at the same time differ from each other according to the degrees of their ontological strength, whereby the measure of the "being that is most of all," the *summum ens,* itself vacillates and is problematic. It is perhaps a prejudice to cling to an equal status of all things in principle for the perspective of thought, just as, conversely, it may also be a prejudice to insist solely on a graduated hierarchy of things. Both moments, which appear to exclude each other, belong to the problematic ontological constitution of worldly beings. All hierarchical ordering of things presupposes the equality of all beings as beings—and, conversely, things do not vanish into a uniform sameness. Difference and contradiction pervade the unity of worldwide Being.

According to this seemingly abstract but thoroughly preliminary characterization of philosophy, insofar as it asks about beings as such and as a whole and about the highest being (a questioning that from time immemorial bears the name "metaphysics"), we again take up the consideration as to whether *play,* too, is a worthy topic for philosophy. Can it, like any thing or occurrence whatsoever, matter for philosophy, insofar as nothing may be too paltry for thinking? Is play just as valid, just as indifferent, as the algae-covered pebble on the seashore? Or is it distinctive in belonging to the human being, in being a special mode of human understanding? The weighty and great emphases of human life lie not in play, not in the unencumbered, cheerful pastime, but rather in the earnest carrying out of our existence, in the toil of work, in the hardship of battle, in the firmness of ethical institutions, in the struggle to prove oneself, in the conflict of duties, in sacrifice and in prayer. Does not the dream-woven world of play disperse as soon as sorrow, need, and deprivation afflict us, but also as soon as we proceed to free actions, to the self-actualization of our freedom in the harsh world of affairs? Does play have a human reality worthy of the name—beyond the years of childhood? Even the human status of play appears slight. The title of this text, however, designates, alongside the "human" problem, also a "worldly" problem of play. Can, then, what appears so peripheral in human life have, beyond that, a cosmic significance? Does play belong not merely to the finite human being but also to the world-totality? This idea initially appears absurd to us, at best allowable as a poetic way of speaking, as an illicit metaphor, which—applied to what happens in the world—conveys a primitive anthropomorphism. That human play is an identifiable "phenomenon," attested to time and again, doubtless no one will deny. We can observe and ascertain it on a daily basis. And we do not thereby maintain the distance of someone observing unfamiliar beings; we never regard child's play in our surroundings in the way in which we, as for instance biologists, watch the "dance of the bees." We see animal behavior only from the outside and attempt to discover the secret of its objective purposiveness; presented with child's play, however, we understand it from the start within a horizon shared with other human beings, understand it from within, as it were, from out of our own knowledge about how to play. And not only because each adult has already at some time played and knows about the activity of play from his own experience. Understanding the fundamental human possibility of playing is not an empirical result but rather belongs to a primordial clarity of understanding in which human existence is open to itself. No one is likely to contest that play exists as a human possibility of a special, imaginatively exhilarated comportment. As an anthropological phenomenon play is considered to be verified, even if controversy may reign over its "phenomenological" interpretations. The indisputable phenomenon of play in no way presents itself as readily evident and transparent; on the contrary: this phenomenon standing more or less on the margins of life offers a surprising opposition to conceptual penetration as soon one undertakes to analyze its structure. What is so buoyantly light and easy to do is hard and recalcitrant for the concept.

However, while human play is recognized as a phenomenon, cosmic play is never encountered and corroborated as an objectively present and intersubjectively identifiable occurrence. World-play is no phenomenon. One cannot point it out or make it the object of a scientific method of research. It is initially a thought and nothing more. But just what a "thought" is remains itself a problem rife with questions. Is a thought something merely "imagined," a phantasm, something our soul has dreamed up—a representation that does not correspond to anything actual? Or does the power of thought reach deeper into the essence of Being than sensuous representation, in which so-called "actual things" evince themselves to us? Plato's "idea" cannot be ascertained by seeing, hearing, tasting, or smelling—and yet it counts for him as "having more being [*seiender*]," as stronger in its Being than sensible things. It is only thinking as genuine apprehension that is associated with the Platonic idea. Platonic ideas, too, are not phenomena. Of course one may not simply invert the situation and maintain that everything that does not identifiably announce itself as a phenomenon is an actuality of higher rank; for one would thereby open the door to the wildest fanaticism and lose the rigor of the philosophical concept. Now, in order to "interpret [*deuten*]" the total movement of the world's actuality in analogy to human play, one could perhaps say that the concept of a "world-play" primarily signifies a speculative symbol. It would be a matter of a "transference" of structures belonging to a specific enactment of human life to the worlded whole of all beings, a matter of a *meta-pherein*, a metaphor—indeed a matter of a correspondence between an innerworldly being and the world itself. This "transference," one might say, has its basis in the phenomenon of play, which is indeed a human reality—philosophical thought leaps from this basis when it attempts to think the whole movement of the world from the concept of play; in such a leap it must necessarily change and transform itself, if it becomes at all expressly conscious of the difference between an innerworldly thing and the world itself. The differentiated elaboration of the phenomenal structures of human play then appears as the most urgent task, while the examination of the question whether the concept of play can be transferred in a symbolic analogy to the happening of the world—and to what extent such a metaphor at all has value for philosophical knowledge—then appears as a subordinate matter. The argument of "common sense," which, with its chubby-cheeked health, moves about with the difference between thing and world as with a self-evident state of affairs, runs something like this. However, perhaps here it hinges not only on the difference between thing and world but at the same time on the question as to how a peculiar innerworldly thing, the human being who understands Being, relates to the world-totality. In the end, nothing is accomplished by our distinguishing human play and world-play, the one designated as a phenomenon, the other as a speculative thought. The world-relation of human existence is not an affair that is already previously known and ascertained in such a way that we could apply the distinction between the human being and the world, as it were, to play. It is rather the converse. In a discussion of play we perhaps achieve the conceptual resources to think and conceive primordially[3] the difference and belonging together of the human being and the world.

If from the slightest things a path always leads to philosophy, one may expect that a reflection on play, on this folly of children, could even ultimately one day unsettle the self-assured knowledge of adults.

2. The World-Significance of Human Play

Each of us is acquainted with play—acquainted with it from the testimony of our own experience and from our observation of the everyday human environment. Play is well known as a phenomenon, familiar to us and commonplace. It does not need to be brought forth out of concealment into the light; we do not need to "uncover" it like some remote, alien thing. Playing is a familiar possibility of carrying out our lives in a manner that is at times relaxed and likewise joyfully exhilarated in itself. As adults we marvel, perhaps with muted envy, at the play of children, the blissful devotion with which they engage in it, the wealth of imagination, the abundance of the forms and freely chosen rules. We marvel in this at the freely unencumbered élan for life. To be sure, even in adult life we are acquainted with manifold "games," practices for "whiling away" idle hours, events resembling the ancient circus[4] that serve as entertainment and conversational material for the masses. We are acquainted with playful situations in the midst of life's serious business, when adventurous or fairy-tale-like features suddenly descend on human existence. We are acquainted with playful moments in "flirting," in sports, in all sorts of ventures and risks, and of course we are also acquainted with explicitly delimited events involving play [*Spielveranstaltungen*] in the theater and cinema, and on the radio and television. Familiarity with the phenomenon of play is incontestable. It is extensive and multifarious, encompassing an immense abundance of forms and structures. And yet we are not able to "express" this already familiar knowledge of play in a sufficient way and to formulate it with conceptual rigor. We live conversant with an understanding of play; understanding has a use-character. As soon as we reflect on it the immediate "use" is disturbed, it loses its fluent "self-evidence," and the light of understanding is clouded. That is, however, a basic process in all contemplation.

As long as we live wrapped up uncritically in the naïve, natural attitude of life and restrict ourselves to the public, general interpretation of the world, which is given to us in advance through common language and tradition in the broadest sense, we "know" who we are, what our task and our goal are, what duty and right, custom and law are; we know what the human is in the midst of things, what his status and his mission are, what "nature" and what "history" are, what "necessity" and what "freedom" are, what in general a thing, a substance[5] is, what "institutions" such as the state and church are—we know, too, what the seriousness of life and play are. Such "knowledge" in the mode of conversantly employed understanding has its "practical intelligibility," its use-value, and finds itself continually confirmed in the changing situations of life. One gets by with it, if one merely "lives," uses one's common sense, in order to arrange one's life as favorably as possible and to "succeed." However, as soon as one contemplates, the commonplace certainty of the immediate interpretation of the world vanishes. When the lightning bolt of wonder strikes us, mysterious amazement bursts open, for which everything familiar suddenly becomes unfamiliar and questionworthy. When the philosophical question arises, the human being does not immediately become more knowing but rather more unknowing, is thrown back into a not-knowing that shocks and terrifies. And the uncanniness of this situation consists in his having to regard his earlier knowledge as nugatory and untenable, as ungrounded and delusional, as a not-knowing that took itself for knowing and labored under a delusional blindness, and it consists in the fact that he initially feels that he is plunged into a poverty that knows that it knows nothing. When the contemplativeness of thought comes over us we fall from former certainties; we no longer know who we are, what a human being is, what custom and right, thing and world are. There is, perhaps, no more essential allegory for this transformation of humanity than the fate of Laius's unfortunate son. Oedipus stands in radiant glory, the ruler of the city, who won Thebes and the hand of the queen when he was able to solve the riddle of the sphinx and to her question could answer: that is the human being. Oedipus knows who the human being is; this knowledge brought him into kingship. He is able to see better, is more clear-sighted than the others; he understands best of all, so far as understanding comes from the wisdom proper to human beings. He takes this knowledge to be certain, his happiness to be abiding and firm. The uncanniness of his situation lies not least in this situation presenting itself precisely as native security. Oedipus lives with an undaunted trust in Being: his world is valid, his rule stands, sons and daughters are the assurance of the continuity of his family line; his knowledge is reliable and provides guidance for fellow citizens. Then the pestilence breaks out in the city, a sign of the wrath of the gods, and with terror the citizens of the city and Oedipus himself suspect that, seen from the higher knowledge of the gods, things are not as good as human beings supposed. This suspicion becomes the impetus for a radical search for truth. And gradually the uncanny unveiling is carried out; the seer, mouthpiece of the gods, is compelled by the king to reveal the horror little by little. Oedipus initially seeks the murderer of the king outside—and finds him inside, in his very self, revealed to be the defiler of his mother. It is a compelling symbol that he gouges out his eyes and thereby blots out the sensuous truth that kept him in the dark. Only when he no longer sensuously sees and the light of day is extinguished for him does he see truly and essentially what is. Bereft of his eyesight, shattered by the death of his mother-wife, deserted by his sons, void of power and driven out from the city, he travels the long, bitter road to Colonus in order, absolved, to be transported away by the gods.

In the fate of Oedipus the fate of the human passion for truth has been depicted in its monumental greatness and simplicity. The son of the earth does violence to his mother when he rises against her and aspires to subject her with the clever cunning of his skillfulness, when he builds houses and cities, makes devices, machines, and celebrates the triumph of his industry and ingenuity. Is such knowledge already knowledge enough? Is it not surpassable by a more terrible knowledge in which, perhaps, an inexhaustibility of maternal nature would be known, an inexhaustibility of which the human being never takes measure? Does not practical-technical know-how with regard to beings suddenly collapse once the question actually arises and is held on to, the question, namely, of what beings are? The not-knowing into which an incipient contemplation plunges us is no "state" in which we could tarry; it is rather characterized by an unbearable tension; the negativity in *not*-knowing becomes the unrest of an spiritual wandering and odyssey where we are never sure of reaching a Colonus. If the tragedy of Oedipus is a symbolic allegory for the human being's radical will to truth and thereby for philosophy, then philosophy is thus brought to presence in a play. A play can suggestively portray, in an essential sense, what philosophy is and in what way it is. We thereby have a peculiar reversal. Instead of philosophically saying what play is, what philosophy itself is can be said in the play of an ancient tragedy. The philosophical statement concerning play can even be encompassed by a play's interpretation of philosophizing. These are noteworthy connections which we do not easily see through and which are full of questions. But initially it comes down to conveying a pre-understanding of the problematic. Of course a methodical procedure could be conceived according to which one would first begin with an analysis of the phenomenon of play, would draw out and clarify step by step the structures of this phenomenon, familiar to us all, and only then could one transition to posing and developing the more fundamental questions. We choose another path. We are attempting a preview of the fundamental dimension of the *philosophical* problem of play. Play is—as was already explained—a possible and worthy topic for philosophy. It is possible as a "theme" because thinking that questions wants especially to grasp that which is unquestionable in itself—it is worthy as theme because in play, in a unique way, the connection between the human being and the world is opened up. Human play has world-significance, has a cosmic transparency—it is one of the clearest world-figures of our finite existence. While playing, the human being does not remain in himself, does not remain in an enclosed domain of his psychic interiority—rather, he ecstatically steps out of and beyond himself in a cosmic gesture and interprets the whole of the world in a manner that is suffused with sense.

Precisely as a human problem, human play is worldly—and as a worldly problem it points to the human being. The relationship between the human being and the world cannot be adequately thought on the model of the relation between two things, two beings. The relations that we are acquainted with and that are transparent in their structure are connections between intraworldly things. To each thing *in* the world there belongs the fundamental character of being related to itself, of identity, and at the same time of being related to another being. To the identity of that which is identical there belongs, in a way that is constitutive for sense, being different from another. Sameness and difference belong indivisibly together; a thing can only be the same to the extent that it is different; and, on the other hand, being different in each case presupposes being the same. Plato, in the *Sophist,* already saw and expressed these fundamental ontological connections. Not only must things in each case be the same in order to be able to be distinguished from one another, but being the same cannot be thought at all without being different. *Tauton* and *heteron* are bound up with each other. In grand fashion this motif of thought is again taken up in Hegel's *Logic* and unfolded as an inner dialectic of the concepts constitutive of the thing. The human being as an innerworldly being is also determined in his connections and relations to other innerworldly beings surrounding him by this interweaving of "sameness" and "difference" and is "conditioned [*be-dingt*]" by the universal ontological constitution of things [*Dinge*]. But the question remains whether such a conditioning of the human being determines him fully and exclusively—or whether he is still not stamped in his essence by another heterogeneous connection, namely by his connection to the world-totality. The world-totality is not an outermost limit of the innerworldly field of things, not a "frame" and not a "container"; beings are not positioned in the world like a worm in an apple or gold in the bank. All well-known and familiar modes of the being-in of things in greater things surrounding them cannot be applied to things' being in the universe or a fortiori to the being-in of the human being, who understands Being, in the ontological whole of the world. The world is no object—rather it is perhaps the region of all regions, space of all spaces, and time of all times. We survey in each case only a delimited section, never seeing the whole. And if we extend our own space of experience, stretch the spans of time experienced by us, by assuming our fellow human beings' knowledge of other spaces and other times, then we still never arrive at an objective knowledge of the world. The world is also not the total object of the united human consciousness. All two and half billion human beings together are not closer to the world itself than a single one. We have our sojourn "in the world," live wrapped up in it and toward things that we encounter and that come to be objects. Nevertheless, we never find the world confronting us like a thing, like a being, like an object. But if it does not itself come into contact with us, how can we then know about it at all? Does it not belong in the realm of fables? What is given objectively and as evident are things and configurations of things, broad realms of inanimate and living Being. These realms are not "self-contained," they are "open"; only the human scope of cognition is limited. We can represent and imagine to ourselves a more powerful intellect that would have a much greater field of cognition than the human being. But could this intellect have the world itself as a complete object? Obviously not. It would indeed have a much greater realm of experience than we do, just not the world as an object, though. If the world thus does not offer itself to any experience, however greatly conceived, then in the end it is nothing at all. After all, we can make no justified statements about something that withdraws from all accessibility. Now, one could, however, oppose this skepticism by saying that not everything that is must be an object of experience, that we do not draw all of our knowledge solely from experience. For, in order to be able to have experiences at all, we must already be in possession of prior knowledge about what can be experienced as such. An "a priori" knowledge about the objectivity of all objects, a categorial pre-understanding, and, furthermore, a knowledge about spatiality and temporality precedes every cognition of experience as a condition of its possibility. Kant has set forth and explicated such "conditions of the possibility of experience" in the *Critique of Pure Reason*. But the a priori conditions of experience prove themselves precisely in their "making experience possible," in their validity. That a system of open horizons belongs to every manner of experience and that what is thus factically experienced therefore implicitly refers to an endless progression is itself still a phenomenal structure. Knowledge about the world, however, has no attestation in the objectivity of experience. If it is supposed to be an a priori possession of human reason, then it would be at best an "idea" without objective foothold in the phenomenon, an idea that contributes nothing to the cognition of things, that is not realized or falsified in any experience—and would perhaps be best entirely forgotten if that were possible.

Now, however, our human reason has the remarkable fate of becoming worried and continually overwhelmed by thoughts of the totality of that which is. The thought of the "totality" does not let us go; the thought of the immense and the sublime inhabits our spirit and wrests it from every modest establishment. This thought of the world is initially less a theoretical concept than an "attunement," an attunement of longing reaching out into the limitless, an oceanic feeling in gazing over the "wide sea" or in contemplating the "starry heavens" above us.[6] This attunement is not a kind of "sentimentality" or "edification"—it is an attunement of thought, perhaps *the* attunement of thought. The entire section in Kant's *Critique of Pure Reason* on the dialectic is an attempt to be finished with the a priori of the thought of the world, in which the exposition of the problem in Kant is more essential than his "solution." Ultimately, "world" becomes in Kant something subjective, a "regulative idea" that we cannot do without in order to guide the progress of experience, yet something that we can also never "redeem" and realize in actual experience. As space and time become subjective forms of the subject's faculty of intuition, so the world becomes a necessary, subjective idea that is, however, never given in experience and that only comes to have a functional value for the architectonic completion of the process of cognition. Kant clearly recognizes (and it is a highly significant event in the history of the problem of world) that the world is not a massive thing and not a massively powerful object—that the relation between the human subject and the world cannot be assessed as a relation between two beings. On the other hand, however, there is no possibility for him to conceptually determine a relation that is in play not between two innerworldly things, but rather between the innerworldly human who has an understanding of Being and the universal whole of Being. For this reason, Kant had to "subjectivize" the world, to make it into a structure of the subject that represents by means of ideas. Kant thereby closes again the problem that, in a magnificent way, he himself wrenched open. Nevertheless, a "world-pathos" remains vital in his philosophy—comes to expression, for instance, in that which he names philosophy's "world-concept," by which he does not mean a piece of scholarly erudition but rather a mode of existence, the human being's way of life, which is present in his highest goals, and recalls the "divine man in us."

However, if it actually belongs to the human being's essence to exist in relation to the world-totality, to stand out with understanding into the whole of Being, then the difficulty arises of our lacking the concepts, not only in everyday understanding but also, in large measure, in philosophy, too, to characterize such a "relation." The lack here, however, is not an unfortunate accident or a flaw of our language; it has its deeper basis in the fact that in the course of the history of Western philosophy the world-relation of human existence increasingly fell under the shadow of another relation, namely the relation of the human being to the divinity. The theological character of metaphysics has increasingly obscured and concealed the world-relation of human nature. Yet wouldn't a meditation harking back to the earliest dawn of Western thought then still be a road, or yet a narrower and more fragile footpath, to arrive at a primordial thinking of the world? Interpreting the early Greeks is a peculiar case. We do not simply return to them when we read the ancient texts; we bring ourselves along when we turn toward them. We cannot simply shake off the tradition as though it were a bothersome speck of dust, a tradition that binds us to the ancient giants of thought just as much as it separates us from them. Let that be said for our own self-critical caution and modesty. We turn to a saying of Heraclitus—to point the way for our own thought—namely, Fragment 30 in Diels's collection of the *Fragments of the Presocratics*. It runs (translated): "This world-order, the same for every multiplicity, neither one of the gods nor humans have brought forth, but rather it always was and is and will eternally be living fire, lighting up in measures, going out in measures."[7] The obscurity of the sayings of Heraclitus the obscure was already famous and notorious in antiquity. We cannot claim to fathom the depths of this saying.[8] "World-order," *kosmos*, is the beautiful dispensation of things and events that links them all together, that impresses a character of totality upon them and gathers them into a structured unity. All things do not seethe through each other in disorderly tumult: land and sea are separate; mountains and valleys; stars, moon, and sun; plants, animals, and human beings; heaven and earth are in equilibrium. An order and a beautiful radiance prevail through everything that is. But neither one of the gods nor a human being brought forth this beautiful dispensation of the whole. This declaration is astonishing. We must, of course, strictly keep the idea of a "world-creator" distinct from the Greek concept of God. But why are gods and humans named at all? What is decisive is not that they are excluded as producers of the beautiful world-order, but rather that they can at all be named in connection with the production of the *kosmos*. For, initially, the gods, like human beings, are in each case beings in the world. The gods inhabit the region of the heavens, the realm of the stars and the heavenly fire; they are of all innerworldly things the "nearest to fire." The gods exercise governance in the cosmos from their sidereal perch; they direct and guide the fates of mortals, send signs to them of their favor and disfavor. Human beings dwell below on the heavy and dark earth and are still close to the realm of animals. With much effort they learn from their divine masters the right way of life and good customs. Notwithstanding the great difference between the immortal gods and mortal human beings, both coincide in having at their disposal the power of production. The gods produce by governing the processes in the land of human beings; human beings produce by building houses, clearing primeval forests, taming and breeding animals, forging iron and fabricating a thousand kinds of devices. As an artisan the human being produces things that without him would not exist in nature at all; he has a delimited, finite creativity. And this is at work not merely in the formed products of his handicraft but also in the constructs of his social volition, thus when he forms states and founds cities and empires. Politics is a sort of *technē*. Having a productive power at one's disposal is proper to gods and human beings as a common, basic feature. Gods and human beings have the capacity for *poiēsis*. But do they have this capacity as an endowment that belongs to them, as a firm possession? Or are they, of all innerworldly beings, "productive" and "creative" because in the end they alone are determined by a relation to the productive power of the omni-potent? Is it because they extend with understanding into the production, into the *poiēsis*, that belongs to the world-clearing [*weltlichtenden*] and world-arranging fire? To put it explicitly, that the ordering, clearing-producing power of gods and human beings has not produced the total order of all that is, only has meaning if gods and human beings in some sense stand in proximity to the world-arranging *poiēsis*. What initially sounds like a harsh dismissal in the saying of Heraclitus is at bottom an honor. What is ultimately productive is the world-light [*Weltlicht*] of fire. This Heraclitean basic concept of fire, of *pyr*, would be thought too tersely, however, if one wanted to explicate it in the direction of an ultimate "world-stuff." Fire does not mean that out of which all things exist, but rather the arranging power that strikes all individuated beings with the character of a beautiful, gleaming total dispensation. Therefore, Heraclitus uses the names of specific fires synonymously: lightning, *keraunos*, and *helios*, the sun. Spoken metaphorically: in night and darkness everything becomes indistinguishable, all articulation is extinguished. In the stroke of lightning, however, obscured dispensation suddenly comes to light again. And when the sun returns after night and darkness, everything shines anew in its precise contours and its connection with other beings. Clearing is a mode of letting a conjoined order of things come forth. The sunlight, however, is also temporal movement, the world-clock, as it were, that measures hours and days, years of individuals and peoples. Clearing and time must be thought together in the fundamental Heraclitean concept of *pyr*, of fire. That also comes to expression in the fact that it is said of this world-fire that it always was and is and will be. Is it only continuous *in* time—or is it even time itself with its dimensions of past, present, and future?

A deeper interpretation, which, above all, would be responsive to the context of world-fire, *helios, horēn,* and *aiōn,* could draw out how a connection between Being and time is thought in the doctrine of fire. The world-relationality of innerworldly gods and human beings has become important for us in Fragment 30. They are *in the world* in a different way than the stone and wave, than the flower and tree, than the hawk and deer are—also in a different way than the artifacts made by human beings are and in a different way than numbers and figures are. Gods and human beings are in the world in such a way that they comport themselves with understanding to the all-giving and all-taking fundamental power that arranges the *kosmos* and regulates the flux and course of things. And from such a relation of understanding they are still able to be "productive" in a certain derivative sense, the gods more than human beings—but still less than the world-fire that enflames and drives the course of all individual things, lets them rise and fall, emerge and pass away. The world-fire is the course of the world itself. The Greek word *aiōn* initially, pre-philosophically, signifies the course of a human being's life, his lifetime with all its content. Heraclitus appropriates this word *aiōn* and merely names fire in another way once more, calling it the course of the world. And of this course of the world he says in Fragment 52: "The course of the world is a child playing, who moves the pieces on the board here and there, is a child's kingdom."[9] The whole of beings, as the prevailing world, is addressed in the symbolic metaphor of the "playing child," the *pais paizōn.* The most primordial production has the character of play. The world prevails as play. Gods and human beings are what they are not according to a proper constitution of Being resting in itself—they are not closed in on themselves like other things in the world; they are in an irrupted, ecstatic relation to *pyr* and *aiōn.* They have derived all their power to exercise control, all capacity for production, from the play of the world. Gods and human beings are citizens of the world, even if of different rank.

But where and when does this play happen? Can one point to it in some place or at some point in time? Every place and every point in time are already occupied by innerworldly things. The play of the world does not appear anywhere or at any time among things. Does this play, then, of which Heraclitus speaks, not at all exist? Is it an arbitrary dream of thought, a phantasmagoria of speculative thinking? Perhaps a beautiful poetic sentiment—and nothing more? That Heraclitus's world-play does not appear anywhere at any time among *given* things has its basis in the fact that it is what ultimately *gives,* the omni-potent, which brings all beings to pass,[10] granting them place and duration. However, what problem lies in his using the name of a human comportment, which is familiar as a phenomenon, for the giving, world-arranging, conjoining power, which is not a present, describable, and immediately addressable finding, but rather something completely ineffable? Has he just more or less used human play as a "cosmic metaphor" by chance—could he have just as well chosen another metaphor? Or is there already in human play, taken up as a phenomenon, a peculiar reference to the whole of the world? Is play essentially determined by a representational function? That is, in fact, the case—and it is the more profound reason for Heraclitus's cosmological metaphor. We must still clarify this and in the process elucidate play as an especially intense mode of the human relation to the world. In Heraclitus, gods and human beings stood in relation to "ever-living fire," were emulators and re-creators of the productive omni-potence. Their poietic power was grounded in the play of the world. As a result they were essentially players. As long as gods and human beings exist from out of their respective relation to the world, the difference separating them was great, to be sure, but nevertheless not unbridgeable, as Heraclitus's Fragment 62 shows.[11] Yet the more the relation to the world that is common to gods and human beings is no longer thought on its own terms, the more starkly does the distinction between divine and mortal beings come to the fore; the human being is then interpreted on the basis of his distance from God. This tendency becomes preponderant at the beginning of Western metaphysics. But even Plato still conceives the relation of the gods to human beings—as a game. He calls the human being a "plaything of God," a *paignion theou*.[12]

3. Methodological Considerations

Our attempt to think about play does not find itself in the fortunate position of having in advance a firm and recognized methodology that would merely need to be applied to a particular case. The problem of play does not even exist firmly for us in its character as a problem. Now, we are, however, acquainted with a typology of problems; we are acquainted in our historical situation with two types of theoretical questions: they are, firstly, the questions of "science," and then the questions of "philosophy." If we distinguish between science and philosophy in this way, we do not mean a sharp division, let alone an antagonistic opposition, and certainly not the vulgar antithesis of rational composure and irrational emotion. Reason is not the cold, pale light that appears to an anemic, withered humanity cut off from the authentic experiences of existence; it is the most passionate passion and the wildest desire, thoroughly aglow with *erōs* down to its roots, as Plato's dialogues show. Science and philosophy are essentially connected, despite their being distinguished. Each needs the other. Science [*Wissenschaft*], taken as an individual discipline [*Einzelwissenschaft*], is strictly bound to its subject matter [*Sache*], thereby proving its objectivity [*Sachlichkeit*]; as a positive individual discipline it has something posited, something established, in advance, an object-domain [*Sachbereich*] in which its research moves and maintains itself. In this presupposed object-domain it finds beings showing themselves, it finds them as phenomena in various modes of manifestation and makes them into objects of a consistent determination. The positive sciences initially take up their object-domains from the pre-scientific awareness of the manifold articulation of beings—but they do not stop at the approximate classification of things. They discuss their own basic concepts, which they use to address their respective object-domains. They mark themselves off from neighboring disciplines and continually supersede the methodological expectations with which they delimit their courses of research. The positive individual disciplines thoroughly relate to beings—but they do not question what beings as beings are. They bind themselves strictly to their subject-matters—but do not determine what it means to be a subject matter. They adhere to the phenomena—without interrogating phenomenality itself. They proceed with the universal articulation of things according to species and genera, they operate with the distinction between actuality and potentiality, without ever conceiving thereby what the specification of beings is and what in general thingliness is, what actuality and potentiality as modalities of Being are.

To ask about everything that the positive individual discipline thus puts aside, or better, what it implicitly "presupposes," is a task of philosophy. Even so, whether philosophy is exhausted in bringing to light the presuppositions of science that are not thematized by the sciences is another matter. In any case, the connection just characterized, which has for us a certain typical familiarity, exists between the problems of philosophy and those of individual disciplines. Some matters come down to being either philosophical problems or those of a single discipline. The manner of formulating a question scientifically is determined by the intention to ascertain first of all the "phenomenon," to hold the matter fast in its pure self-showing and revealing and, so far as it is at all possible, to generate the explicative concepts from the matter itself. The perspective of philosophy is determined by having its eye on the ontological constitution of questionable beings; this ontological constitution adheres to a matter not simply like an enduring property that would merely need to be named and described. The ontological clarification of any matter whatsoever always leads back to the fundamental philosophical questions because the measure by which we assess the ontological status of a being remains what is most questionworthy.

If we now wished to subject our theme of play to the previously noted typology of problems, then two lines of questioning would be prefigured: the question of an individual discipline would have to proceed from the "phenomenon" of play; as a phenomenon it is an anthropological datum that would initially have to be secured in contrast to the modes of behavior of animals appearing biologically similar, in order then to be interpreted in terms of its own content and its own phenomenal richness. A manifold of structures could be elaborated and appreciated in their cultural significance. The philosophical question would then aim at the ontological constitution of human play, at the particular way in which play exists; for it is indeed immediately apparent that play "is" not in the way in which the serious human pursuits of life are—that it is an exhilarated "doing as if," that it contains within itself a peculiar "appearance," a noteworthy sphere of "non-actuality." Play—as a strange interpenetration of "Being" and "appearance"—is, as it were, an appearing Being and an existing appearance. A thorough ontological clarification of play requires an insight, not easy to attain, into the "interplay" of Being and appearance. Our attempt to think about play is neither that of an "individual discipline" nor "philosophical" in the sense indicated earlier. Here it is not a matter of examining an ontic phenomenon and holding it fast in descriptive concepts nor of characterizing "ontologically" the ontic phenomenon of human play, of determining it in its complex ontological constitution in an ontological-conceptual way; here it is a matter of something simpler and more primordial: grasping the human being's world-position under the guidance of a specific understanding of play.

The expression "world-position [*Weltstellung*]" is initially unclear and polysemous. A "position" has something as its spatial location in an environment, in a region—as well as a temporal position within a manifold of positions. A thing, a matter, a being has a spatial-temporal position within a system of positions. This position has a specific positional value in relation to a system of coordinates that must be well known in order for us to be able to identify near and far, in general the distantiality of specific things within the system. Now, the things in our environment are already, to a certain degree, oriented around us, are things near and things far, have distance from us; the whole field of perception is gradated in terms of depth, structured in concentric circles and zones around us. We are the zero-point of the perceptual realm, so to speak—we, that is: our embodiment. Foreign things stand and situate themselves around our body; every individual thing has its place within the system of positions of the perceptual field and a "position" therein, a relation directed toward us. But things do not remain motionless; there are manifold motions in the perceptual field. Things can draw near to us and can distance themselves from us, can thus change their position in our field of vision. Their position is variable. The distance of things to us is at the same time our distance to things. And this distance can be altered not merely through a motion that things carry out; we can also move ourselves. Our body is not firmly rooted; it is mobile. We can draw close to certain things in our perceptual field and can distance ourselves from them. But when we speak in this way of our own movement of our body, we have already gone beyond the environmental space of orientation and have presupposed a system of positions that is not centered in our body. The domestic house, the settlement in which we live, now perhaps functions as a "zero-point." Things are situated around it: the fields that we cultivate, the river that flows by and disappears in the distance. In this system of things near and far we can move around and have a position ourselves, a changing and variable position in relation to the zero-point. To be sure, this system of positions is also "oriented": things have their position from the relation to the distinctive thing that is taken to be the point of relation for all relations of things near and far. Now, there are many such oriented systems of positions in which the opposition between spheres of nearness and farness, between "domestic" and "foreign," is reiterated in manifold ways. The inhabited earth is, as it were, humankind's domestic sphere of nearness, from which it seeks to reach out into the stellar expanses with the projectiles of the most modern technology. Space as it is thought scientifically emerges for us, however, in a certain way, when we abstain from a determinate, firmly fixed orientation, when we consider no thing to be the distinctive zero-point, but rather regard all things as possible zero-points of an arbitrarily determinable system of coordinates; space then becomes "homogenous." The selection of the zero-point is arbitrary; nevertheless one must choose some point in order to be able to determine the location of all other things in relation to this fixed point. The homogenous system of positions is distinct from the "oriented" system insofar as one is able to choose all things purely and simply as zero-points. Yet both in the oriented and in the homogenous system of spatial positions, the "place" of each being is determined by a relation to *another being,* whether this be a fixed or an arbitrary zero-point of a system of coordinates. The position of each intraworldly thing is expressed by a relation to a specific intraworldly thing. Not merely individual things but also the system in which the former are in each case marked in their position is assessed in an intraworldly manner and remains fundamentally intraworldly—without it being the case, however, that this intraworldliness is explicitly recognized or taken into consideration. The whole of beings attains the shape of a comprehensive context of things, which is conceived as an articulated, architectonic structure—as a system of locations, of intervals and distances with respect to a distinctive being.

In the concept of the "position" of a being, not only is a spatial relation thought as well, but perhaps still more a hierarchical relation. As has already been said, the hierarchical relation of things is initially asserted *pre*-philosophically according to some distinction of power, beauty, or the like, and then philosophically interpreted with regard to constancy in time, strength of Being, and rationality, whereby what is most continuous and most rational counts as most being. To be sure, philosophy does not "dogmatically" determine what or who the most constant and rational is—it maintains a critical reserve with respect to itself and keeps the measure according to which it assesses the Being of phenomenal things included in the problem. It knows about the provisionality of such statements when it addresses the *summum ens,* the highest being, with the venerable and holy name *God*—it knows that it thereby "takes the Lord's name in vain." Nevertheless what is more profoundly questionworthy is whether that from which the ontological status of all existing things is determined would itself have to be a highest being, whether it as *summum* would have to be an *ens.* If philosophy determines the hierarchy from a relation of things to a highest being, then this hierarchy, however much it is held to be problematic, nevertheless fundamentally has an intraworldly character. The ontological status of all things is determined from the relation to a being that is just as much "in the world" as they themselves are. The ontological hierarchy likewise becomes an intraworldly relation between things as previously was the case for the spatial location of a thing, insofar as it is designated from its distance to the fixed or arbitrary zero/middle-point of a system of coordinates. But is the *world-position* of a being actually in view when we can specify its location in an intra-worldly total system? Things are "in" space, they are "spaced" within the one, all-encompassing space; the being-in-space of things, their being-spaced-within, however, is still not at all grasped when we pay attention to distances, stretches, lines, and points. A material, corporeal thing has its figure, its outlines, corners, and edges; a block of stone, for instance, contains in itself parts of different sorts that we could break off. As a large thing it comprises many smaller things in itself. In its own filled space it contains the filled spaces belonging to its smaller constituent parts. And similarly the block of stone in the mining heap and the mining heap in the mountain and the mountain in the mountain range and the mountain range in the earth's crust and this on the globe and this in the solar system, this in the Milky Way, and so forth. But what, then, does this "and so forth" mean? Are we actually able to conceive and to grasp it? We can elevate the everyday positional descriptions of the immediate things of our life-world by means of scientific "determinations of position"; we can choose the solar system instead of the domestic house as a zero/middle-point—but we thereby achieve as a result only a greater intraworldly sphere and not the world itself. Do things in the world exist in the same way as small things in larger things? Or is there a completely other way of being-in that holds intraworldly things as a totality in their relation to the whole of the world? Are the manifold spaces of things in the space of the world like smaller spaces of things in larger spaces of things, are times and durations, in which intraworldly beings emerge and pass away and have limited existence, in the time of the world as shorter stretches of time are contained in longer stretches of time? Or do such intraworldly relations of containment miss the mark here? And a similar consideration should also be raised in regard to the hierarchy. Can the hierarchy that exists between things according to the variously thought exemplariness of a highest being at all serve as a guiding model to expose, even merely as a question, the hierarchical position of things in relation to the world-totality? Everything here is initially obscure. And, above all, it comes down to enduring the strangeness of posing questions in such a way and to letting this strangeness resonate—and not at once eliminating it with a hasty "answer."

This was also the motive for thinking back to Heraclitus. In both of the aforementioned fragments the human being's position in the world and the connection with play was the essential thought, under whose guidance and escort we sought to set our own stammering reflections in motion. Gods and human beings are not what they are from their relation to an innerworldly being—but rather from their relation to "ever-living world-fire" that, in clearing, stamps every individuated thing into the finite contours of its appearance, allocates its form, place and duration, and brings it into and removes it from presence. Thus gods and human beings are like participating witnesses of the clearing, temporalizing, and productive play of the world-fire, and, from such witnessing, they themselves attain in a derivative manner characteristics of the world-fire: they are poietic, are disclosing, and they understand time. Heraclitus always thinks the same thing in all his obscure sayings, but in ever different ways. He addresses fire both as lightning and *hēlios*—and the life of fire as the play of *aiōn*. However, the fact that what is manifoldly named is not merely the same, but has a sameness of a completely peculiar and unique sort and cannot be understood in its "identity" from the identity of things, comes clearly to expression when Heraclitus contrasts *pyr,* fire, to all beings, *ta panta,* with the metaphor of "gold" and "wares."[13] Things in their multiplicity are related to the golden sheen of the fiery, all-gathering light of world—as are the many purchasable objects to gold. The unity of the All, in gathering and dispersing, encompasses the multiplicity of intraworldly beings. And Heraclitus also calls the worlded unity the "one, alone wise," *hen to sophon mounon.*[14] The fiery world-light is thus to be thought less on the model of an elementary original stuff than on the model of a clearing understanding. Fire, light, time, play, and reason are different names for the same prevailing of the world. And to the extent that it is precisely gods and human beings who stand in a peculiar relation to this prevailing, they also participate in the reason of the universe. Of the "one, alone wise," Heraclitus says in Fragment 32 that it is not willing and nevertheless is willing to be called by the name of Zeus. Highly significant in this formulation is the precedence of the resistance to concession. The rational play of the world, which is imbued with fire, time, and light, *is not willing* to be addressed by the name of the highest god. But, insofar as the highest god stands closest to it and in its finite determination is more speakable and thinkable than the world itself, it is in a certain way also the will of the totality to enter into speakability in the name of the being nearest to the world and therefore highest, to appear therein just as much as to disappear. The history of Western philosophy could be written as a commentary on this thirty-second fragment of Heraclitus, insofar as the primordial openness of human thinking to the world is ever more strongly transformed into the theological orientation of metaphysics and aims at the "absolute," at the *summum ens* and conceives itself in the most extreme culmination, in Hegel's philosophy, even as the "self-consciousness of God." In closest connection with this tendency is the fact that intraworldly relations decide the "position" and "status" of the human being, and that the human relation to the world sinks into the shadows of an oblivion lasting centuries. Gods and human beings in Heraclitus are not determined from their own standing, nor from what they each already are of their own accord, from what they bring with them, but rather they are conceived from a unique and hardly addressable openedness for the reason of the totality and the fire-play of the universe.

That is something which is almost inconceivable for us, not merely because of the "obscurity" of the Heraclitean manner of thought, but above all because of the traditional ways in which we are accustomed to think. We are accustomed by a long tradition to make statements concerning beings. Beings lie before us; we experience, observe, investigate them. From our insight into their concrete content, we take the facts of the matter pertaining to them and formulate this in language. The thing becomes the "about-which" of our statements, becomes the underlying thing for our speech—which is about or on it. We thereby grasp what is given to experience in things, empirical contents—but we can also, in another orientation of interest, attune ourselves to what we know in a previously familiar knowledge about things, their general structure, their makeup, and their manifold realms independent of and before all experiential encounters with them; we can attempt to bring what we know a priori to the concept. Nevertheless, in this empirical knowledge, as in a priori knowledge, we are guided by the conception that all known, cognized, and grasped determinations belong to the things and themselves depend on them, are, so to speak, "attached" to them. Things are what they are precisely in their essential and inessential properties. The thing is a bearer of properties. Beings have the fundamental structure of substantiality. That need not always mean that there is something persistent in the alteration of conditions. Even "events," processes, and occurrences have the aforementioned structure of being bearers of the determinations of their properties. Admittedly, the manner in which "properties" belong to a substantial bearer is not identical in all things. There are many sorts of properties and there are many ways in which, respectively, a property comes to belong to the bearer. The realm of the inanimate, the mineral realm, not only delimits the widest possible region; it also characterizes a certain manner of relation between material substrate and property. In the field of living things, of organisms, other forms of being a property show themselves—and still others in the case of the human being, insofar as he is not exhausted by biological-organic observation. The human being, one says, is not merely an "animal," a living being, that is determined by metabolism, generation, sensation, memory, and the capacity for perception. The animal has all that to a certain degree as well. The human being does not merely perceive "better" than the animal, but rather in another way. Many animals surpass us in the keenness of their sensation. The human being, however, has specific capacities that raise him above every animal. He has the capacity for the practically formative activity of work; he can produce things that would otherwise not be, which in their Being depend completely on the Being of the human. He has the capacity for forming concepts and abstract thinking and thereby a rational method in the mastery of the necessities for his life. He has, further, a sense for the distinction between "good" and "evil," a moral conscience, an acquaintance with the basic shapes of the ethical world and their manifold institutions. He also has the capacity for language and hence the means for a structured and multidimensional understanding of Being. The human being has an understanding of Being. To be sure, not in the completely clear and unclouded way that we surmise is the case for the gods. Our understanding of Being always remains troublesome; we indeed never entirely grasp Being and we never fail to grasp it. We go around with the understanding of Being, make use of it, call things beings in manifold respects—and yet we do not grasp without remainder the understanding of Being that we ourselves practice. *In* this understanding of Being there lies, among other things, too, the a priori pre-projection of the being-a-thing of things, of their structure as substrate and property. Accordingly, we comport ourselves in an unreflected and self-evident understanding to things in such a way that we thereby continually "presuppose" the thing-structure of substrate and property. In the case of the clod of earth, the tree, the house, the cow in the pasture, the triangle, and the number, we can "attribute" the properties of these objects to the beings determined by them in a firm and reliable manner. The properties are "borne" by the thing's standing on its own. Certainly, all corporeal things exist in a causal interconnection and continually receive determinations from this interconnection that do not lie in themselves. But being entwined in the causal nexus itself belongs to the concrete content of material things.

Now the question is whether the universal ontological model of a thing also holds in general for the human being himself, whether he has a self-standing independence that bears his "properties" in the manner of a substrate. One will initially find such a question odd and superfluous, totally beside the point. For, if the human being is just a subject matter, a thing, a being, he must also have the same basic structure that belongs to all things. His "properties" may be different, richer and more complex than those of a stone, plant, or animal—as properties they adhere to a substrate that bears them. They do not drift away in that which is groundless; they are affixed to the remarkable and hardly graspable "substance" that the human being is. But the question posed just now was aimed at the doubt as to *whether* the human being is, in truth, a substance standing in itself. In an elementary sense, the stone, the tree, and the animal "stand in themselves"; they indeed appear in the context of the all-encompassing unity of the universe, but they are not determined by a comportment to this all-encompassing unity. They are "in the world," but in such a way that they are closed off, as it were, to the world. Yet the expression "closed off to the world" is also not applicable here in the strict sense; for we do not find anything in them that would indicate that they turn away, or are closed off *from* the world. They exist in a simple, plain, and immediate mode. Such things repose in themselves, so to speak. One would have to examine whether the things resting in themselves and standing on their own have not above all[15] provided a guiding perspective for the conceptual explication of our ontological understanding of the structure of the thing. Here, properties belong to the substrates of things. Certainly, a difficult issue always remains, the issue of saying more precisely and rigorously in which way properties adhere and cling to the substantial substrate. Nevertheless, for us the point here is mainly the difference with regard to the human being.

The human being is not present at hand simply and plainly, merely immediately: he comports himself continually and unremittingly to his own Being and to the Being of all things; the human being exists *in* the understanding of Being. He is, while he goes about with his Being, concerned for himself, and this not just in reflective self-relatedness but rather from out of openness to the whole of the world. Now, one could object, and one would thereby only express in another way what one has always already said, that the human being has the capacity for language, reason, intellect [*Geist*]. As an intellectual being he is very sharply distinguished from all other natural creatures and assumes a special position. That should not at all be contested. What is questionworthy now is merely *how* the human being stands in regard to his oft-mentioned and well-known "privileges." Does he stand to them in a "relation of possession," like an owner to his property? Does the human being have language, reason, and understanding of Being—like the table has a black color or an elephant its trunk? Or does language have the human being? Is modest, finite human reason the reflection of world-reason? Do we already dwell in the light of Being when we form and express concepts of Being? Even with an impressive "inversion" of the customary representation, nothing yet has actually been grasped. The relation of language, reason, and Being to the human could still be construed as a relation between two beings or still on the model of such a relation—only it would now be read from the other end. And thus such an approach would also still be *intraworldly.* Provided, however, that Heraclitus's sagacious saying refers us to a world-relation of gods and human beings, from which alone they are what they are—from which they are participants in the productive power, in *poiēsis,* in the clearing, in temporalization, in the prevailing play and in the world-reason—then the human being could not really be thought any longer as a thing that would moreover still stand in a "relation," but would rather have to be conceived, if still as a thing, then as such a thing that is first and above all a relation—one which would have nothing self-standing or resting-in-itself about it, but rather would exist as an ecstatic openness. The situation of the human being would then not be something to be determined in an objective system of places, which would be oriented toward the place and the ontological status of a highest being. The relation of the human being to something that is no being and nevertheless is not nothing, that embraces, pervades [*durchmachtet*],[16] and plays throughout all things and never itself appears in a finite shape, but gives space and grants time to everything that appears—this relation characterizes and comprises the world-position of the human being. That means: the relation between the human being and the world can never be fixed from without in any objective sort of determination. The human being, living *in* the world-relation, must determine this relation through thinking. According to Heraclitus this also holds for the gods; they, too, have their sounder and more successful Being from the understanding proximity to the prevailing world. With Plato and Aristotle the view comes to triumph that the gods are at home in the veil-less, unrestricted, and complete truth, that they know everything entirely, that for them the cosmos is changed into radiant clarity and all darkness is obliterated. Absolute knowing, *sophia,* is then ascribed to God; to the finite human being, however, only impotent striving toward it: *philo-sophia,* love of wisdom. For Heraclitus, God's knowing is still appraised as a participation in the rational world-fire of the *sophon* above the divine, of the "one, alone wise." Humans and gods are believed to be capable of the same thing, even if in different ways. The knowing that belongs to both is at most[17] philosophy as love, as *philia* for *sophon.*

4. The Position of the Human Being in the Centauresque Metaphysics of the West

The human being's position in the world, which we are attempting to contemplate, is not a "theme" that is familiar in its accessibility, is not a "state of affairs" that lies before us, is not a "phenomenon" that is given, not a relation in the manner of the relations between beings. Only through the human being's openness to the world do we have possible themes for our consideration and treatment at all, do we discover states of affairs, are phenomena given to us, can we identify specific relations between innerworldly things. Thus, our thinking here must return to the ground of its own possibility, must consider the medium in which it itself oscillates. The human being's position in the world is not an objective location in a space understood as a homogenous system of positions, is not an extent of time in a constant manifold of extensions, is neither specifiable by the proximity to certain things nor by a fixed distance from a highest being, and thus does not signify any location in a hierarchy or graded architecture of all things. Formulated less abstractly: our question concerning the human being's position in the world cannot be answered in the traditional manner with the assurance that the human being is the highest of all natural creatures, the biological apex of living beings, the peak of the pyramid, which is built on the broad foundation of inorganic things, the narrower stratum of the realm of plants, the still more narrow one of animals, in order to reach in humanity the apotheosis in the intellect [*Geist*]. But also where one sees the distinctness of the human being in the power of production, thus in *homo faber,* or in freedom and moral self-determination, or in an "immortality of the soul" and being a child of God, which makes him master of the earth and all things, or in his intellectuality, his reason: in all these places the dimension of the human relation to the world is not reached. The human being is conceived as a "possessor" and "owner," as a "holder" of marvelous properties that allow him to be favorably contrasted with most other things that become his footstool, are plunder for him, material for his labor, means for his own self-assertion. From his superiority over the stone, plant, and animal the human being derives great pride; he makes the earth subservient, overcomes the power of the free wilderness with his self-forged plowshare, separates herb and weed, tames wild animals and transforms the face of the earth in the long history of the economic process. In his work activity he stamps the brand of his mastery on the things of his environment. Nevertheless, this human power of mastery is, as one says, a finite and limited one; not merely because we are not able to subjugate all things and because our powers of production become exhausted in the immensity of nature—we believe we are surpassed by more powerful beings that are invisible, that are not given as evident phenomena in our environment, that have more subtle modes of announcing themselves, that speak in the mysterious voice of conscience in our heart or visit blows of fate upon us. In our ultimate inability to dispose over turns of fortune in life, which are removed from the deliberate, planning grasp of the human being, the prevailing of heavenly powers is intimated. Before them the proud human being becomes small and conscious of his frailty. Now, doesn't the human being become aware of his true position when he knows, at one and the same time, what he has at his disposal, what is subordinate and exposed to his force, and what he never has at his disposal, what rather has him at its disposal as the force of fate? Does he validly understand himself when he feels himself to be the master of things and the servant of God and lives amid all his domination of nature in the fear of the Lord? Is not the true "place" of the human being between the animal and God? This conception of the human being determines to a high degree our intellectual tradition—in religion and philosophy and their hybrids. Thereby the "intermediate position" of the human being between the animal and God is, for the most part, not merely conceived as an objective determination of location that would be fixed by an observer beyond the human, as it were. One says: the human being stands not merely between the animal and God like a stair step between their neighboring steps; rather he comports himself in an understanding manner to the animal and God; his situation is opened up for him. And again this, too, not in a calm manner without tension; on the contrary, he is rent asunder in his Being by opposing tendencies—he has the animal and the divine in himself, not merely next to himself—he has animal needs and desires, burns with passion, has wildness, rage, and fury, but knows also the calm of the soul in the contemplating gaze, knows the yearning for nonsensuous happiness, the enigmatic homesickness that drives us out beyond ourselves. The human being is thus conceived as the animal with the divine spark in it, as the uppermost natural creature that already borders on the spirit realm, is a citizen of an intelligible world: a sensing being that knows about pure intellect and from out of the world of sense aspires to that which is above the sensuous, has an intimation of an intellectual hinter-world, a *meta-physis,* behind nature that is manifest to the senses, *physis*. The human being is interpreted as an existing tension between the animal and God, as a tension that is a continual struggle, a discord between the animal and the divine inside us. The human being is not regarded as an equilibrium at rest, but rather as swaying scales, where at one time the animal, at another the divine spark of light preponderates.

We are familiar with, in countless manifestations, this interpretation of the human essence that determines the image of the human being in Western metaphysics, which indeed operates with the fundamental distinctions between the sensible world and the intellectual world, *mundus sensibilis* and *mundus intelligibilis,* and determines the place of the human being on the dividing line of both "worlds." The metaphysical interpretation of the human being makes him into a being that is torn asunder and constantly disquieted by this fact, a being that is sensuous and intellectual, animal and divine, at the same time striving back below himself into the animal realm and above himself in the direction of God. The human being thus appears as an intellect stained with sensuousness and as an animal perturbed by intellectuality—as a double-being, so to speak, made up of parts that conflict with each other, as a centaur. As the mythical creature "centaur" consists of an animal lower body and a human upper body, so Western metaphysics thinks of the human being as simultaneously half-animal and half-divine. This centauresque basic feature of the traditional image of the human being is a disastrous legacy, inasmuch as human existence's essential relation to the world was thereby concealed and obscured by the human being's innerworldly distance from the animal and God. An intraworldly relation, which doubtless has great significance, had thereby bound and consumed the ecstatic power of human existence. Now, one could, however, say in defense of the metaphysical image of the human being that he is not at all located in his position by simple relations of proximity to other beings; if he is conceived as an intermediary being between animal and God, then this signifies not primarily distance from other beings but rather a twofold and tense relation to the world of the senses and the pure world of the intellect. Precisely a *world-position* of the human being would here be recognized and retained, his position between the *mundus sensibilis* and the *mundus intelligibilis.* The human being would be conceived as at home in *two* worlds, even understood in his ambivalent Being from out of a doubled world-relation. But is such an argument correct? "World" is here used in the plural—and this plural is suspicious enough. The concept of world in the plural usage is a metaphor, an analogical mode of speaking, intends a context of wholeness, a comprehensive grasp [*Inbegriff*], a *totum.* The world, however, is not just any whole, not a total realm, not a region of things, not "a" *totum,* but rather "the" *totum,* the single, all-encompassing *totum* plain and simple. The world-totality is not a case of totality in general, is not like specific and generic totality or that of an infinite quantity—the world-totality is incomparable with all intraworldly "totalities" (of a relative sort). However, we metaphorically use the expression "world" when we want to indicate a comprehensively enclosed, relative total context. The world of the senses and the world of the intellect are, strictly speaking, not worlds; they are realms *in* the world, dimensions of specific beings. It is significant that the thinker who tears open the cleft between the sensuous and the intellectual—between that which we see, touch, smell, and taste and that which only thinking apprehends—does not at all speak of dual worlds. Plato calls the realm of the senses the "visible place," *horatos topos,* or also the "genus of the visible," *horaton genos;* he calls that which is apprehensible through thought the *noētos topos* or also *noēton genos.* That these contrasting Platonic realms of sensuous things and ideas were later characterized as two "worlds" indicates not merely the decline of the Platonic problem into a vulgar Platonism that was regrettably powerful in its cultural-historical effect, a Platonism that has as little to do with Plato as so-called platonic love—it indicates still more the closure of the problem of world. That, however, the problem of world could be closed at all in the concepts of metaphysics has its ground precisely in the fact that the ecstatic character of the human being was always, in a certain abbreviated way, thought of there at the same time. The human being was interpreted as self-surpassing, as a movement of a transcending, an upsurge: he did not remain in himself, was not encapsulated in his egoity, he was thought of as a living being that is always more than itself, which burns in yearning and has its highest possibility in enthusiastic rapture. But that up toward which such a self-surpassing happens was reckoned as the highest being, expressed mythologically: as God. The ecstasis toward the being that is most proximate to the world consumed the ecstasis toward the world. The god of metaphysics disguises the world, and he disguises it all the more the further he is moved beyond every graven image, every appearance manifest to the senses, every comprehensibility in the concept and, in a continually increasing manner, becomes the *deus absconditus.* Rightly understood, this holds only for the god of the philosophers, of the metaphysicians—not for the "God of Abraham, Isaac, and Jacob," not for Zeus and Apollo, not for the father of all, Odin, not for Isis and Osiris. Nevertheless, it was understood precisely in the metaphysicians' concept of God that the god who withdraws from the slightest human access draws the human being on precisely through this withdrawal, rouses him out of his everyday comfort, snatches him up and dis-lodges [*entsetzt*] him from his displacement [*Versetztheit*] amid things. To the extent that and as long as the human being was characterized by his relation to God, his highest and best properties came to be attributed to him from this relation to God. The spark of light in the human soul was considered to be a light from the divine light, human reason to be a reflected splendor and faint echo of divine reason; the human soul was considered to be divinely determined. According to the conception of the Christian religion, all things, indeed, depend on God, insofar as they are created and maintained in Being through the omnipotence of God—the human being is in a special way related to God, is breath of the divine breath and must therefore strive to reunite with God. What the human being is, he is not purely in himself, so to speak, but rather is on the basis of the ecstatic relation in which he exists.

That holds in another, perhaps still more primordial way for the human being's relation to the world. Not only do we not "possess" our understanding of *Being* in the form of an ultimate and perfect "science"; we do not at all have our understanding of Being as a firm, available "possession." Our understanding of Being is thoroughly worlded. Not only is our knowledge about things' belonging to the world already included in any understanding of the Being of a particular being; the understanding of intraworldly beings comes to us from the open expanse of the world. We never initially find worldless things and gradually attain to a comprehensive representation of the whole by progressively stringing together single things and indefinitely extending this sequential process into infinity; the first thing that we become aware of at all is already "in" the world, just as much as our very becoming aware of it belongs "within" the world. Our understanding swings out in advance into the expanse of the entirety of space and time and apprehends, from out of primordial farness, every nearness, every nearness and intraworldly farness of things. Our understanding is opened in advance to the space-giving and time-allowing of the prevailing world and returns from it to things. Before we know what is here and what is now we know the here and the now. The human being is a strange creature, a being in the world—and at the same time a being that is characterized in advance by its relation to the world; he is an innerworldly thing to which the whole of all Being is thrown, in order to come to light and to shine [*zum Leuchten und Scheinen*] in him. We can summarize this in two propositions: 1. All things in general are intraworldly—or: the Being of all existing things must be conceived as "being-in-the-world"; 2. the human being is the innerworldly thing that exists in an ecstatic relation to the totality of the world, is addressed by the universe and is turned toward it with understanding—and hence must be understood in an entirely special way as "being-in-the-world." With the title "being-in-the-world," a fundamental concept of Heidegger's philosophy is named, which found systematic exposition in Heidegger's great breakthrough work *Being and Time.* There, the term "being-in-the-world" does *not* mean a basic feature concealed in all beings in general, nor the belonging of everything that is to the all-encompassing embrace of the universe. The Heideggerian concept of being-in-the-world indicates rather the basic constitution of that being which we ourselves are, the basic constitution of human existence [*Dasein*]. Methodically, Heidegger proceeds in such a manner that he identifies and neutralizes specific conceptual ideas of "world." In the prephilosophical and everyday understanding, we take "world" initially to be the sum of all things. This cumulative concept of the world is rejected straightaway, and likewise the idea is brushed aside that wants to interpret the world as a framework, a container, a gigantic vessel for manifold beings. In contrast, a view that understands the world as the whole of human accessibility is already assessed positively. Beings in the mode of human access, in the play space in which our understanding may encounter them, can be taken as an indication of a more essential world-concept. For instance, we already speak in an everyday manner of the "world of the Middle Ages," of the "world of the Europeans, of the Asians," and so forth, of the "world of the child," of the "world of men" and the "world of women." In such turns of phrase "world" is understood in reference to the human being's specific mode of lived experience; it becomes a modal determination of human existence [*Existenz*]. One can call this the existentiell world-concept. Every fundamental possibility of human existence [*Dasein*] has the world of experience that belongs to and is characteristic of it. The variety of such worlds of lived experience nevertheless is grounded in one fundamental constitution: existence must, as existence, have a sphere of sense that belongs to it and is ranged around it as a field within which it can then encounter things as objects. Existence has a world-field of the a priori understanding of Being in advance, has it as a field and structure proper to it, and existence finds things as "objects" of its representing and acting in the realm that is pre-projected and held out by it. This field, which is spread out in advance as an understanding of Being, is not a proper determination of things themselves but is rather the antecedent subjective condition under which they can show and present themselves to us. The world as a field of the understanding of Being is—according to Heidegger—an "existential." By "existentials" he understands fundamental determinations of the constitution of the Being of the human. For him, the concept opposed to this is the "category" as the a priori determination of the Being of non-human things. Insofar as the "world" is assessed as an existential it becomes a structure of existence—though certainly no simple structure; the world-field of the understanding of Being does not belong to human existence like appendages to the body, like weight to our *corpus,* indeed not even like the body belongs to us. In the short work *On the Essence of Ground,* Heidegger characterizes the human's worlded and fielded understanding of Being as "transcendence," as "surpassing." The human being, who has an understanding of Being, does not remain enclosed in the interiority of his soul, but is rather essentially always already outside and is before all external things, which can only appear for him in the spatial and temporal field held out by the human being. Heidegger's interpretation of the existentially understood world as "transcendence," as surpassing, converges in a certain way with Kant's concept of subjectivity. The human subject for Kant is not just any being in space and time, although, of course, one cannot dispute that we in each case occupy a determinate place and last for a determinate period. Space and time for Kant are a priori forms of intuition that belong to the subject and essentially co-constitute its subjectivity. Space and time according to him are not determinations of things in themselves nor are they themselves some sort of independently existing non-things or super-things. Space and time together form a field held out and pre-projected by the subject for all things sensuously appearing to us. Taken pre-philosophically, the human being, for example, is the thing speaking here at the lectern—thought philosophically (in Kant's sense), however, he reaches with the pure forms of his sensibility belonging to him all the way to the most distant stars. If space and time form the human subject's field of understanding and belong to him in truth, then the "transcendental subject" goes beyond and surpasses the empirical subject in an immense way—the human being, thought philosophically, to whom space and time belong as *his* structures, lies far beyond the diminutive human being who in space and time occupies a virtually minuscule and insignificant place. However, while in Kant space and time as fixed and finished systems of the manifold, so to speak, constitute the static form of the pure sensibility of the subject, Heidegger conceives space and time in the aforementioned writing as an existential [*daseinsmäßiges*] happening, as the formation of space and as temporalization. Space and time, likewise, are assessed as existentials, as structures of human existence like the "world," like the "understanding of Being." This existential concept of the world in early Heidegger is determined "transcendental-philosophically" and understands the worldness of the world from the perspective of *alētheia,* of the manifestness of beings-for-the-human-being. The world is where beings are understood, recognized, and handled. Beings are not necessarily in themselves in the world. Heidegger speaks in *On the Essence of Ground* of the fact that beings as nature could never become manifest, "unless they found *occasion* to enter into the world. . . . Only if, amid beings in their totality, beings come to be 'more in being' in the manner of the temporalizing of Dasein are there the hours and days of beings' entry into the world. And only if this primordial history, namely, transcendence, occurs, i.e., only if beings having the character of being-in-the-world irrupt into beings, is there the possibility of beings manifesting themselves."[18]

On the basis of this position the cosmological problem of the world is no longer posed; the individuated being does not have its individuation as an effect of the world; it is "worldless" and never appears anywhere—unless it is unconcealed by the human who understands Being, unless it attains a derivative space and a derivative time from the primordial spatiality and temporality of existence [*Dasein*], unless it enters into the existential [*daseinsmäßige*] world. The human is understood as "being-in-the-world" itself. In the strict sense he is not "in" the world, he is the world, is world-forming and projects the spatio-temporal structural field within which he himself then establishes himself; he "founds" the open realm in which he then "takes root"; "to found" and "to take root" are for Heidegger two essential modes of "grounding." However, if the world is thus transferred to the subject, if the human being is taken to be the distinguished site where the world is formed, where it emerges and where even the appearance emerges that all things would be gathered in the one world and be encompassed by it, then the human being, as the genuine "place" of the world, space, time, and the understanding of Being, obtains an ontological significance that is situated high above all the other familiar ontic privileges. "Ontic" privileges are, for instance, such markers of humanity as *homo faber,* "ethical personhood," "immortal soul" and "child of God," "rational being," freedom," and so forth. The significance of the human being is formulated by Heidegger in *Being and Time* in a twofold manner. Human existence has an ontic precedence above all other beings, because it is the questioning being, because all questioning about the manifold constitution of the Being of manifold things and realms of things proceeds from the human being, serves his understanding of life, happens ultimately for his sake and "recoils" into the existence that questions. However, the human being also has an "ontological precedence" over all other things, because he is innately "ontological," that is, exists with an understanding of Being—he is the being who himself is distinguished by his understanding of Being. With regard to this double precedence of human existence, it is advisable, in terms of the course and path of thought, before determining the ontological constitution of any subject area thematically, to begin with the interpretation of that being which is the one that understands and interprets. The human being's self-understanding, once thoroughly clarified concerning its possibility of naming Being, of articulating it with language, and of referring to things, must manifestly provide the fundament for every ontology of specific domains of things and can hence be called "fundamental ontology." In this context Heidegger, in *Being and Time,* refers to the interpretation of the human being, to the "existential analytic," as fundamental ontology. The following may be said, critically, in response to this approach that is driven by a radical question: 1. because the world as a universe, as a *kosmos,* was discussed only in terms of the massive-ontic ideas of a "cumulative whole," a "framework" or "container," thus in terms of the easily dismissible, mistaken form of a gigantic thing or of an objective system of positions, the single totality of the world-totality was not at all able to appear more clearly in its complete embrace of everything that is at all, be it wretched earthworms or the radiant gods. Above all, the power of the world as the play of individuation, through which individual things come to a "stand" in a particular state of Being, was not taken into view; the universe was represented in the inanimate, motionless form, as it were, of a more or less questionable total structure. In contrast, the world, understood existentially, was interpreted as a primordial movement of world-formation, of temporalization and spatialization, and the essential features of the world itself were ascribed to human existence. The constitution of the Being of existence was not interpreted from its openness to the prevailing world, but rather, conversely, the world was interpreted from the structure of existential [*daseinsmäßigen*] world-formation. 2. The human being's world-relatedness as the primordial openness of our essence for the universe inevitably had to be covered over when the world was regarded as something adhering and belonging to the human being—as a space-time-field projected by him, or otherwise as a referential structure of human "involvements." The ecstatic character of existence almost became a "property," the human being the owner of the "understanding of Being." It had not been[19] elucidated how human nature, along with its existential constitution of "being-in-the-world," is itself *in* the world as the world-totality and is therein exposed and sheltered in a strangely ambiguous way. 3. Also connected with this is the fact that the concept of existence [*Dasein*] in Heidegger remains "transcendental-philosophically" abstract in the aforementioned writings. If the human being is expected to actually be the world itself, to be the broadly oscillating whole that is imbued with space and time, to be the site of the temporalization and coming to appearance of all that is, then the human being does become different from the way he is conceived of in "absolute idealism"; nevertheless he is just as strongly overtaxed as he is in absolute idealism, where he provides the finitely frail vessel of the absolute—and, as "Napoleon," is supposed to depict the world-spirit on horseback and, as Professor Hegel, spirit thinking itself. The "world-historical individual" or the "epoch-making" peoples are not the only valid and legitimate world-shapes of human existence.

Many forms of community are based on a genuine and sustaining relation to the world. In the ways in which we know about death and about the absence of the departed who have returned into the elementary clan's universal ground in consanguinity; in which we know about the interwovenness of our mutual activities and about the fraternity of work activity; in which we know about struggle and war, power and ruling; in which we know about the immortality of life in procreation and birth; in which we know about the enchantment of the mask, the beguilement of beauty, and the conjuring presentation of pure images in the elevated buskin—in such ways we are *communally* opened up and opened to the profundity of the world in all things. The less the human being wants to be the world itself, the more he finds his way into its primordial nearness. The human, who has an understanding of Being, cannot posit what Being and beings are from his own complete power; he must comply with a claim that comes to him from the world's expanse. The world is not "merely" something human, not merely an existential structure, not merely a determinate form of the human's ontological constitution—yet it is true that the world is in a peculiar way turned toward the intraworldly human being and in such turning-toward is also in an enigmatic sense "human"; it is "human" because the human is first "worldly."

The "critique" of a decisive position of *Being and Time* that we just sketched is not primarily ours—it is first of all Heidegger's self-critique, which was carried out in the famous *turn* [Kehre] of his thinking, according to which the understanding of Being is not to be interpreted from the human being as a fixed point of reference, but rather above all from the horizon of the openness of the human essence for Being itself. And something like this holds also for the other fundamental existentials: for truth, world, temporalization. Truth, world, and temporalization no longer have their "place," so to speak, in the human being, but rather the human being has his noteworthy and thoughtworthy "place"—which is not determinable in any objective system of positioning—in the disclosure and temporalization of the world. We lack the appropriate concepts for this relation to the world. The human is the paradoxical being who is occupied by the thought of the immense and the immeasurable, who lives in the slipstream of the universe, in the shadow of death, in the toil of work, in the struggle for dominion, in the fragile happiness of love—and in play that portrays. Perhaps contemplating play is a thread that will not, indeed, lead us out of the labyrinth of questions, but deeper into them.

5. The World as Play? An Approach in the Appearance of the Playworld

The path of our meditation on the theme of play, up to now, seems like a detour. Instead of arriving at the "matter at hand," we have spoken longwindedly about philosophy in general, about its problematic assessment of all things according to their ontological status, about the structure of the relation between things in objective systems of positions, about a few obscure sayings of Heraclitus and the human being's position in the world indicated in them, about the "centauresque" interpretation of the human being within Western metaphysics as the intermediary being between animal and God, in order to finally turn to the concept of being-in-the-world. Play may be connected with the human's being-in-the-world and may perhaps even be an especially distinctive mode of such being-in, yet it nevertheless appears "like a detour" to initially approach such a problem-laden concept as being-in-the-world in order to consider from that point the universally familiar phenomenon of play. Frankly, a procedure that holds itself more closely to the phenomenon and seizes and thoughtfully expands on the character of already being interpreted that lies within it is more prone to persuade as a method. Nevertheless, what is chiefly at issue here for us is not so much the apprehension of a subject matter, is not a "phenomenology" of play, but rather the world-significance of play, the recognition of play as a key phenomenon of a truly universal status. It could be that its world-significance is not located in the manner of an identifiable moment in the everyday, familiar phenomenon of play that would be "dimmed," as it were, in the routine, normal contact with play. Then the dimension in which a world-significance of play could come to light would still have to be gained in the first place. And we are still on the way toward this. In the course of our preliminary reflections we reached the concept of "being-in-the-world," a term that Heidegger coined and determined as the ontological constitution of human existence. We have briefly discussed the inner difficulties of this speculative basic concept—and have suggested how the methodological outline of Heideggerian philosophy depends on a specific interpretation of "being-in-the-world": such as whether philosophy begins with the analytic of human existence as that being which is distinguished by the "understanding of Being," or whether it begins with a thinking that stands out into self-clearing Being and first finds itself as "understanding Being" from out of such openness. We have, for our part, proposed the concept of being-in-the-world as a title for a twofold speculative problem: firstly for the being-in of all finite beings in general in the world-totality, and then for the particular way in which the human being, who exists as open to the world from out of his relation to the world, is in the cosmos. The human's being-in-the-world is not, in our view, an "ontological constitution" that belongs or is proper to him, which he has like the stone has its solidity and its weight, and it can thus not be primarily conceived from the independent Being of the human. Rather, the human being is the intraworldly being addressed by the world itself, is taken in and inhabited by the thought of the immense. Human existence is being-in-the-world with understanding, because the world has irrupted into the human being. Hence he also does not "have" world-openness in the same way as he has his senses, his body and other possessions. World-openness does not belong to the human being, but rather the converse: the human being belongs to world-openness; he exists in ecstatically turning toward the circumoscillating expanse of the universe, from which the light of reason, of language, of the understanding of Being comes to belong to him in the first place. We do not have the "world" because we inherently "possess" reason, language, and the understanding of Being. Rather, because we are open to the world, drawn out forcefully into the in-finite—because we are opened up to the assembling-structuring *logos* of the whole—we can think and speak with an understanding of Being. The human's being-in-the-world is not a mode of Being belonging to his "nature," nor is the human being the being for whom "world," "truth," and "temporalization" are structural moments, so-called existentials, that adhere to him. When we distinguished a twofold concept of being-in-the-world: 1. the being-in of all things in the universe and 2. the being-in of the human being in the cosmos, a being who is marked by his relation to the world with understanding—we did not mean to distinguish two separate kinds of being-in in general; for the human being's being-in, too, is included in the being-in of all finite things in the world. All finite things have their place and duration, are somewhere and at some time granted place and flow in the stream of time, emerge, increase and diminish, change constantly, and in the end pass away. Everything that has a look, a delimited outline, an aspect, and thus as something delimited is nameable and effable, has its ascent and decline, gleams for a while in the light of appearing, and sinks back down again. Finite things are above all finite and exhaustible in their power to hold themselves in Being. When they emerge into existence, they have a reserve of power, as it were, with which they must economize, but they can exist only by consuming and using up this reserve; they exist as self-consuming. Nothing finite abides forever, even though there are certainly enormous differences in the length of time in which finite things abide. Everything living is of the fleeting sort—more firm and lasting are land and sea, mountains and waves, the stars revolving in the sky. But even their duration is exhausted at some point. Everything that appears *in* the space and time of the all-encompassing world is transitory—what "comes to be / Deserves to perish wretchedly,"[20]—what goes up must also come down; even the most powerful thing that appears under the heavens must go down into Orcus: the most powerful human beings as well as the most wretched slaves, the thriving, thalassocratic cities as well as the village of helots, the pyramids as well as the mountains and seas, the gods as well as the celestial bodies. But where one finite being goes down, another rises up; where one is extinguished, another steps into the light of appearance; where one decreases, another increases; where one departs, another arrives. The emergence and decline of finite things are joined to each other. From where emergence comes to belong to existing individual things, to there goes their passing away. The course of all finite things in the space and time of the world is a manifoldly joined [*verfugte*], interlocked, total dispensation [*Gesamtfügung*] of emergence and decline, of increasing and decreasing, coming and going, of life and death. The human being is integrated [*eingefügt*] in this course of the world, too, he has a place and duration in it as an individual, as a people and as humanity. The course of the world enjoins [*verfügt*] all individual beings; it allows them to emerge and perish, to grow and to shrivel; it brings things into their individuation and takes them away from it again—it occurs as the universal individuation of all finitely existing beings. The universal being-in-the-world of all finite things in general as a belonging within the cosmos does not therefore mean a static, stationary relation, but rather the belonging of things within the prevailing of worldwide individuation, within the cosmic process of individuation. The human being, too, belongs within this process. Undeniably, he is a finite thing. He is even the "most" finite thing.

To what extent? Are not all finite things "finite" in the same way, that is, delimited, hemmed in by borders and thereby closed off from all other things, marked by an outlined aspect, addressable by a proper name—all, too, emerging and perishing in the same way, exhaustible in their power of Being? What might it mean here to call one being "more finite" than others? We already said that there are differences between intraworldly things in regard to their temporal duration. But if the rocky mountains last longer than the mountain forests and the animals in them, are they perhaps less "finite"? The human being is not even the most fleeting of living beings. Many animals have a shorter life span. And yet the human being is "more finite" than they are. Animals live out their life, flow in the stream of time for as long as it is apportioned for them—though existing transitorily they know nothing of their decay; they are in time but they do not comport themselves *to* time, they do not comport themselves to their own transience. They grow up in the calm and regular rhythm of nature, which never fully exposes them; they flourish—and in so doing know nothing about their demise. The human being is not so immediately at one with his own Being—as is the animal. The human being stands "over and against" himself, as it were: he is not only in time, he comports himself to time. He knows in the now about what is to come, knows in vitality about decline, in youth about old age, in life about death. We are not "at one" like the animal that is sheltered in its nature is. We experience our disintegration against the background of the more intact Being of animals. Thus we read in the fourth *Duino Elegy* of Rilke: "Flowering and fading come to us both at once. / And somewhere lions still roam and never know, / in their majestic power, of any weakness."[21] The human being knows already in his most mighty power of his future powerlessness and his own deterioration, knows in the highest fullness of life that he is doomed to die, knows in his persisting that he is inexorably decaying, fading away in his abiding, knows that he is the most evanescent of all evanescent things. But if the human being is thus not merely in time, but rather knows about time and transience—is not merely simply present at hand like the stone or the cloud but rather comports himself to his own Being, indeed is even unsettled by his own questionableness and seeks to grasp his existence—then he knows himself in this way not merely as "different" and "of another sort" against the background of animality, but rather thereby also comports himself to what is intransitory, to what steers all perishing, all emergence and decline of finite things. He comports himself to the world, comports himself to the process of individuation, to the course of the world—as to the way in which the omni-potent operates. The most finite being knows precisely about the power of the totality. Transience as such can only become known if at the same time the intransient is known. But do we not thereby end up taking the path of the traditional metaphysical division of the whole of actuality into an upper, as it were, "divine" realm of changeless and perpetual Being and a lower realm of changeable things that would be the dwelling-place of the human being? Metaphysics, however, has established the difference between the intransient and the transitory in beings and upheld two regions of beings, the divine region of perpetual ideas and the lower region of changeable sensuous things. But the difference between the intransitory and the transitory is, primordially, the difference between the space-giving and time-granting world and all intraworldly things, whether these be grains of sand or gods. The world itself is never intransitory on the model of an innerworldly duration, it does not abide and persevere like some indestructible stuff that only exchanges its aggregate states. The world does not abide—as something within time abides. At most it abides as time itself does. There is always something obscure in the self-understanding of human transience, even if it be the unelaborated understanding of the intransience of the world.

Now, one might be tempted to elucidate in the following way the connection between the two concepts of being-in-the-world we initially distinguished: the human's being-in-the-world is a special case of the general being-in-the-world of all finite things. All things in general, in the broadest sense, are in the world, inasmuch as they belong within a total dispensation of the course of the world that brings about and takes away individual things. That holds also for the human being. Even he is integrated into the world's course, has in it a place and a duration for his appearance. Only the way *in which* he is integrated is distinct from the way in which all other things are; he is integrated in such a way that he comports himself to his being-here and being-now with understanding, that he knows himself and thus has "self-consciousness," that he is concerned with himself, is directed toward his "felicity," pursues goals that converge in one final goal, that he is not merely plainly and simply present at hand, but rather comports himself to his Being and to the Being of the things surrounding him, lives in an understanding of Being, not, to be sure, in a finished understanding but rather in a restless and questionworthy one that longs for conceptual clarity, and so forth. But if the human's being-in-the-world is thus conceived as a "special case" of the general being-in-the-world of all finite things, then the emphasis is placed on the distinction between the human being and all non-human beings. The human being—one then says—exists differently in space, in time, differently in the light of appearance above the earth than the mountain and the tree and the bird in the air. Certainly, this difference does exist. Nevertheless, inasmuch as the human being comports himself to time as such, to space and to Being as such, he stands precisely in a coruscating relation of understanding to the imperishable world, a world that nevertheless prevails as a process of individuation. That is, he understands in a first glimmer and flash of light the power of individuation in all individuated things. A relation of understanding to the being-in-the-world of all finite things lies in the human's being-in-the-world. The highest human self-consciousness includes the worldedness of all beings as well. Accordingly, we cannot treat the two concepts of the general being-in-the-world of things as such and of the special being-in-the-world of the human who understands Being as two separate problems, but rather must recognize and acknowledge the necessary interconnection of both questions. A philosophical self-interpretation of the human being includes an unfolding of human knowledge about the world-process of individuation. A self-knowledge of the human being cannot be achieved sufficiently by thematically delimiting *only* the human being and bracketing out infringing sense-contexts. Self-knowledge of the human being is always simultaneously also a question concerning the whole of beings. The most finite thing is inhabited by the thought of the universe. The thought of the world is the thought of all thoughts—it first makes human thinking possible as a questioning and thoughtful determination of innerworldly beings.

Nevertheless, these connections are for the most part not at all known to us. Everything that we expressed until now concerning the primal relation between the human being and the world (in a provisional and prefigurative sense) cannot be culled immediately from the phenomena given to us. Indeed, because the so-called phenomena that one likes to invoke as the highest court of appeals are themselves determined by a unique "world-dwindling." This dwindling is nothing other than the power of "the self-evident." We all know vaguely and superficially that each thing stands in a thing-context and that all thing-contexts stand in a universal total-context, are included in it; whatever we call a "being": the earth, the bright sky, the land and the sea, the mountains and the plains, cities, fields, trees, houses, furniture, vehicles, and so forth—each being is together with other beings; none is alone, for itself, and fully separated from others. Each has its separateness and its determinate outline enclosed within firm borders only by being enclosed together with other things, too, by the borders which enclose it. Each thing is contiguous with other things, each is situated—and everything that is situated stands in a common, all-encompassing presencing [*Anwesen*]. Yet, initially, only the environing situation is of interest, that is, things in their manifold characteristics of utility and serviceability. If the vital interest in utility is relaxed and a wider space for our contemplation of things is enabled, new theoretical guiding interests emerge, which again establish a determinate perspective on things. We are thus practically and also theoretically interested in beings—led by an anticipation of determinate situations. The total situation, the world, however, is too "self-evident" to be immediately posed as a problem. We no longer see the forest for the trees. And even if we have raised ourselves above working-practical contact and have transcended the perspectives of the positive sciences and ask after *beings as such,* we mostly take it as "self-evident" that from the world-expanse of space and time, beings as such lie before us. This "beings as such," the *on hēi on,* is interpreted according to its structure as an individual thing with a universal species-character and as set into a process of motion that one finds just as manifest as finite things themselves. Insofar as the finitude of things is thus treated like a discovery that one makes immediately and can again exemplify in anything whatsoever, precisely the provenance of the finitude of finite things from out of the prevailing of the world is concealed and falls into oblivion. Finitude itself becomes, so to speak, a "phenomenon," a datum in things. "Being" is interpreted as the Being of finitely existing beings; the problem of Being loses its tension vis-à-vis the in-finite, at best is proclaimed as a particular, highest being, God or the absolute as the possessor of "in-finite Being." And that happens all the more, the more the question recedes (or better: is not posed at all) as to how individual things reside within the world-whole. And so long as this question is not posed, the finitude of things cannot be thought back into the world's process of individuation. "Being-in-the-world" as the cosmological, fundamental character of beings in general cannot immediately be found in, and read off, intraworldly things and be described as a manifest "phenomenon"—it first lights up when the thought of the world assumes control over human thinking. And in an analogous way this also holds for the particular being-in-the-world of the human being. Initially there is the self-evident tendency to pass off the human being's understanding of Being, his knowing about space and time, as an independent property of our mind; the human relation to the world comes under the sway of guiding representations that are oriented to the belonging of properties to a substance. That can even take effect within philosophy itself and far beyond it if one, for example, reinterprets this relation to the world in terms of a transcendental field-structure or an existential constitution. That, nevertheless, the primordial world-openness of the human being first makes possible our capacity for language, reason, and the understanding of Being is difficult to recognize and even more difficult to explain, because there are still no categories available for the ecstasis of the human being toward the world. Being-in-the-world in *both* of the meanings that we have distinguished forms a speculative problem of great difficulty. Both meanings, moreover, are connected with each other and must also be thought through together. The process of universal individuation, in which each being in general obtains place and duration, emergence and demise, growth and dwindling, splendor and opacity, is the course of the world. What kind of a "course" is this? Is it a movement of the same sort as the circuit of the stars, as the waves of the tides of the sea or the flight of the clouds, as the growth of plants, the hunting of animals, the activity of human beings? Movements of that kind are innerworldly, are known to us to some extent according to their laws; we commonly distinguish mechanical motions from vegetative ones and these in turn from deliberately controlled ones. We speak, for instance, of the mechanical course of a struck ball and in another way of the sporting course of the athlete. The "course" is initially an innerworldly concept—to "apply" it to the whole and likewise to what is not presentable as a phenomenon but rather only thinkable and attainable for thinking, namely, the cosmic total-movement, is certainly a tricky matter. And it becomes all the trickier the less we know about the trickiness of an intraworldly model of movement for the world-movement. The course of the world is not a course in some already familiar type of movement belonging to things. And yet early thought called this course of the world the *aiōn,* "a child playing—a kingdom of the child."[22] The process of individuation is thought in the image of play. Play comes to be a "cosmic metaphor" for the total appearance and disappearance of existing things in the time-space of the world. The frothing, intoxicated tide of life, which elevates living beings in the delight in reproducing, is secretly one with the dark surge that drags the living down into death. Life and death, birth and dying, womb and tomb are twinned: it is the same moving force of the totality that brings forth[23] and annihilates, that begets and kills, that unites the highest delight and the deepest grief. "For if it were not Dionysus for whom they arrange the procession and sing the phallus-song"—so reads Fragment 15 of Heraclitus—"it would be an entirely shameless activity. But Hades and Dionysus are the same, the one for whom they rave there and celebrate their Lenaia."[24] The god of the erotic exuberance of life is at the same time the god of death—but he is also the god of the mask and of play. Are these merely mythic and poetic images—for a world-motion that cannot be attained by an intraworldly concept? Or does a special indication lie in play, a special, world-containing metaphorical power? These are open questions.

Now, according to conventional ideas, a procedure that appears plausible and well tested imposes itself: namely, to investigate human play first of all and to ask afterward whether it could be applicable as a critically scaled-down model for a characterization of the "course of the world." Yet the sole purpose of our long methodological preliminary consideration was to neutralize this procedure. We are thereby guided by the conviction that a comprehensive interpretation of human play already presupposes ecstatic openness to the world, and thus must move within a knowledge about the world, even if it is an obscure knowledge. In order to understand *play* we must be acquainted with the *world,* and in order to understand *the world as play* we must achieve a still much *deeper insight into the world.* With this observation, which is intended to be fundamental and expresses the guiding thought of the treatise, we conclude our preliminary considerations.

We are attempting to turn to play itself. This turn of phrase sounds like it could be misunderstood. One turns to an instance of play when one watches the play of others or plays along. But to reflect upon play is obviously neither itself an instance of play nor conducive to our delight in play. One does not become more inclined to play by thinking; rather one becomes less inclined, one loses the unconcerned naïveté of life, the impulsive verve and the unrestrained cheerfulness, the delight in the unreflective and uninterrupted carrying out of life. So one says, at least—and psychology appears to confirm this. Children still play in unrestrained merriment; adults do so in many cases already with a bad conscience, considering play as a restorative free-time activity that relaxes our mind, frees us for a time from the burden of our obligations. Thus play shifts suspiciously close to idleness. In other ways of carrying out life, thought occasionally facilitates an improvement. A deliberating, planning, rationalizing "thought" can better the methods of work in various ways, but also the methods of ruling. Surely it cannot do this for play in the same sense. To be sure, new games can be made up, devised, but these contrivances are obviously good "flights of fancy" rather than methodical results of thinking. There appears to exist a "hostility" between the image-laden, creative imaginative powers of play and conceptual thought. The human being at play does not think, and the thinking human being does not play. That need not signify an opposition of human types; the same human being indeed lives in many basic forms of life—he works and plays, fights and loves, and does many other things besides. Is the consideration of play only ever possible from the perspective of the "spectator," so to speak, of the spectator of another's life as well as his own? Or is there also a genuine and truthful thinking about play that remains in the enactment of play—which is maintained in the human being's openness to the world that is determined by play? These are no idly posed, more or less rhetorically intended questions.[25]

For the moment, however, our task is to find an approach for our thinking about play. For if we are not simply and cheerfully to describe and depict the phenomenon of play, but rather wish to direct a thoughtful question to it, we must seek to understand what is understood in it on its own terms. Playing is an actual carrying out of life by an actual human being; he now plays, for example, just as he earlier worked. In the activity of work he dealt with things that offer resistance to his deliberate forming, resistance that he overrode with just the efforts of his body or with the help of machines. In the activity of play, above all, insofar as it involves playing a role [*Darstellugsspiel*], the role-player also performs actual activities—but they have, so to speak, a "double ground": they are activities of the one who is role-playing and in another way also activities of the player according to the "role" that he has assumed in the instance of play. Everything that he does proceeds in a strange "simultaneity" on two "levels," is an actual comportment of a human being in the "actual world" and is at the same time an activity in accordance with roles in a "non-actual world of appearance." The actor [*Schauspieler*] on the stage is as actual as the spectators, the mise en scène, the lights, the theater building, but he is at the same time "Hamlet," the prince of Denmark, who wants to avenge the death of his father and for sheer thinking cannot act. Is Hamlet less actual than the actor—does the talk here of less and more have any specifiable sense? If we call the theater-appearance, the playworld, merely "non-actual," have we thereby already sufficiently characterized it? The "non-actual" as the simple antonym of the "actual" is indeed that which is utterly nugatory, that which is not at all. The "appearance-world" of the theater is, however, nevertheless something that is, which as appearance has precisely a special sort of actuality. Now, however, the Danish prince has the event of the king's death presented on the open stage, so that the culprits will understand that he knows of their guilt. There thus comes to be another theater played out in the theater, and a double "non-actuality" is introduced. What kind of remarkable and strange "appearance" is this, an appearance that belongs to the kind of play that involves playing a role, indeed in a certain way to play in general, which is, to be sure, actual but presents nothing actual? Can the "non-actuality" of such worlds of appearance be arbitrarily repeated? How can a non-actuality be actual at all? Don't all conceptual demarcations then get mixed up, as soon as one approaches even the first attempt to clarify such entanglements? Play with the playworldly appearance proper to it is quite a nuisance for philosophy. For here, otherwise separated and neatly divided concepts pass over into each other unexpectedly and outlandishly—and this not from carelessness, but rather in the course of expressing the matter itself. With a wholly self-evident assurance, the everyday understanding of life moves about in the multidimensionality of play. Children already go about with distinctions that are of the most difficult questionworthiness for thinking. Perhaps the strange "non-actuality" that belongs to play is *more* than merely a negative character of the dream-woven construct of sense that, in its negativity, is measured from its distance to the actuality of tangible things.

Chapter Two
The Metaphysical Interpretation of Play

6. The Non-Actual Character of Play

Our question concerning play is led by a fundamental philosophical problem. This problem is the relation between the human being and the world. And this relation is a special manifestation of the relation of innerworldly beings to the all-encompassing world-totality. While we are accustomed to observe the processes of motion in animate and inanimate nature as lawfully regulated sequences, and to speak of a mechanical and even biological causality, we assume that human activities—at least in part—do not belong to a lawfully determined sequential continuity but rather proceed from independent acts of freedom, that they present creative incursions into a context of events otherwise determined according to rules. We are already, in an innerworldly way, familiar with the phenomenal difference between an event that is bound to occur and one that is not. We, of course, do not remain content with this familiarity; this difference unsettles and disconcerts us as soon as we contemplate it. How are natural causality and freedom compatible with each other? Can both exist together in a comprehensive actuality that encompasses them? Is not the rule-governed coherence of natural occurrences continually "punctured" by human activities that actively encroach on the course of nature? Many an attempt has been made in philosophy to come to terms with this difficulty. One attempt at a solution is the denial of human free will. One says: "free will" is an illusion; in our activities we are no less lawfully determined than the stone when it falls, only the determinative laws of human psychical life are still not sufficiently known to us. The assertion of the "illusory character" of human freedom is more a naturalistic "dogma" than something known—above all, the proof is still lacking as to how and from which lawfully determined motives the illusion of freedom can emerge at all, of how it is possible for the deterministic character of human activity to conceal itself, so to speak, in the feeling of freedom. Another attempt at a solution is the division into spheres: one relegates the self-enclosed natural realm to what happens causally, and "ethics" to what happens freely, and carves the human being himself into a sensuous being belonging to nature and into a "moral being" belonging to the intelligible realm of the spirit. Artful theorems have been developed in order to determine the juxtaposition of the two spheres and the corresponding relations between them, as already in the Cartesian dualism of *res extensa* and *res cogitans,* in the system of "occasional causes" in Geulincx and Malebranche, in the doctrine of the "pre-established harmony" between the realm of nature and the realm of grace in Leibniz, and in the Kantian separation between the human being as a member of the world of appearance and the human being as a "citizen" of the noumenal world.

Yet in all these divisions into spheres it cannot be clarified how the human being, who freely determines himself in his embodied activities, intervenes in the actuality of nature. Free action is indeed not merely ethical self-legislation, not merely a moral phenomenon; the freedom of the human being reveals itself also in sensuous deeds; it objectifies and materializes itself in what the activity of work is able to construct. The human being in his freedom deliberately produces indeed not merely the forms in his soul; he produces artifacts that are then situated in space and time, he transforms the face of the earth and stamps his traces on it in a thousand different monuments of his power. Technical production streams into nature, already presupposes nature as a setting, as material for its work; this technical production cannot at all be thought of as housed in a sphere separated off from nature. It was perhaps a disastrous, "idealistic" one-sidedness to interpret human freedom predominantly from out of morality. Already in the first reference to the intraworldly motion of things it becomes clear how the distinction, initially familiar to us, between a lawful boundedness and a free unboundedness of occurrences becomes problematic—and how from there motifs of thought emerge to determine the manner of motion belonging to all motions in a total and comprehensive way. These motifs press toward a cosmic understanding of motion. The question arises as to whether the motion of the whole of the world can be appropriately grasped and explicated with the categories of the innerworldly understanding of motion. The motions of inanimate nature, the course of the stars, the ebb and flow of the sea, the gust of wind, rainfall, and so forth are included in the total motion, but so are the motions of growth, the blooming and wilting of plants, animals and human beings, conservation in the exchange of matter, the passing on of life through the generations—as well as, on the other hand, the form of motion of human activities, the ethical deeds and activities of work: all that belongs, too, within the total motion. But *how* are these manifold motions of things in the *one* universal motion of the whole? Are single motions added to a sum of motions, are they entwined into a unified fabric? Or must the obscure distinction between world and thing be supposed here?

This distinction is "obscure" because we are all familiar with it and at the same time misconstrue it. We move about with it where and whenever we understand beings, but we are not able to grasp it: we slide into representations and models of thought that are oriented to what is intraworldly. We try to think of the total motion of the cosmos, for instance, in terms of celestial orbits, of the sun's course, or otherwise in the image of a great "growth," a *natura naturans,* or, like the early materialists, as a shower of atoms, or as a deliberate rule of the gods or a divine world-architect, or as the *creatio continua* of a creator god—or perhaps also as a *game.* If the world's movement is to be grasped as play, the play of the world cannot be understood and interpreted simply without tension according to the image of the innerworldly play of human beings. To be sure, the human being is an innerworldly thing of a special sort, insofar as he comports himself in his very Being to the cosmos, stands forth with understanding into the whole of the world. But nevertheless it is in no way already certain that the whole has a structural constitution like the intraworldly thing, which is stamped by an ecstatic openness to the whole. The "play of the world" is a speculative formula that does not express phenomenal results but rather points out a way of thinking. Human play, in contrast, is a tangible phenomenon with which everyone is acquainted, that is universally familiar, and of which each has an intimate knowledge from the testimony of his own lived experience. We are conversant with a manifold of individual features, are familiar with a wealth of examples of forms of play, rules of the game, and customs of every kind, and we are able, without further ado, to cite specific structures of play-comportment. However, because our view of human play is subordinate to the fundamental question concerning the connection between the human being and the world, we cannot commence arbitrarily. We begin with the question concerning the "non-actual" character of play. For, as we initially only suspected, a special reference to the world is hiding in this odd character of play. Such a suspicion appears incredible at first. For how, precisely in the "non-actual" aspect of play, is an indication of the most actual of everything actual, of the world itself, supposed to be contained? Yet here it would have to first be clarified and understood in what sense the talk of "non-actuality" in play is meant. We usually distinguish in a common and tangible manner between "actuality" and "non-actuality." Without an explicit ontological clarification, we make use of these concepts in an approximate and conversant mode of understanding. "Actual" and "non-actual" is a simple and rigorous opposition. This opposition is more rigorous than that between "large" and "small," "warm" and "cold"; for the large and small, the warm and cold "are"; they are, in each case, actual. To be sure, the same thing cannot be large and small, warm and cold at the same time; when one determination applies the other cannot apply; when the one is "actual," the other is "non-actual." Admittedly, if we take large and small, warm and cold as determinations of degree, then a thing can very well be both large (larger than other things) and small (in relation to larger things). Then what it actually is, is expressed in its degree of magnitude or heat. The actual determination of a thing in regard to its own properties of magnitude and temperature presupposes the actuality of the thing, its existence, its *existentia*. The actuality of properties is only possible on the basis of the actuality of a substantial bearer of properties. Actuality, for its part, is not a property that can belong to a matter or a thing—or even be left out. If the actuality is left out, the whole thing with all its properties vanishes. What kind of remarkable character is this: the "actuality" of a thing? Is it anything *in the thing* at all? We can see actual things, feel them—but can we also see and touch the actuality of these visible, tangible things? The sensuous perceptibility of a thing often counts as proof of its being actual—and yet the actuality of beings is never sensuously perceived. Actuality is a determinate, fundamental manner of the Being of beings, an ontological modality—and stands in a relation to "possibility" and "necessity." Everything that is actual is at the very least also "possible" but does not at all need to be "necessary." Thus conceived, "actuality" is taken to be an ontological modality of existing things, is assessed as the being actual (as the *existentia*) of beings. Philosophy finds itself seriously perplexed when it is supposed to specify in what this character of being actual, of *existentia,* might consist. It finds help, for instance, by referring objective beings back to the representing subject. If the connection of representations is not subordinate to the arbitrariness of the subject, if the latter cannot capriciously combine representational contents, but rather experiences a concrete restriction in attempting to do so, then the object is manifestly actual. Or one says that there must exist a connection with subjective reception—or that the experience of resistance guarantees for us the being actual of represented objects. Or one says in general: the occurrence of a spatial and temporal position constitutes the being actual of actual things; space and time are the two *principia individuationis,* the principles of individuation, and being individuated is synonymous with being actual.

But—one will perhaps ask—is actuality nothing other than the being actual of things, let alone of objects, for the representing subject? Is this subject not also for its part actual—and is its self-experience characterized by the aforementioned criteria of actuality? Does it experience itself "receptively" or as "resistance" or as positioned within space and time? Clearly not. But is, then, the actuality of the subject another sort of actuality than that of objective things? Is it not more radical to ask whether actuality in general is primarily a determination of *beings,* a character of things and states of affairs that enigmatically adheres to them, or a total character of a universal presencing [*Anwesen*]? We also speak, for example, of actuality *tout court* and do not mean thereby an actuality of these or those things, but rather the total field of the actual. There is only *one* actuality, however many dimensions it may have. The *one* total actuality is not first assembled from many individual actual things, however, but rather actuality *tout court* gathers together every individual-actual thing in advance. The concept of actuality is polysemous and problematic. And indeed the concept of "non-actuality" is just as polysemous and full of questions. When, as was said, we go about unreservedly with our everyday understanding of the distinction between "actual" and "non-actual," we live, as it were, in the conviction that this alternative is exhaustive. Either something "is"—or it "is not." Something is "actual" or it is "non-actual." There is no third option. The either-or is exhaustive, *tertium non datur.* That is clear without further ado. But must we not hesitate and become apprehensive if we take a closer look at what we have formulated to be so "clear"? Either something is or it is not! What does "something" mean here? Not a thing or a state of affairs; for if we think of a thing or a state of affairs, we think of something that is a *being,* and a being is something *actual.* Only in an improper way do we speak of the possibility of a being. But we can represent "things" and "states of affairs," imagine them, have them as representational images in our soul, "merely think of" something—and say that what is thus merely represented, merely imagined, merely thought of, exists only in our soul and not in "actuality." Because we can "intend" and "imagine" beings and because it is sometimes difficult to separate what is merely in our soul and what is both intended by us and also actually existing, we can therefore ask whether "something" is actual or non-actual. What is imagined is nugatory; it cannot be recognized in its claim to be actual. But what is merely imagined and therefore nugatory is nevertheless not simply nothing. It exists as imagined, as a phantasm, as a representational content. What is merely represented is not something actual, but it is nevertheless itself actual as an intentional moment of an act of representing. An actual act of representing contains a sense of "non-actuality." We thereby see how the statement "either something is actual or non-actual" contradicts itself in its operative presuppositions; for the "something which is not actual" is nevertheless, for all that, itself actual as the act of representing something non-actual. The unreserved, blunt, and immediate harshness of the common distinction between actuality and non-actuality cannot be maintained. There are not only actual and non-actual things—or, formulated more precisely, there *is* the "actual" and there *is not* the "non-actual"—but there is also the mediation between both; there is something actual that contains something non-actual as a represented, meaningful content. The chimera and other mythical creatures do not exist, but there is the poetic, imaginary production of such mythical creatures, an actual consciousness of non-actual content. That is a harmless affair, as long as the human being understands how to reliably separate his actual imagining from the non-actual figments of his imagination. Where imagining is not aware of its contrast to the apprehension of actual things, where it is infatuated by the impressive power of its images, the danger always exists of taking the non-actual to be actual, indeed even to be something more ontologically actual than common everyday actuality. And this danger is most dangerous when we surmise a realm of superhuman beings, when we populate the land beyond Acheron with the dreams and anxieties of our heart. Precisely in the relations that concern us most of all, in the relation to the divine and to the realm of the dead, we also become most confused by actual representations of non-actual objects. Here it is perhaps most difficult to specify what the characteristic of truly actual Being is—what distinguishes a mere dream of the heart from the truth.

We now ask: how and in what sense is human play determined by a peculiar "non-actuality"? Play as a comportment and an activity is just as actual as other human activities. All activities are "actual." Initially, one might well say that activities as such have no special distinction, that they are no more actual than passive comportments. In an actual human being, an inaction in which he, for instance, pauses for a moment, is just as "actual" as a subsequent lively bustle. Doing and leaving undone, movement and rest are only different modes of the continually actual human being. But already early on in philosophy the essence of being actual is elucidated by way of the model of activity. We find manifold "capacities" in an organism: it has, for example, the capability of nourishing itself, of growth, of sensuous perception. On occasion, "capabilities" can persist when they are not used. The capability to see exists as a capability even when we are asleep. Our seeing is then potential. Seeing exists *in potentia*. It exists *in actualitas* when one opens one's eyes, in their activation. The being-at-work, the *energeia* of the sense of sight determines its active actuality. Aristotle used the phenomenal distinction between the readiness and the use of a capability as an analogical guiding model for an interpretation of Being as power and an interpretation of actuality as the *energeia* of the power of Being. Since then activity has a privileged actuality-character, as it were. To be sure, the human being is also "actual" as an animal, as a living being, but he achieves his particular human actuality in self-actualization through his deeds. "Being actual" does not simply belong to the human being—as it does to the stone, the blade of grass, the slowworm; he instead actualizes himself in the decisions of his freedom. Taken as activity, as a spontaneous enactment of life, play is also a mode of human self-actualization. And yet we hesitate to say this. Why? For the most part we have an idea of the meaningfulness of human life. The individual does not know with complete clarity and distinctness what he is aiming for in his inmost will to live—but he does know that he is aiming for something, that a striving urges him on. Each human being is a vital project; each brings a unique tone to the immemorial, eternal melody of existence. The individual's life project is not at all openly disclosed to this individual himself; his inner goal does not lie unconcealed before his eyes; most seek their way errantly. Only a few go with unswerving certainty through life and see the star toward which they are going. Human beings, however, are as a rule guided by common interpretations of the right path for the human being, are determined by intersubjective ideals, morals, and doctrines of faith. All seek the path to human felicity; the majority attach themselves to communal hordes that seek disparate paths to *eudaimonia*. The human being cannot rest content with simply existing on the earth, without questions like the animal; he seeks a sense, asks why and wherefore. His earthly sojourn is unsettled by the perpetual concern to find the right and valid sense of life and thereby true happiness. In everything that he does and leaves undone, he assesses, he evaluates his life circumstances according to a pre-projected ideal. He does not simply live out his life; he comports himself to his life by continuously taking a position with respect to it—and in doing so he is by no means certain and assured of the measure according to which he assesses. This tension of the uncertain search for happiness overshadows all the works and days of the human being and at a deeper level of understanding constitutes that which one calls the "seriousness of life." We are aware of this seriousness in the harsh struggle for our daily bread, in laborious confrontation with formidable nature, in subduing the passions and desires, in the needs of the soul, in the despair of our conscience—but also where we painstakingly learn, where the human being seeks to understand and to fraternally help his fellow man. The seriousness of life determines all activities that mediately point to the final goal, which are done and persevered in for the sake of human felicity. The activities that have a shade of the seriousness of life count for us as serious activity, as an activity that "makes sense" and is imbricated in the highest sense of existence. However, a non-serious activity stands over and against such serious activity, a non-serious activity that does not receive its sense from the architectonically structured total configuration of human goals but rather appears to a certain degree to be "senseless." Activity then has a peculiarly non-binding character; it is not derived from the totality of that which is foreseen, nor from the project of life—it is "aimless." Of course this is not to say that we would thereby act without any plans whatsoever. Yet such a plan of action has no anchor in the project of life otherwise guiding us. Serious activity is, as it were, "sporadically" interrupted by "islands" of a non-serious way of carrying life out. Of course, no one will fail to recognize that an enormous significance belongs to such intermittent pauses in the economy of our life, that we relax in the non-seriousness of play, recover, renew ourselves once more, that we plunge back into the untroubled lightheartedness and mirthful idleness as into a refreshing pool. If play itself, in this sense of a higher economy, thus serves the serious life and is a "means" of renewal, then play itself still has certain serious elements. Yet playing activity in itself is non-serious, is without the weight and the burdensome character of human actuality as the task of self-actualization—it is relieved of seriousness and with its floating lightness has an enticing power for the human being. It entices us into an "aesthetic" bearing toward life and thus into an underdetermination of the reality of the human being. The "playful" is a well-known category for in-sincere, non-serious activity, for an "acting as if" without obligation, without commitment. The posture of play can be revoked at any time, the rules of the game rendered void. When there is merely a semblance of occupation, for instance, a self-important demeanor without real industriousness, we say that one is "playing around." We call a flirt "playful." For the most part the concept of the playful has a negative undertone and means an insincere, illusory activity, an acting-as-if. There are playful variations on the serious ways in which we carry out our life, as when we pretend to work, pretend to fight, and pretend to love. But it is not settled that the playful consists only in such variations on the seriousness of life or that it has its domain therein. The customary and typical conception of play concedes a positive significance to the play of children and tends to judge dismissively the play of adults, unless it should serve indirectly as restorative play.[1] All play activities thereby fall under the aspect of the "not-serious." To be sure, no one would dispute that play activities are actual, but, as activities of non-seriousness, they bring with them a sense of "non-actuality." This non-actuality belongs to them even if they are kinds of play that do not involve roles. This is not entirely easy to see. Human action is not merely an actual process like the flight of a cloud. The billowy cloud is, to be sure, seen and understood by human beings, but it is understood in such a way that it does not thereby evince its own "sense." But surely each human action—be it the most insignificant enactment—evinces the goal intended by it. Nearly every action of the human being is a gesture that has a sense [*Sinn-Gebärde*] and that refers to the whole of existence and the final goal governing it. Play is an action that, in its sense-gesture, does not have this reference, that instead withdraws precisely from such a reference and displays itself as non-serious and illusory. That holds for the countless games of amusement with which we while away our time. The pastime is already a case of non-seriousness that has a unique structure: we fill up free time; in doing so it is quite a matter of indifference with what we fill it up, how we best escape a menacing boredom; we fill in a stretch of life not with what we genuinely want and aim at but rather with trifles. Each human being has only a finite supply of time. The number of hours and days is measured for each; only we do not know how great this number is. But we do know that it flies by with each day, with each hour of this one life that we each get—that we cannot get anything back again which we missed out on. And yet we spend portions of this precious and irreplaceable time of our lives in non-serious, illusory activity, "move the pieces on the board back and forth." According to the common conception of play, "non-actuality," as an existentiell non-seriousness and as an "acting as if," forms a characteristic moment of actual play. In its being actual, play thus bears within itself as a constitutive feature the illusory variation on serious life.

The moment of non-actuality of course emerges more starkly in those kinds of play involving portrayal. Wherever the player slips into a "role" and wraps himself up therein, the activity of play becomes two-dimensional: there is at the same time the activity of the player and the activity of the human being *in* the playworld. What sort of strange character of "non-actuality" belongs to a playworld? This non-actuality is not simply nothing, it is an "appearance" that *is*, an existing appearance. But in what way and where is this appearance of the playworld? Is it similar to an imaginary representation, where we indeed actually imagine but in doing so do not represent anything actual? The imaginary object is only in the imagining soul, is a psychic reality, not an objective and intersubjective one. But what is going on in the appearance of the playworld? Is this only an imaginary product of a solitary soul? Is there not here a certain objective reality? Or does this playworld-appearance exist for all those playing together—and to a certain degree also for the spectators of such play? If we see a scene in the theater, then together with this we see the events on stage—but we nevertheless, together with this, see not merely that which is simply actual in these events, human beings of flesh and blood, their dress, the mise en scène; we also see, together with this, the playworld and understand the roles of the players. And this not because each, having himself been stimulated by the movements and words of the actors, would elicit the imaginary representation in and for himself. We see the play simultaneously as a play of simply actual human beings and as the portrayed life of the playworldly figures. Here, of course, the great question arises as to whether we grasp the playworld essentially enough when we view it as an objectively present mirror-appearance of actual life, so to speak. Certainly, it displays itself to an impartial observation of the phenomenon of play as a sort of mirror-appearance. The principal categories should be drawn from a discussion of mirroring in general in order to be able to characterize in more detail the relation between actuality and non-actuality in play. Yet this is not without danger. The mirror-image displays itself in its very self as "derivative" of the archetype, as an imitation of the archetype. When philosophical confrontation with the Dionysian violent play [*Spielgewalt*] of human life and the world was led into a primal animosity and extreme fervor—in Plato's battle with the poets, with Homer and the tragic Muse—critical thinking began with the mirror-character of play and thereby already reached the verdict that all poetry is only imitation. The interpretation of poetic art as *mimēsis* governs the metaphysical interpretation of art for a long time hence. The poet, says Plato, resembles the painter, and the painter resembles a mirror. So long as we suppose play to be derivative appearance, to be mirroring, and suppose mirroring to be a reproduction of archetypical things in residual silhouettes, we are all held under the spell of the Platonic interpretation. We must free ourselves from this spell.

7. Play and the Other Regions of Human Life. Plato's Blending of Being and Nothing

The aspect of "non-actuality" belongs to play in a manner that is generally well known. Every reflection on human play, however preliminary, somehow makes use of this well-known essential feature in its statements. Playing is considered to be a comportment that is characterized by a certain "non-seriousness" and "in-sincerity," to be an "acting as if," to be a neutralized acting that does not make any decisions, does not bind us in our deeds, an acting that remains "non-binding," is, as it were, a mere trying out of possibilities that does not entail inevitable consequences. We can call off an activity of play at any time—nothing at all has been changed thereby in our serious life. As long as we are only "playing," we cross over no Rubicon—neither in war nor in love. What we do when we play, we do only for fun. The carefree cheerfulness that we feel in the enactment of play, the transformation of the entire attunement of life into something bright and light, almost floating, has its ground in being taken away from the existentielly heavy dimensions of life: occasionally, for all too fleeting hours, play relieves us of the burden of life's cares; we plunge back again, as it were, into the insouciance of childhood, rejuvenate ourselves in this dreamlike happiness as in a refreshing sleep. Certainly, not every form of cheerfulness and jesting in the communal life of humans is connected to play or is even merely of a playful sort, but conversely we can still say that every game is attuned with excitement in its enactment of life, is an exhilarated way to enjoy life. This delight we take in play [*Spiellust*] need not at all be a primitive joviality [*Lustigkeit*]; as delight, it can embrace, encompass, and to a certain extent include all feelings of the human heart—it extends to the dark delight in tragedy. In play we experience a peculiar creativity, a creative and happy fortune: we can be everything, all possibilities stand open, and we have the illusion of a free, unrestricted beginning. In other cases we are determined by the history of our course of life; we find ourselves in a situation that is no longer open to choice; we are the product of our earlier deeds and omissions; we have chosen in a variety of ways and have thereby lost countless possibilities. The path of life, so to speak, is determined by an uncanny, accompanying contraction of our possibilities. Every activity that we earnestly carry out makes us more determinate and at the same time less possible. We continually determine ourselves, do irrevocable things. The more we attain to determinate actuality in the self-actualization accomplished through our deeds, the slighter do our possibilities become. The child *is* potentially: that does not mean that it is not yet this or that but rather that it is still "everything," that it still has a thousand open possibilities, that the whole of life still oscillates in it before all determination. The old man has the history of his self-actualization behind him; he has in one way or another squandered the thousand possibilities, has realized himself, and with each step in the course of life has narrowed the open range. Perhaps the old man, if he looks back, senses the unlived possibilities wistfully, the omitted life that is something entirely different than the neglected and misused one. What we have "neglected" is indeed judged from the sense-context of our self-actualization; we then regret not having chosen decisively enough in a particular case. But when the old man looks back on his life that has passed by, perhaps an insight into the lot of the human being in general, that of only being able to become "actual" in the perpetual loss of possibilities, unsettles him. The child is indeterminately everything, the old man is determinately little—we are born as many and die as one. The inexorable contraction of our possibilities, which accompanies our course of life and is the implacable law of serious life, is alleviated in its sadness—by play. For in play we enjoy the possibility of retrieving lost possibilities—indeed, even far beyond this, of attaining the openness of a mode of existence that is not determined and not bound. We are able to cast off the burden of our own life history, can "choose" what we wish to be, can slip into any role of existence. However, we are precisely not able to do this actually and truly, but rather *only* "in make-believe." We can only escape our actual and decided life in an illusory way. Liberation is a mere dream. The rapture pertaining to play transposes us into "non-actuality." In the mode of non-actuality we can, so to speak, begin anew, without history; we can choose in an imaginary space and an imaginary time. We again attain unwasted freedom as freedom in the dimension of a mere "appearance." That playing as playing is an actual, real enactment of life, that it occurs amid and among the serious activities of life, no one would contest—but the actuality of playing is determined as such precisely by the fundamental character of a non-serious acting-as-if. Playing is an illusionary variation on human self-actualization. Playing itself decides nothing, but it copies in manifold ways the enactment of life in which each moment decides in one way or another. The non-seriousness of play frequently consists in precisely the illusionary imitation of serious life. Play is imitation in the space of the imaginary. Indeed, the character of a creative transformation, a fantastical variation on serious life, in playful imitation must not be misconstrued. Play does not exhaust itself in a slavish reproduction; it also brings forth entirely new motifs, gets new possibilities to flare up, possibilities with which we are not acquainted in the space in which we otherwise carry out our lives. As a variation play is creative—but its productive power can only unfold in the useless realm of the "non-actual." The non-seriousness of play does not stand as an autonomous sphere "alongside" the realm of serious life. Certainly there are a plethora of activities that occur specifically in the realm of play and that do not as such have the character of providing a variation. That is the case, for instance, in kinetic games that arise from the joy in limb-loosening movement and that effect an amplified consciousness of the body, a sensuous bodily delight. Modern sports present a clear and methodically developed expression of this play that arises from the predominance of the body. It does not provide a "variation" on something and also bears no moment of non-actuality in itself. It is initially a sign for a new relation to nature, a truthful discovery of the sensuously embodied rootedness of the human being in the elementary media of air and light, a performance training on a magnificent scale. But manifold motifs of the more general phenomenon of play enter into this sphere of sports, for instance in the way that competition in sports ever more comes to be a playful variation on the real battles of nations and occasionally an exhibition resembling the ancient circus. And thus events that are initially about sports attain, via superimposition, a mediate play character that is now also determined by the contrast to so-called serious life. The contrast to serious life is generally determined in play not merely as distance but also as imitation. In its zone of non-actuality[2] play repeats "serious life"—but takes all burdensome weight away from it, raises compulsory life, so to speak, into the light, floating ether of the "non-binding."

Human life is structured in elementary dimensions. It is difficult and arduous in the field of work, whether it be harsh physical work or the intellectual types of work; it is brutal in the field of ruling, where the tense difference between those who command and those who obey, between masters and servants, rends brotherhood asunder; it is unsatisfactory and full of disappointments in the meeting of the sexes; it is bitter in sickness, sorrow, and loneliness; it is full of terror and uncertainty in relation to superhuman powers—but it is cheerful and weightless, light and exhilarating in play. To be sure, play does not bring us the profound happiness that is perhaps necessarily bound up with profound sorrow, but it confers a certain pleasurably attuned feeling of happiness, even when we play out [*erspielen*] the awful horrors of tragedy. The happiness of play is connected most closely with the "non-actuality" belonging to it. To be sure, it is an actual, if also ephemeral happiness, but an actual happiness in regard to the illusionary non-actuality that lies in its very self. This shows itself clearly in those instances of play in which roles are played explicitly [*eigentlichen Darstellungsspielen*], which contain a scene, a stage, and a portrayed sense of action that encompasses an enclosed "playworld" with specifically chosen types of roles. The theater is the clearest form of play involving roles, but it is not the only one. In every kind of play in which the role-character of the players predominates and one moves about with a fictive conception of oneself, a "non-actual comportment" is portrayed in an actual comportment, and such self-rapture in the realm of an "appearance" is felt with excitement and pleasure. The "appearance," this thoroughly nugatory and unstable formation, has the secret power to carry us away, to lift us above and beyond the life that is so thoroughly determined by care—to a place where we can freely shape our lives and yet not deprive ourselves of any possibilities with a decision. We live from the inexhaustible, fundamental source of the imagination, but such an unresisting and spontaneously creative life is enacted only in the impoverished dimension of the "as if." We are rich at the price of poverty—rich, inasmuch as we can all still slip from one skin into another, can make our deeds undone; poor, inasmuch as this existence is played out not in true actuality but rather in the land of the imaginary.

Seen in this manner, "non-actuality" is thus an essential, fundamental feature of human play. And it is not merely *a* fundamental feature; it is the decisive fundamental feature. The actuality of play activity is a perpetual, continual, productive comportment to the "non-actuality" of the playworld. Wherever there are philosophical questions about play that are connected to the general problem of Being, it is precisely the moment of actual "non-actuality," the strange entwinement of Being and appearance, that requires conceptual mastery. How can something even be "non-actual"? The most obvious answer is initially always that which is related to human cognition, that which reflects on the fact that we can represent mythical creatures in our power of imagination, although these beings do not exist in connection with actual things and events. One then says that what is actual as an act of representation need not be actual as what is represented by it. The creatures of myth only have a "mental existence," are only in our head, so to speak—as "fancies," as illusory thoughts, as poetic inventions; they are not out there among actual things—among houses and streets, human beings and vehicles. We can obviously think of many things that do not exist at all. As just one example among many, we form the concept of the "nothing"—we think of something that is not some existing, actual thing; we think an object of thought that does not exist at all, that is the comprehensive concept, as it were, for all that "is not"—we think it actually, without thereby positing it as something actual. But the nothing presents certain difficulties. Does it have only a mental existence? Is it a thing belonging only to thought, an *ens rationis,* in Kant's terms? Is the nothing only in our thinking, or in our empty intending and imagining? Does the nothing have no significance and no relevance for beings themselves, for the being-a-being of existing things [*das Seiendsein der seienden Dinge*]? Can we understand the "Being [*Sein*]" of beings without understanding it from the horizon of the nothing? Isn't the nothing also a cosmic power against which the totality of the All [*Allheit des Alls*] gathers itself and comes into relief in the first place? In view of the theme to which we have restricted ourselves, we cannot begin a speculative treatment of the problem of the nothing. But in any case the problem occupying us, of "non-actuality" as an essential feature of play, has some connection with the fundamental problem of the nothing. It nevertheless becomes clear in a still wholly preliminary interpretation of play that the "non-actuality" emerging here in no way bespeaks absence in the sphere of external things or a merely "mental" existence in the representing soul. Instead the non-actuality of the playworld, the scenery with its figures in their roles, truly occurs in the midst of the objective actuality of things, not indeed like a simply actual thing alongside other simply actual things, but rather as an objectively present "appearance," which rests on simply actual things and overlays them in an entirely unique way. The play-appearance is not merely in the human soul; it is in the midst of and among things and is nevertheless separated from all other things. It is objective—and yet not an object alongside other objects. It has no immediate vicinity to its surroundings. It is delimited in a strange way, framed and "enclosed" in itself.

All this requires closer interpretation. In the history of philosophy, critical confrontation with the enigmatic actuality of play, which keeps open an existing appearance, a dimension of "non-actuality," in itself, begins in the thought of Plato, thus at the beginning of Western metaphysics. Although Heraclitus had, in monumental simplicity, characterized the course of the world as a playing child, employing a cosmic metaphor of unbelievable boldness, nowhere did he unfold the ontological constitution of play; he did not provide the categories for the interpretation of its marvelous symbolism [*Sinnbildes*]. The explicit groundwork of metaphysics is carried out in Plato in a manner that always operates with the distinction between archetypical actuality and the reproduction of afterimages [*urbildlicher Wirklichkeit und nachbildlicher Abbildung*], in order to carry out fundamental ontological separations, but the operative models of thought themselves are also to a certain degree taken into consideration and called into question. Plato's thought, which was rooted in Heraclitus and Parmenides, could not stick with the brusque Eleatic separation between Being and nothing: he conceived things, which were already commonly called "beings," as mixtures, as an intertwining of Being and nothing, as an existing nothing and a nugatory Being. All things emerging and passing away, the *onta gignomena,* sensible things in the broadest sense, simultaneously are and are not; they are, but they are not really, continuously and without change; they are not truly, are not being in the mode of being [*in seiender Weise seiend*]; they are not *ontōs on.* Transitory things only are to the extent that they, in a manner difficult to explain, "participate" in the stronger Being of the ideas, of the formative powers of light that bring all finite things into their character, conferring on them a face and aspect. Each finite and transitory thing refers to the idea and bears witness to it, manifesting itself as an imperfect reproduction and afterimage. What is decisive here is that such reproducing and afterimaging pass through the dimension of a qualitative differentiation. The transitory sensible thing is a reproduction of the non-transitory idea. The resemblance between the sensible thing and the idea is maintained within the space of the non-resemblance between the transitory and the non-transitory. The sensible thing only resembles the idea insofar as something transitory can at all resemble something non-transitory.

In order to indicate this correspondence of resemblance between the sensible thing and the idea, a correspondence that is broken by an unbridgeable non-resemblance, Plato takes up particular phenomena from the realm of sensible things—phenomena that prove to be derivative in themselves and furthermore are determined by a moment of reproduction. Such phenomena are, as it were, existing "non-actualities." Plato operates with the phenomena of the "shadow," the "reproduction," and "mirroring." Shadows, reproductions, and mirror-images occur as specific appearances within the total realm of sensible things. We commonly distinguish a corporeal thing itself from its shadow, from its image and its mirror-image. Shadows and mirror-images refer to the actual thing itself; they manifest themselves as derivative of, dependent on, and conditioned by it. *As* the shadow refers to the actual sensible thing, *so* does the sensible thing analogously refer to the idea. The relation of the Being of the sensible thing to the Being of the idea is thus explained by Plato metaphorically through a familiar relation of reproduction that on the whole is played out in the sphere of sensuous actuality. Plato thus draws the models for the ontological devaluation of the sensuous sphere from precisely the very sphere he wishes to devalue. In order to demonstrate the sensible thing speculatively as a mixture of Being and nothing, he takes up a sensible phenomenon in which a mixture of actuality and non-actuality is attested to phenomenally. The shadow, the reproduction, the mirror-image serve as operative models of thought for the formulation of the metaphysical problem of Being in Plato. The founder of metaphysics does not thereby proceed in such a way that he first investigates his guiding model of thought—the structures of reproduction—and only then makes speculative use of them. Rather, the clarification of the guiding model is carried out—to the extent that it is advanced at all—in the course of his central philosophical questions. We already said that play, too (above all when it is taken as the play of the tragic Muse and as the *poiēsis* of the poets in general), assumes the aspect of a reproduced imitation, of a *mimēsis*. The "non-actuality" that belongs to every instance of play as one of its moments appears, after all, to point in this direction. That, however, is the question that is to be examined. Is the so-called non-actuality of play determined as a certain kind of afterimaging, a certain kind of imitative mirroring of serious human life? Is play a mimetic repetition of *non*-playing existence? If our first, provisional descriptions are correct, which spoke of a variation on serious enactment and also of a scene portraying an imaginary playworld, then the "non-actuality" that constitutively belongs to play must manifestly be interpreted as *mimēsis*. But are these descriptions correct? Have they been taken from the pure phenomenon in a sufficiently impartial manner? Could it not be that the Platonic tradition still dominates us, even when we "describe" given phenomena that appear to be entirely "ahistorical"? The dominance of metaphysics does not merely overpower those who, in the wake of the ancient thinkers, contemplate what they had thought, but rather is documented in an intellectual legacy that holds us inconspicuously under its spell through the power of self-evident notions.

Before we can more properly and rigorously pose the question as to whether play is a reproduction of an actuality, a real mirroring of human life in the irreality of a peculiar appearance, we must first make clear to ourselves what a "mirror-image" even is. If the mirror functions as the guiding model for the interpretation of play as *mimēsis,* and the categorial concepts for the exegesis of play are attained with recourse to mirroring, the problems for understanding thus begin already with this guiding model. We know well enough what a mirror is when it comes to using one in an everyday manner, but we lack the concepts that would suffice for interpreting it in a way that would enable us to understand and grasp it. We thus initially pose to ourselves the question concerning what *mirroring* is at all. Now, one might think that this question can be answered by reference to the theory of optical natural occurrences in physics. Here, the laws of refraction of light rays in translucent media and deflection in reflecting surfaces and all optical effects in general would be determined precisely and with scientific reliability. However, mirroring is indeed not merely and exclusively a problem in physics; it is also a question of our understanding of perception. And an onto-conceptual distinction is at work in this perception of a mirror-appearance when we separate the thing itself from its mirror-image and characterize the thing itself as "actual" and, conversely, the reproduction of the thing in the mirror-appearance as "non-actual." In what sense do we use the ontological concepts "actual" and "non-actual" here? In terms of the onto-conceptual understanding, which is already at work in the conception of a mirror-image, we are attempting to carry out a meditation—a meditation on something that everyone is familiar with, but something that, despite all familiarity, cannot be explicated sufficiently enough. What is a mirror-image? Let us therefore take up this question not in the way that a physicist would understand the issue, where it is obviously a legitimate problem, but rather let us take it up ontologically. The things in nature all around us are diverse and abundant, belong to different realms, and are for us innumerable. We roughly distinguish the realms of inanimate things, plants, animals, human beings, and things made by human beings. As diversified as such things are according to their realms, they nevertheless exist as mixed together, so to speak, in the one all-encompassing total actuality. In no way do all inanimate things exist in a heap, with all living beings together separated off from it; rather, the inanimate and the living are intermingled according to a dispensation that is imbued with sense; for example, in a human settlement the sustaining earth as a setting, houses as dwellings, human beings and their apparatuses, tools and vehicles, domesticated animals, but also the space of the air and the bright sky are all "together." All things of this sort "are," are actual. Now, it belongs to the particular conditions of corporeal things in light that they cast shadows, delineate a silhouette of their appearance, so to speak, to their surroundings in the direction facing away from the source of light. The shadow is, as a shadow, no less actual than the thing casting the shadow. Or, in other words: trees on the lakeshore are mirrored in the water. The mirrored reflection as such is just as actual as the mirroring tree. In the moment, however, when we view not merely the shadow, not merely the mirrored reflection as a phenomenon of light, but rather perceive in this phenomenon of light a "reproduction [*Abbild*]" of the tree, a silhouette of its appearance, a mirror-"*image*" [*Spiegel*-"Bild"], a peculiar differentiation is carried out: a new dimension is opened up, so to speak. We recognize in the shadow an image of the tree, in the mirroring even a faithful reproduction. The shadow presents us with the outline of the shape; the mirroring even gives back the colors of the tree on the lakeshore. We say the mirror-image lies on the surface of the water; it extends out upon it. Yet the mirrored tree does not lie on the water like an actual log floats on it; the mirrored tree is there and is also not there. Its image never "covers up" the water. The mirror-image does not lie on the water like a piece of cloth, like a coat of paint, a speck of oil, or the like; it lies on it in such a way that we see at the same time its irreality. We say it is only a mirror-image. We distinguish between the real tree and its reproduction on the water. We do not confuse the two. It is not at all easy to characterize the way in which a mirror-image lies on a real being, here the tree image on the surface of the water. We see through the mirror-image—it does not prevent us from recognizing the actual water. As the effect of radiance on the water, it is a particular circumstance of this water, but as an "image" it is the presentation of a thing that is not "in the water." The image is an irreal thing presented in the real radiance on the water.

But how can this irreal thing overlay, so to speak, an actual thing without covering it up? Is this a relationship similar to what otherwise occurs in cases of translucent materials? For example, we see through glass and we also as a rule see the glass at the same time. Does the mirror-image lie on top of the water to some extent like a translucent glass? By no means. When we see through glass and in doing so see also this translucent medium, the glass that is being looked through is just as real as the thing seen behind the glass. Here there is no difference between irreality and reality. In contrast, the tree is nothing actual at all in the mirror appearance on the water; it is an actual reproduction of the simply actual tree on the lakeshore. And yet the irreal image extends out on the real surface of the water. And even if this extension of the image does not cover up the surface of the water, indeed does not at all disguise it in its pure self-showing, but rather gives way without resistance, the image is nevertheless dependent on the real image-bearer, here the surface of the water. An image, as a real phenomenon of the presentation of another real thing in the mode of a remarkable irreality, needs a simply actual basis in order to provide expanse for the image appearance; it needs lines, shapes, and colors of a simply actual sort in order to be able to present in them the outlines, figure, and colors of the thing imaged by it. Lines, figures, and colors become two-dimensional, as it were, are lines and shades of color playing on the light on the water, and are "at the same time" the outlines and colors of the tree in the image. The talk of "two-dimensionality" is admittedly misleading here; there are not two dimensions of simple actuality, but rather the dimensions of the simply actual and of the irreality imaged by it. The mirror-image manifests itself, however, in a thoroughgoing dependence on the original. It produces no new lines, shapes, or colors, except where the medium of presentation with its own colors darkens the colors of the original thing in its rendering in the image world; colored things are mirrored in a darkened manner in the dark blue or peat-brown water. The mirror-image that is there of its own accord, so to speak, in nature—but needs the human being who perceives it in order to be recognized in its irreal content—is an imagistic repetition of the thing itself, is dependent in everything on the thing that is mirrored, and on the circumstances of light between the things. The mirror-image copies. But insofar as it copies and is dependent on the original, it opens in the first place a region of a strange "appearance":[3] we see into, so to speak, an irreal realm. The mirror-image works on us like a "window" into a non-actual and yet visible land. If we stand on the shore and look down into the water, the green depths and their mute life may stir us in a mysterious way—but it is still more mysterious that the trees of the mirror world, and beyond that the lofty sky and the flight of white clouds, once again appear on the water and yet are not really attached to it. The human being who bent over the water for the first time and recognized himself in the mirror-image opened up a mysterious and enchanting domain: the mirroring of actuality in itself. In the *Sonnets to Orpheus* one reads, "Mirrors, no one has ever yet described / you, figured out what you honestly are. / You are merely a few sieve holes inscribed / on sliced regions of time hopelessly far. // You are the prodigals of the empty chamber / when dusk spreads on the woods enormously . . . / Like a sixteen-pointer stag the chandelier / strides through your impenetrability. // Sometimes you're full of paintings. And a few / seem to be brushed right into your background / while others you've sent timidly away. // But the most beautiful of them will stay / till bright Narcissus catches and breaks through / to her chaste lips hidden in the beyond."[4]

To ask what it means to mirror is not simply to pose an arbitrary ontological question. It is through mirroring that beings separated into originals and reproductions and first became ambivalent for the human being, so that he could ask what beings are.

8. Plato's Interpretation of Play by Way of the Mirror. His Critique of the Poets

With its grand beginning in Plato, metaphysical philosophy's relation to play is one of a stimulating ambiguity. On the one hand, Plato's thought oscillates in the element of the playful, is a high, sublime play of thoughts, is in all seriousness and rigor detached in the free distance it takes from itself, serious in its jests and jesting in its seriousness, full of Socratic irony and subtlety, familiar with and enjoying the allure of the mask. The playfulness of this thinking is much more than a merely artful stylistic element. However, on the other hand, Plato struggles passionately against the world-significance of play, against the wisdom of the mysteries and tragedy, against the poets, who base their claim to speak the truth on the inspiration received from the Muses and Apollo. This struggle does not consist in the simple denial or rejection of the possibility of *mania,* of enthusiastic inspiration from the god; Plato does not oppose an "enlightened" reason to poetic intoxication, but rather a reason that is itself ecstatic—which signifies the true *mania.* What poetry claims to be, philosophy *is* for Plato. It is a passion that is inflamed at the sight of the beautiful form of the young man, intensifies in conversation with youths and looks out from the beautiful forms and the magnanimous souls to the beautiful in itself, to the uniform beauty of the *idea,* and ultimately finds its way from the sensuous sheen of beauty in general to the non-sensuous truth only accessible to thought. To the poets' myth that the beautiful is true, Plato does not simply oppose another myth, that the true is what is really beautiful. Rather, he interprets the beautiful as a path and step toward the true, as a prefiguration of the true that opens itself up to pure thinking. He takes the beautiful to be the veiling of what is really true, to be a sensuous reflection and glimmering. What comes to light within the realm of sensible things in the enchanting luminosity of the beautiful is a beacon, as it were, lighting the way toward that which truly is. The radiant flame of the heavens that lights up our day and allows the plants of the earth to grow and grants them visibility and flourishing is the visible, derivative image of the highest idea, the idea of the good. As the visible in general is related to the invisible realm of thought, so the beautiful is related to the true. The beauty of the beautiful is in itself already a reference above and beyond itself. Or to put it differently: in beauty the terrestrially visible already gleams as though touched by the non-sensuous light of the idea. The intensification of being beautiful is therefore of the greatest import for Plato. Beauty is gradated in itself and points from one step to the next, has the tendency to point beyond itself. The well-formed body is beautiful, the soul more beautiful, thought more beautiful than that and more beautiful still the true Being of the idea that is accessible to thought alone. The comparison of the beautiful becomes the path into philosophy. The power of beauty is interpreted as an escort to the truth. The beautiful is the *psychopompos,* the guide of souls. In many dialogues Plato lauds this soul-guiding force of the beautiful and, in connection with it, the daemonic enchantment by *erōs.* Philosophy is erotic passion—for Plato a passion that arises in the sensuous and leaps from it. The guidance of souls by the *kalon,* by the beautiful, is—like everything high and mighty—also exposed to the greatest danger: the guidance [*Führung*] can be perverted into something that leads one astray [*Ver-führung*]. This happens when sensuous beauty is not recognized in its referential character, when we fall prey to it and become more strongly bound to the sensuous by it. And Plato sees just this danger in poetry, which does not understand itself as a *prefiguration* of philosophy and as able to be superseded by it, but rather poses as the most autonomous and primordial mode of interpreting the world, indeed even as an inspiration from the god. Plato reinterprets the concept of the *theion,* the divine: the gods represented in traditional myths, who behave in a manner human-all-too-human, who are jealous and contentious, engaging in amours and appearing in all sorts of altered forms, are not truly divine. The god is essentially good, without weaknesses and wretched human features, is unchangeable, constant, continuously identical in his very self. The god is like the idea—or, more precisely, the idea is the true god. And from this speculative concept of God, which conceives of God from the idea, Plato now also grasps the essence of *mania,* the essence of what it means for a human to be seized by the force of the god. True *mania* is philosophy. The way in which Plato presents this intoxication of reason, the ecstasy of spirit, nevertheless bears many features that appear to be taken precisely from the *mania* that is being combated. On behalf of philosophy, Plato speaks the language of passion, of erotic frenzy, of yearning and rapture. That is no contradiction; for sensuous pathos belongs indeed to the path of philosophy—as the beautiful shows the way to the true. Or at least *can* show it. If the beautiful is conceived in its true soul-guiding function, then philosophy can determine the provisional prefiguration of the true that is concealed in the sensible image, as it is brought about by the art of poetry. It is then on the basis of philosophy that one must[5] put art in its place and determine its character.

That is the sense of Plato's critique of the poets. This critique does not condemn poetry absolutely, it condemns only the claim of poetry to its own primordial truth, which would be outside or even above philosophy. Like beauty in general, poetry, which indeed moves in the element of the beautiful, is a preliminary sensuous likeness of veritable truth. Still having obscure intimations, thus not yet actually knowing, it imitates true knowledge. Poetry is essentially mimetic. Yet it is an imitation, a *mimēsis,* of philosophy, only as long as it allows philosophy to determine its character. In contrast, if it wants to speak the genuine truth itself and present itself as the independent wisdom of tragedy, it thus becomes—according to Plato—the imitator of pre- and extraphilosophical life, and insofar as this is already an unknowing imitation, because in it we are referred to sensible things, the art of poetry becomes an imitation of an imitation. The sensible thing is a reproduction of the idea. Poetry is a reproduction of life entangled in reproductions—and thus a reproduction of reproductions, indeed without knowing it; it is even caught up in the delusion that it is hitting on the truly actual. The Platonic critique of the poets amounts to a world-historical decision, insofar as the metaphysics of art, of play, was thereby established for a long time to come—it was decided in advance that the beautiful is subordinate to the true and is a sensuous image for pure non-sensuous thought. That has had great consequences not only for the conception of human beings, but also for the representation of the whole of beings. The human being was interpreted mainly in regard to his "reason," and the world was interpreted as a rational construct and a moral order. War and play were denied to be fundamental cosmic movements, and the cosmos was interpreted as an ordered structure that emerged as a result of the methodical operation of a reason at work. The world is understood as an architecture structured by gradations: at the top the realm of ideas only accessible to thought, supremely highest of which is the idea of the good, the *agathon,* or also *nous,* the world-reason; under it the particular ideas, the archetypes of the same, the different, rest and movement, the inanimate and the animate, species and genera—then follows the *cosmos* as the reproduction of the idea of the good; it came into being through the dispensation of *nous* at work, but is imperishable and is thus something intermediate between the eternal ideas and sensible things that emerge and perish, which it contains within itself; and then at the bottom lies the *chōra,* the dark material that provides the stuff for all the formative activity of world-architectural reason and represents the primal principle of the sensible and what is alien to the intellect. The whole of actuality is interpreted as a universal triumph of the principle of reason and as an effect of a cosmogonic *technē.* As an artisan methodically brings his work into existence, so *nous* brings forth the total structure of all beings. And that which comes about through reason is itself rational: is *not* a vast aimless play, not a dance of things, not an inconceivable ascent and decline of everything transitory. The Platonic conception of the world does not leave play to the side; it does not overlook it—but it banishes it from the essence, displaces it from the heart of the world, pushes it away into the sphere of sensuous appearance, assigns it an intermediate role, a pointing-out-the-way, in which it points beyond itself and away from itself. And yet one can say that Plato does not bring his great confrontation with the power of play, which so captivates human beings, with the art of poetry in general and with tragedy in particular—that he does not bring this confrontation to the victorious conclusion that his theory would indicate.

Until the late writings the problem disconcerts him. And in the *Laws,* that work of old age, which death prevented him from completing, the relation of the human being to the gods is interpreted from the horizon of play: the human being is called a plaything of the god. Play is thus here not merely a preconceptual and preliminary way of understanding the relation of human beings to the gods—such as the elevated association with divine powers in the community of the festival—but rather play is the mode in which the gods handle human beings: we are delivered over to them like playthings to the child. The gods play—they do not work onerously like mortals; they do not struggle for sustenance; they do not forcefully wrest from the earth stones to build houses, clay for jugs; they do not clear the wilderness; they do not sow in order to reap, nor gather the harvest into barns; they do not stand their ground against one another in a battle for life and death; they are immortal, cannot starve, and are not killed. And if they procreate and love, then this does not have among them the sense of a striving after "immortality" as it does for mortal human beings who can only live on in children and grandchildren, but as individuals themselves pass away. What is the activity of the gods supposed to be? The human being initially tends to represent them as similar to human beings, albeit much elevated. Only a purer sensibility [*Sinn*] catches an intimation of the gap that exists between mortals and immortals, attributing governance of the world to the gods. And in Plato's late text this governance of the gods over human beings is interpreted as a game, as a handling of playthings. Playing is the activity that happens in leisure relieved of all need. Because the god is without need, he is able to play continually. Another direction for the interpretation of the activity of the gods—which determines to a greater degree the history of metaphysics—aims at the activity of thinking. It is already found in the pre-metaphysical thinkers but comes to lasting predominance with the foundation of metaphysics by Plato and Aristotle. If one is not willing to accept that the gods sleep—says Aristotle—and yet do not need to work and do not have to conduct wars, then the only thing left to believe is that they are continually concerned with the highest matters, with which the human being only occasionally and in the highest upsurge may concern himself, when his mind is free from need and is gathered together in leisure: namely, pure thinking. The god of metaphysics thinks. He thinks that which is accessible to pure thinking alone: the imperishable Being of the ideas; he himself is the world-reason in whose thinking the ideas are housed. And for this reason the metaphysical god thinks himself: is the thinking of thinking, *noēsis noēseōs*. This determination of the divine is retained through the history of metaphysics all the way up to Hegel's "absolute knowing," up to the concept conceiving itself. When the activity of the gods, divine being, shifts primarily into thinking, play, as the other great possibility of leisure, falls under the aspect of a *prefiguration* of the true, just as in the Platonic critique of the poets. The beautiful becomes the appearance of the idea—a conception that also governs Hegel's *Aesthetics*. But if what it means to be divine shifts to play, then other interpretations of Being, of truth, and of the world result. Both interpretations determine the history of Western thought, in which undoubtedly the interpretation of divine being as pure thought is guiding and the other interpretation of divinity as play accompanies it below the surface, in a noteworthy relationship that is fraught with tension. And yet the late modern thinker who attempts to think the death of the metaphysical god, namely, Nietzsche, says in *Zarathustra:* "—because the earth is a gods' table, and it trembles with creative new words and gods' throws [of the dice]—."[6]

The problem of play stands for us in the background of this history. We began with the question concerning the "non-actuality" characterizing play. How must this be understood? Is it an afterimage and a reproduction, an imitation, a *mimēsis?* And furthermore, is it an imitation of the really and truly actual thing or an imitation of something that is already derivative and residual in itself? Or is play in the end brought into a wrong orientation when one interprets it as some sort of imitation of serious life and of things and events belonging to the serious actuality of human life? The guiding model for an interpretation of play as *mimēsis* is, already in Plato, the mirror. The mirror is the metaphor for the painter and the painter is the metaphor for the poet. We must inquire into this graduated structure of references. The mirror-image is already not easy to understand and to analyze conceptually. To be sure, everyone knows what a mirror is, yet it is not easy to express this knowledge. We initially left aside the sort of observation a physicist makes; for in our context we are not interested in which laws of reflection are operative for beams of light, but rather in how a mirror-image is seen and understood in this seeing. Mirror-images that are not seen with human eyes, which move to and fro as physical processes between the tree on the shore and the surface of the water, for instance, do not contain a positing of an actual "non-actuality"—which is indeed what we think merits interrogation. The human being sees the image as an image, sees on the actual water an actual phenomenon of light that contains something "non-actual" in itself, sees therein the trees on the shore and the clouds of the sky. But in seeing such things he does not believe that these are actual trees and actual clouds; he knows of their illusoriness, of their irreality. The mysterious dimension of "irreality" is something marvelous, with which we are now concerned.

We have approached the matter with the most natural mirror that occurs clearly and purely in nature without any human assistance, that is, the reflective surface of water. Ever since the earth existed, the light of the sky had its reflection in oceans, lakes, rivers, and ponds, and thus the cloud formations and the brightness of the sky have drawn their opposing traces over the surface of water night and day for a very long time. But only the perceptive living being, primarily the human being, who is able to distinguish between actual water and the non-actual things projected in the form of images on the water, sees images in such opposed traces. But there are still several other things that mirror, that render surrounding things in images on a smooth, shining surface. Yet for the most part these are things artificially produced by human beings: polished surfaces of marble or bronze, for instance, or glass windowpanes—and ultimately, sheets of glass underlaid with a reflective coating, that is, industrially produced mirrors. In his critique of the poets, where Plato posits the equivalence of the mirror, painter, and poet, he begins with an artificially produced mirror. That is not without significance. For the perspective that guides the consideration there is *technē*. The artisan of some *technē*, the craftsman of a handicraft, produces his piece of work judiciously: the potter the pot, the weaver cloth, the smith the horseshoe, and so forth. Each makes what is appropriate to his profession. And he does so well the more he sticks to it and perfects himself in his art. The shoemaker who sticks to it in his task will become an ever better shoemaker. Technical ability is developed in specialization. A particular capacity is developed in a good way precisely in the renunciation of being able to do everything to some extent and roughly and to tinker in all skills and tasks more poorly than properly. The "jack of all trades," if he does not happen to be a renaissance man, is more likely a "master of none." And Plato lets the artist of a thousand talents appear, who not only makes one thing, but all things, and "makes" not merely artificial things but also natural things. Already in this skipping over of the difference between artificial things and natural things one can see that this "making" of the artist of a thousand talents is no genuine making. For indeed natural things are exempted from the human's ability to make; they form a precondition for human making. Plato's supposed artist of a thousand talents "makes" all things by fiddling around with a mirror and capturing mirror-images of all things, natural and artificial. He thus "makes" in the manner of reproductive imitation. Insofar as he makes mirror-images, he does not at all make actual things like the shoemaker and the smith, but rather makes that which is non-actual in the strange dimension of appearance. But the making of such a non-actual thing is itself a powerless, impotent making, is a making of mere semblance. Such making brings nothing into existence, allows nothing to become independent of the activity of work as a self-standing product—it only leads one to believe, merely lets an appearance arise that is only an image of a thing but is not itself an independent thing. The maker of everything in truth makes nothing. The Platonic characterization of the mirror-artisan has features that are clearly caricatures, pointing in advance to an interpretation that devalues the painter and the poet. The painter and poet produce nothing actual; they bring forth only images, only powerless mirror-images—indeed mirror-images of the ordinary actuality of things evident to the senses—and do not at all notice that these sensible things are already reproductions, reproductions and afterimages of the ideas, of that which truly is. The distorting tendency in the way Plato unfolds his thoughts is shown by the fact that Plato characterizes the man manipulating the mirror as, in general, an artisan. A mirror-artisan, though, is in the first place a producer of mirrors, not a producer of mirror-images. And even if Plato distinguishes a producing and a using *technē* and furthermore places the using *technē* over the producing one, nevertheless, the manipulator of the mirror is not a "user" in the proper sense. However, Plato treats the one using the mirror as someone who makes a thing. He attributes to use an aspect of production that does not exist at all in the use. Yet no one is so foolish as to ever maintain that in fiddling around with a mirror he produces, fabricates, or confects any kind of things. In the most customary understanding of the use of a mirror there is the knowledge that they are *only* images that appear on the gleaming surface. Obviously Plato, too, knows this, but by distorting the customary understanding, by passing off the user of the mirror as a producer of merely "apparent" things, he is able to assess the problem in a more incisive form, that is, to pose the question concerning the ontological character of the mirror-appearance. And above all he obtains a determination of place for such appearance in the framework of his principal perspective, which is oriented on the model of *technē*. The mirror-image is a reproduction of a reproduction, *mimēsis mimēseōs*. Yet the reproduction has a respectively different sense in the two stages. The sensible thing that is still an actual thing—for example, the ore from which a smith makes an anchor chain—is, as an actual thing, a reproduction of a higher actuality, namely that of the idea. The mirror-image of an anchor chain contains no "actual anchor chain" in itself but rather a non-actual one within the image. One could pose a counter-question to Plato: is the sensible thing related to the idea in which it "participates" as the mirror-image to the original thing? Is the distinction between the idea and the sensible thing not "greater" than that between a thing in the light and its mirror-image? Yet the mirror-image is an accurate and reliable reproduction, only flipped. And if in the image on the water there are five trees on the shoreline to be seen, then there actually stand five trees on the shoreline, too. In contrast, however, Plato thinks of the relation of sensible things to the idea essentially as a relation of the manifold to the one. The one idea of the table appears in manifold brokenness and turbidity, but above all pluralized into all tables. We cannot infer back to the multiplicity of accompanying ideas from the multiplicity of certain sensible things. But a mirror-image, however, shows the same number of reproduced things as there are in the original actuality. These considerations show how, in Plato, there is a specifically guided description of the phenomenon of the mirror—and also shows that the categories for an explication of mirroring were developed with a certain deliberate one-sidedness. We must free ourselves from this. Above all we must make clear to ourselves that in seeing a mirror-image the illusoriness and irreality of things within the image are known; this appearance is an acknowledged appearance that does not pass itself off as immediate actuality; we do not confuse genuine and merely reproduced things. Of course, such confusion can occasionally occur through a sophisticated arrangement, through cunningly applied optical effects, but then in that case we are not at all conscious of the image. However, where we understand an image as an image, we are never tempted to confuse original and reproduction. To be sure, the mirror-image is actual as a mirroring, but it contains in itself, in the space of its image, something "non-actual." This "non-actual" thing, however, continually has a referential relationship to actual things outside the image in itself. The mirror-image indeed only reproduces; it cannot reproduce anything that does not exist. Indirectly, it has an indicative character. For example, if Hagen of Tronje had entered clumsily to the side of and behind the drinking Siegfried, so that the latter would have seen in the mirror of the pool the raised spear in Hagen's hand aiming at the Linden leaf spot, he would not have been pacified in the thought that this was only a non-actual image on the gleaming mirror of the water, but rather would have leapt up in order to ward off the attack. A mirror shows "in the image" what is actual outside the image. A mirror-image is not, *as* an image, merely something actual, an actual thing with the peculiar structure of containing in itself something "non-actual," but rather this "non-actual" thing refers indirectly to actual things in a reliable manner. The referential relations are familiar and common to us; we make use of them in various ways. They constitute the particular reproductive character of the mirror. We call what is "non-actual" *in* the mirror-image the mirror-image-world. It is nothing real that one can grasp, touch, smell, or taste, but one can "see" it. More precisely, one can "see into" it; it is visible and is nevertheless not existent. Then is it the case that, by another sense than seeing, we again actually apprehend something that itself is not actual? We can certainly have auditory hallucinations, sense-impressions that simulate objective impressions to us,[7] but then the "appearance" is merely subjective, is in our soul and not in the midst of things. But the mirror-image is intersubjectively perceptible; it can be seen by many, indeed in such a way that they can mutually check their perceptions. The sense of sight alone truly has the possibility of becoming aware of such an objectively present "appearance." But is this due to the sense of sight as such—or to that within which the sense of sight operates: light? In any case, this is a question that has yet to be treated sufficiently. The approach to the question of Being in ancient philosophy is perhaps co-determined in an essential way by the bifurcation of Being and appearance that is possible in the space in which there is light and the sense of sight. We see into the mirror-world, similar and in turn not similar to the way in which we see through a "window." The mirror-world "opens" itself to our actual world; it is not closed or closed off; it is "broken open" for us, as it were, released to the observer. And yet it does not anywhere pass over into the actual world, is not like the actual room behind a window. One cannot "reach into" the mirror-world, one cannot step into it, it is "inaccessible"—but one can peer into it; it provides us with an "insight." The mirror-world is nowhere else at all than in such "insight"; it is only the "window," so to speak, through which we look in. But it has its own irreal space that does not pass over into our space, although it is "opened up" to us. In this irreal space of the mirror-world there are the mirror-worldly "things," which have a place and a nexus of positions in it; and in it, too, irreal movements run by like a flight of clouds in that sky that we see in the image on the water. The space of the mirror-world has an irreal "depth." But the whole mirror-world rests on a real bearer of images, cannot exist at all without it. The bearer of images is a constitutive moment of the image that is just as important as the image-world is. Both moments together, in their opposed tension, first yield concrete imagery. The Platonic interpretation of the phenomenon of the image jumps restlessly back and forth between both moments, without distinguishing them explicitly enough. That amounts to a not inconsiderable breach of theory at significant points in the course of his thought.

A further ambiguity remains in the concept of re-production [*Ab-Bildes*]. We can ask: is each image [*Bild*] a reproduction [*Abbild*], and further, is each reproduction a mirror-image [*Spiegelbild*]? The mirror-image is a reproduction that is essentially determined by the simultaneity of imagistic depiction and the depicted original. The tree on the shore and its image on the water are "simultaneous." In contrast, one can very well produce an image that re-produces a thing and nevertheless remains as an image, when perhaps the thing no longer exists. Such a reproduction depicts an actual thing, rendering it in the way it looks—and is nevertheless not bound to a simultaneity. But in the sense of such a reproduction lies the fact that a simultaneity existed at the time of its production. The original must have determined the imagistic copy. A photograph, for instance, is a reproduction in the sense now meant. It is otherwise in a painting (of representational art). Here, too, the image depicts something; we recognize things in it, can describe them with names, but we do not recognize uniquely individual things. It doesn't matter what the painter took for his "model." The image makes, so to speak, no declaration concerning something factual—it indeed reproduces but does not exactly reproduce a specific, unique thing. The significance of the image does not lie in the reference back to the incidental model. The image can have been freely formed at a thorough remove from a factual model—and still depict something objective. And again in another sense an image can be a configuration of forms and colors in tension with one another—without the character of reproduction. How is play an image? Is it a mirror-image, a reproduction at all—or an image without a reference back to an original? That remains to be asked.

9. The Lens of the Disenchanted. Critique of the Platonic Model of the Mirror

The confrontation of metaphysical philosophy with the power of play belonging to existence established the perspective in which afterward all questions of its human and cosmic significance were already predetermined. Its dangerous enchanting power was banned—insofar as play was shown to be an essentially derivative and secondhand phenomenon. It had to come down from the elevated buskin in which it had strutted on the tragic stage; it was exposed in its merely feigned mask of the god, put in its place by the rigor of the concept for its arrogant wisdom. The poet of the Homeric epic and of Attic tragedy was the typical player, against whom the vehement attack of metaphysical thinking was waged. The Platonic critique of the poets, however, is not merely an external action of philosophy; it is an essential moment in the process of philosophical self-consciousness: metaphysics, at its beginning, finds its self-understanding by asserting itself against play's mythic-tragic understanding of the world. Self-assertion, however, is always still incomplete when it leaves the opponent "outside" and lets it exist as an independent, if also suppressed, power. Complete triumph is evidently attained if it succeeds in completely melting down the oppositional element and converting it completely to itself. Platonic-Aristotelian metaphysics strives after this triumph by assigning a subordinate rank in the hierarchy of truth to the poetic art and reinforcing this determination of place with a poetics. Play is explained fundamentally as reproduction and imitation, is determined to be *mimēsis.* This concept of *mimēsis* signifies the veritable disenchantment of play. The metaphysical thinkers' competition with Homer and the tragic poets seems to be[8] won with the insight into the mimetic nature of play.

But what kind of triumph is this? Is it a clear and unquestionable success? Or do unmastered questions remain here? The murkiest question is whether play is comprehended in its full and primordial sense when the moment of *mimēsis* attains privileged[9] prominence. Play indisputably has a mimetic character—but is that all it amounts to? And above all, is this imitation something that refers to ontic events and activities? Initially we are not really acquainted with another schema of an "imitation." A human being imitates another—he repeats his motions, gestures, way of speaking, and so forth. Or human beings imitate the extrahuman processes of nature, attempt to portray gods or beasts. An imitation thus appears to be thoroughly related to an exemplary [*vorbildlich*] being that is then copied [*nachgebildet*]. A craftsman imitates a pattern when he manufactures a product. Such a pattern can be a natural form or another product or, ultimately, the "idea." For Plato every *technē* is essentially mimetic. In another way, we imitate in moral conduct certain exemplary human beings, who have indicated to us the paths, as it were, to right living, or we imitate guiding images, ideals, in following such ethical authoritative models. The human being's whole practical and technical conduct is characterized by relations of imitation: but some *being* or other is always thereby imitated, whether human beings or ideas or ideals. Insofar as Plato interprets play, in the representative form of the poetic art, from the horizon of *technē* and *praxis* in the broadest sense, he restricts it to an imitation of *beings.* And because play is indeed less capable than any simple handicraft, which can, after all, produce actual shoes and actual tables as after-images of the genuinely existing ideas—because the poetic art only produces in the space of the imaginary, so to speak—it can only be an imitation of imitation in *praxis* and *technē.* Thus is play unmasked for the critical gaze of metaphysical thought. And if we want to pose the question as to whether this unmasking is ultimately right, then we cannot do so from a standpoint outside this one: the situation of our question is already stamped and co-determined by the history of the metaphysical tradition.

That means we must formulate our question with regard to what the metaphysical tradition takes to be the basic feature of play in general, that is, *mimēsis*. Is the imitative character of play actually the decisive basic feature, the substance of its essence? And is imitating an imitating of innerworldly beings? We cannot proceed from the assumption that the interpretation of play at the beginning of metaphysics is false—and that for this reason one could skip over it. It has its strict truth, even if this is a truth of a limited kind. Now, in what does this limitation consist? It does not consist in a partial view, nor in an incomplete conception of the phenomenon, but rather in a completely disillusioned mode of observation. The whole phenomenon of play stands in view, but in the view of a disenchanted spectator. Disenchantment in general is a curious process. It transforms things without the things themselves actually being changed. But all at once they appear to us in a cold light. As long as we are enthused, enraptured by human beings or things, as long as we see them with the eyes of love, they are, as it were, transfigured, elevated, glowing with a deep significance; we are as though affected by a spell, struck by a more secret beam. Such captivation can be perceived from time to time as a daemonic power that leads us to believe a false image; but for the most part it is experienced as a deeper truth; inspiration leads us into the heart of all things. Yet captivation can suddenly and incomprehensibly vanish, the spell can be broken—and we then see all at once the beloved human being "all too humanly"; the teetering bridges between us no longer hold, the dream is over, we are disillusioned. Everyone is familiar with this uncanny transformation of the scenery of human life. All at once, the disenchanted one sees things differently. It is not correct to say that he sees "more truly"; he is more critical, more mistrustful, and he more sharply sees everything that mistrust sees, no longer seeing what the eyes of love see. The enthused spectator who was seized by the captivating power of play and remained under its spell saw the deeds and sufferings of the god on the stage; he became the epopt[10] of an epiphany. To be sure, he still knows about the performance, but the performer disappears for him into the god or hero. The essential thing is that which appears through the finitely frail human being. Yet when the play is "over" and everyday human beings materialize once more out of their roles, when the actor removes his makeup, disillusionment returns: the play contains the fatal character of "mere play." The "god" or "demigod" becomes a mere "role," the mask a prop. Disenchanted disillusionment has its own lens. It takes in the whole play—but precisely under a disillusioned perspective. The measure of actuality is now the actor who "imitates" a god or hero and in truth is neither—the role of the hero is understood from the perspective of the actor, who is not conceived as a means for the manifestation of the hero. Two perspectives stand opposed to each other: the understanding of play under the spell of play and an understanding of play that withdraws from such a spell and speaks from disillusionment. Plato's critique of the poets is a great example of the lens of disenchantment. Only when the mask of the god has fallen from the human being's face can play be unmasked as an imitation of an imitation.

The Platonic critique interprets play as a reproduction. In this, the concept of the mirror-image in fact predominates. To construe the character of reproduction as mirroring amounts to a peculiar overspecification of the course of thought. Initially, the mirror is a natural phenomenon, as a reflection in water, for instance, and is characterized by a simultaneity of original and reproduction. A mirror can only reproduce for as long as the original exists. In the case of a mirror-image we have the same processes in the original actuality and in the mirror-world. Only when something happens in the original can something also take place in the mirror-world. Or conversely: when events run their course in the mirror-world, events of the same kind must also happen in the original actuality. Can this relation between the mirror-image and the original be applied to human play without further ado? Certainly there is the possibility that some kinds of playing operate as an imitation of a simultaneous serious activity; for example, children can imitate the simultaneous life processes of adults. As a rule, however, play does not mirror simultaneous events of the serious sphere. It is no slavish imitation. In no way can we play merely in such a way that we at once do the same thing in the serious realm as we do in play. Taken in all strictness, mirroring cannot offer the appropriate model of play, for playing is not necessarily coupled with a parallel activity in the serious sphere. One does not escape this parallelism of mirror-image and original if one posits, as Plato does, an artificially produced mirror as a guiding model instead of a natural mirror. The artificial mirror represents no less slavishly than the natural one. If play is a *mimēsis*, it is nevertheless not mirrorlike in the strict sense. The poet, the *poiētēs*, does not at all relate to the lawgivers, generals, and statesmen like a slavishly, faithfully reproducing mirror that would, moreover, be reliant on legislators, generals, and statesmen acting as seriously during the poetic mirroring—as the poet does toward appearance. If the poet reproduces such forms of life, then this still happens freely—at the very least he is not dependent on the simultaneous presence of his model. He can reproduce from his memory, from his imagination, without the reproduced thing being actual at precisely the same time. One could say that Plato does not intend the mirror-model in the entirely strict sense—we would overspecify his thought to the point of absurdity if we should insist on the simultaneity of original and reproduction. But this simultaneity is not just any moment, not a peripheral feature of the mirror, but is rather *the* feature that distinguishes the mirror-image from all other reproductions. It is not some vague relatedness to an "original" that constitutes the mirror as such, and also not the exactitude of the rendering, but rather the indissoluble simultaneity of the archetype [*Urbild*] and its reproduction [*Abbild*]. This "simultaneity" has its great difficulties as soon as we attempt to grasp it conceptually. There exists spatial and temporal proximity between the tree on the shoreline and its mirror-image in the water. But the mirror-world "in" this mirror-image has its own irreal space that we see into, to be sure, yet remains "inaccessible." And events occur in this inaccessible, irreal space—clouds sail by in the sky; the mirror-image-world manifestly has its own irreal time. But in the way that the space of the mirror-world opens onto actual space in the manner of a window, so, too, does the time of events in the mirror-world open itself onto the time of actual events. Thus it is rather a simultaneity of two times than a simultaneity within one and the same time. And yet it is the latter, too. For the actual cloud-drifts in the firmament and their luminously conveyed traces on the surface of the water are simultaneous events in one time, in the time of actuality. With the moment of the "image-bearer," the mirror-image extends into real space and real time; with the moment of the "image-world," in contrast, an irreal space and an irreal time is posited. Yet it is precisely this irreal image-world that is in a firm relation of dependence on the original; the former renders the latter's reflection inversely, but otherwise faithfully according to all aspects of the appearance, indeed in immediate "simultaneity." Mirror-images can last only as long as their archetypes stand in the light; they are bound to them and cannot at all exist on their own. The fixing of a mirror-image in a material receptive to light, as, for instance, in a photograph, is something else. The mirroring of things in natural mirrors was surely a motive for human beings to capture reproductions of human beings and things by means of an artificial fabrication of images. In mirroring one was able to observe the graphic means of nature itself, to study the manner in which it depicts the outlines and colors of an irreal, image-worldly thing in real lines and real colors. Insofar as the reproduction is fabricated in a methodical, technical fashion and receives a lasting form in a specific material, the detachment of the image from the original is accomplished. To be sure, it is still a "reproduction"; it refers in itself to something whose image is captured. But if the image is given, the original no longer needs to be given immediately, too. Indeed, the possibility emerges, in increasing measure, that the formation of the afterimage is also already detached from the exemplar to a certain degree during production; formal elements are combined, characteristic individual features are overemphasized, other ones recede—in a word, it treats the original freely and eschews the character of mirror-resemblance in favor of capturing essential features. The image, although it is still a reproduction, already provides a "variation" on actuality; it does not mirror, it interprets. And, finally, an image can also free itself entirely from every reproductive function, can present a combination of colors and figures without an objective sense. What is it then? Is it then only an expression of tensions in the soul of the image-maker, only a manifestation of psychic reality—or is it a free and at the same time necessary play of colors and forms? Does not play itself here enter into the image-character of the image—perhaps not only a human, all-too-human play? It is not an accident that the Platonic critique of the poets is oriented by the paradigm of the mirror, by that image that, so to speak, contains no elements of play in itself, which in the strongest sense is a reproduction. Plato took up the image-form, which is devoid of all relation to play, in order to use it as the paradigm for the determination of the mimetic nature of play or the poetic art. The mirror is, as it were, *mimēsis* most of all; it is the unsurpassable extreme of a merely imitative repetition. The human being makes nothing at all with the mirror, so to speak—light itself depicts the counter-images of visible things on the surfaces of the mirror; here the human being can only comport himself by observing in a purely passive way. And if the mirror becomes the disillusioning metaphor for poetic art, then what is thereby implicitly expressed is that the poet produces nothing independent and actual at all—he merely makes mirror-images, repeats in an impotent and merely copying way what already is, repeats beings merely according to their superficial appearance, and only produces something illusory in a nugatory sphere of appearance. All moments in the phenomenon of the mirror that exhibit slavish reproduction and a lack of creativity are singled out by Plato in order to devalue the poet in his claim to truth. Only he skips over the characteristic of the essential simultaneity between original and reproduction in the mirror. And he must skip over it, if he wants to hold on to his destructive paradigm for the devaluation of the poets. Had he also acknowledged this moment, an interpretation of the poet as someone who merely mirrors the serious life of human beings would have scarcely been possible. This counter-critique of the Platonic critique of the poets is not, as one perhaps could suppose, dependent on the overestimation of a single feature in the phenomenon of the mirror. Plato's condemnation of the poets brings together two moments that are at odds with each other: the productivity of the poet on the one hand, and the completely unproductive function of a mirror to repeat on the other hand. The real force of his critique consists in the thesis that the poetic productivity of which the poets are so proud is precisely the most uncreative and cheapest repetition, is, as it were, a pale imitation [*Spiegelabklatsch*] of everyday actuality, which for its part is already a reproduction of the archetypal idea. It is not the poets who conceive of themselves as mirrors, but rather in the eyes of the philosopher who knows the stages of truth and of the truly actual, the productive power of poets merely resembles the impotence of a mirror—play resembles the mirror-image. Platonic thought does not have its subject matter in the universal relation between play and the image in general, which is represented by the ancient gods of play, Dionysus and Apollo, by the god of the mask and the god of the lyre; nor does it have its subject matter in the pictorial powers of play and in the elements of play in the free formation of the image—but rather it has its subject matter solely and in the strongest sense in the attempted "exposure" of play as a mirrorlike impotence. This exposure does not succeed, however, as an evident phenomenal proof that persuades those who only ever retrace the course of thought. Plato cites an abundance of good arguments for his thesis—and yet these arguments for the most part operate with awkward[11] analogies of play to image.

However, Plato was not able explain incontrovertibly how the image as an analogue of play could only be a mirror-image. Only if he were right that play and poetry are mirroring, and indeed in the sense of a completely impotent afterimage and reproduction of another, ontologically stronger being, only then would the overcoming of the power of play belonging to existence be achieved. The interpretation of poetry as *mimēsis* is expressed from the vantage point of disenchantment. Plato certainly does not become a sober-minded philistine; he is never completely removed, even in his loftiest thinking, from the vital élan of play. But his enthusiasm is broken by Socratic irony. Enthusiasm that is not conceptually broken cannot and may not count for him as the higher form of life—he must subordinate it to thought. And the interpretation of play as *mimēsis* becomes the weapon in this war. Now if we, however, for our part, pose the question as to what extent there exists an analogy between the structures of the image and the structures of play, a certain parallelism cannot be denied. In play we produce an image of life, we provide a "variation" on the serious enactment of existence, we cultivate [*bilden . . . aus*] as-if-comportments in which we exist only jokingly and playfully, but do not enter into them with the existentiell gravitas of our life. To this extent, a fictive element belongs to every kind of play, even to the most ordinary pastimes. But far and away most kinds of play "portray something." The character of portrayal can sometimes belong only to the plaything, but as a rule it encompasses the player himself; in the instance of play, this player has a "role," a specific, sense-imbued function, and in this role stands both for himself and his fellow players. The play-companions, who have been embraced by a sense-imbued interplay and whose respective roles are coordinated with each other in it, live in a communal and a communally apportioned "playworld." This playworld is itself something irreal, although it involves actual human beings. But it involves them precisely with regard to the characteristics of their roles, and thus as having imaginary attributes. The "playworld" is not an actual/real situation of actual/real human beings; it has a peculiar "illusoriness"—it is nothing actual and yet not nothing. And it also by no means exists only in the souls of the players; these players do not dream a collective dream. If they perform the life-enactment of playing in the real actuality of life, they are precisely at the same time enraptured in an irreal sphere and have therein a communal, "intersubjectively" recognized continuity of sense depending in each case on the overall sense of the instance of play. The "playworld" in fact has a remarkable structural similarity to the "image-world." It is similarly enclosed in itself and set off against external surroundings. But as the image-world does not, indeed, signify a disruption of the real context of things, and where the image-world appears, simple actuality does not have a gap but rather is continued in the "image-bearer"—as the water qua water passes through the mirror-image of the tree on the shoreline without being disturbed by the irreality of the image-world—*so* the playworld, too, does not disrupt the real context of human beings and things. The playworld in itself is indeed located in a closed-off space, yet in the midst of this real context as an irreal appearance; it has its real substrate in the playing human beings and their material playthings, which function as "bearers," as it were. A playworld can never exist alone by itself; it is always reliant on the simple actuality of players and playthings. In a manner that is difficult to describe, it "overlays" a group of actual human beings who are united by the fact that they are playing together, and yet in doing so it does not cover them up. Both the player and the spectator of the play understand the difference between the actual actors and the functions of the roles in play. The one playing enters into his role, so to speak, but he does not lose himself thereby. We are well acquainted with the manifold phenomena of the intensive identification of player and role, but even in extreme devotion the player does not confuse himself with the character that he portrays according to the role. He can "awaken" at any time from his immersion in play. The playworld is an irreal appearance that "embraces" the ones playing, overlays them with the roles of characters and yet does not thereby cover them up in reality. As we still see the water, on which the mirrored appearance gleams, through the mirror-image of the tree on the shoreline, so we can always see the real players through all irreal roles. As the image-world necessarily has a real bearer, so, too, does the playworld. This is perhaps most recognizable in the play activity of the theater. As the frame delimits the image, so the stage delimits the irreal space and the irreal time of the playworld. The playworld-space and playworld-time have neither place nor duration in actual space and time. They do not at all appear in a system of positions of actual spaces and times, no more than the painted landscape in the image on the wall has a local and temporal connection with this wall. But as the irreal space of the image-world needs the surface of the canvas and the bit of wall on which it can appear in its peculiar "non-actuality," so the playworld, too, needs a bit of simply actual space in order to appear, and thereby takes up actual time, too. And furthermore, each playworld, too, opens—analogously to an image-world—onto the context of actuality; like every image-world, it, too, is a "window." One could formulate this general analogy between the image and play more precisely with the proposition that the image-world corresponds to the playworld as the bearer of the image to the real persons who play, and that in general the image-bearer relates to the image-world as, analogously, the actor to his role.

But if we thus emphasize the doubtlessly existing "analogies," then we also ought not to overlook, on the other hand, the essential differences. The image is an irreal appearance; it depends on a *thing*. This "dependence" can occur in two ways: first, as a natural image that is grounded in specific circumstances of light and its reflection on blank surfaces, but in order to be an "image" it needs the human being who takes it in. Second, an artificial, manmade image of a thing can be produced; the irreal appearance is then deliberately manufactured. We can for now leave aside the difference between immobile and moving artificial images. But a production process and a terminating conclusion belong to the fabrication of an image. The finished image is an artificial thing of an entirely peculiar sort; it differs from a tool, a weapon, a piece of jewelry, and the like. It is, to be sure, something effectuated, an artificial thing produced in the activity of work, but bears in itself an irreal dimension. This is fixed, so to speak, in the image-thing. The "image," as an artificial thing, is a product. One must perhaps distinguish the production of products that still encompass an irreal dimension in their actual content from the fabrication of other artificial things. But at any rate, production thereby terminates in the result of fabrication. The image-world-appearance of the artificially produced image is a result that has left the process of production behind. But this is not the case with play. Playing is not an activity of fabrication, which would come to an end in a result detachable from the process of fabrication. We do not play after we have fabricated the game or the playworld, but rather we play only so long as we produce the playworld. The production of play does not come down to a result. Or in other words and formulated in a sharper antithesis: playing exists *as* the producing of playworldly appearance. The production of play primarily concerns human beings themselves, is a relation of enactment to a continually cultivated non-actual sphere of human roles—it only indirectly concerns things, insofar as they are used as playthings. The image is essentially a product, play essentially the act of producing. This fundamental distinction between the human being and the thing also restricts, in a certain way, the previously discussed "analogies" between the image and play. Above all, it should thus become clear that such analogies are still most readily "tenable" when they are not based on a comparison between human play and the pure natural image, but rather on such images in which the human being's producing power has been documented. That means the mirror-image is most unsuitable for the analogical comparison. Human play does not mirror passively, does not repeat an original as a mere reproduction. In play there is in the strict sense no mirroring. That Plato's critique of the poets operates with the equivalence mirror = painter = poet signifies, beyond all eristic, the "evil eye" of the disenchanted. It cannot be denied that equivalences between play and the image can be drawn and that a certain understanding of the structure of play even thereby emerges. But the question is whether an interpretation of play under the guidance of the paradigm of the *image* could bring about a primordial understanding—even if Plato's malign orientation to the *mirror*-image were avoided. Everything here hinges on how we conceive the "non-actuality" of the playworld—whether from the role's distance from the real actor, thus from the vantage point of unmasking, or from the enraptured upsurge of the player who vanishes into the god, that is, from the enchanting spell. In the one case the "non-actual" is such as to remain behind innerworldly things and has an entirely diminished, impotent, indeed almost nugatory Being. In the other case the region of the irreal playworld could be the mysterious and ambiguous sphere where what is more existent and more powerful than all things would come to appearance amid things. The Platonic critique of play encounters play in a late form of culture, as the play of a cult that is no longer truly believed in, as an ironic distance from life, as making fun of a sublime spirituality. Certainly these are features that belong to play, *too*. But do they constitute its essence? And, above all, can the categories drawn from the phenomenon of the image be used to formulate a valid concept of play? We must proceed further in the direction of these questions.

10. The Ontological Devaluation of Play at the Beginning of Metaphysics. The Problem of the Symbol

The interpretation of play as *mimēsis*, as imitation, and the further exposition of imitation as reproduction—and the elucidation of reproduction as mirroring—these were the essential steps in the formation of the concept, which already the founders of metaphysical philosophy had accomplished so as to determine the place of play and the beautiful: play is associated with the beautiful and the beautiful with play, and both become a prefiguration of the true and are related to that which is veritably true as appearance is to Being. The ontological status of play and the beautiful is determined from their distance to the proper Being of the *idea;* its positive significance is seen solely in mediation, in the transitional character of beautiful appearance, in its referral to what properly is. The metaphysical assertion concerning the transitional nature of play and the beautiful remains itself somehow transitional, moves restlessly back and forth between recognition and rejection, sometimes emphasizing their distance, at other times their nearness to the truth. Beautiful play and playful beauty are conceived as harbingers. However, a harbinger has a perilous ambiguity: it can indicate and it can dissimulate—it indicates when it points out beyond itself, brings tidings of something that is different and more essential, and, in indicating, itself recedes; it dissimulates when it passes itself off as the true thing. Play in the beautiful *can* be a harbinger of philosophy as the guide and escort of the soul, as the "handmaid of the Lord," so to speak, the *ancilla philosophiae,* but it can also be the worst adversary, a seductive daemonic power that opposes thinking and leads it astray. The metaphysical interpretation of play ever orbits around this referential character, play's exceeding of itself, the moment of a strange transcendence, but it interprets this transcendence in terms of a *paideia* that is thought philosophically, as the drawing and e-ducating pull toward the true Being of the idea. And the perspective provided by the model of *technē* is employed to this end. Insofar as play is taken as a *technē* and *technē* in general is already understood as imitation of an archetypical idea, play manifests itself as an altogether derivative *technē,* as a completely impotent and illusory production, namely as a production of mere appearance and thus as an imitation of an imitation. In this conceptual mastering of play, in which metaphysical thinking grounded itself and asserted itself against a great antagonist, the categories were formed that extensively dominate the traditional understanding of play and Western aesthetics and thereby also determine in advance the situation of our *question* concerning play. For this reason, negotiating the ancient quarrel between the poets and the thinkers is no antiquated affair, which over and done with would lie behind us, but rather remains a *task.* And this task consists not least in keeping alive[12] a suspicious doubt concerning the intellectual domination of play by metaphysics.

We have already said that the interpretation of the phenomenon of play by way of the phenomenon of the image incontestably has a genuine, concrete ground, and thus does not present an arbitrary, let alone malicious distortion of the facts. In fact, many structural similarities exist between play and the image, which manifest themselves in the analogical parallel between the world of the image and the world of play, between the bearer of an image and the player preceding his role, and so forth. The structural analogies could of course be worked out with much more discrimination and subtlety than we have done in our rough preliminary sketch. We have only gone as far as we have in this direction in order to accentuate the legitimacy in the metaphysical interpretation of play, its *fundamentum in re.* It is indeed not false, even if it is perhaps fatefully one-sided in overemphasizing subordinate features of play while suppressing the essential ones. The structural affinity of play with the characteristics of the image was the entry point for the metaphysical critique and overpowering of play. Here leverage could be applied so as to topple old idols. That the analogy between play and the image was thereby overemphasized with a view to destruction, and indeed was "overextended" with the orientation to the mirror-image, must be understood from the bellicose situation of metaphysics: metaphysics could only bring its conception of the world as a universal, tiered, rational structure of beings to completion through the suppression of the view that the prevailing whole of the world was a game. "Rational order" or "play"—that was now the question. Work of methodical and technical *nous*—or the tragicomedy of the ascent and decline of all finite things from the nameless nocturnal womb and tomb of every individuation? Are beings as a whole a *taxis,* a meaningful structure of universal reason, of the concept conceiving itself, or are they the ultimately inconceivable play "of the child who moves the pieces on the board back and forth"?[13] If the founding of Western metaphysics was carried out precisely according to a projection of Being that subordinates Being to thinking, *einai* to *noein,* then its position on play had to attain paradigmatic significance. And thus even play was subsumed under the universal principle of reason as a prefiguration of the rational. As the child plays and is rational in a still irrational way, as it prepares and practices for future adulthood, as child's play is, so to speak, the instinctive anticipation of the later form of reason, so play in general—according to the metaphysical interpretation—is reason that is still disguised, a reason that is disguised in the sensuous, but already shimmering with the gleam of truth. It is precisely Plato's thematic explications of the play of the child in the *Laws* that show with all clarity the basic features of the metaphysical understanding of play. And, likewise, all his magnificent interpretations of the erotic moments in philosophy, of the role of the beautiful in the soul's path to the true, of playful appearance as referring to deeper seriousness and the like, reveal the unconditional will of this thinker to become master over this countervailing power. Interpreting play as an image has legitimacy; interpreting play as a mirror-image, however, is false—it is Plato's overly trenchant, polemical anti-thesis.

However, what is actually conceived when play is interpreted with the categories drawn from the phenomenon of the image? Is play adequately understood from itself and in its ontological sense when it is described as a reproduction, as some imagistic portrayal of serious life? Play "corresponds." Correspondence is a basic feature that is proper to it. Only it is questionable whether correspondence must be determined as a reproduction of *beings*. That, to a certain extent, play has structures analogous to the image and even a correspondence within the framework of these structures nevertheless does not preclude that the *most essential* correspondence of play precisely does *not* occur as a re-production. Yet precisely the traditional categories for play at our disposal have been drawn from the analogical relation to reproduction. But what "reproduction" even *is* remains in the background, unasked in this conceptual formulation. For reproduction as such is indeed not yet sufficiently understood and brought to light when one determines it as a reference back to an original. Certainly there does exist such a reference back to the original; a reproduction is always a correspondence to an archetype. But it is not always such a slavishly unfree one as in the case of the mirror. Reproduction [*Abbild*] is an image-from [*Bild-von*]; it bears in itself the referral to something else, is derivative and secondhand in relation to the archetype [*Urbild*]. And Plato does not tire of emphasizing this aspect of the image's derivation and non-originality. It is the aspect that interests him most of all, because a grading, a gradation of Being can thereby be conceived as a system of references. Yet is the imagistic character of the image thereby sufficiently determined? Is information concerning the Being of the image sufficient if one always speaks of *what* has been reproduced? We understand the image's intention to portray if we recognize the thing portrayed, if we can label it. That suffices for a practical association with images but does not suffice for a theoretical answer as to what an image is as an image. *Of what* a reproduction is, is now not the essential question, but rather what *reproductivity,* as something that is apparent and lets appear, is. The dimension of the imagistic itself must indeed also be determined in regard to what it itself is, and not only in respect of that to which the image refers. Although an image in its function of reproduction points away from itself, presents itself as "not being original," and "expresses," so to speak, its distance from the original, its non-originality is nevertheless itself an independent mode of Being. As an image it is "original." And just as little is play that is put in parallel with the image already conceived in itself when it is discussed as a variation or portrayal of serious life. What ought to be asked in the first place is not what is varied and portrayed, but rather what variation, what playful portrayal as such is. For if we only keep in view what the original model for the playful imitation is, then we can indeed characterize play according to its intended content, but we move thereby in a vague and incautious pre-understanding of playing in general, and then we precisely do not experience play as what is genuinely questionworthy. Here it would be especially instructive to investigate forms of encapsulation in which instances of play occur within instances of play, and in which it is therefore not a matter of characterizing play only from its distance from imitated serious life. However much intellectual energy, conceptual subtlety, and contentious passion may lie in Plato's critique of the poets, the fundamental feature of his thoughts is thereby still predominantly determined from the perspective of the graded reference of archetype and reproduction, original and afterimage—without the dimension of the reproductive in itself receiving a sufficient ontological characterization.

And that holds still more for play, which ultimately is interpreted in an analogical manner by the categories drawn from the phenomenon of the image. Yet the Platonic categories of the image are not sufficient for an understanding of the nature of the image—and even less sufficient, then, for a comprehension of play. This assessment has nothing to do with arrogant, know-it-all one-upmanship. It is a task for contemporary thought—as for every thought that is timely—to put the tradition into question and to whittle away our predetermination by a traditional inheritance that we have more or less thoughtlessly taken up. We have attempted to approach the question of play by way of the marvelous moment of the playworld's "non-actuality." Can this irreality be explicated by way of a comparison with the image? One can doubtless make such a comparison—and the Platonic critique of the poets indeed, as we saw, is based on this comparison—but it remains problematic as to whether the irreality of play is thereby understood *essentially.* The comparison between play and the image forces the interpretation of play into the fatal direction of an ontological devaluation. The gradation of the Being of beings as the slope from the highest idea of the good down to transitory sensible things is expressed by Plato with the help of the phenomenon of the image, which is thereby understood above all as a function of reproduction. As a reproduction or shadow relates to the thing itself, so the sensible thing relates to the idea, so sensuous belief relates to true knowledge. The reproduction is "less" than the archetype, the sensible thing less than the idea, the imagistic appearance less than the simple Being of a thing. The "non-actuality" of the playworld that belongs to play as a constitutive moment is understood as a residual reproduction of a more valid actuality and thus contains a negative accent. In play, one then says, we reproduce actual and serious activities, repeat them in an illusory and unserious way. The non-actuality of play is thereby less than the actuality of serious life. But "non-actuality" and "actuality" are here determined as *ontological modes* of *beings*. Here is the critical point. Thought with respect to beings, an imagistic appearance is undoubtedly less than the original thing. The image gives us only the *semblance* of a being, not the being itself. Yet, measured by actual Being, the semblance is not this either. In relation to actual Being, the semblance is a derivation.[14] *If* human play is primarily an afterimage of innerworldly actual activities of a serious kind or of some original things, then Plato's critique is justified. But precisely this "presupposition" has become doubtful to us. In play the features of reproduction emerge in a conspicuous form when it is seen with the eyes of the disenchanted. It stands to reason that ultimately the "non-actuality" of play acquires a transformed sense if it is conceived in the mode of its primordiality. Perhaps, then, the "non-actuality" is not *less*, but rather *more* than the simple actuality of things. The "appearance" could be something other than only a mere semblance.

In order to point out in advance the direction in which we see a problem here, we will briefly turn once more to the image as such. Even in the case of the image, we are acquainted with the possibility that the reproduction may recede: the reproductive character of the image is at its strongest in the mirror-image; it is already weaker in the case of the artificial image, for which it is not a question of photographic fidelity but rather one of capturing essential features. And it has almost disappeared in the case of the pure composition of colors and figures. The less "reproductive," the more strongly "symbolic" an image is. We certainly ought not thereby to misunderstand the symbol as a sign and to replace the graphic function of the image by the abstract[15] function of the sign. A sign need not be similar in appearance to the thing signified. Traffic signposts in the streets, for example, are signs whose meaning has been determined by convention and can now be read by those in traffic. "Symbols" themselves can appear in various things, in simple things, but also in images and even in signs as well. It is wrong, however, to want to elucidate the symbolic character of the symbol by what pertains to the image or the sign.

But this claim appears to be contradicted by the fact that the "symbol" was initially precisely a sign, indeed an identifying sign, for instance a broken coin whose halves were given to friends separated by great distances. If one sent a visitor to his friend, he gave him the one half to take along as infallible proof: the places where the coin had been split into two had to be matched to each other, the one half had to be completed by the other. Now, both features were significant for the symbol: the "fragmentation" and the "completion." *Symbolon* comes from *symballein*, "coinciding," and signifies a coinciding of the fragment with what completes it. Now, there are certainly many kinds of forms and possibilities of fragments coinciding into a complete unity. In the coarsest and at the same time subtlest way, Plato offers in the *Symposium*, in the speech of Aristophanes, an allegorical interpretation of love: the halves of the human being cut apart by the gods seek each other, wandering around, the man the woman and the woman the man; they are *symbola*, halves of life arranged for completion, which first constitute the whole human being only when they fit together properly. But the male-female completion of the unity of human life does not remove the limitation of even the "whole" human being. In a deeper sense, all finite things in general are fragments—whether they are determined to be maimed or intact, whole or in privation. Each finite being is not everything, is only this, is confined within limits, separated from surrounding beings, is not everywhere, but rather in precisely a specific place, is not for all time, but rather only within a delimited duration. Being, to the extent that it belongs to finite things, is a variously fractured and restricted Being; it is fragmentary, splintered, rent apart and cleaved asunder. Numerous and polymorphous beings look like the rubble of Being. But all such rubble and fragments are at the same time subtended by the omnipresence of the one, worldwide Being, which is everywhere and for all time, which in its simple rest embraces the ravages of opposition and contradiction, the power of negativity. It gathers the fragments and yet does not afterward first piece itself together from them. The whole, in which all finite things appear, is not assembled from finite building blocks—it precedes all dismemberment and contains it *within itself*. The world-whole is the first and the last whole, which is ahead of all individual things and also lies above and beyond them all. Yet we never find it at all, so to speak, immediately in or among things. It holds itself at a remove from us. We ourselves are finite and are also attuned to finite things in our understanding of Being. When we use the word "Being," we use it initially and for the most part as the Being of beings, that is, as fragmentary, ruptured Being, as the Being of individuated things. And yet at the same time we always have an intimation of a more primordial unity of Being—and occasionally this worldedness of Being flashes in some finite and frail individual thing; as a fragment the latter experiences a "com-pletion" of a peculiar kind. Not just any kind of completion, but rather *the* completion by *the* whole: the light of the world falls on an innerworldly thing and raises it into the great radiance of the universe. The finite thing, the fragment of Being, becomes "transparent," as it were. Yet we must beware of an unfitting interpretation; we ought not to make the finite thing into a metaphor, a sign for another being. "What is destructible / Is but a metaphor"[16]—that holds for metaphysics in its distinction between the temporal and the eternal but does not hold for a thinking that strives after world-wisdom, for which the finite is no refuse of the idea and no nugatory appearance, but is rather essentially the *intraworldly*, which, however, now and then can flare up in the light of the world. The completion here brings nothing along in addition, does not add something that until now was missing and outstanding, does not bring some being to another being, does not in general get rid of the fragmentary character of finite things—rather it more expressly puts them, precisely as these finite individuations, back into the encompassing world-whole. Thus, we must think the completion from the world-whole and not from an intraworldly wholeness. Here it is not a matter of making some rubble whole again in the sense of the wholeness of inner-worldly things, but rather precisely of conceiving innerworldly wholeness as such as a fragment. Things then become *symbola*—not as signs for something different; they are *symbola* as themselves, inasmuch as they exhibit their finitude as intraworldliness. We customarily live in a peculiar captivation and blindness: we perpetually deal with beings, with finite and delimited things, but we do not concern ourselves with what such finitude is in general. We live for the day, live immersed in the world and do not at all think to ask wherein and on what basis we live. We are assailed by the incessant intrusion of the things surrounding us, but we do not consider the field, the space and the time of such intrusion. Only seldom and for the most part also briefly do things become "world-profound" for us, attain a reference to the prevailing whole without our being led away by them to something else; rather, in these exceptional cases, we still remain among them, but turn to them more profoundly and experience how the whole resonates through them. In becoming world-profound, a thing becomes a symbol; the *symballein* of the being and the universe takes place. And this is the most primordial enchantment: the unnamable power of the totality appears in the midst of frail things. The stars of the night sky can revolve around a pair of twinkling eyes, the world-light can shine on a weapon—as on Odysseus's bow after the slaying of the suitors—and the simple breaking of bread can be a symbol in the highest sense. The human being cannot freely bring about such transformations of things whenever he wishes. The gleam of the world-light on intraworldly things comes unbeckoned—like an avalanche.

And yet there is a strange[17] mode of comportment in which a human being's "influence" takes place in a certain way, that is, the magical practice of enchantment. We are used to viewing this as a possibility done away with long ago, which has been suppressed and overcome by rational culture and only infrequently still occurs as a vestige of the superstitious way of thinking. We no longer believe in magic. But the early human being practiced magic in cultic play, and the child, too, in its play-activity behaves surprisingly like the "primitive." That at any rate provides an indication of deeper connections. For magical savages and for the child, play is not characterized as a sphere of non-actuality that is determined to be "less worthy" on account of its distance from customary things and their tangible actuality. On the contrary. The "non-actual" has here an emphatically positive character, is a mode in which something that is more powerful and ontologically stronger enters into the customary sphere of life. The non-actual is characterized as the elevated and genuine. The "fairytale-like" and the "wondrous" is that which has validity in the best sense. However, that does not mean that the child and the primitive do not see simply actual things, going around, so to speak, as though in a dream, "sleepwalkers," as it were. They instead actually have a very distinctive feeling for the difference between customary things and the "fairytale-like." Only this difference is evaluated in a different manner—differently than as otherwise occurs in the rational culture of human beings and adults. "Non-actuality" is no objection, no degradation. In play they feel closer to what is essential and genuine. Their play has an entirely peculiar and strange seriousness. We lack the proper concepts for it, although we still commonly enough go about with the difference between play and work, play and seriousness. But these schemata break down when it becomes necessary to actually grasp the magical cult-play of the primitive and the play of the child. We will initially try to attain a first preliminary conception of the cult. In doing so, we will first have to address the *human* side.

The cult in general is indeed a relation between human beings and gods and thus cannot be adequately determined from the human side alone. The human-all-too-human statements about this can always be surpassed and outdone by what the god himself announces through the mouth of his prophets and messengers. However, the cult indisputably has human roots, too. And for the moment we wish to ask about these. The human being in general is, at all times of his earthly history and prehistory, a being that relates itself to itself. The self-relation of human existence is the basic feature that separates us from the animals. This self-relation, to be sure, has a different character in the archaic past than it does in the historical times of culture. It is not yet determined by a differentiated understanding of Being, by a richly developed language, by a rational tailoring of the whole conduct of life. Existence is still simple, yet it is also whole; all primordial fields of life exist for the primitive, too: he loves, he works, he struggles, he fears daemons and the formless, incomprehensible power to which he knows he is exposed, he has the urge to venerate, and he buries his dead. Hunts and war campaigns, nomadic wandering or the earliest form of agriculture, weddings and funerals, sickness, need, joys and sorrows constitute the course of his life. He does not merely live out this life, does not just simply carry on with it—he relates himself in his life to his life. Perhaps not so much as an "individual," but rather as a tribe, as a horde, as a clan. And such self-relation is thereby also less a specific action than an abiding within traditional interpretations, a maintenance through rites and prescriptions, through rules governing what is taboo. The strict bondage of primitive existence by the taboo, however, does not exclude the fact that now and then the self-relation "actualizes" itself, so to speak, brings itself to life, and renews itself. That happens in festivals. The festival does not have the pragmatic sense of only a relaxation from the monotonous routine of the everyday, an unharnessing from the yoke of work—it is above all the bringing to presence of the whole sense of life, an orientation of the human being concerning his position, concerning the relations determining him: concerning his relations to the gods and to the departed dead, to the daemonic powers who offer fertility to the fields and to women, and who can also send famine and sickness, who can conceal themselves in animals and trees and appear in countless forms. That which incessantly determines the life of the primitive human being to such an extent is both alarming and consoling: he cannot "think" in a non-sensuous way even the prevailing of natural daemons; he must "see" it, "behold" it, have it before his eyes, in order to understand how it pertains to him. And such beholding happens in cultic play. Here the prevailing of the forces under whose power the human being finds himself becomes visible. The sense-context that encompasses him[18] becomes lucid. Cultic play stands in close proximity to the consecrating activity of sacrifice and is a grand ritualized gesture, an image of the whole. And precisely therein lies its genuine paradox. It does not reproduce determinate regions, so to speak; it rather lets the whole arise, and in a delimited scene. The whole shines back within itself, so to speak, and shines forth "in the image": it is made finite in a finite thing—this image is a symbol in the primordial sense. And on account of this, the moment of non-actuality is here grasped entirely otherwise. The cultic dancer, player, or priest is not conceived of as "more actual" than his role of representing the daemon; rather the daemon appearing on the cultic scene is much more actual, forceful, and powerful than the man who portrays him. Portraying has the character of being entranced, of being taken over by the power that is portrayed. The irreality of the scenic image is the space of admission, as it were, for an overwhelming superiority. The whole of all the prevailing powers imposes, so to speak, scenic representation on a delimited, small space *within* this whole. The whole, which is never visible as a whole, appears in a field within itself. It is reflected back [*reluzent*] into itself. The *totum* goes back into a part of itself and elevates this innerworldly part through the proof of the shining back [*Rückschein*] of the whole. Because of that, everything here is different than in a conception of play as a reproduction of something actual in the medium of a "non-actuality." Here "non-actuality" is[19] the basic feature of the symbolic representation of the whole of the world in an innerworldly being. Cultic play brings to presence the universal sense-context of primitive existence, is an expression of its world-relation. The world becomes lucid here; here play is truly a world-view.

Chapter Three
The Interpretation of Play in Myth

11. Basic Features of Mythical Cult-Play

In the course of our thoughts we have arrived at a critical point: we must attempt to free ourselves from the traditional condemnation of play as a mere reproduction of "actuality," thus to free ourselves from the lens of the disenchanted and the Platonic "evil eye" for tragedy. This is by no means an easy matter. For, conceptual penetration into the phenomenon of play has been carried out in a philosophically radical form precisely from the viewpoint of disenchantment and in the closest connection with the foundation of Western metaphysics. Plato's struggle with Homer and the tragedians is no peripheral motif, no ornamental arabesque; it is a life-and-death struggle, more essential, harsher, and sharper than the strife with the sophists. The sophist is only the caricature [*Zerrbild*] of the philosopher, able to be exposed in his impotent illusoriness by a more rigorous conversance with the very same *logos* that he manipulates in an merely eristic, instrumental way. The sophist is exposed by relentlessly being referred to the truth of the *logos*. The philosopher and the sophist, in their strife, remain within the dimension of the concept. The poet, as the representative player, is the seer, the spectator of the great game in which all things are put at stake, in which they have their emergence and decline, their fortune and downfall, their radiance and extinguishment. The poet is the spectator of the drama [*Schauspiel*] of the prevailing of the gods, of the deeds of heroes, of the sufferings of human beings; in his song, he allows everyone to see what he has seen. Plato's critique of the poets claims that the poet only sees images, and images [*Bilder*] are mere re-productions [*Ab-Bilder*] and after-images [*Nach-Bilder*] of customary things and events that for their part are already poor afterimages of the ideas that alone truly exist. Plato's critique of the poets has its ontological emphasis in the interpretation of the image as such. The imagistic character of all poetry has thereby been subjected to an aggressive, indeed a demolishing critique, which was able to summon its power from the immense conceptual energy that was released in *thinking through* mere *seeing* [Schauens]. However, one cannot postulate as a universal formula that the concept prevails over intuition. For in Plato thought itself, in its highest apex, *after* it has passed through the dialectic and in view of the highest idea, the idea of the good, has the character of seeing. Admittedly, this is a seeing of thought. He also calls it a "touching," in order to indicate this ultimate and highest immediacy of the enactment of thought. Such "immediacy" does not exist before mediation but rather after it, and can only be attained over a long and arduous course of thought. The poets, however, purport to immediately see what is genuinely real in their visions and to be able to place it before the eyes of their fellow human beings in the poetic word; they lie, insofar as they pass off mere reproductions as what is essential. From the perspective of the metaphysical critique of play, as we conceive Plato's critique of the poets more generally, the "non-actuality" constitutively belonging to play as a "mere reproduction," that is, as something that has a *lesser* ontological status than the things that belong to the typical reality of our lives, is less than the house, the table, the bed. But how can we free ourselves from this perspective? How do we remove the metaphysical lens in relation to play? Can we, so to speak, leap out of the situation of disenchantment with a single bound, transpose ourselves into the position of the enchanted, and from there recognize new conceptual determinations concerning play? If this were so, such a leap would have already been carried out often and even resulted in new conceptual categories for play. The Western metaphysical understanding of Being, to which the interpretation of play as reproduction belongs, too, cannot be arbitrarily abandoned, so to speak. We cannot simply "step off the trolley." The historically transmitted understanding of Being is the dimly lit house of the human being in the gloom of the world-night, as it were, which shelters and protects him and affords him a dwelling—a house, admittedly, that he must time and again repair, that remains exposed to continual ruin, that perpetually falls into disrepair. A restructuring of this understanding of Being, of even a minor sort, can only be carried out as a confrontation with the tradition. And the more primordial such a restructuring would be, the more severe the historical displacement must be, too. The philosophical question concerning play cannot be explicated without explicit reference to the Platonic critique of the poets. For that reason, we have tarried for so long in our discussions about the image, the mirror, and the like. That may appear to be a superfluous addition; however, thought strictly from the matter itself, it was necessary. For what we have said about play in a different way, for instance, must be able to stand up to the critical spirit of Plato's train of thought. The moment at which Plato's critique began is with the peculiar "non-actuality" that, as a playworld, belongs to play. Is this non-actuality grasped decisively when it is taken as a reproduction? That is the question that concerns us. "Non-actuality" here does not mean "non-being," as probably everyone will acknowledge, does not mean a sheer nothing, but rather an enigmatic something, which does not exist like customary existing things but is also not nugatory like a hallucination or a merely subjective delusion. The "non-actuality" of the playworld is an appearance of its own kind. Plato has an answer, an answer to the question as to what sort of odd appearance it is: this appearance is only an image. And an image is determined, above all to the extent that it is a reproduction, from its own derivative resemblance to the original. The appearance of the playworld is thus explained as a reproductive relation of resemblance between two *beings*. We can express the fundamental sense of this Platonic interpretation with the formula: the playworldly appearance is interpreted from the relational space of an *intraworldly* relation—play mirrors, as it were, real processes of serious life, copying them in the medium of a unique appearance. As long as play is thus interpreted from the relation to innerworldly beings, the conception of it as a reproduction inevitably presses on and imposes itself.

But here we are attempting to insert a question mark. For is play primordially a reproduction of innerworldly processes and events, a repetition and imitation? Or is it a particularly emphatic form of the human relation to the *world?* The world-relation of human existence, although it defines and thoroughly attunes us in an essential manner, has remained furthermost from a conceptual clarification. Hence, we do not have at our disposal an adequately cultivated conceptuality to express with the necessary clarity the world-relation of human play and the relation of understanding to the play of the world itself that is concealed therein. For the moment, we will sketch out the direction of our question. We have already begun to do so by briefly discussing and formally indicating the concept of the *symbol.* We do not understand by this any sort of sign that indicates, depicts, represents, stands in for something, and so forth. A *symbolon* is a fragment that has been determined for completion. But the philosophical concept of the symbol does not pertain to inner-worldly completions of fragmentary forms of life. Rather, it is precisely each innerworldly being that is conceived as a fragment of Being, as finite individuality split off from the one, all-encompassing Being. Each finite thing as such is a fragment, is exposed in its individuation, is torn away from all others, is enclosed within its limits, is only this—and not everything else. It is it itself, and through its selfhood and its self-standing is removed from the one primal ground of life, from which it emerges and into which it will again someday be submerged. And yet it is never alone as this self-standing thing; not only does it stand in proximity to other self-standing things that form its surroundings. It and its neighboring things are gathered all together into a presencing [*Anwesen*] that encompasses them all—one Being runs through every being, subtending all the limits and divisions of individual things, holding and gathering them, exposing and sheltering them, letting them emerge and pass away, bearing their change and passage. We ordinarily have no eyes for this *one* and *unifying* Being of the whole that subtends all limits of things, no ears for the music of the world: we are captivated by beings, distracted by the variety of things, we are turned toward the finite without essentially understanding the finite in its finitude. We do not perceive the power that gives and takes away finite things, binds them together and divides them, gathers and separates them. We gape at individuated beings in their incalculable multiplicity but ordinarily do not thereby catch sight of the fundamental process of individuation. We move about as a thing among other things, comport ourselves with understanding to things in all domains, but do not ordinarily understand the prevailing force that unifies beings in their multiplicity and at the same time tears them apart in their delimitation. In the customary understanding of Being we deal with fragments of Being without experiencing them *as* fragments. Philosophy as world-wisdom awakens when the finite thing flares up in its *intraworldliness* and thus refers to the world-whole, when the fragmentary character of beings shines forth in the light of the world. That need not always be an event of *theōria*. There are manifold ways in which finite beings become truthful symbols and can experience a primordial, worlded "completion"—in which the fragment is returned to the intact whole. In all great upsurges of the human heart and spirit the transformation of things occurs. They are not thereby "altered," not metamorphosed; they remain finite Being, but this finite Being of things reveals itself in its finitude on the basis[1] of the more primordial, more intact Being of the world. And this Being of the world does not lie like a realm of stronger and more powerful things next to or behind or above ordinary things, is not a sphere of the eternal beyond the sphere of the transient. The Being of the world prevails and reigns *in* finite things, prevails as finitization, individuation, which is simultaneously gathering and dispersal. Wherever this force of the gathering-dispersing prevailing of the whole is experienced as the "war" and "peace" of the world, all things gleam in a new light, become *symbola*. This glimpse or lightning flash of the world mostly comes as an onslaught. It can come to appear in all human fields of life: in love, in work, in ruling, in the remembrance of the dead—and in play. In the coming together of man and woman both these halves of life become the symbol for the great cosmic harmony of all oppositions, and they then feel themselves blessedly aglow from the flame of the life of the totality and can say with Hölderlin's "Hyperion": "The dissonances of the world are like lovers' strife. In the midst of the quarrel is reconciliation, and all that is separated comes together again. / The arteries part and return in the heart, and all is one eternal, glowing life."[2] Deep as the world, however, are not only the life attunements of cosmic harmony—the harshest ruptures can be world-profound, too, if they are conceived as pointing to the strife intimately raging through the one whole, pointing to the negativity endemic to Being, to the world-structuring power of rupture, to war, which according to the words of Heraclitus is the father of all things. Even where the human being tills the barren earth by the sweat of his brow, the world-light can gleam in the simple activities of sowing or reaping, and the nearness to the bounteous power of the earth can be experienced. Or when we bury the dead, give them back to the elements, this activity, too, becomes a symbol for us: in the case of this one fellow human being whom we return to the earth, the return of all exposed things into the nameless, ineffable, sheltering ground can become clear and significant for us. This, however, does not happen in such a way that the individual case could be recognized as an example of a universal rule. Rather, the very distinction between the individual and the universal, between the example and the rule, disappears in the genuine symbol. Now, one could, however, object that here an elevated and intensified association with human things, the admission to its more mysterious significance, would overshadow the everyday praxis of life; that such a description would not apply in everyday life, but would only hold for the particular life praxis of the cult. An important problem is touched on with this objection.

But the question is whether the human being can apprehend the world-significance of finite things only in the cult—or whether the cult is the collective memory of world-profound things. If ever a golden age existed in the dawning morning of the human race, then this race had *no cult,* because all things were still world-profound, because the shimmering of the farthest stars lay on each blade of grass and everything was full of gods. Only when in the course of time things were exploited, when human beings cultivated their customs and thought and felt according to custom, when customs disguised and clouded the primordial dwelling of the human race on the solid earth under the open sky—only then did it become the task of a special praxis to break through the trivialization of life through customs, which was perceived to be a danger, and to again hoist the things that were sunk into the all-too-familiar upward into their lost radiance. The cult elevated customary things by consecrating single instances of them and giving them a cultic relevance. The cult is the attempt to restore the primordial world-light to all individuated, finite things.

This attempt has a remarkable structure: it appears to want to contradict itself. For, initially, it is precisely the *demarcating exclusion* that is striking about the human cult. The counter-move against trivialization through customs, against the banalization of human existence, is begun in the cult as the demarcation of a sacred sphere. A grove, a forested area like any other, a hilltop or a special precinct in the city is demarcated, is separated off by sacred borders from the rest of the soil, is held to be consecrated ground, to be a site for the appearance and self-manifestation of the gods. On such ground a temple is erected. And it is arranged in proper alignment with the cardinal directions of the heavens: the rising and setting of the sun, the starry vault and much of this sort of thing finds its counterpart in the measurements of the most ancient temples. And some individuals are marked off from the mass of ordinary human beings, removed from the ordinary course of life. This seclusion of priests, however,[3] is not sufficiently grasped if one sees it only as part of the universal specification of human activities, which goes along with the division of labor. The priest relates to his fellow human beings like the awe-inspiring temple precinct to the surrounding land.

The chosen one is also secluded. He is singled out and removed, has been transported by his consecration of universal human ordinariness, is raised beyond the customary human measure. He becomes the administrator of the mysteries and sacraments, promulgator of the holy, executor of sacrifices. This sacrificer is himself the first sacrifice—he belongs, to cite the words of Hegel, among "those solitary individuals, whom their people had sacrificed and exiled from the world and dedicated to the contemplation of the eternal. . . . Theirs was a life devoted exclusively to the service of contemplation, without practical gain but only for the sake of blessedness."[4] The priest, who sacrifices and consecrates, is himself sacrificed and consecrated—is marked off from the mass of everyday human beings stirred by desire and passion. But he is marked off for those things—as the demarcated temple ground has been spared as a site of divine epiphany *for* the surrounding land. Precisely by there being a space that remains free, indeed even furnished with a significance that raises it beyond all ordinary places, in the midst of fields where human beings toil for sustenance, or among the houses in which they live, procreate, and die, this sacred space can take on the function of hallowing all places of the countryside or city. It stands then for all other spaces, stands in their stead, operates vicariously. And, similarly, the priest acts vicariously for his fellow human beings; he takes the relation to the sacred upon himself in order, from such a relation, to have an influence on the lives of his fellow countrymen. The sacred things of the cult, whether they be the temple precinct, the priest, the altar and the chalice, the sacrificial lamb, or the consecrated bread, operate, on the whole, vicariously for profane things: for the house of the human being, for his dinner table, for the wine that he drinks and the bread that he eats. Cultic consecration divides sacred and profane things in order to ultimately consecrate the profane. The cult must initially draw out and wrest a sphere free from the generally prevailing ordinariness of life, separate and delimit it from the everyday, in order to be able to penetrate the everyday itself from out of the sacred site that is thus elevated. Regarded in this manner, it is an immense stratagem of life to withdraw from instrumentality and superficiality in order to return to the primordial sources. That is initially thought of in a purely human sense, the cult conceived as a phenomenon of human self-relation. Yet it is certainly more. It is indeed not merely a relation to his own originality of life that the human being who is threatened by the danger of stultification in customary routine attempts to produce. In the cult the immortal gods appear to mortal human beings. So, at least, the priests, prophets, and saviors of all peoples and times tell us. The finite human wisdom of philosophy has removed this divine aspect of the cult from consideration; here only silence remains for us. But we can direct our gaze to the human phenomenon of priestly self-consciousness: the priest understands himself as a mediator between humans and gods, as a representative, as a mouthpiece of God, as his herald and promulgator—as a proxy of God on the earth, to whom extraordinary authority is granted, to whom it is promised that everything that he establishes as binding on earth is also binding in heaven and everything that he dissolves on earth is also dissolved in heaven. If the essence of the priest is thus thought of as a vicariousness of God on earth, even if hierarchically graded, then in such a conception the divine must still be represented in a certain sense as distant and absent. The distance and absence are not absolute: perhaps they only exist for the dull senses of human beings or for the indolence of their hearts. What is always there does not arrive at epiphany. Land and sea, the elements and the most familiar things have no epiphany. The sun rises every day anew in the eastern sky, traces its golden track in the firmament and sinks into the west; its appearance and receding are quotidian. The appearance of the sun is no epiphany. The Greek god dwells at a distance from human beings, perhaps on the shimmering heights of Olympus or even in the highest regions of the stars, in the depths of the earth or way out on the uncharted sea. But he can come among human beings, sometimes appear to them in disguised forms in order to protect mortals and to save them from the fate of Semele. He can also manifest himself in the gentle charm of natural impressions and stir the soul: in the moonlight over mountain forests as Artemis, in the gleaming glare of the sun as Phoebus Apollo, in the white-maned, storming steed-waves of the sea as Poseidon. The Christian god, thought of as the creator of the world, remains on the one hand transcendent from the created world; on the other hand he continually and ubiquitously suffuses it with his omnipresence and omnipotence. He is simultaneously present and absent. His presence is only accessible to faith, not to the natural knowledge of the finite human being. The Christian does not see his god with physical eyes during his life on earth, except perhaps[5] the first Christians as disciples of Christ. But these physical eyes, too, did not see the glory of their lord; they trusted his word, while their eyes saw a human being who died on the cross. Because the Christian god actually dwells in heaven and invisibly pervades the earthly world with his omnipotence and omnipresence, proxies of God are needed for *visibility;* prophets and priests are needed. The Greek gods had a place *in* the world, were at home in the magnificent sphere of the highest radiance of Being, which mortals never reach; the Christian god has *no place in the world*—rather the world has a place in him. There always also belongs to the cult as a phenomenal structure a proxy of things or human beings in relation to the gods. It can be the "graven image" that one worships, the "exalted serpent," the marble form of Pallas Athena, the holy book, the altar, or the sacrificial lamb and the sacrificing priest. Because such things "stand in for" the gods, they, hallowed from such a relation, are for their part able "to stand in for" all the profane, earthly things, that is, they keep the relation to the sacred alive *for the latter.*

The most difficult problem in interpreting the cult is the relation to the world-whole that resonates in all these proxies. The vicariousness of profane things in sacred things and the vicariousness of the gods in priestly human beings, statues, temples, and cult equipment—these are, in each case, *relationships between beings.* The world-relation, in contrast, is a relation between *an intraworldly thing and the world.* What can this mean here: a thing stands in for the whole? A finite thing stands in for the infinite? And, to be sure, not *an* infinite thing that is thought by the highest intensification and denial of finite properties, by the combined *via eminentiae et negationis,* which amounts to the traditional concept of the "absolute." The world is near and far in a different way than a being can ever be near and far. All nearness and farness of beings is made possible by the spatiality and temporality of the world. Only in the space-time of the world are innerworldly things near to and far from one another. Thing and world have no gap, no remoteness between them: each thing is in the world, and yet all things together do not fill up the world. Expressed figuratively, the world is farther outside than each conceivable thing, and yet it is also closer to each being than the nearest thing; indeed it prevails in and through them. The world is what is nearest and farthest at the same time, is the force of the universal movement of Being in all beings, the passage as emergence and decline of all finite beings—the throwing that throws them into existence and the predation of all-producing, all-consuming time. Whenever we understand a single thing from out of this passage of Being, it becomes "world-profound" and flashes in an infinite significance. It does not point away from itself and out to another thing—it points into its very ground, into the movement of transience that flows through it. Such insights into the fundamental movement in which all finite things are placed are rare; they have an unsettling force for the human heart and the human spirit. We thereby perceive the immense power of the negative, the inexorability of death, but also the inexhaustibility of the womb, from which all individual things emerge. In the cult we preserve and retain the world-profound, lived experiences of our existence. When *all* things no longer flash in the light of the world—as perhaps in the fabled golden age—when things become used up and custom replaces the primordial, entrancing, enigmatic character of intraworldly beings and the dust of the everyday deposits itself everywhere, the cult must elevate *a few* things and interpret them as *symbola,* in order to retain the memory of world-open existence. That means the cult is already a derivative comportment of the human race, the recollection of a world-relation that was *not yet* determined by the distinction between the sacred and the profane and by the human being's conscious distance from the gods. The cult seeks to retrieve, to restore the world-relation, but it is capable of such restoration only in a mediated way: precisely in the elevation of a few things that it wrests into an in-finite significance. When the whole earth is no longer full of productive power and fecund growth, then a place must be set aside as a sacred precinct, where the festival of recurring Persephone can be celebrated as an invocatory summoning to presence of all worldly powers of growth. When all human beings no longer live in concord with the peace and the war of the world, then the priest as the sacrifice for all must seclude himself from the natural and ingenuous community and must ponder the prevailing fate of the whole. When each house, each table and each bed, each finite piece of bread and each finite drink of wine is no longer known to be intact [*heil*] and to belong to the whole, then a specific single house, a specific table, a specific piece of bread, and a specific portion of wine must take on the reference to what is intact—as a temple, as an altar, as an offering. Where intactness [*das Heile*] as a fundamental feature of the worldliness of all beings is denied or is obscured by the dust of custom, the "sacred" [*das "Heilige"*] must appear. The sacred is an echo of worlded intactness [*des welthaft Heilen*].

This is the fundamental conception that guides our recourse to the phenomenon of the cult. This conception, with its briefly outlined theses, has of course still by no means been given its due. But once more it should be emphasized that we are dealing only with the purely human side of the cult, not with its super-human partners, who fall under the jurisdiction of the theologians. In our opinion, to put it cautiously, the cult preserves the recollection of the human world-relation, but it disguises it, too, in preserving it: the cult reinterprets its meaning in terms of a relation to a higher being, yet at bottom and in general the human world-relation is not at all a relation to any intraworldly things, not even of the highest kind. And that holds already for the early forms of cult, for the archaic practices of enchantment and magical rites. Even the early cult is an indirect recollection of the world-relation. That does not make it any easier for us to understand; for the conspicuous thing in archaic existence is indeed precisely the belief in daemons, the paralyzing horror in the face of uncanny, spectral beings, the panic-stricken anxiety before numinous powers. No warrior's bravery helps against this primal anxiety, no diligence and exertion at work helps. Precisely the two serious activities in which the human otherwise asserts himself, belligerent struggle and the toil of work, remain inconsequential here. One cannot battle with daemons and one cannot break their resistance by working. But *the* activity that one for the most part regards as the least serious and that one commonly believes to have no power, namely, play, becomes the sole possibility for the human being to counteract the magic power of the daemons or to turn their malevolence around. The mask of the player itself becomes a magical force. What that means philosophically is a most difficult problem.

12. The Cultic Sense-Image and Its Veiled World-Reference. Association with Daemons

If meditation on human play is carried out through the lens of the disenchanted,[6] then play takes on the aspect of reproduction, which in any case is acknowledged as having a mediating function, as Plato's critique of the poets had shown. To be sure, it still remains a phenomenon of life with status, but it must recede behind more essential ways of carrying out existence. In what its light of understanding makes manifest, it is taken to be inferior to work and struggle and love, for instance. It becomes a way to "recover" from the ways in which life is difficult and grave, it becomes lighthearted idleness, a cheerful and pretty variation on bitter seriousness. It mirrors in an impotent way the powerful pursuits of life, makes present merely as a reproduction every dark sorrow and every harsh pain of our heart, and thus has the capacity to safely discharge the dangerously pent-up affects, passions and desires, tribulations and anxieties, to purify the soul of dark forces. We are always in danger of losing the proper composure and calmness that belong to the character of life, of reacting intemperately to the threatening character of our environment, of exceeding the degree of fear appropriate for us or, on the other hand, of giving ourselves over too much to being with our fellow human beings and of losing ourselves in the process. We preserve the soul from an excess of fear and compassion by giving an outlet in play to these self-destructive affects, letting them peter out, so to speak, in the playworld-appearance. In the economy of life, play's task becomes to minimize the excess of imagination that serious life cannot utilize for its own creative tasks and to find a use for the harmless discharge of aggressive and destructive impulses of the soul and at the same time to thereby hold a mirror before the human being, to help provide him with a view of himself "in the image" and to thus promote his self-understanding. It is evident that play has a significance in the life-economy of the human being that is similar to the dream—seen from the vantage point of depth psychology. Playing is a kind of waking dream, distinct from the ordinary dream in sleep by its being carried out collectively. When we dream in sleep, we can, to be sure, very well stand in diverse communal relations in the dream-world; the dream-world-I is together with other dream-world-fellows. But the dreaming-I is alone. In contrast, in play we have not merely a community of persons according to the playworldly roles, but always also an actually existent community of real players, who are open to one another in the communal activity of playing. One ascribes to the dream—similarly to play—a cathartic function: it purifies the soul of drives that well up from the most submerged and darkest depths of life, from the wish for incest to the desire for murder; it diverts the excessive imagination and at the same time, however, keeps the imaginative power of the soul alive and in full swing. It is precisely the imposition that the dream experiences from the perspective of waking sobriety that has become decisive for the conception of play. Just as the one who is awake judges in the clear sobriety of the morning the wild, colorful dream of the night, *so too* has metaphysical philosophy all the way back to its beginning judged play—and it has passed judgment on it as a "mere reproduction."

A completely different perspective on play opens up for us when we understand the "non-actuality" of its playworld not as a "reproduction," not as an imagistic rendering and portrayal of an original being, but rather as a "symbol"—and thus think the essence of the symbol from the *world-relation.* A being, a finite thing, becomes a symbol when it experiences "completion" by the world-whole, when the totality shines forth and gleams in it, when it becomes representative of the universe—when the finite is translucent in its intraworldliness, sets the gaze free, as it were, into the prevailing force that flows through the finite, brings it about, and annihilates it. Each thing in the vicinity of the human being *can* become a symbol, *can* wrench us from the *fixed* limitation of our gaze that sees for the most part only *beings:* finished, fixed things and finished, fixed events in and with things, but not Being itself, which structures and destroys, which only "sojourns" in the thing, so to speak, and which ultimately conditions all things [*das letztlich Bedingende für alle Dinge*]. This direction of the symbol, its world-sense, the completion of all finite fragments of Being by the world-whole, is for the most part concealed from us by an understanding of the symbol and symbolism that we have from the cult. The connection between cult and play is extremely significant. We have initially touched on it in a preliminary fashion with our brief discussion concerning the symbol and the cult.

The cult—considered only according to its human side—belongs already to a stance of existence that is determined by a kind of curious world-oblivion. To be sure, the human being, as a human being, is never without a knowledge of the world. He is, simply, the world-open being; the thought of the totality occupies him—and makes possible his understanding of Being, his reason, his language, his bearing toward the actual and the possible, to Being and non-being, makes possible his art of producing artificial things, makes work possible—the thought of the totality glimmers in the human wish for the immortality of mortals in children and grandchildren and fuels the struggle for rule within the state. Because the human being is the world-open living being, he is also the rational, the speaking, the erotic, the skilled and political living being who understands Being. These are quite simply features that fundamentally separate him from the rest of the natural creatures. But even though he owes these fundamental features of his existence to his world-relation, he is nevertheless, for the most part, just not open in an explicit and eager way to the world *as such.* On the contrary, as a rule he lives turned away from the world, lives immersed, "blind to the world," as it were. Yet even the human being's world-blindness is a mode of his world-relation, the mode in which he predominantly comports himself in his everyday form of life to the all-prevailing whole; he does not live attentive to the universe; he moves about, all too self-evidently, within space and time and within the general appearing of beings and pays no attention to space-time as such nor to appearing as such. In each instance he is turned by myriad interests to specific things that he desires, strives for, chases after; in his everyday form of life, the human being lives *immersed within the world,* but *without regard to the world.* On account of myriad things that interest us, we do not pay attention to the whole that thoroughly attunes and resonates around everything. But we ourselves and everything with which we are concerned in such an interested manner in the manifold dimensions of life are finite things that we understand in a twilit vagueness as finite. However, in the understanding of beings in regard to their finitude there always lies an obscure, albeit undeveloped, knowledge of the world, the world-intimation that is the pricking thorn of our spiritual unrest, as it were. We mostly leave it at that in this world-intimation, go about our business, concern ourselves with the particular affairs that matter to us, with our property, our money and well-being, with our nearest and dearest, our family members, our nation—perhaps in a noble and almost noncommittal feeling also with "humanity." The world for us is still much further removed from the interests of our life than humanity is. We usually do not concern ourselves with it at all; it is the most self-evident of all self-evident things, is the scene of our sojourn, but goes endlessly on beyond into unthinkable distances of space and depths of time. We are at home on a small wandering star. Our most audacious technical projects dream of a rocket flight to neighboring celestial bodies. But even then we would still have only colonized a small island in the immensity of the universe. If we but ponder it, this immensity makes an impression on us with mixed feelings of shudder and sublimity, terrifies and enraptures our understanding with the chilling emptiness in which the thought of the world remains for us. And after such an occasional intermezzo with the "starry heavens above me"[7] and the elevation in the feeling of the sublime that is morally tied to it, one turns all too gladly once more to nearby and tangible things, to what is interesting, useful, and dear. The world recedes into the uninteresting; it is no theme for our action, no object for the praxis of our lives—it is at most the theme of a theoretical contemplation.

World-wisdom arises when the everyday certainty of interest-bound association with innerworldly beings breaks down, when distance is gained, when astonishment releases us from our captivated enthrallment to things and we attempt in a questioning manner to think the being-in of beings in the world-whole. Philosophy as the thoughtful relation of the human being to the world has been decisively determined in its historical trajectory by the fact that an initial openness to the prevailing world-whole was closed off; by the fact that a theoretical regard for intraworldly beings, things, and substances gained supremacy; and by the fact that the unity of things was conceived as a thinglike unity, as a system and as an architecture of lesser and greater ontologically powerful things, as a hierarchy that culminates in a highest being and descends in stages. In connection with this, the finitude of beings was then conceived as distance from the highest being, to which alone "infinity" was ascribed. The "highest being" of metaphysical philosophy was called by the name of God. "Infinity" became a theological attribute and lost its primordial[8] cosmic sense. The history of the transformation of world-wisdom into a theologically stamped ontology does not come to an end, however, with the Platonic-Aristotelian foundation of metaphysics, but rather runs through the course of philosophy up to the present day as a latent tension and strife between the world-closure and world-openness of Western thought.

The cult, however, is older than philosophy. Before human beings were able to think in a rigorous way, before they could avail themselves of concepts, they beheld in images that which is, that which *is* genuinely and *is* essentially, what their task on earth was, their fate and their purpose. These images [*Bilder*] of myth, however, were no "re-productions [*Ab-bilder*]" of something previously existing and previously known in the manner of afterimages or depictions, as if what came to expression in them could also have been known independently of these images. Mythical images are primordial experiences themselves, so to speak, not belated renditions of experiences. Nor do they serve as means of communication, as aids for a collective agreement concerning the questions about the sense of human life. In ordinary circumstances one can communicate something to someone very well with an image; an image can function as a means of communication. For instance, in a criminal affair a witness produces a sketch of the crime scene and a drawing of the culprit and thereby communicates important particulars to the police. He makes objective in the optical visibility of the image a knowledge that he already previously had. Insofar as it is a reproduction of an original that is thereby disclosed, the image communicates. However, the mythical image is precisely *not* a reproduction. We can rather say that it is a sense-image. The sense that lies in it does not become apparent to the mythical human being "imagelessly" in order afterward to be preserved and expressed for the first time in an image. Rather, the beholding [*Schau*] of the image is the creative visionary act of understanding the sense of life. And this productive act of beholding has been already originally enacted in a collective communication. Mythical existence lives in collective enactments much more intensely than we can generally imagine; it lives from out of archetypical grounds of the soul. But once again, not in such a way that any individual differentiation would be absolutely impossible. The archaic human being is neither a beast that lives simply like the ant, immersed in an objectively purposive organic union of life without a relation *to* this purposiveness, nor is he a "modern individual." The archaic human being, too, comports himself to his life in the world, strives for an insight into the obscure sense of life, but he is bound much more strongly and sympathetically to the fellows of his tribe, his horde, his people, than the historical human being of late culture. The rhythm and feeling of life pulsates through all members of a clan and perhaps even flickers through them at times with the same visionary energy, makes them into epopts of the same sense-image. The sense that is communally understood is condensed as an image. The image as sense-image in the atmosphere of the mythical cult need not be an image in the strict sense of the word; it is not at all a matter of it looking identical or even similar to something that is portrayed. In general, it is a question of whether the mythical image refers to "things [*Sachen*]," points to other beings. Anything can become a sense-image: a human gesture, a plant, an animal, a word, a piece of writing, natural things without any artificiality. Yet artificial things, too, can become sense-images: pillars, a statue, two crossed pieces of timber—and ultimately, too, images and figures in the ordinary sense. Such things are then altogether "significant"; they represent a suffusion of sense to which the mythical human being cannot comport himself independently of the representation—a suffusion of sense that opens up to him in the representation. To be sure, with some justification, one can say that things that originally have an ordinary significance would thereby be overloaded with new and much more profound characteristics, that they would be reinterpreted as "metaphors," as sense-bearers of a sense that a sober and impartial attitude could not find in them. However, that is spoken from the perspective of the spectator, who understands myth as an anthropological reality, but not as a still valid, true expression of the sense of life. For us—the late skeptics—the mythical world appears to be an enchanted landscape of fairy tales that the dream-sense of the human being has created. For the mythical human being himself, in contrast, things "are" their "meaning"; for him there is no distinction between a mere bearer of meaning and a meaningful sense persisting alongside it. The thing and the sense of the sense-image secretly coincide. The mythically significant thing *is* a metaphor. But that precisely does not mean that it is something other than that which is signified by it. That which signifies and that which is signified coincide—or better, continually cross over into each other. If in a lyrical mood we compare small clouds in the sky with a flock of sheep, then that is an entirely superficial metaphor in which no relation exists between the things compared; it is a conceiving together of different things by the human being who compares them. We can compare many such things in this way—and the hackneyed schemata of popular metaphors are universally known. The genuine, primordial metaphor [*Gleichnis*] can only be beheld and expressed by the human being where actual "equivalences [*Gleichungen*]" come to pass, where transitions take place in the things themselves—where, perhaps still more primordially, transitions are carried out between the world and things. The human being of myth beholds equivalences prevailing through the world when innerworldly things become a metaphor for him. We alluded to this aspect with the notion of being a proxy, of representation. The symbol is the finite thing [*Ding*] in its inner transparency with regard to the prevailing force of the world that conditions [*bedingende*] it.

It may be that all historical time was preceded by a prehistory in which all things were still aglow in the light of the world, when beings themselves had not yet been so released from Being as to occlude it, and the human being still oscillated in the knowledge of the all-encompassing unity of everything divided and individuated. No knowledge is able to reach back into that fabled prehistory—not even the cult's knowledge. When we said that the cult was to a certain degree the memory of that golden age, we did not mean that in the cult the human being returned to prehistory, as we return to yesterday with our memory today. The cult "remembers," insofar as it invokes in a fragmentary way, as it were, a submerged world-openness. It is the memory of "paradise lost" from the vantage point of loss. In the cult the partial and incomplete memory of the worldliness of beings is enacted—indeed, paradigmatically, in *a few* things. The cult is structured by the exclusiveness of sacred things—of the temple precinct, the priest, the sacrificial altar—thus by the strict separation of the sacred from the profane. But the narrow realm of the sacred stands, vicariously, for all non-sacred, for all profane and ordinary things. And, secondly, the priest stands vicariously for the gods. That can still be spoken from the self-understanding of *homo religiosus*. And if, from the perspective of the human being, from the human side of religion, it is also thought that the elevation of a few things to the status of symbols amounts to a human proxy for what is super-human, then in this conception one still remains within the horizon of the religious interpretation of the world. Religion appears to be divided into two sides, the incommensurability of which presents the genuine miracle of religious existence. The human being comports himself to the divine, and the divine comports itself to human beings. Now, if one makes the cut in such a way as to only take into account philosophically what religion for its part recognizes as the human side of its essence, if one leaves out of consideration everything that concerns the divine and the gods and keeps silent about them out of reverence, then not much remains for philosophy in religion than an odd psychology. But vis-à-vis religion, philosophy, as one may declare as a freethinking opinion,[9] does not itself need to take the standpoint of religion and to recognize without question its demarcations between the human and the superhuman. On the contrary, it must attempt to extend its own competence even to that which is denied it by religion: it must attempt to understand religion itself as a symbol, as a metaphor, which is traced back to the world-relation of human existence. Therefore, it must venture the attempt to reduce the gods to sense-images of the world-totality—to see traces of the universe in the dimension of the divine. Such an approach exceeds the basis of phenomena that are given in psychological findings regarding religious consciousness, for instance. However, a depiction of given facts does not concern us here, but rather an explication of human play as an ecstatic relation to the play of the world. The human being and the world can be reached by philosophical thinking; gods cannot. It follows from this[10] that philosophy should not treat the existence or nonexistence of the gods, that it should make declarations neither of a dogmatic theism nor of a dogmatic atheism.

We are acquainted with beings; they reveal themselves to us in manifold ways: each person is familiar with the elements—earthy solidity, fluid water, air, and fiery light—and is familiar with the things that are mixed together from these elements in myriad ways: the lifeless stone, the blooming tree, the swift deer, and aside from these pure natural things the human being and the works of his hands and intellect. We call all of that collectively "things." Of these things, however, we know that they are gathered within an all-encompassing total unity—that they exist within a common, ordered, and structured presencing, exist in space and in time, appear therein and vanish from there again. To be sure, we never discover, as a being, the world in which each being is; we cannot even discover it because it is itself the space-time of all discoverability. And yet we do not suspect that it could be a mere figment of our imagination; indeed, it is in all things and beyond all things. For us, the gods are neither simply present in the manner of things in our environment nor uniquely non-objective, but a mode of conditioning that enables all objects. The world gives space and grants time for beings; it is the space-giving and time-granting for all that exists in the mode of individuation. The rule of the gods, however, is "believed in." This faith may perhaps move mountains—but it remains faith.

In no way do I thus mean to say something detrimental about the truth of religion, only that its truth must be thought in an entirely different manner than the truth that belongs to the human understanding of Being and to the human world-relation. Only the truth of the understanding of Being and of world-openness belongs to philosophy. The truth of religion certainly does not relate to the truth of philosophy as the "representation" to the "concept"—as it did in Hegel's hybrid conception, which thought that philosophy is "absolute knowledge" and for this reason could leave no truth external to it, but rather had to include everything within itself. Philosophy does not think in the intense brilliance of the concept what religion believes in representative images. Each attempt to dissolve religion into philosophy leads to a theologization of philosophy. In fact, here we find that he who "takes the sword, perishes by the sword."[11] There is no wickeder, more deadly poison than that of the dead gods. Like a dreadful symbol, therefore, is Nietzsche's lament of Ariadne over the god of play. The herald of the "death of God" entered into the night with the formula "*Dionysus versus the crucified.*"[12]

If we now attempt to discuss the cult from philosophy's vantage point, we do so only insofar as it appears as human to us, yet we do not consider "what is human" to be in the subjective acts of religious consciousness alone,[13] but above all, too, in cultic symbols. The cult appears to us to be a derivation of a more primordial world-relation. For the one who is situated *in* the cult, such an interpretation is not acceptable; for him the cult is the primordial association with the sacred, the divine, with the gods, with God. For the humans practicing in a cult, being a proxy, which counts as foremost,[14] means the priestly promulgator's proxy for God. Since God appears in the "burning bush," lowers himself down into the flames, the ground on which the human being kneels down before him is sacred; the character of the sacred that belongs to certain places and things, to certain human beings and states of affairs, belongs to them only on account of God. For *homo religiosus* the symbol is not a coincidence between a finite thing and the infinite world, but rather between a thing and divine consecration. For mythically bound human beings the manifestation of the numinous power has the ambivalent character of blessed terror and disturbing exaltation. The sacred becomes the *mysterium tremendum*. We must first simply bring this self-conception of the cultic human being into view, without wishing to somehow "explain" it.

However, it is important for the train of thought we are pursuing here to explicitly and incisively pay attention to how the association with the numinous and the daemonic happens. The archaic human being does not deploy, against the force of daemons to which he knows himself exposed, the powers by which he otherwise asserts and defends his everyday existence. He does not work and struggle against the superior daemonic power. From the meager earth he can gain an abundant harvest by the toil of work, by irrigation and many such arts, by the improvement of his tools, by making use of the powers of animals, by observation of the proper, appropriate times for sowing, and so forth. With a weapon he can defend his fields, pastures, lands, and herds against plundering neighboring tribes. By his own effort and his own power he sets himself in opposition to the resistance of nature and human beings. But all his exertions can, so he believes, come to ruin through the disfavor of daemons; they send sickness, poor growth, unfruitfulness for land and people. And they have free rein over human beings not in the way that the human being cultivates the wilderness, not in the way that he battles enemies. The daemons do not work and struggle against human beings; they have no trouble with them. They effortlessly do what they like with human beings. We could characterize this effortless, arbitrary, and unpredictable association of daemonic powers with human beings most readily as a game. They play with us. We are like marionettes in their hands; we are their powerless playthings. And they do not show themselves to the archaic human being as they are, as they truly are; they do not show themselves in their true, valid, reliable form. They play an everlasting game of hide-and-seek, a masquerade of an uncanny sort—they can be hidden in things that appear entirely harmless; they do not allow themselves to be gotten hold of and recognized in a form; they do not reveal themselves to us as they genuinely are; they do not reveal what their true form, their non-deceptive appearance is. They are always masked, keep themselves disguised behind many masks; we do not succeed in unmasking them. They have a magical power, not merely over lesser beings like humans and animals, but above all over themselves; they are engaged in perpetual transformation, in transitions, in metamorphoses. Daemons are incomprehensible for us as long as we are simply and plainly what we are: a hunter, a warrior, a worker, a man or a woman—a human being. As long as human beings live immersed in simple obviousness they are completely and powerlessly at the mercy of daemons—in ancient times.

But—one could ask critically—how does a representation of daemons come about at all? If indeed they do not show themselves as they are in truth, if we always receive only concealing masks for a face, the tree in which the dryad is hidden, the green depths of the sea in which the tritons and nereids live, the storm clouds from which Zeus's avenging bolt of lightning flashes, why do we not simply remain at the level of the tree, the depths of water, the storm clouds? What tempts us to presume something more behind them, a power that conceals itself and has made itself unrecognizable in such concealment? The event of human death has certainly come to have the greatest significance for a daemonic conception of nature. When a fellow human being dies, one with whom we were acquainted for a long time, who was known in his gesture and body language, in his disposition and style of demeanor, he is then transformed in death into something sublimely uncanny. He has vanished into the inconceivable, into a land without place or name. He has slipped into what is without essence. And yet he is not nothing for us: he leaves behind an emptiness that is felt, which, as infinite resonance, seizes hold of the hearts of those who have loved him. The dead one remains unreachable by the love of the living; this love is no longer fulfilled, it can only honor and preserve the memory. Nevertheless, the dead one comes at night in the dream. He manifestly has another form of existence, which is uncanny and at the same time consoling to us. And this peculiar mode of Being of the dead, to be sometimes "present" in an inconceivable manner, to rise up into the land of the living, is—perhaps—the prototypical paradigm for all daemons. The archetype of everything daemonic—is it in the end the dead human being? Here we are not propounding the thesis that everything daemonic stems from the root of the human dead.[15] The archaic human being, however, who does not reach daemons with work and struggle, achieves another, more restricted, dangerous, and even exhilarating association with superhuman powers when he disguises and masks himself, relinquishes the obviousness of his existence, slips into the polysemy of the mask—when he participates in the daemonic power as a player, becomes himself the enchanter.

13. Cosmic Status of the Symbolism of Play—Ancient Belief in Daemons. The Enchantment of Masks

We are asking about the connection between cult and play—not with a religious-philosophical intention, to which we do not at all feel entitled, but rather because in the cult perhaps the most primeval form of human play appears, and because the aspect of "non-actuality" belonging to every kind of play here signifies an elevation and intensification beyond customarily actual things. We are above all concerned with gaining an insight into the human sense of the cultic symbol. The cultic symbol dissembles the cosmic status of the symbolism of play. Nevertheless, this dissemblance and occlusion is by no means a drawback that would have to be corrected, is not a prejudice that one would have to put aside in order to achieve true insight into valid facts. The gods dissemble and occlude the prevailing world from human beings. We recall Fragment 30 of Heraclitus, which we cited earlier. It says of gods and human beings that neither the one nor the other could have produced the world-dispensation of all things, but precisely by means of this demurral it distinguished both the gods and human beings as poietic beings who are near to the world. Gods and human beings are thereby singled out from all other intraworldly things in that they not merely are *in* the world but comport themselves to their being-in-the-world. Among human beings this takes the acute and tense form of knowing about their own finitude and transience, about our existence's being doomed to death. In human openness to the world our own individual finiteness is known against the background of the unthinkably endless time of the whole, and we comport ourselves to this unceasing time in the love whose obscure desire for procreation impels us to the immortality of the human race. We are in the midst of things, are moved in diverse ways like they are, have been taken along for our planet's ride, taken along by the vegetative life processes—and yet do not exist like the plant and animal do. We act from freedom, work, and are political: we produce things that are not given by nature; we fabricate in a finite and fragile manner; we bring about and effect artificial things, in alien matter and in ourselves; we manufacture technical constructs and states. Human labor overruns the globe with its traces, and the struggle for rule rages through cities and empires.[16] However, in work and struggle the human being is close to the generative prevailing of the cosmos that structures and configures. Because we are opened up to the prevailing whole, experience our finitude from out of its in-finitude, we know we will perish and we know about the imperishability of the race; we are able to fabricate and to form politically. As the knowing, understanding world-dweller, as *politēs tou kosmou,* as cosmopolitan, the human being is the mortal, the lover, the worker, and the fighter. These basic phenomena of our existence are grounded in our world-relation. The animal is intraworldly, without understanding its intraworldliness; it therefore is not aware of death and does not know love, work, and ruling.

But how do things stand with the gods? Are they not similar to human beings insofar as they, too, are open to the world, indeed perhaps stand closer to the whole in a higher and more essential sense? What we understand in only a cloudy and twilit sort of way, that is, that remarkable Being that is comprehensively unified and at the same time appears to be broken in itself in myriad ways and divided into finite things, may perhaps stand before their serenely gazing eyes in effortless clarity. But it is not so much in the difference of a clearer view that they have the advantage over us, not in the knowledge that is more aware and in their greater creative power. What abyssally separates them from everything human is this: that they do not know death, that they are immortal. In the case of the human being, everything that he does has the character of transience, is overshadowed by death. That holds for human love, human work, and the human struggle for rule. And if the myths of peoples speak of the death of the gods, this is a death that is followed by a resurrection, not an actual, final death. Everything the gods do is stamped by immortality, whether it be the way they produce artificial things, the way they invent skills and teach them to human beings, or the way they contend with each other and vie for supremacy in ruling the world. They do not produce their life by producing required, necessary means for life, they do not have to work in order to keep themselves alive, they are not threatened with the danger of starving, they do not suffer the hardships of the weather, they do not need home and hearth like human beings—and they foster their love as an amusement rather than as the preservation of the race of gods. They exist—in the sense of a perpetual perdurance. And because they are imperishable, they do not need, strictly speaking, to love, to work, or to struggle. Human seriousness is missing in their love, work, and struggle. Everything becomes easy and effortless for them. Love, work, and struggle—as depicted in the myths of the gods—are rather a kind of pastime; indeed, we can say, a kind of play. The gods play, they live in blessed leisure, they not only play their games, they also play at love, work, and struggle. They play at the human-all-too-human. The strife of the goddesses over the apple of discord was not merely a divinely ironic portrayal of human bickering; it involved human beings, led to the judgment of Paris and thus to the Trojan War. And if in the course of this the heavenly ones themselves took sides, some fighting on the side of the Achaeans, some on the side of the Trojans, they themselves did not fight a battle for life and death against each other. Indeed they could not die at all; they could at best wound one another. Their struggle was a game—with playthings. And these playthings were the human beings who risked their finite lives, who actually fought and suffered and experienced heartbreaking grief. It is a flagrant idea that all human hardship and trouble is a spectacle, a dramatic play, in the eyes of the gods, that it is elevated to an ultimate buoyant lightness. Play is thus what appears to be raised up above all human measure into the super-human. It is a difficult question as to whether we know about play because we understand the divinity of the gods in the manner of an intimation and from the distance of privation—or whether the human being attained the idea of divine, superhuman, immortal beings who are without needs because he is familiar with play and in play experiences a liberation and release from the heavy, oppressive weight of existence—and ascribed this experience to those imagined beings as a lasting condition. Is human play a reflected radiance of divine Being in our life—or are the gods phantasmagoria of the human drive to play? We cannot answer this question. Theology has no place within philosophy, insofar as the latter conceives of itself as the finite world-wisdom of the human being. At any rate, it is incontestable that the problem of God was central to entire history of Western metaphysics—from Aristotle to Hegel. Yet this entire metaphysical tradition was determined by the suppression of the world-problem. Our reference to the mythical representations of the Being and prevailing of the gods in connection with play thus refers to the merely human side of religion and of the cult and deliberately brackets the question concerning the existence of the gods or God. The cultic symbol dissembles and occludes the more primordial world-sense of the symbol as the coincidence of thing and world. The cultic symbol is characterized by the mysterious presence of divine forces and powers in an elect and demarcated thing, which thus attains an elevated significance and function. The table becomes an altar, bread and wine a sacrament. Through the consecration that the priest as the mouthpiece of the divine pronounces, certain things that otherwise stand in everyday relations to the human being are used and required by him; they can be elevated to the status of harboring a superhuman power. The thing then does not cease to appear as it was appearing hitherto. It does not change its form but remains what it was. It is always still itself and yet at the same time not itself. That should not be misconstrued as though a meaningful sense were bound to any kind of finite thing by collective agreement, as though the thing pointed away from itself toward something else. A signpost is a board that has been written on to indicate directions and attached to a post by the wayside: on it the piece of wood and the "meaning" are clearly to be distinguished. However, the bread that two or three who are assembled in the name of God break is not an external sign for a psychological sense that is thereby intended, but is rather, as this bread, the hidden god. The bread does not cease to appear to be bread and to taste like bread, and yet it coincides with God himself in a mysterious identity. God does not break through in his heavenly radiance by means of the inconspicuous loaf of bread; he remains concealed in it. By his superior, indeed, most superior actuality, he does not obliterate the actuality of the bread-thing with which we are ordinarily familiar: he does not himself go into the phenomenon but holds himself at a remove from the unbelieving gaze. He is inaccessible to the everyday gaze, for which he is but a "non-actuality." But it is precisely this structure that, in our context, interests us: how, so long as ordinary, everyday things are held to be the standard of being actual, something that is held to be "non-actual" can be conceived as a higher, superior mode of Being—how what is stronger in Being can conceal itself in the semblance of what is weaker in Being. The interpretation of play by Platonic metaphysics conceives the "playworld" merely as an imitative reproduction, thus as inferior when compared to the things that the craftsman manufactures. To be sure, Plato does not take everyday sensible things to be the standard of valid Being. The standard for him is the Being of the idea that is only accessible to thinking. Measured by their duration, all ordinary natural and artificial things are not genuinely existent. But for him the playworld is only a reproduction of sensible things and therefore even less existent than these. If the playworld, however, is not conceived as a reproduction but rather as a symbol, then despite its "non-actuality" it has a higher ontological status than the tangible things of everyday actuality. As a symbol the playworld of human play is initially understood in the cult. The cult is the comprehensive concept [*Inbegriff*] for all comportments carried out by human beings toward the divine, the comprehensive concept for the representations of God, for the rites and ceremonies of a veneration quaking with terror. The cult—as the human relation to the gods—dissembles human existence's deeper relation to the world. We, as the world-open being, comport ourselves indirectly and in a mediated manner to the world itself, insofar as we "believe" in a superhuman being that is more open to the world, and insofar as we secretly take the properties of the gods to characterize the world, we think the totality of the world through the power and knowledge of the gods and speak of omnipotence and omniscience. And to the extent that the cult (considered only in a purely human sense) is a mediate form of human existence's ecstatic relation to the world, the cultic symbol, too, is an early form of the most primordial symbol—it is a symbol of the symbol.

We are approaching the problem from within this perspective. This perspective is one-sided and perhaps all-too-human, because it only takes up the cult according to its human form of appearance and ignores its own truth as a revelation of the divine itself. But the truth of religion remains inaccessible to philosophy. It is another matter whether this has as its consequence a subordination of philosophy to religion or the resolute indifference of the thinking human intellect vis-à-vis all religion. In early antiquity the human being is disturbed and is shaken to the core, agitated, excited, made anxious, and uplifted by his belief in daemons. His sojourn in the world is not exclusively, indeed not even primarily, determined by what he sees, feels, smells, or tastes; it is not characterized by the apprehension of perceived things; it is not ruled by the visible. Much more strongly is he concerned with the invisible, the suspected, the intimated, that which is felt as uncanny power. He is not safe and sound at home in a small but firm circumscribed sphere of familiar things. The shadow of inconceivable powers can always unexpectedly and suddenly fall over all that is familiar and well known. The landscape of his life can suddenly become clouded over; horror can arise from the closest things. It is already even the case for the archaic "savages" that the Being of things in which we believe ourselves to be well versed can incomprehensibly "veer" into a mysteriously dark strangeness that shocks and horrifies. Only the savage does not formulate such veering with the categories of the problem of Being. Even for him the Being of existent things and of his very self is profoundly familiar and at the same time profoundly strange and uncanny. But he calls such experiences the workings of daemons. Early historical existence, to a degree scarcely still imaginable for us, is full of association with daemons. They are everywhere and nowhere, are here and yet not visible; they lurk behind each bush and tree, materialize in diverse disguises, appear in the most impossible and unbelievable forms, mask themselves in the figure of the friend and, from out of the most benign disguise, pounce maliciously, or, with the ghastly forms of ghosts, turn out to be helpful, beneficial powers. Daemons are so unpredictable that one can scarcely arm oneself against them. They are incomprehensible and mask themselves in ever new metamorphoses; they are manifold and variable, capricious and shifting like the weather: sometimes good, sometimes wicked, sometimes helpful, sometimes horrible, sometimes generous, sometimes rapacious. Daemons lie like a monstrous nightmare on the archaic collective soul. And, to be sure, the most uncanny thing is that one does not know why they involve themselves with human beings, why they continually play with them sometimes for good and sometimes for evil, why they interfere everywhere in human affairs, why they confuse and bring into order again and confuse once more. Indeed, daemons do not need human beings, in any case not in the way that the human being needs domesticated animals such as the ox, which he has draw the plow, or the horse, with which he rides out on hunting expeditions and military campaigns. Daemons would be fine without continually disturbing human beings. But they do not let the human being out of their clutches, nor out of the sight of their sometimes malicious, sometimes benevolent eyes, which see without being seen by human beings. The early human being, in everything that he does, lives with the basic feeling of being furtively watched by superhuman witnesses of his deeds and omissions. But these witnesses—what do they actually want from him? They do not want his work, nor his spoils of war, nor his pleasures of love; they also do not want to rule over him as human beings rule over human beings. The human being, compared to daemons, is less than the slave compared to his master. They reign over him in a wholly inconceivable manner. They are, indeed, not only outside, concealed in external things; they also conceal themselves within the depths of the human being's soul, make him possessed, a person running amok in every sense of the word. Daemons are unrelenting, impossible to ward off, but concealed and disguised witnesses of the course of human life. They obviously take pleasure in forcing open every recess of human self-consciousness, in spying into the furthest nook of each soul, in dabbling in every human craft, in thwarting him from attaining any sort of free selfhood. What do daemons do? We said already that they play, as it were, with human beings, but not like a player does with other playmates; rather, they play with them like a player plays with a plaything. But that does not yet say enough. For a lifeless plaything, it is entirely a matter of indifference how it is manipulated. One can handle them carefully or carelessly. Among children of a certain age it is often the greatest playful delight to take a plaything apart into its constituent parts. One can also play with a living plaything, for instance, animals, which presents a particularly complicated problem.

The human being documents his dominant position compared to all non-human things by "looking at" them. In his vision, other things become his objects. The human being is the universal witness to the Being of non-human things, which surround us as animals, plants, and rocks. But this witness and spectator is himself the spectacle for an uncanny gaze, which he always feels on the back of his neck—which he never sees unconcealed and as it is in itself, no matter how quickly he may turn around. The belief in daemons is always a belief in such superhuman witnesses to humanity's life. In the course of human history the primeval belief in daemons becomes clarified. Above all the ambivalent character of the daemonic recedes more and more—or better, separates into "good" and "evil" powers. Daemons lose their characteristic feature of exhibiting an inconceivable reversal of opposites into each other; more and more, they become "housed" in determinate forms and are thought of as "settled" into these forms, even if the latter are still viewed as disguises of their true essence. Daemons become local spirits, local deities, and are distinguished according to their functions and effects, which they exercise on human beings. To be sure, even the "good daemons" retain the enigmatic double aspect of the benign and the formidable; in the awe before them the fear that is near to all reverence still resonates. With this progressive restructuring of the representation of daemons also comes a restructuring of the human relation to daemonic forces. They are represented as "able to be influenced"—able to be influenced by a right and upright conduct of human life, by prayers, requests, and sacrificial offerings. And, in alliance with good daemons that he has moved to favor him, the human being can then avoid the evil daemons' stalking, tricks, and wicked deeds. The belief in daemons becomes a healing practice with manifold applications. In the course of this trajectory—as is often[17] said—a purification comes about, that is, the belief in daemons progresses to the genuine belief in gods, indeed finally to monotheism. We can thus distinguish two main motifs: on the one hand, the tendency to personify the divine. The relation between divine power and the human being who is at the mercy of and handed over to it is determined according to categories of human sociality. "God" is experienced as the personal, overpowering "thou" who takes us up into his goodness and whom the human being approaches with complete trust—like a child approaches its father. God, then, forms a "bond," for example, with human beings, with his chosen tribe; he is the god of his people as this people is the people of its god. The other motif in the purification of the representation of God is operative in metaphysics, indeed already in its founders. Plato's critique of the poets was not least a critique of daemonology, too; the god of metaphysics is not the dark power that pursues and hunts human beings, plunges them into fortune and misfortune, casts them into patricide and maternal defilement—the metaphysical god is essentially only good and is for human beings only the cause of good things, never the cause of what is bad and evil. The cause of evil deeds, of errors and transgressions, is always the human being alone. The metaphysical god does not veil himself, does not conceal himself in diverse forms, does not change like a Proteus; he remains unaltered in himself, is pure self-persistence, is changeless constancy, self-identity; nor does he reveal himself in such a way that he sends his son into the world and announces himself in the latter's words. He is always manifest and always announced in the *logos,* which prevails through all beings. But he is not visible to human beings' sense of sight; he is only accessible in pure thinking. And this metaphysical god of thought, this philosopher-god of Plato and Aristotle up to Hegel's "world-spirit," is not amenable to supplications and requests, to any sacrificial aromas. He is not moved by human pleading, is not moved by promises and good intentions. He is the demiurge and the sovereign of the cosmos, but not the loving father who forgives and draws near to his heart. And even if Plato says that the human being is "the plaything of the god,"[18] this divine play that is thought by Plato is already as moralized as is the play of the poets whom he does allow in his state. The two main motifs of a "purification of the representation of God," that is, Jewish monotheism and the metaphysical concept of God, came to be united in the history of European humanity and combined under diverse inner tensions. But the representation that the human being lives under the eyes of God, exists in front of his invisible observation, always has a superhuman observer, witness and examiner of the heart over him—that he is never alone in the cosmos—has remained preserved up to the most sublime forms. As long as this representation prevails, all human play is reinforced in its cultic derivation, is a kind of play before God, is not yet immediately worldly.

Now what does the cultic derivation of play look like? By "the cultic derivation of human play," we are in no way implying that all play is originally rooted in the cult. But considering the archaic cult offers a distinct possibility to understand the "non-actuality" that belongs to play as the playworld in terms of a reference to a higher, not a lower, kind of Being, as measured by the Being of things we ordinarily experience. If the early human being initially knows himself to be uncannily exposed to unpredictable, capricious, and fickle daemons that are sometimes well disposed and sometimes malevolently disposed, then he can oppose to them no force of his own that would come from his own undaunted Being. As long as he *simply* is what he is, he remains a ball for daemons to play with. However, he *is* "simply" when he loves, works, struggles. But already death brings along a peculiar bifurcation of the human essence. We distinguish the living and the departed. It would be an all too cheap, pseudo-rationalistic explanation if one were to say that such a bifurcation does not truly take place. In this view, there are only living human beings. Dead human beings are, at most, corpses, relics, from which being-human has departed. Dead human beings *are* not human beings, they were human beings. That is certainly correct, even if in an entirely superficial sense. Were being-dead only simple being-annihilated, it would then be completely senseless to comport oneself at all to the dead; one would comport oneself to an entirely empty nothing. But the cult of the departed is perhaps the most ancient cult on earth; the memory that we retain of those who have returned home binds our day above ground to a mysterious night from which all life comes and into which it sinks again. The living know themselves to be members of an endless chain, with the deceased behind them and the unborn in front of them. In knowing about the difference between life and death a difference of world-dimensions is understood: the dimension of manifestation and the dimension of absence. The reciprocal relation of manifestation and absence prevails through everything that is. It is evident in a conspicuous manner in the human association with daemons. They are present in the mode of a thousandfold veiling. They manifest themselves in the mask. When the human being lives without masks, thus simply, for instance in the harshness of work and of struggle, he cannot confront daemons; he is at their mercy, exposed to their curse or their blessing. However, the human being has the peculiar possibility of being able to mask himself. Of course, he masks himself differently than the daemon does. Anything whatsoever can be a mask of the daemon. He can appear as a bull, as a swan, as rain, and seduce earthly women—as Zeus used to do. However, what he *is in himself,* no mortal eye sees, for it would perish like Semele. The human being who masks himself indeed remains in the form that nature has given to him; he cannot escape from it. He masks himself by covering himself, dressing up, wrapping himself in animal skins, concealing his true face in carved masks. He uses the mask as a thing that is distinct from himself, as a cloak, as camouflage. The mask is thus a prop that is different from the masked human being. Obviously we cannot in the same sense say of the daemon that he uses the things in which he temporarily appears as the human being uses his artificial masks. These things become masks by virtue of the god or daemon temporarily appearing in individual things—but by means of masks, which the human being makes for himself or which he finds, the human being is for the very first time transposed into the possibility of *appearing* ambiguously and polysemously.

In any case, one must guard against an interpretation that would understand the mask that the human being procures for himself as only a reproduction or afterimage. The mask can always be reinterpreted in this way, but it is not originally so. The donning of a mask is an elementary form of enchantment. The basic purpose of the human mask is not to deceive one's fellow human beings in order to lead them to believe something, in order to appear to be something for others that one in fact is not. One wants to appear multifarious for oneself; one wants with the mask to enter into the magic spell of the daemonic, to participate in a minor way in the incomprehensible transformative power of daemons. The mask is not supposed to mislead; it is supposed to enchant. To a certain degree the mask releases us from the inescapable fixity and rigidity of our life's situation. One can be everything again. With the mask, the human being even attains daemonic force and power, to a certain extent. In the play of masks he can confront daemons, dispose them to be friendly or drive back the malevolent ones. At issue here is not outwitting the daemons, who would be deceived by a mask, as it were. Beings who are experts at such a high degree of dissimulation do not really allow themselves to be misled by some animal skins and face masks. That which they shrink back from is the magical power of the human being, which he achieves in the masking, in the cancellation of simplicity, and in the passage to a multifariousness of existence. As a player the human being becomes more powerfully and essentially commensurate with the superhuman daemons than in other fields of life; he is able to confront them with the same power, even if in a lesser magnitude. The masking of the human being in ancient periods of humanity has by no means been understood as an optional, arbitrary, or harmless play, for instance as an amusement or cheerful masquerade. On the contrary, it is considered to be a dangerous risk, a provocation of daemons. It was not open to everyone; it was the privilege of the skilled enchanter-priest, the medicine man. The mask became a ritual prop of a cultic invocation that put human society into the full circuit of all the beneficial and terrifying forces of terrestrial and chthonic daemons. The peculiar "non-actuality" of the "appearance" achieved with the mask can be understood, in a more primordial way, not as a deceptive effect but rather as enchantment, as magic. Cultic play at its most fundamental level is the enchantment of masks. What it is beyond this remains for us to ask in what follows.

14. Sacred Technique, Cosmic Metaphor, Initiatory Enchantment. Transition to Cult-Play

The enchantment of the mask is the most ancient prop of human play—it belongs to the early form of the cult in an entirely essential way. Strictly speaking, the mask is not a plaything, is not something with which one plays but rather something in which one plays, something that constitutes cultic play in the very first place. The mask is the enchanted item whose possession transforms the human being—the spell's power adheres to it, as it were; it has a magical quality. But it does not have this like the stone has its weight or like the tool has its usefulness;

its magical quality is not a property that belongs to a thing in itself or that belongs to a thing in relation to the human being. Heaviness belongs to the stone (to be sure, not in an absolute sense but rather only insofar as it is in the gravitational field of a body with mass) under ordinary terrestrial conditions. The usefulness of a stone axe or a bow as a weapon exists for *that* human being who is experienced in handling tools and weapons, who is well versed in such practical things, who understands how to wield them. The practical quality of such artifacts produced by human beings, however, is more than merely the character of being taken up that a thing has for the one grasping it. Anything can have a special "sense" for any human being beyond its general, objective properties: as a memento, as a gift, for instance; it has a reverential value and the like. The things in one's environment are enveloped in countless sense-qualities of diverse kinds that have wholly different ways of belonging to the thing itself. In a hike on untrodden paths, for instance, we take conspicuous and prominent things as path markers in order to find our way back again. In that case these things have the meaning of pathmarking only for us. However, every alpinist in the high mountains understands the path-directing meaning of so-called cairns; these already have an "intersubjective" meaning, even if it pertains to the limited intersubjectivity of those who understand it. It would be a great and vast challenge to go through the objectivity of the sense-characters in the things within our environment and to determine its many forms and stages appropriately. The human being does not stand on one side and objective things on the other—the human being is interwoven with his environment in a way that is both complex and difficult to disentangle; he has deposited and objectified his understanding, his thinking, his feelings, above all, however, his activity, in things. There are human sense-qualities in things that are only accessible to a few, that display private significations, so to speak, that are not able to be recognized at all by other fellow human beings, such as secret signs and the like. However, there are also sense-characters that exist as private significance for the public, as do the hearts carved into the bark of trees, for instance. Furthermore, there are characteristic significations that exist for wider society: national memorial sites, flags, and so forth. From the mere significances in things, we must distinguish significations that are secure and fixed for a secure and fixed circuit of those who understand them and that are connected with specific things, such as the value of goods, exchange value, commercial value, and monetary value. In these "values" the utility of these things is expressed for all. Obviously, the "objectivity" of the monetary value of a house[19] is of a different sort than the objectivity of the value of piety; monetary value is, so to speak, more public and universal, more intersubjective, and more "objective" than the value of piety. Monetary value has a socioeconomic reality, while the value of piety exists for the few for whom the house was a home. Of course, the greater or lesser publicity of a value-quality does not yet tell us anything about the status of such significations.

Clearer than the sense-qualities that "invisibly," so to speak, adhere to things are the characters in things that point back to a shaping, transformative activity of the human being. All artificial constructs in the broadest sense bear the human act of formation in themselves; human formation is documented in their form and has itself been reified. This human action that has been objectified in things is, for the community of practical users themselves, an objective feature that co-constitutes the objectivity of the practical object. The utility, suitability, serviceability of things produced artificially is by no means a "mere conception," but rather belongs to the ontological constitution of the artificial construct. To be sure, its utility exists *for* the human being, exists only for that living being that is determined by the incarnation of freedom. The animal is corporeal but not free—and the angel is free but not corporeal. Neither the animal nor the angel can have a self-created artificial environment. Only the human being works and produces artificial things through his work activity. The animal and the angel do not know what it means to work. They both lack the capacity for *technē*. Neither is dependent in its Being on the products of its own production. The human being alone is the odd terrestrial creature who does not live out in a predetermined way the life granted him, but rather incessantly transforms the conditions of his earthly sojourn, rises up against maternal nature, and wrests from her a place for settlement, stone for the construction of a house, clay for pottery, bronze for tools and equipment, wild plants for refinement, and wild beasts for taming and domestication. But in work the human being not only produces food and equipment for the production of food, he also, by means of work, produces all the artificial things that he uses in the other basic dimensions of his embodied existence: the necessary, requisite things for battle, for love, for remembering the dead, for honoring the gods—he produces weapons and beds, jugs used for libations. Work creates things of which battle, love, the cult of the dead, and the cult of the gods must always make use in order to have, as it were, a "site." That is also profoundly connected with the embodiment of human existence: we do not battle in a merely intellectual way, not as one pure intellectual being against other intellectual beings, we battle with weapons. We do not love soul to soul, lifted out of all sensuality; we love the whole, other, beloved human being in a bodily way and we use the bed for procreation and childbirth. Even our deaths are carried out not as a purely "intellectual event" but rather in the full concretion of our embodied existence; the one who dies departs and leaves behind his corpse. The coffin as a hollowed-out tree trunk, in which one is borne out of the community of the living, is likewise a product of labor, a fabrication of *homo faber*. And similarly, all the devices with which we accomplish the remembrance of the dead are human workpieces.

The temple for the god, the ornamented columns in which he comes to epiphany, the votive offerings and cultic devices—all this stems from the laboring activity of the human being as a worker. The worker produces all the artificial things in which the fundamental dimensions of our existence manifest themselves. Without the labor of the worker the human being would be without hearth and home—he would be like a lover without a bed, like a warrior without a weapon, like a suppliant without a sacred precinct and temple, like one who has departed without a tomb. The significance of these necessary things, which provide the sites for basic human phenomena, has for the most part not been sufficiently grasped. In most cases, one takes them as more or less contingent constructs of a merely incidental kind. The incalculable wealth of forms allows the aspect of arbitrariness to thus come to the fore. To be sure, the particular form of weapon, bed, cultic device, or tomb is certainly not at all "necessary"; human history has brought to light an immense richness of forms and in the course of its progress will also bring entirely new and unexpected forms to light. But these are always variations on the same fundamental themes. As long as the human being exists bodily as finite freedom on the earth, he will work and use the devices of work; he will love and have need of the bed for congress; he will erect a house for the gods, who for their part have no need of housing; he will put the corpses of the dead into coffins or consign them to the funeral pyre. Precisely in such things as plow and sword, bed and temple, cradle and coffin, an eternally human sense comes to light: we are interwoven with the Being of such things; they belong to the human being's furnishings for life, belong to us, are not to be thought away by us without destroying the specific humanity of the human being. They certainly do not themselves have the human being's mode of Being; they are artificial things—but the human being as a producer cannot be understood at all without his products. The human being as worker objectifies himself in his works, in the constructs of his work activity. Yet the human significance of the temple is not exhausted by its being a house erected by human labor. The temple is necessary for the human being's need to worship superhuman forces. The temple pertains to the suppliant, not primarily to the worker, even if it only comes into being through the worker. Insofar as the human being produces artificial things in accordance with skilled labor, it appears to be in his power whether such constructs come about or not. He is the efficient cause for such things, which are his "effects." As effects, as results of labor, they depend on him, the worker. But is it up to the human being whether he wants to be a worker? And is it up to him whether he wants to be a warrior, a lover, and one who prays? Are they not fundamental needs of our existence, which first open up the realm of our free creative activity? Certainly, there are only pots because there are potters—but there must be potters because the human being needs vessels. To be sure, there are only temples because there are builders—but there must be builders because the human being needs, besides a house for himself, a house for the gods, needs to have a consecrated site in order to concentrate on the highest being and to bind his terrestrial day to the heavens. The openness of the human being for his basic needs and the purposive understanding that is contained therein first motivates his work activity. The causality of the *causa finalis* here precedes the *causa efficiens*. The human being is creative and industrious because he is placed into the elementary basic needs of his finite existence, because he is exposed to the unsettling questionworthiness of beings, because he knows about Being and nothingness, feels his subjugation to death and at the same time the inexhaustibility of the swelling ground of life, because he recognizes the supremacy of the gods. In battle, in love, and in the cult he exists just as primordially as in work. And yet work, insofar as it builds a human environment and stamps a formation on natural things from out of the human spirit, in a certain way becomes more prominent than the other basic phenomena. The economic process then appears to be the genuine history of the human being. However, in truth, the human essence is structured much more complexly; it forms a reciprocal interpenetration of the basic phenomena. Work makes possible the sites of battle, love, and the cult—but battle, too, avails itself of love, cult, and work in total martial mobilization. Love is likewise a comprehensive aspect of existence: because we obtain earthly immortality through love, we need the bed, the cradle, dwellings for the family, labor as the provision of subsistence, and the cult as the ethical preservation of the depth of the intimacy of familial life in the shadowy realm of the Penates and Lares. And, finally, the cult hallows the tools of the worker, blesses the weapons of the warrior, consecrates the matrimony of husband and wife, and bears offerings for the dead.

The imbrication and joining together of the elementary dimensions of existence is a problem of the greatest philosophical significance and also of the greatest methodological difficulty. We do not yet[20] have the adequate categories at our disposal to formulate with sufficient conceptual acuity the being-with-one-another and the reciprocal interpenetration of the fields of human life. It does not suffice to simply distinguish concepts of existence from concepts of things. For, in the first place, human existence is not at all to be understood apart from its involvement with things; it does not hover like a pure spirit, is not like the disembodied, disincarnate angel above spatio-temporal things—the human being exists in the midst of things, exists in the space and time of the world and is deposited therein. He "founds" by cultivating the earth, erecting living quarters, and wresting the things necessary for his basic needs into his realm of life. And, in the second place, all human relation to intraworldly things is already directed by a world-relation, even if an obscure one. The human being is a worker, warrior, lover, and worshipper of the omni-potent because he exists open to the world. The being-together of the basic phenomena of existence ultimately cannot be determined at all from the mere contrast to forms of configurations and constellations that are thought naturalistically, but rather presupposes insight into the connection between the human being and the world. Human labor, however, also produces the plaything for play, and also produces the mask, that is, the enchanted item, without itself being the sort of thing that enchants.

First we must elucidate why the mask is not a plaything—and, to be sure, we must do this within the horizon of the primeval, archaic life of the human being. There one does not play with the mask, one plays in the mask. The mask is not a thing suitable for play, to which an imaginary play-sense can be easily attached, so to speak—as, for instance, the hobbyhorse made out of wood has the play-sense of "war-horse" for the boy who is playing. The wooden thing becomes a plaything insofar as it is given a made-up signification within the context of an enclosed playworld. In this, the resemblance of appearance between the plaything and the represented thing itself is not even absolutely necessary, but a resemblance does facilitate the player's imaginative bestowal of sense when he designates the wooden thing as a spirited horse and himself as the gallant rider. The plaything is positioned within the encompassing sense-context of the whole playworld, in which it has its imaginary signification, its role-function. The mask of the primitive, in contrast, opens up the play-space for his cultic play in the first place. By masking himself therein the play first begins—a kind of play that indeed has a fearful, dangerous and uncanny seriousness. The masked human being becomes ambivalent, polysemous, unrecognizable. Precisely by concealing himself, he appears as a power equal to the daemons. The mask is thus something like an invisibility cloak, an enchanted ring, a magic wand. It is not so much a matter of what or whom the mask is supposed to portray, to which daemon, to which superhuman helper it is assigned. The face of daemons is indeed inaccessible and unrecognizable for human beings, even if they repeatedly attempt "to make a graven image" of it. The daemon-mask can make no concretely grounded pretension to "resemble" the represented daemon itself; it can at most express more or less precisely a collective representation. The reproductive character is not the essential thing here. Rather, the dissolution of human straightforwardness and unambiguousness is essential. When we escape the firm characterization according to which we must be identical with ourselves, when the primitive early human being can at the same time be a human and a leopard, he is able to resist hostile daemons and to bring the well-disposed ones into closer contact with him. The mask is the enchanted item that is not a means of enchantment, not a means to help the enchanter, but rather is the spell itself. But the mask must be worn by the human being; it does not by itself have the power that belongs to it when it is worn. Taken by itself alone, to be sure, it is still something to be shunned, something on which a heavy taboo is laid—the forbidden thing that may not be touched. But not until the medicine man wears the mask and becomes the ritual mask-dancer within the circle of his helpers does the horde that fears the daemon take courage and gain confidence; through their magic priest they are in a certain way able to participate in the superhuman power of daemons, to which they would otherwise be helplessly delivered over. As someone who is elevated in a superhuman manner in the mask, the medicine man is, to be sure, not himself taken to be a daemonic being by his tribesmen; they know who is concealed under the mask, but they also know that the person concealed there is not the genuine truth of the mask. The truth of the mask for them is the daemonic polysemy as such. And this is not a result of work, so to speak,[21] as one for instance produces the beauty of a ceramic piece in the process of producing ceramics. The mask is not a means for producing a polysemy in the mask-wearing human being, and it is not a means for bringing about an enchanting power. If we were to understand the situation in this way, then the labor of the human being would have generative functions for the other equally fundamental fields of life. The production of the mask is itself almost a cultic activity, which is performed according to a transmitted secret knowledge; in this case the cultic aspect also overlays the work processes that lead to the cult's props. The production of the mask that imparts daemonic power occurs for the most part in a ritually stylized process of work and remains separated from the everyday and profane activity of work. In the finished product, an appearance [*Schein*] refers back [*fällt . . . zurück*] to the *technē* that leads to sacred artifacts. The enchantment of masks operates by shining back [*rückscheinend*] on the production of masks. Technique thus becomes hallowed, but only the technique that leads to cult objects becomes sacred technique.

However, this is only *one* concept of sacred technique. This concept is also used—precisely in the explication of the primeval cult—in a sense that is meant completely differently: namely, as a title for the activities, practices, and actions of the medicine man who is endowed with the enchanting power of daemons. Perhaps here, too, in the beginning was the deed. The cult, conceived in its archaic root as an association with daemons, was less an observation and a tranquil tarrying before things or great contexts, was less a contemplative overview of the whole structure of the world and its order, than an attempt to save ourselves from terrible distress, from actual dangers and occasionally, too, from imaginary ones. The human being of early times was, to a degree scarcely still perceptible to us, exposed to the ravages of the elements, to the wildfire of the steppes, to floods of the sea, to adverse weather that destroyed his seeds. He was also exposed to the blows of fate falling incomprehensibly, to the whims of those who dwell in the heavens, who send sickness and blight. At every turn he felt himself secretly observed by resentful kobolds. Life's decisive question for him was whether he could ward off the evil and hostile influence of sinister daemons and how he could secure for himself the help and assistance of the well-disposed spirits. The human being first lifted his gaze to gods and daemons from deep need, which he was no longer able to master from his own powers. Need taught him to pray. Not the astonished admiration for the grandeur of the world, not the rapture before the shimmering starry night, not the uplifting and sublime view of the wide sea when dawn breaks in the distance brought the human being to fall on his knees, but rather bitter need and obscure suffering, anxiety and concern for those near and dear, fear of the uncanny, trembling before superhuman forces. The archaic cult emerges not so much from a freer[22] openness to the world than it does from the fear of the Lord. It is essentially practical. For that reason this cult is predominantly activity, a ritual enactment, but precisely not activity in the customary and ordinary sense. It is the activity of enchantment that for the most part is carried out under the spell of mask-enchantment. The medicine man has extraordinary powers and abilities—yet not from himself, insofar as and to the extent that he is a member of the horde, the tribe, the clan; he has them thanks to the mask, by means of which he can touch and move the daemonic sphere. Ritual activity thus has an entirely peculiar structure: it is a "likening [*Gleichung*]." What is meant by this requires elucidation.

The ritual activity of the medicine man is to bring to presence in the small, finite circuit of the primitive horde that which prevails through *everything* as a greater, overarching event. To a certain degree, the comprehensive event finds a reflection in the vicarious activity of the enchanter. However, the reflection is not simply a reproduction of the whole, for the whole is indeed not given as an original. The significant connections in the counterplay of benevolent and malevolent daemons are rather divined than clearly seen, and the ritual gesture is the way in which this intimation is brought into a specific and clear form. The activity of enchantment is just as much intimation [*vor-ahmend*] as it is imitation [*nach-ahmend*]; it represents, yet not in the way a reproduction represents an original, but rather in the way a part represents the whole. A mysterious harmony in some way prevails between the part and the whole. The whole shines back into the part and expresses itself in the part, even if in a fragmented manner. The light of the whole falls on the part; the fragment is "completed" by the whole. The *totum* is *in parte*. That they have in themselves a symbolic representation of the whole without simply and merely reproducing the whole by no means occurs in all things or all activities. The whole exceeds every possibility of reproduction. But it is representable in the symbolic figure. The medicine man endowed with the enchantment of masks knows the strong symbolic gestures that move the daemons, he knows the secret significations that are based on likenesses between whole and part, and he understands how to handle them ritually. He becomes a practitioner of a magical art; he holds in his hand the "key," as it were, that unlocks the relations between whole and part. The hunt, the youthful squad's military campaign, wedding celebrations, funerals—he brings all of this together in the correct and valid gesture, in the ritual ceremony, and he joins the humble life of his tribe to the more powerful orders of the daemonic realm, thereby providing an anchor for it in the superhuman. His activity, however, is by no means an impotent "knowing" about the human's situation of being threatened by daemons, about the human's precarious and uncanny position, which he would elucidate in interpretative gestures. The gestures of the rite have above all a practical sense; they ward off hostile powers and, on the other hand, "call the arms of the gods to one's side."[23] The rite invokes, rendering the evil and good spirits spellbound; it is a magical technique, as it were—in the primitive community the most important of all techniques, more important than the construction of houses and cultivation of the land, domestication of animals, and the art of war, more important than the production of devices, tools, clothing, and jewelry. For all the effort of human beings is in vain, and all their skills count for nothing, if the practice of enchantment and the priest's magical technique do not assure a small garden for human industry. Most ritual gestures have this sense of a return of all human things to the supremacy of divine operation, to the blessing of the good powers and protection from the evil ones.

But there are also distinct activities in the early cult that have a significance that exceeds what we have discussed to this point—and within which the structure of sense belonging to the symbolic likening is emphasized more sharply. We mean by this the actions that are genuinely enchanting. If the medicine man generally portrays the blessing of heavenly rain for human fields in the ritual pouring of holy water and makes clear to all what the heavenly power of blessing is, such a gesture indeed always has a practical sense, which, however, primarily serves to orient the members of the tribe and to help them come to an understanding regarding the powers on which their life is dependent. However, if drought settles over the land and the seeds go to ruin under the scorching sun, then perhaps the medicine man ventures a great reversal. If the whole symbolically recurs in the part, then the part's influence on the whole must be possible, too. The symbolic likening must be able to be "reversed." What happens vicariously in the part must recur in the greater whole. It is not only that the whole shines back in partial things, which are capable of a symbolic representation of the whole, but the parts thus distinguished are also able to influence the whole: *pars pro toto.* The rainmaker pours the precious and rare water uselessly onto the dust—but he thereby compels the all-prevailing daemons to repeat his activity now on a greater scale and to send rainfall. This idea of an initiatory enchantment lies at the basis of the magic practice of many primitive peoples.[24]

There are, to some extent, stages in the development of the cult that we have distinguished up to now. The oldest stage appears to be the enchantment of masks; then on that is based magical technique, above all in the impressive form of initiatory enchantment, which is a reversal of symbolic likening. Over this then arises the third stage, which we can call cult-play in the genuine sense. By no means do the two first stages disappear when the cult has taken on the character of cultic play. The mask and magic technique remain preserved in cult-play, too, but they are arranged within its context of sense and attain a function within its total meaning. Cult-play likewise retains an eminently practical sense, becomes a mode of association with divine powers, is a solitary appeal, as it were, a solemn prayer, a plea for heavenly help and blessing. However, it is detached from the immediate situation of crisis, from the entirely concrete cause in an acute crisis; it belongs within the course of the sacred calendar, within the rhythmic recurrence of the seasons, within the revolution of the moon, sun, celestial bodies—it already has a cosmic vastness, even though it is not the symbolic representation of the prevailing of the world but rather of the rule of the gods, of the coming and going of Persephone. In cult-play there is also already to a high degree a beholding, a rapt *theōria,* a wondering at and astonished admiration of the divine governance in the world-totality. Cult-play allows one to see how things stand with the human being, with his putative power and grandeur, with his pride and his knowledge—how small and nugatory he is before the gods, how he must be shattered by guilt and abysmal suffering, how he must sink into disgrace and madness, in order to experience the most bitter dregs of our existence, the limits of the human, as did Oedipus and Ajax, as did Niobe. Cultic play becomes the dramatic play or spectacle of the communal festival of a god, becomes an epiphany of divine power and a paradigm of human suffering. And in the play that human players perform and carry out as a festive service for the gods and proffer as a votive offering, they play, oddly enough, their own "being-played," their own human roles of being the ball and the plaything of those who dwell in the heavens. In human play there occurs the representation and the symbolic recurrence of a far greater, more encompassing play, whose two-faced character we divine throughout[25] the tragedy and comedy of human existence.

15. Cult-Play as a Dissembling of the World-Relation. Play of the Gods and Play of the World

The cultic origin of play is of the utmost importance for the philosophical clarification of the phenomenon of play, primarily for three reasons. As cult-play, as priestly activity, play is drawn into the inmost core of the archaic human being's life; it is not a "marginal phenomenon," not a peripheral appearance without which life would be able to be carried out in more serious occupations. Cult-play forms the center of the primitive lifeworld, the fundamental act of its self-understanding and self-interpretation. This early life does not yet speak for itself in concepts and logical syntaxes. It speaks in visionary images, in gestures, in elevated and stylized rituals; it must act and behold, "understand" with the eye and bodily movement how things stand with it—how it is admitted into powerful, overarching forces, exposed and abandoned to them, how it "depends" on what is beyond the human. Cult-play informs the cult community about what is essential and about human beings' position in the midst of cosmic forces, about the "invisible powers" that bestow blessings and send calamity, whose enigmatic and unsettling presence is felt and yet not directly seen, grasped, or conceived, which in their proximity remain inconceivable and mysterious and lurk around small human settlements in the midst of the wilderness as though concealed and lying in ambush. But cult-play not only gives an orientation, it is above all an activity in the sense of a magical technique, as a cooperation or counteraction vis-à-vis daemonic forces. The most important deed in the primitive tribe's framework of life is the activity of those who understand how to correctly deal with daemons, who best know their secrets, who understand how to distinguish between good and evil spirits, who know the correct incantatory formulas and in the enchantment of the mask dare to oppose overwhelming forces and detain them. The deed of the medicine man, of the enchanter-priest, is a salvational deed on which the weal and woe of the entire social organization depends. For this reason he has an elevated, privileged status, is the administrator of consecration and sacramental sanctifications; he gives his blessing to weddings, births, and deaths, to hunting expeditions and military campaigns; he conducts the festivals in which the whole of life, which has been disintegrated and scattered into the quotidian, gathers itself again in the coming to presence of the gods. The magical technique of the enchanter-priest is the most important *technē* in the diversely structured system of primeval practices; divination binds together heaven and earth, gods and human beings, places human things collectively and explicitly within the horizon of the whole. And it is highly significant that the human being's historical trajectory does not merely begin with purely economic activities, through which he produces his means of life and thus preserves his existence in a "mediated" fashion, but that in the earliest dawn of the historical trajectory the phenomenon of the cult already emerges, in which the intellectual [*geistige*] activity of making sense of life appears, precisely as the praxis of the enchanter-priest with his secret knowledge and secret arts. The primal form of "knowledge" is priestly and is initially beset with the taboo of the sacred and what ought to be shunned. The "ones who know" are the "initiated," who are aware of the true relations that exist between heaven and earth, who are aware of the fundamental processes: the governance of gods and daemons, the right time for sacrifice and offering, for sowing and reaping, for military campaigns against enemies. And it is a long trajectory accompanied by dramatic transformations of sense, a trajectory in which human knowledge frees itself from its sacred, priestly roots and becomes the knowledge of philosophy and of the sciences. But in any case, the most cursory glance at the phenomenon of the early cult already demonstrates that human history cannot be conceived *only* as a history of labor. Intellectual activity does not emerge until labor is "divided" and separated off into manual and intellectual work processes, into performing and directing modes of work. In the early form of priestly knowledge within the horizon of the archaic practice of magic, the motivation for knowledge and the intellectual activity of interpreting life as distinct from work-activity have already become apparent. And one can even say that until late in historical times magical ideas have implicitly co-determined even the human esteem for the sciences. The peculiar solemn seriousness of early play, its sacrosanct ceremoniousness, its priestly dignity, is grounded in the close connection that play has with the primeval cult. Such play does not provide a variation on the serious life of human beings; it is itself the most serious seriousness, insofar as it has to do with the safeguarding of the social community in relation to invisible powers.

The second reason for the particular philosophical relevance of cultic play is the positivity of playworldly "appearance [*Schein*]" that emerges here. Every spectator knows that a human being is behind the mask, but this knowledge does not disillusion; the point is not that a human being has disguised himself but rather that within a human disguise the daemonic itself comes into view. The awareness of semblance [*Scheinhaften*] in a mask, play, or scene does not lead to the dissolution of the intention to portray or to a "rupture" of ontological belief. The awareness of semblance is rather just the presupposition for the symbol's ability to come to light. When an event is "only played," when it only "appears" in the imaginary circuit of the scenario before the spectators, it is not thereby devalued and deemed to be less than the actual actors [*Schauspieler*] or to be less existent than the spectators' stone benches. On the contrary, the "non-actuality," in the sense of the magical representation, becomes the distinctive "breach" for a deeper and truer, genuine actuality, precisely the actuality of powers and forces at work everywhere. For the first time ever, the concept of actuality thus attains a deep dimensionality with many levels. To be sure, the symbol, taken as a thing, does not, in its signification, have the solid actuality of everyday things. But in being distanced from solidly actual things through the "non-actuality" of the play-appearance belonging to it, it can point back to a more primordial power of Being. The "non-actual" becomes the locus of the hyper-actual. In the cult, the hyper-actual or the actual to the highest degree for the most part has the character of the daemonic and the divine. The symbolism of cult-play remains in the relation of the human being to the god. Symbolism here represents the relation between two *beings*. And this is the third reason for the extraordinary significance of cultic play. Cult-play brings to presence the governance of the gods, their ordering and steering activity, which without effort and without exertion dominates the transformation and passage of all innerworldly things—and it interprets the prevailing of the gods not merely *in* human play but also in many ways *as* a kind of play. Cult-play, as it were, lets the play of the world-governing gods "appear" in the visionary symbolism of the scene, that is, lets it emerge before weak human eyes in a metaphorical visibility. The magical invocation of the highest actuality brings something supremely actual to appearance before human eyes.

But that is just the question we have already repeatedly touched on: whether the human-god-relation, which pervades and attunes the cult, sustaining it in all its forms of appearance, is the most primordial symbol-relation (in the philosophical sense) or only a reflection of the relation between the human being and the world. The world is never *one* actual thing [ein *Wirkliches*], nor the *highest* actual thing in a hierarchy of ontological intensity; yet it is ultimately the all-encompassing *actuality* [Wirklichkeit], the *fabric* [Gewirk]. In the fabric of the world each finite being has its place and its duration, its emergence and decline—it is made fit and forfeited [*erwirkt und verwirkt*]. And the all-encompassing working [*Wirken*] of the world: does it come to a symbolic presence in a human kind of play—and does it thereby also, *as* a kind of play, attain the clarity of something that has come to presence on the stage? That is the decisive question that we prepared in our reflection on the cult, more precisely on the human side of the cult. We need cult-play in order to pose our problem, because in it play is experienced as the most serious seriousness; its "non-actuality" is experienced as an entry point to a more genuine actuality. These are features of the greatest significance for understanding play. And, furthermore, cult-play in a peculiar way dissembles the play of the prevailing world, insofar as it allows the governance of the gods to "appear," sometimes even *as* a kind of play.

We have hitherto characterized cult-play in three stages: first, as the enchantment of masks; then, as magical technique; and finally as the festival-play of a cultic community. Festival-play can assume a variety of forms: it can be the sacred activity of consecration, the solemn service to the god in the great ritual that affords all spectators the sight of a magical-technical interaction of the priest skilled in enchantment with daemons and gods, making those spectators into witnesses of his heavenly contact. With a mixture of dread, anxiety, and hope, primitive human beings watch their medicine man venture to detain the invisible ones, to spellbind, to influence them with mystical formulas and magic spells, to ascertain the ordained future from the flight of birds, from the blood of sacrificial animals, from the convulsions of the torn-out heart of the human sacrificial victim. But festival-play can also be a trustful attempt to invite the gods to partake in fellowship, to produce a community of mortals and immortals in the joy of the feast, amid the sound of musical instruments and songs that sing the glory and praise of the gods. At the end, such festive-celebratory feasts occasionally transition into an orgiastic delirium, a bacchanalian frenzy: human beings become certain of their contact with daemonic supremacy when they lose control of themselves, when they fall into a trance and shed daytime's sober consciousness.

By no means is the orgy of such festivals merely degeneracy, a debauchery of inebriating drink and unbridled eroticism. What may appear to the outside observer as "debauchery" is for the participants of the cult a rapture that lifts them out of the ordinariness of everyday life. And in an entirely different manner, cult-play can have the feature of bringing the divine sphere to presence on the stage; it then becomes ritual dramatic play or spectacle, which narrates the mythos and lets it become visible. Festival play determines the playful from the perspective of the festival, that is, from the presence of the gods that is believed in, intimated, felt. Play then has for the most part an obscure, cumbersome, gloomy character. The overwhelming power of the gods unsettles the human heart with sublime terror. Even the good news of heavenly succor and of the favor of the gods, which is perhaps proclaimed in such festival play, is not entirely able to brighten up the gloomy seriousness. The distance that separates mortals from immortals is too great. Cultic dramatic play or spectacle becomes tragedy. However, with this indication, we do not wish to provide an interpretation of "Attic tragedy," that unique flowering of the human spirit. We take the term "tragedy" here in a more general sense, according to which it means the somber interpretation of human fate in the face of the happiness of the gods without need. As long as festival-play is primarily characterized from the perspective of the festival as the mysterious presence of the gods and the playfulness of cult-play is thus overshadowed by the magic of the cult, a dark seriousness governs the stage. Yet the aspect of play in festival-play can occasionally come into its own so strongly and powerfully that all at once the festival is stamped from the perspective of play, is governed by mirthful delight and lighthearted grace, by the jocular character of free, pure play, by its imaginative exuberance. The satyr-play follows the tragic formulation of the mythos; liberating laughter, the ironic distance to our very selves—comedy—follows the heavy, serious bringing to presence of human suffering and the demise of heroes. And it very much depends on how a mythos supposes the gods to be, whether as serious, formidable powers, in whose proximity no unseemly sound is permitted, or as themselves ambiguous beings, whose sacredness is not profaned by Homeric laughter. And if the festival-play of the cult offers not merely the prevailing gods' coming to presence on the stage, but an elucidation of their peculiar prevailing as a kind of play, then the sense of this elucidation ultimately depends on *how* divine play is characterized. For the ideas we have about such play of the gods can be emphasized in various ways.

To start, let us take, for example, the play-metaphor to describe the unlimited supremacy of the gods vis-à-vis human beings. They interact with us—as with playthings. What does that mean? Is such a characterization sufficiently clear—or does it still allow for different interpretations? How does the playing human being interact with the plaything? What is the characteristic feature of such interaction? And here we must precisely say that human interaction with the plaything can be manifold, not because there are all sorts of playthings, but rather insofar as the interaction may be carried out in different ways. In "playing," we can manipulate any given thing, and in doing so we can even "switch gears" as we please; we can use things we have come across for the ends of our play. We do not need to be especially "attentive" in doing so. The play-use is an entirely different relation to things than, for instance, the utilization-use—at more of a distance, more unbound, freer. When the human being recognizes things in his environment for their utility and prepares them for usage through his work, he is to a high degree bound to the peculiar character of such things, depends on them. He cannot interact and switch gears with respect to them arbitrarily and in any manner. The peasant must look after the soil, which he cultivates for use; he may not work it to exhaustion without destroying its fecundity. The artisan must comply with the material that he works on and presses into artisanal form; his work activity is "materially conditioned" in many ways. Each work is faced with the resistance of the things that are to be formed by the work. It is precisely the rigor of work, its travail, that should be understood from its relation to the independence and indestructibility of formable material. Because the human being must invest so much energy, time, and effort into the products of work, he interacts with them attentively, economically, and frugally. He makes rational, economic use of them. Both in the manufacture and in the utilization of the manufactured product, the arbitrariness of the human being is strictly limited by concrete exigencies. In contrast, playful interaction with things in one's environment is characterized by an extraordinary breadth of arbitrariness and caprice. To handle anything as a plaything hardly demands effort and exertion; it is not at all necessary that natural things first be prepared for play. Certainly, "playing" can also be present when one forms, shapes, and creatively transforms pre-given objects, can experience rapturous delight in the alteration of the given—but transforming is here not work, not travail, not an in-forming [*Ein-Bildung*] of objective forms that are ends and are required by objective needs; rather, forming is the outcome of a plastic drive to play. The child who makes a mud pie plays—but the homeworker who produces dolls and the mechanic who is occupied with the industrial manufacturing of toys for children do not play; they work, and do so no less than those who produce foodstuffs, tools, machines. A plaything can be an artificial thing, formed from human labor, but it can also be any natural thing. For the playing human being can "designate" anything whatsoever as a plaything, thanks to his creative imaginative play. Imaginative play "works magic," bestows an imaginary sense on entirely ordinary things and thus decks them out with magical significations for the players. Of course, there are also playthings that are prepared quite beautifully and that are expensive and have collector's value. Yet the most beautiful and most expensive doll that is to be gotten hold of in a toy store has no more *playworldly* reality than a poor girl's measly rag doll.

The playing human being does not necessarily have to handle his playthings as attentively as his other products of labor, for he can at any time use his imagination to add what has not concretely come to objective form. Play is characterized by this lack of consideration, by this free unboundedness with respect to the material of play. If it is said of the gods that they interact with human beings as with playthings, this unboundedness of their interaction is what is chiefly meant: they can switch gears with respect to mortals according to caprice, whim, and discretion; they *need* have no consideration for mortals, not even as much as the farmer has for the cow that he wants to milk; they *can* plunge human beings into pain, need, misery, and misfortune, and can destroy them, break them down, and devastate them however they please. They are not bound by any consideration or constrained by any dependency; they do not need human beings for their continued existence as the human being needs plants and animals for sustenance. Indeed, they are not nourished by fatted offerings but demand these in order to make the human being conscious of his dependency on divine power, in order to make use of the riven self-consciousness of the children of the earth as the dim mirror of their own glory. The gods play—with human beings as their playthings.

Completely separate from the already touched-on problem of a purification of the archaic representations of God in the direction of the essentially good deity, there is an ambiguity in using the play-metaphor for the activity of the gods—and that is the case because the human enactment of play already includes a twofold relation to the plaything. The interaction with the plaything does not always and perpetually have the just-described fundamental feature of free caprice and arbitrariness, but rather chiefly does when we are assured of our own "self-mastery" in the instance of play, when we delightfully gauge the play-space of our imaginary production in this lived experience. The plaything is then revealed to us in its complete lack of resistance. To a certain degree we can make everything out of it; what we are not able to connect to it in an objective way we can at any time ascribe to it as its imagined sense-property. Now, the freedom of the gods in their interaction with human beings is obviously analogous to this unbound freedom of the human being interacting with the plaything. To know ourselves to be the plaything of those who dwell in the heavens, then, is the acute consciousness of *being at their mercy.* Our fate is not in our power. Whatever we do, however much we try, however hard we work and however valiantly we struggle, the human being is defenseless against the supremacy of the gods. Above all, the play-metaphor characterizes divine Being in its utter supremacy.

But there is also a somewhat differently structured interaction with playthings, in which the feeling of caprice and limitless arbitrariness does not predominate, where the one playing does not experience himself as the free lord of his game. There is also immersion in play, being carried away into the sphere of play, where the player does not reign supreme over his game, but rather to a certain degree is "pulled into it," loses himself in it, "vanishes" in his magical role, is himself held spellbound by the mask that he wears. In carrying out this kind of play the player does not relate to his plaything with the sovereign distance of the ruler, but rather is captivated by his plaything, fascinated by it and bound by it, as it were. Do the gods play—as the human being overwhelmed by play does? Do they play as the child plays, enthralled and taken in by play's spell? Are the gods superior players because of their freedom, because they maintain a distanced relation of free arbitrariness toward the plaything—or are they themselves enchanted players who fall under the power of the magical world? Obviously, the meaning of the human being as a "divine plaything" is to be interpreted in completely different ways depending on whether the play of the gods is assessed as "distance" or as "subjugation." As a rule, the play of the gods is interpreted in mythical representations of God as an unlimited, free disposal over human beings, as a "play of freedom" in relation to them, these marionettes in the hands of God. The play-metaphor, then, does not express much more than the complete exposure of the human being and the complete, unrestricted arbitrariness of divine prevailing. However, here the claim is not being made that the gods are essentially "players," that they need human beings. As a pastime in their endless lives they occupy themselves with the fates of human beings and with reigning over all innerworldly things in general. Their ruling resembles a kind of play and their play a kind of ruling. In only a few myths is the prevailing of the gods understood as being enchanted by a kind of play that also spellbinds them—and thus, at the same time, referred to a still more primordial kind of play, in which even the gods are playthings. In general, however, we have to say that human play that is enacted as archaic cult-activity is a clear example of an enactment of play that spellbinds and enchants the ones playing. The plaything of cult-play does not have the character of arbitrary caprice; on the contrary, it has the character of a profound necessity. Indeed, it is the symbol-laden things—such as the altar, sacrificial offerings, and signs standing in for the presencing of the gods. By means of this cult-play, we relate ourselves with understanding to a divine kind of play, which has a different structure than cult-play itself. By means of a kind of play experienced as "subjugation," we relate ourselves to an almost infinitely distant "play of freedom." Admittedly, this relation takes place in "belief"; it can be described and considered by philosophy as a human belief but is not validly assessed in its claim to truth.

In our context it depends on what implicit relational categories are inherent to the self-understanding of mythological cult-play. Hence we have to distinguish two questions: first, the question of the play-character of cultic play as such, and then the question of the play of the gods who are brought to presence by cult-play. The early human cult has a play-character because it is first and foremost the enchantment of masks. And it is precisely the enchantment of masks because only through the disguise can the human being lose his unambiguity and "participate" in the polysemy characteristic of the daemonic being. Participation in the daemonic in turn makes possible the magical practice of the medicine man and the enchanter-priest. But only in fully developed cult-play with its ritual can the total bringing to presence of the mythos on the stage come to pass, can the history of gods, demigods, heroes, and champions come to appearance in the play-community of the festival. The setting, marked off from ordinary locations and places, becomes the site of manifestation for the total context of all that happens: the whole comes to appear in exemplary fashion in one place within the whole, which thereby obtains an in-finite representative. The separated off, delimited location of the cultic setting becomes a metaphor for the limitless. And as cultic play enfolds the most serious and most sacred events and stories, so too does a play-interpretation of the event enfold all incidents emerging within the total event. By no means does the mythos interpret everything that happens simply as play, not even where it seeks to understand, in the play-metaphor, the prevailing of the gods.

The expression "everything that happens" is easy to misunderstand. It can mean two different things: in the first place, *each* happening, each single process, but then also the comprehensive total-happening that subtends all single events, sustains them, keeps them in motion, and is not simply pieced together as their sum. Even the archaic human being is familiar with many kinds of motion, is familiar with the thrust, throw, fall, even if he could never enumerate them in this way; he is familiar with the kind of motion of lifeless things, the way in which plants grow, the way in which animals prowl, the way in which human beings go about in the spaces of their life. And he understands in an experienced and unreflective manner how such motions are "effected." He understands it when he himself produces, in work, artificial things for his benefit and utility, when he slays the enemy with his weapon. He is aware of the different modes of being a cause, although he does not have a concept of cause that has been thought out. His environment operates in a typical manner. It does not change its *modus operandi* from moment to moment; it persists in a characteristic way, and as a result, it is clear and recognizable in some contexts. Certainly, the human being of early times does not yet have a rigorous concept of causality, which posits an inviolable lawfulness within nature. Nature may still be conceived as entirely full of spirits, in "animistic" terms; one may still suppose a culprit behind every deed, yet this schema of attributing events to culprits is an interpretation, too, which posits a specific style of causation. Every single event is "effected"; each has its "ground." To be sure, thought does not yet pose the question for itself of what the ground of the ground is in each case and thus regressively backward to infinity. Theoretical thought has not yet been awakened. Yet there is already an obscure intimation that the total-happening in its comprehensive wholeness must be understood differently—than incidents *within* the whole. And this happens above all where the prevailing whole is interpreted in its form of motion as play. Things are dependent on one another in their coming and going, their growth and diminishment, their transformation and their exchanging places. They are interwoven in myriad ways; each is the "effect" of an effecting "cause," whether these causes be natural powers, "purposes" endemic to things or even activities of daemons. Here, it is not a matter of the distinction between scientific and mythical understanding but rather of the distinction between a conception of the comprehensive connection of all events, which is "groundless" as such, and the always grounded single events.[26] The whole has no ground and no purpose; it also has no "sense," no task, no goal. The prevailing whole is grasped in the interpretive metaphor of a game. To be sure, one can, of course, also interpret individual processes and incidents as a kind of play; behind anything that happens, one can suspect as culprits kobolds, daemons, or even gods who play their jokes and pranks on us, but then play is only a particular interpretation of the culprit-schema. Instead of gods ruling methodically, one can also suppose that there are "spirits" who delight in games and seek pastimes, who more confuse our human world than order it. However, the play-motif in cultic play first attains its more profound significance when it is referred to the totality and thereby "transcends" innerworldly processes. The truth of the play of the gods is the play of the world.

16. Play and Consecration—Cult-Play and Religion. The Play of the Gods Is Not Itself Cult-Play

The connection between play and cult, which we sought to bring into view primarily in archaic, mythical human existence, opened up for us as an essential imbrication of primordial human phenomena. The human being's drive to worship, at its root, is bound up with the drive to play; the association with superhuman powers is carried out in early historical time in a play-ritual. That is a strange and extraordinary state of affairs that appears more bizarre the more we "self-evidently" proceed from the everyday, current understanding of play and thus emphasize play's features of unboundedness, of arbitrary fancy, of unserious, relaxed merriment and a vagabond levity, and oppose play to the solemn ways of carrying out our lives. For this reason it surprises us to encounter play in the most serious and most solemn activity of the archaic human being's life, in his association with gods and daemons. How could play achieve this status, this elevated significance? Perhaps this question is falsely posed. Perhaps it has nothing at all to do with the fact that human play retains a meaning, which it does not at all have itself, from religion's dimension of sense. Perhaps even that which, in an everyday manner, we call "play" and contrast disparagingly with serious areas of life is already a fallen mode of an erstwhile primordial state. In any case, we need to be clear: cultic play first and foremost must be interrogated in its playfulness and in no way may it be subsumed under the popular concept of play. The cult is not merely "primordial" in its religious aspect but also in its playful aspect. Here, not only is play "consecrated"; "consecration" is also played. Consecration and play permeate one another in the phenomenon of the archaic cult in an almost indissoluble intimacy. Consecration is determined by play and play by consecration. We have sought to make this clear in reference to the enchantment of masks, magical technique, and the dramatic play or *spectacle* that brings the mythos to presence. Insofar as these are aspects of the cult, the cult as such is a playful praxis. It is carried out as an elevated kind of human play that does not merely move within a "sense," maintain itself in an understanding, or stand in an openness to the revelation [*Offenbarkeit*] of prevailing powers; it gives to be understood the sense that is understood, it interprets the revelation, it imparts its knowledge. The cult is always also a making-known, a life-teaching, proclamation. Proclamation is not thereby restricted to the word. It is not confined to the transmission of knowledge by the discourse that imparts. In the realm of the sacred, discourse has a peculiar powerlessness and impotence. We can easily discuss what is readily given to our senses, what lies before our hands and eyes, the things that we work on, the everyday given thing: here everything has its fixed name, its nameability; everything takes an understood, understandable course; everything is already interpreted in language and pre-formed, pre-known, in its typical modes of relation. We have names for inanimate things, for plants and animals, for land and sea and the celestial bodies in the sky—for the devices that we use, for the paths we take, and in general for our whole well-trodden association with beings in our environment. We reside in the midst of things in such a way that in each case we understand, are acquainted with, and designate them not only as solitary individuals. We are placed within a communal public familiarity; we are installed in a language that encompasses us; we reside in a continual social conversation about things that concern us in various ways. Each field of human life has its own modes of understanding and of co-existentiell conversation. The possibilities of making statements about beings and of expressing things with one's fellow human beings are thus not everywhere the same. What is familiar in an everyday sense has the easiest possibility of appearing in the word and being discussed in the small talk of neighbors. To be sure, a spate of words stands ready in the everyday realm even for the sacred; it is initially flattened out into a common familiarity. However, it does not actually allow itself to be held fast therein. It withdraws from availability, from the exploitative utility of everyday conversation. The words that designate the sacred do not indicate plainly present phenomena that are perceptible by everyone at all times; they rather point to a breach[27] of the actuality that is familiar in an everyday manner, to deeper and more primordial grounds of Being. The words that designate the sacred are themselves thoroughly attuned by the terror of the sacred. The human being is not supposed to take the name of the Lord, his God, in vain. The sacred word is beset with taboos. What holds for the cult in general holds once more for the cultic word. It is removed by being excluded from ordinary speech—as the temple precinct is from ordinary land. It is lifted into an elevated, intensified significance, becoming an invocating sign and magical symbol. The magic word also belongs to the cult in its most primordial form—as an invocatory spellbinding of superhuman powers, as a naming of the unnamable. Hierophantic[28] discourse hovers on the verge of saying the unsayable, of invoking in a comprehending and defining word that which, in its incomprehensibility, is above and beyond all comprehension and definition, and of experiencing in the rupturing word the supremacy of the sacred. Cultic knowledge is initially safeguarded as a secret knowledge, transmitted as priestly wisdom, handed down in sacred texts and sealed words; it has an esoteric character and must be protected from all profanation. It is structured in a gradual descent and has a manifold of circles in itself. The inmost circle of knowledge is accessible only to the few who are "initiated" to the highest degree; around it are formed gradually descending steps, in which knowing loses its genuineness and its mystery more and more and finally ends by becoming universally superficial [*Veräußerlichung*]. The consecration that determines the priest for serving the sacred is before all else an initiation, a revelation cloaked in mystery. In its primitive elementary form, for instance, it is the transmission of the medicine man's magical formulas to his younger successor.

Because the cult's language is primordially hierophantic[29] and is determined only for the priesthood in the highest tension between saying and the unsayable, the proclamation of religious teachings on life does not exclusively happen in the word—it initially happens far more in signs and gestures, in ritual activities of an immediate, heart-rending symbolic power. The cultic community is witness to the enchantment of masks, to the magical techniques of priests who perform sacrifices, and, above all, to the dramatic play or spectacle that places the mythos visibly before their eyes. What the sacred and its irruption into the light of day are becomes clear to the cultic community by more than the expressed word when they see symbolic activities. The burying of the grain seed, its sinking into the dark, lightless ground of earth, and the offering of the ripe ear of corn brings the connection of downfall and resurrection, of death and life, into a simple, valid metaphor for the simple soul [*Gemüt*]. And if at the high point of sacred activity in the cult of Demeter the cult members put their hands into the *kistē*, into the womb of the great mother, then, run through by a shudder of enraptured anxiety, they surely perceived the inexhaustibility of existence vouched for in the power of giving birth. And the spectators of the sacred play, which brought the mythos into visibility, were situated as spectators, as eyewitnesses before the epiphany of the divine. As spectators they played along. Still, the cult community in festival-play does not resemble the ancient circus. In the historical trajectory of humanity it comes to pass in various ways that the cultic ritual fades more and more, recedes further and further, while what takes the upper hand is the doctrine, the promulgation in the words of the prophet and preacher. Priestly knowledge loses its basic esoteric feature, becoming a universally issued revelation that only needs to be explained in the proper manner from sacred texts. The more religion becomes a religion of the promulgated word, a kind of good news, and the more it maintains its emphasis in what is sayable, the more does the magical substance, the mythical dramatic play or spectacle, that which is playful in the cult in general, vanish. Certainly there remain relics, remnants in the ceremonial gestures of a liturgy, which, however, are an exhausted ceremoniousness rather than a genuine ritual play. The religious community appears in only a few sacramental activities as a witness and co-player. The connection between play and cult in the archaic early forms of religion is much more starkly given and more decisively discernible than in the historically advanced religions. However, if the early cult is carried out as a kind of human play that is rich in meaning, then this play expresses a total interpretation of life, expresses it more in ritual gestures, in metaphorical activities, than in words. Cult-play gives something to be understood. It is addressed to its community. What it gives to be understood in its symbols, metaphors, and mythological activities is the way in which the gods reign, the way in which they conduct their regime over human beings and finite things in general, the way in which they steer and direct the fate of individuals, of heroes and demigods, but also of the most wretched servant, the way in which they bring about the splendor and downfall of peoples and empires, the way in which they send weather and thereby dispense favor or disfavor for the fields, the way in which they give all and take all. Certainly, the cult always clarifies the great connections of sense that prevail throughout everything that lives and that secure borders within the inanimate realm between land and sea, between the open heavens and the sealed earth. Every cult has an overarching sense, a universal signification. But the cult variously interprets the total context of all things and the particular position of the human being in the midst of nature and in the sight of the gods. The cult is a play of sense-interpretation [*Sinn-Deutungsspiel*].

By far most cults, being in each case such a play of interpretation, are related to the total character of events insofar as they thereby posit and use human phenomena of existence as paradigms for the movement of the whole. To be sure, we always know that the movement of human beings is interwoven in the encompassing movement of the comprehensive context and is determined from there, but we have no ideas, concepts, or words at hand for the motion of the totality. We can only clarify it for ourselves at all by employing, as metaphorical likenesses, manners of movement that are phenomenally pre-given, but we can at the same time be aware of the inadequacy of such metaphors. The reign of the gods is for the most part posited in the cult on analogy with human phenomena of existence, namely, ruling and work. Human beings imagine the gods to be superhuman rulers and superhuman workers. And the gods are not only imagined in such a way that they accomplish to a far greater extent what human beings do; their ruling and work is not only quantitatively superior to that of the human; they rule in another way and work in another way—divine rule and divine work are qualitatively distinct from all human works. Their rule cannot be resisted; their work is more potent and lasting. In their case, ruling means the establishment of the order of all things in general, the taming of chaos, the regulation of the celestial trajectories and the change of the seasons, the steering of human fates. The rule of the gods is not limited to the human realm; it extends to all beings that stand *under* the highest being, the divine—it extends to the whole gradually descending hierarchy of things, to the human being, beast, plant, and stone. Human ruling is always a precarious and unstable affair; it is always threatened by the revolt of those being ruled, by the rebellion of the oppressed. The human being is not able to rise up against the rule of the gods. They effortlessly crush the transgressor. Their ruling does not contain within it the quaking tension that makes the souls of tyrants and Caesars tremble, with pleasure and at the same time with dread. Gods do not rule over those who are equally free. To be sure, the human being has the freedom to be able to oppose the will of the gods, yet he can only seal this freedom with his own doom. It was not the boast of Niobe that brought the curse on her offspring, nor the blasphemy of Latona, but rather the fact that she had dared to make the highest and fullest happiness of the earthly woman, her fruitful motherhood, distinct from the realm of the gods' blessings and wished to ground it in the earthly power of her almost inexhaustible womb alone. Every attempt of mortals to elude the rule of the gods leads to their doom. And supposing that death is not the complete end of human existence, then the human being, who would sooner choose death than bear the rule of the gods over him, would fall prey to the heavenly ones by this heroic act only still more hopelessly. He can no longer "bail out" of the otherworldly life; he would have to experience, unceasingly and without end, that it "is a fearful thing to fall into the hands of the living God."[30] To be sure, with the representation of a "patriarchal" regime, with the idea of a divine "father," who comports himself to human beings as to his "children," religions often temper these thoughts—which dissolve all human pride—of the inescapable rule of the gods that is impossible to resist. But if human beings feel like children of God, they do not know themselves as young gods, in the way that human children know themselves to be young humans. The human being's divine filiation does not annul the abyssal difference between God and the human being; it only tempers it and dampens the severity of the separation. Because rule, as wielded by the heavenly ones, is not threatened by the opposed tension of those who are ruled and by a possible reversal of the relation of rule, the model for the prevailing of the gods, abstracted and borrowed from human existence, is ultimately a faulty metaphor: they rule, but precisely beyond every standard that is understandable to human beings. And it is similar to those paradigmatic representations that describe the activity of the gods as work. They certainly do not work as we do, we who are able to keep ourselves in existence only by the activity of work. They work in a sense that is heightened beyond every human measure, indeed, beyond every human power of representation. They do not work on beings already existent; they bring things about for the first time. And, to be sure, not any old artificial things, which the human being, too, is able to produce on the basis of pre-given material, by imposing and stamping on natural material a form deriving from the human intellect through the activity of his hands or by means of tools and machines. One says of the gods that they produce natural things, that they do not need pre-given material in order to work on it; rather, the whole of nature, which for human beings is otherwise the scene of their acting and doing, the quarry for their raw materials, is already a divine work. This thought transcends the representational power of our finite understanding and withdraws into religious mystery. In a certain sense, the god of Platonic metaphysics also performs such "work," insofar as he produces the beautiful and well-ordered dispensation of the *cosmos* from the amorphous stuff of the world, interweaving the measureless, the *apeiron,* with the measure, the *peras.* The labor of the Platonic god is an ontogenetic occupation; it is a bringing into shape of nature—but from primordial ontological powers, from matter and intellect, from *chōra* and *nous.* God as conceived by Christianity, on the other hand, is able, by the pronouncement of his omnipotence, to wrest nature and all natural things—from nothing. In regard to the Christian god, the metaphor of work becomes sense-less through an extreme intensification. The creator of the world does not "work," even if the account in Scripture speaks of a "rest" on the seventh day. If the myths tell of works of the gods, these are, nevertheless, far, far removed from the unfortunate exertion of human work; they are effortless and easy. The idea that appears best—from the human side—is the idea that ruling and work among the gods is at bottom a *kind of play.* And in a few cults this vision of the divinity of the gods becomes determinative for their sense. Cult-play then brings to presence the prevailing of the gods as ruling or as work, as effortless holding sway and effortless working, not only *in* a kind of play; it interprets divine life, in the way it is carried out, as a kind of playing. The cult-play of the human being sets the play of the gods into the visibility of the scene, lets them become manifest in regard to their essence, in their inconceivable, effortless success. We already said that such divine play is distinct from all human kinds of playing, that it must be a much freer, indeed an infinitely free playing in comparison to even the most buoyant, dancelike human kinds of play. However, if, in playing, the gods rule nature and all things, then their play, nevertheless, has the character of a causality that conditions the course and transformation of things. Nature and everything that is natural, according to such a perspective, attains the determination of a plaything. The course of nature then is not a kind of play, but rather only the life of the blessed gods, who make use of all other things that are below their sphere as playthings and works of play. As a kind of play, this life of the gods that is blessed with play [*spielselig*] has no ends that lie outside it—it knows only internal ends for play, which the gods posit just as easily as they again annul. Their activity is "without responsibility," is "beyond good and evil," is—to speak with Nietzsche's Zarathustra—"a wheel rolling out of itself."[31] The lack of ends, absence of aims, and senselessness of the life of the gods that is brought forth in play does not exclude the fact that many immanent ends and aims emerge, but they do not thereby give sense and purpose to the whole of life. The course of life of the gods is not determined by a painfully felt lack—as is the case for finite human beings.

We have our daily aims, tasks, and ends, because with our whole life we head toward an aim, toward an end: toward the aim of *eudaimonia*. Our manifold strivings, despite all the diversity of our interests, are nevertheless gathered and conducted by an ultimate and extreme concern with the success or failure of life. We *are* not, we incessantly *become*—and perhaps never arrive at a conclusive form, and until death we are a project for ourselves. We do not live carefree in a peacefully abiding present; we are carried away by the raging stream of time, whose uncanny movement we observe with trepidation: care breathes down our neck and never actually lets us free of its pressing grip. Certainly, from time to time we can numb ourselves, we can abandon ourselves to distractions and forget our needs and tasks—but care overtakes us again, flushes us out of every contrived comfort, pushes us onto the course of our restless strivings, drives, passions, and desires. The human care for life is not only economic, it is also the concern for the "salvation of the soul," for the one thing that is essential, concern for insight and the clarification of life. The pervasively projective manner in which the human conducts his life secures all particular purposes and individual aims to the final aim that is sought after, but not given with infallible certainty. Here only the *child* appears to be an exception, who is in the present, abides peacefully, and almost has eternity in the dreamily assured way of simply being there and not asking why and wherefore. There is only a short span of time in which the child exists no longer merely vegetatively and not yet in intellectual freedom, where it lives purely and in an unbroken way in play. These are golden days in the existence of each human being, memory's most precious treasure, which brightens the whole of life with its radiance—and is unforgettable, even if we are no longer able to imagine the time that has elapsed. This paradise lost of childhood is the paradigm for our belief in blessedly playing gods. From here, in a certain way, we can devise and above all get a feeling for how the play of the gods might be. Their superhuman life would then resemble that of "the child, who moves the pieces back and forth"—it would be a "kingdom of the child."[32]

The saying of Heraclitus we just drew from does not speak of the gods' play, however; it speaks of the play of *aiōn,* of the play of the course of the world. In the metaphor of the playing child, a kind of play is thought that is still more profoundly distinguished from human play in general than human play is from the play of the gods—a *game* in which all things are wagered, all affairs and all persons, whether they be gods or human beings, and which thus has no player. Is this not an absurd and impossible thought: a game without players, a game without a person who is playing, without a who? As long as the orientation to cult-play drives our posing of the question we must inevitably think that, for every kind of play, there is a player playing it as well. Cult-play brings to presence the prevailing of the gods and interprets this "prevailing" as a super-human rule or as a super-human work; in both interpretations rule and work come into an astounding[33] proximity to play, above all through the features of effortlessness, groundlessness, and the impossibility of resistance. And sometimes the mythologem of cult-play interprets the activity of the gods themselves as a free, unencumbered playing of halcyon cheerfulness. The human being coincides with the god from an astronomical distance—both are players, the god wholly, the human being in part, insofar as he is additionally a worker, fighter, lover, and mortal; the god plays with everything that is outside him—as with his plaything; he need not regard anything at all as higher than himself; all other beings stand under him, are positioned as his footstool, are only an embellishment of his throne. And because he is set above all other beings, because he is not surpassed by anything, his playing does not have—as human play does—the character of imaginary representation; he need not open up a site for the symbolic manifestation of omnipotence by means of a "non-actual play-world." The play of the gods, for its part, does not have the features of cult-play. Gods do not believe in gods; they do not religiously revere a highest god. Undeniably, the myths of peoples have told of a hierarchy in the realm of the gods, have spoken of a father or king of the gods; nevertheless, these are completely different manners of relation than those of human beings to the heavenly ones. One can rather say that the gods relate to one another in like manner and yet again relate to one another in an immeasurably inflated fashion, just as human beings relate to other human beings. They are inclined to contend with one another or to enter into amorous liaisons, to be joined by ties of kinship; thus they revere one another, yet not in a religious form. God—as the object of religion—himself has no religion.

It is something else in the case of daemonic intermediate beings, which the human belief in gods posits in various ways: in the case of angels and suchlike. They have religion, albeit not as "belief," but rather as "knowledge," insofar as they live within view of the divinity, in the *visio beatifica*. If through cult-play we thus bring the play of the gods to presence, too, the latter itself can no longer be cult-play. That is an important structural insight. Cult-play does not allow itself to be iterated. However, instances of play can otherwise generally be included in each other in manifold ways.[34]

Let us briefly summarize the results of our reflection on the connection between play and cult. The cult is the distinctive phenomenon of life in which play precisely[35] does not occur in the all-too-popular and all-too-familiar character of the "playful" and is not revealed as "a lack of seriousness" or as "idle"; in the cult it has the urgent, uncanny, and spellbinding basic feature of enchantment, the rapture that removes the human being from his everyday straightforwardness and fixed determinacy. The mask here is not so much concealment for the masked one as it is rather human access, the door to the realm of daemons. It not only enchants the spectators; above all it enchants the wearer of the mask—turns him into an enchanter, into a medicine man, a priest, a mediator between the uncanny and invisible realm of "spirits" and his fellow human beings. Precisely in the case of cultic symbols, the enchanter-priest's praxis is starkly pervaded by elements of play; play is at work in the bringing to presence of the prevailing whole through the proof of the shining back [*Rückschein*] of the whole into what is partial. The initiatory enchantment that belongs to magical technique is based on the reversal of this relation—the whole can be influenced by the part, if the part is the symbol of the whole. And the mythological dramatic play or spectacle must also be brought into this context; not only does it make evident what the dominant, over-powering forces are to which the human being is abandoned, and not only does it orient—it is also efficacious, in a practical manner. If the human being brings the powers to epiphany in the dramatic play or spectacle, powers to which he knows he is fully exposed and handed over, then he accomplishes at the same time an atonement and a purification, a catharsis of the soul—a purification that should be thought of differently than the way in which the aesthetic theory of early metaphysics formulates it in Aristotle's *Poetics*. Cult-play can "purify" an entire city. Cult-play relates to the gods—brings to presence their superhuman rule and work—and their superhuman play, too, in words and in ritual gestures. The play of the gods, however, remains a kind of play that is played by a person. It always has someone playing, whether he is veiled or unveiled, who moves the pieces back and forth. As will become apparent to us, these are important structures that, in such a context, could only come up in cult-play. The entirety of the cult is certainly not playful, and play, too, in its entirety is not primordially only cultic. Already in the earliest human horde there are the games of children; there are aspects of play in the meeting of the sexes, in courtship, in refusal and assent; there are kinds of play with an excessive martial power, such as martial dances and contests; and, finally, the manifold pranks of everyday life.

Yet cult-play predominates in archaic times—and the other modes of play remain subordinated to it and occasionally receive an enchanting sheen from it. If we now leave cult-play aside, we must remain conscious of the fact that a great problem is left behind whose surface has hardly been scratched. To be sure, there is an immense ethnological literature about the early cult and the magical meanings of dances and dramatic plays or spectacles. A philosophical understanding of the assembled facts, however, could first be attained or at least prepared, only once the categorial clarification of the structures of play had made progress. The cult is not only a problem of play—it is above all a theological problem. The genuine theological question is not a concern *for us;* it transcends the framework of a philosophizing self-understanding of the finite human being. Does it do so in the way that pure sunshine transcends the twilit caves in which we dwell, or like the Fata Morgana transcends the desert sand? Who can know this—except God alone or those whom he calls to be the hearers of his word?

17. Nature "Full of Gods" in Myth, Empty of Gods in Late Culture. Critique of Religion on the Model of "Self-Alienation." The Question Concerning the Worldliness of Play Is neither Sacred nor Profane

With the bracketing out of the theological question, cult-play already came into our view in an abridged form; it had revealed itself to us *only* as an anthropological phenomenon. In itself, however, cult-play is a kind of play before God, consecration-activity, archaic practice of enchantment, mantic joining of the human realm with the heavenly powers of fate—is an elevated, solemn, and festive association of the human race with the divine. The intimate binding of religion and play belongs to the wonderful and primordial mysteries of early human existence. The human being of late culture has only sparse memories of this prehistory, when all was still full of gods; they are submerged memories in the collective unconscious that light up from time to time, flash like lightning in our mundane day, which is saturated with the droning of motors, with the workshop din of our technological civilization, with the battle cry of ideologies and with the hectic bustle of our businesses. The human being of our age has a long history full of transformations behind him—a history in the course of which he reorganized himself in increasing measure with the products of his productive power, inserted himself into his self-created environment of artificial things manufactured through work activity, weaved himself into the fabric of his diverse creations of freedom, and perhaps[36] alienated himself from his very self in the objectification of his deed. This historical trajectory is just as magnificent as it is uncanny: the earth is covered over with the traces of human structures and destruction, accomplishments and laying waste, work and war. The globe has been marked by the human being. It is no longer natural wilderness—it has been, on the whole, forcefully pulled into the history of the human being. It is the theater of this restless species, the material for its labor, the field for its battles.

This historicization of the earth in the historical course of human work and the struggles for power and rule occurs, however, at the same time as the human being increasingly becomes "terrestrial": at the same time as there is a dismantling of the religious interpretation of human life and a progressive decline of mythical substance. Certainly, the process of the dwindling of religion has not yet reached its dismal end; powerful life energies still exist in the great religions present today—but the decisive controversy, which cuts humanity in two, revolves around the interpretation of the economic process, around the explication and the proper ordering of the productive forces moving the course of history. This controversy is carried out with religious fervor, or better: it has drawn to itself the most intimate interests of the human being, which otherwise were worked out in religion. One can even formulate the global controversy as follows: it is not at all the case that both world-political camps are only distinguished by their conceptions of the economic process, of the regulation of the economy. They are distinguished above all by their conception of the position of human work activity, whether it is a field of life alongside others or whether it is the central field of life; they are distinguished in the radicality with which they conceive the historicization of the earth as the becoming-terrestrial of the human being. In the time of early humans the earth is predominantly wilderness, hardly scratched by the feeble productive powers of archaic technology. As wilderness, this earth is full of gods and populated by daemons; it radiates in a magical, enchanting light; it affects the human soul with sublimity and terror. And it is only in play, in the form of human play that is elevated by the cult, that the human being who is beguiled by its radiance and made anxious by its terror is able to draw near to the forces prevailing throughout the earth—not in work and not in struggle. The historical trajectory of the human being not only brings along an unfolding of the uniquely human power; it initially brings a purification and an elevated development of the archaic belief in daemons and gods, and thus an unfolding of religion into the great, historical religions, but also then their decline in connection with the shifting of humanity to the spirit of science and the industrial technology thereby made possible. In this the unique power of the human being appears to triumph. The human being becomes "terrestrial," now not in a sense that refers to the earth as wilderness, but rather that understands the earth as the disenchanted dwelling place of humanity producing its own life itself. This earth is empty of gods.

Such a way of speaking is easily misunderstood. No dogmatic claims about the object of religion are intended to be made here. We are not saying that there were gods in archaic human existence and that there are no longer gods in modern human existence. We are speaking only about the human phenomena of belief and disbelief. "Full of gods" and "empty of gods" are meant as anthropological expressions. The numinous shudder that emanated from nature as wilderness wrenched the human being of early times beyond himself, impelled relations to the super-human, motivated offering and sacrifice. The archaic human being interpreted his position, his exposure, in cultic gestures of play and from such knowledge practiced magic healing practices. He could not remain within himself, could not stay in the closed circuit of human things—he had to hold human things out into the storms of heaven and the originating powers of the earth. He had to seek contact with divine forces, had always to surpass himself. In contrast, the human being of scientific late culture appears to be characterized by a closing off of the human essence, by a resolute turning away from superhuman forces in the attempt to ground humanity on itself. At one time this was carried out as the rational critique of religion, as its reinterpretation as a phenomenon of a utopian self-alienation; at another time, however, it was carried out still more decisively as the self-objectification of the human being in the freedom of his work activity. The human being is conceived of as unable to placidly remain in himself like the animal and plant. He is conceived of as having to "go beyond" himself, having to surpass himself—but the "surpassing" is shifted onto the human being himself: in his creative power he first forms the dimensions within which this surpassing happens—his freedom, one says, is not only an interior capacity of the self-determination of his will; it is above all a capacity of sensuous-objective production, the objectification of a human sense in an object. Freedom occurs as work and as struggle. As work and as struggle, human freedom forms the dimensions within which it expresses [*aüßert*] itself and at the same time thereby externalizes [*entäußert*] itself from itself. The field of externalization belongs indissolubly to human freedom; it surpasses itself within itself, so to speak. Admittedly, it thus depends on an environing nature; yet it does not let this stand as it is in itself, but rather imprints on it, from the uniquely human power, the stamp of its free deed, makes it into the material for its work activity, into the site for the externalization [*Veräußerung*] of spirit.

The survey of the structure of the externalization of freedom, as it is achieved above all in the conceptual penetration into work, is now variously projected back even onto religion from polemical motives. One attempts to "interpret" religion from out of work not by interpreting religion as a kind or a prototype of work, but rather by "applying" the schema of the self-objectification and self-externalization of human freedom achieved in work to religion. One then says: the human being in the religious attitude of life first of all forms the dimension of the sacred, which he then populates with the creatures of his subconscious imagination; in the appearance of what is "alien" he transfers to the beyond what the ground of his own soul is; the superhuman is a *Fata Morgana* of the human heart and the dream-woven human act of representation. The truth of religion would be the human being. The human being would not be an image, a likeness

[*Ebenbild*] of God, but God a dreamed-up likeness of the human being. It is an old feature of religious critique to explain the gods from out of the wishful fancies of human beings; it is, however, a more recent feature of the modern critique of religion to leave the structure of "transcendence" to the divine and precisely to derive[37] it, with all its transcendence, from an illusory self-externalization and self-alienation of the human being. This possibility was first prepared by the absolute idealism of Hegel, propagated by Feuerbach in a strident battle slogan, brought by Marx into close connection with the structure of labor, and unfolded by Nietzsche in the attempt at a world-historical unmasking of Christianity, metaphysics and Western morals. Hegel's philosophy opened up the possibility of allowing the harshest and deepest oppositions to cross over into one another; it is a philosophy of universal transition, of mediation, that just as much sets apart as encloses together, a philosophy of the total movement structuring and joining all, a movement of the streaming of Being through all beings. "Everything flows"; flowing Being is the life of Spirit, the concept conceiving itself—however, it is not what is without distinction, but what distinguishes itself within itself, the stream of unity in which negativity is perpetually at work as diremption, as the allowing of oppositions to break open and as the destruction of antitheses. Hegel turns against unity without distinction, against "the night in which all cows are black,"[38] just as much as he turns against rigidly maintaining fixed distinctions. Everything hinges on thinking the "absolute" as a stream and as a delimited determination, as a movement and as a thing, as the one-and-all [*All-Eine*] and as the dirempted. For this reason, for Hegel there are no ultimate, indissoluble distinctions: not the distinction between finite and infinite, nor between the human being and God; the finite being is conceived as self-finitization, as the temporary form of the infinite. The human being is interpreted as God still[39] concealed within his majesty.[40] What essentially "is," is transition. The life of absolute Spirit is determined by a perpetual self-externalization and a perpetual return home to itself. Especially revealing in this connection is Hegel's concept of "self-consciousness." By this is not meant the plain and simple self-knowing of a spiritual being, which can for instance say "I" to itself, thus not ego-consciousness in distinction to object-consciousness, but rather that knowledge which is achieved in the movement of thought, which breaks through the phenomenal alienness of the external object, recognizes itself as Spirit precisely in what is apparently alien to Spirit, finds *itself* in *another,* and thereby conceives the other as its own[41] self-externalization. By means of this, the phenomenal distinction between self-consciousness and alien-consciousness is sublated—and a speculatively elevated model of self-consciousness determines the idea as "absolute knowing." And ultimately Hegel can therefore designate his *Science of Logic* as the "thoughts of God": the thinker has passed over into God, because earlier God had alienated himself into the human being. God and the human being are in the transition, are not entities that are fixed and divided in fixed ways; they are poles of the extensive oscillating movement of Spirit or of the absolute Idea. The difference between God and the human being is ultimately conceived from the perspective of a unity of life that is encompassing, but also self-dirempting and from this diremption self-restoring. The surpassing of the human being toward God is not grasped as a relation to another being that is higher and exceedingly powerful—it is understood as self-transcendence, or, better, as a return from a self-externalization: the relation of alienation is dissolved into a self-relation. Yet this does not succeed in such a way that the "phenomenon" of alienness can be made to disappear entirely by means of speculative thought; it is only "re-interpreted," interpretively turned around [*um-interpretiert*]. Alienness comes into the self-relation as *self-alienation.* The concept of "self-alienation" in Hegel is related to the absolute, to Spirit,[42] to the Idea. The concept of "self-alienation" means a self-alienation of the concept; it alienates itself from itself when it crosses over into "nature," becomes external, sinks into the apparently spiritless, in order to then go from this being-outside-of-itself in the sphere of externality, of spatio-temporal determination, into itself and to "recollect" itself as a movement of knowing and of thinking, to realize its being-one-with-itself, its self-possession through a long course of steps. Self-alienation and self-attainment are stations on the way in the movement of Spirit, which is the actual and the true as the streaming of Being in the Being of all beings, one that is perpetually rent asunder by the negativity endemic to it.

Among the epigones of Hegel who attempted "to put his philosophy on its feet," self-alienation becomes the basic feature of the human essence. If, in Hegel, the human was such as he initially and for the most part understands himself—simply a creature of nature, caught precisely in the self-alienation of absolute Spirit—then the situation is "inverted" by Feuerbach and Marx, and likewise by Nietzsche, too. Idealist philosophy is henceforth taken to be a conceptually ponderous and utopian self-alienation of the human being, a losing of the self in dreamy thoughts without true reality. Philosophy becomes a decided and resolute anthropology—but not even anthropology in the sense of an already familiar individual scientific discipline; philosophy becomes the interpretation of the human being, insofar as all questions converge on it as on a focal point. In the doctrine of the idealist-illusory self-alienation, the dimension of the super-human is retracted into the human being; the human being is interpreted as the actual basis of actual representations of non-actual phantoms—the dimension of environmental things is understood by way of work as material or as a construct of human work activity. Only because this anthropology operates with the basic thought of self-alienation, borrowed from Hegel's philosophy but reinterpreted, can it relate all beings in general to the human being and become that post-idealist philosophy of reflection that purports to grasp, in the human being, the quintessence of all beings.

Two relations of the human being to other beings thus suggest themselves: the relation of alienness and the relation of self-alienation. When the relation of alienness is taken as a basis, the human being is considered separate in his mode of Being from the Being of other things: he exists in a different way than a stone, flower, or horse—but also differently than daemons and gods. He lives in an understanding of alien modes of Being, without being able to be, himself, the alien being of another kind. He surpasses, with understanding, his own Being. For example, in cult-play he comports himself to superhuman powers. The situation of the human being appears to be entirely different when the relation of self-alienation is predominantly taken as a basis in order to elucidate the manifold relations of the human being to things in his environment. In a certain way, the human being is then everything; even what is apparently non-human is nevertheless bound to the human in a latent concealment. The surpassing remains within the realm of the human field of life; the "transcendence" of beings is interpreted as humanity's "transcendental" sense-horizon. Both fundamental possibilities of interpreting the human relation to surrounding beings have become very important for philosophy, because they are conceived as almost fixed alternatives. Either we comport ourselves to alien beings that are in themselves not originally related to the human being and not dependent on him, *or* we comport ourselves to an "in-itself" that is only secretly posited by us; we alienate ourselves into a seemingly self-standing and human-free sense-construct and are only able in the highest effort of philosophical thinking to break through the appearance of "alienness" and to find out that we are the *architects* of such constructions. The alternative runs: the human being comports himself either to beings that determine him or to such beings as he determines—either to things-in-themselves or to constructs of his own self-alienation. This "alternative" has its existentielly sharpest form in the realm of religion: the human being prays to the god who has made him, or prays to the god whom he has himself made.

However, if here, in the context of the question concerning the essence of play, we bracket out the religious connection that thoroughly determined and sustained play in the early years of the human race, and restrict our gaze to only its anthropological content, this does *not* occur by way of the thought of self-alienation. The human being who to a certain degree is everything, who refers the gods, the superhuman beings, back to himself as the spawn of his dreams and who interprets nature as material for work and as a field of his own self-objectification, is no longer left for us. The human being that does remain for us is the one who comports himself to the *totality of the world before* all relations to *beings*, the totality of the world from which the lowest and highest things first arise at all. Such a relation is neither a relation to what is alien nor a relation to the self. What it is in itself must be ascertained [*erfragt*] in the first place. We are attempting to ask about [*fragen*] it by interrogating [*befragen*] human play. The bracketing out of the religious significations does not leave behind a kind of play that would be lacking in significance; sacred cult-play does not become "worldly" through a methodical dimming of its religious motifs—at most it thereby becomes "profane." The profanation of cult-play is a process that comes about in a variety of ways in the history of culture, a process that for the most part happens slowly but is also occasionally actualized in rapid and sudden upheavals, for instance, when one cult prevails over another, achieving an acknowledged predominance; then it can still happen that the cult that had been overcome withdraws into the inconspicuousness of a mere kind of play. What was once an invocation of the gods becomes a song in a children's game [*Spielsang eines Kinderspiels*]; an activity originally intended for ritual becomes the mere convention of playful conduct in a game of entertainment [*Unterhaltungsspiel*]. Much of what in everyday life is only a curious product of play [*Spielwerk*], an ancient tradition of play [*Spielsitte*], is a relic of archaic practices. The ruins of play, too, and not only that of cities and empires, litter the battlefield of history. Admittedly, for the most part, the profaning of cultic play arises from its dissipation in time. To be sure, it is shielded against such dissipation more than everyday customs; its hieratic feature acts to preserve it. But even the most venerable things trickle away in endless time. Life never remains stationary; it is movement.[43] And ultimately religions and mysteries change, too, even if more slowly than the constructs of ruling and of work. Forgetting spreads out over every instance of human knowledge, like a cloud in the sky, initially scarcely visible, but then expanding more and more; every act of knowing is a theft from an original forgottenness, and this theft is avenged, slowly but inevitably. It is a great illusion to believe that the human race in its collective memory retains all cultures that have lived, that it lives in the continuity of an unbroken chain of memory through countless generations. Certainly, possessions are carried forward from one generation to another, and there are amazing cohesive links throughout the centuries.

But much more powerful than every retention and preservation is the power of forgetting, the immense, ruinous power of time. Everything falls victim to its gnawing teeth, the mountains and sea, stellar nebulae—and, in a much more essential sense, the Being of the human being with all his creations, with all his upsurges and deeds, his conquests and his sufferings. What we retain in time and are able to keep for a while is only a fraction of what we lose in it. The trajectory of human history is a trajectory of perpetual losses, and this far more than a course of new conquests and discoveries. Even the hieratically assured cults fall into ruin—not always in such a way that they are simply supplanted by new cults or other life forces. They fall into ruin by starting to become "habit." They become rigid in a popular currency. The sense of brightness that in the beginning suffused them with the most acute tension between what is unsayable and what can be said disappears; the enchanting moment recedes and an apparent "common sense [*Verständigkeit*]" gains the upper hand. Cults die, too, by being "demythologized." The religious festival-play loses its binding character that gathers the community into the presencing of a god; festival-play remains, but the gods withdraw and quietly abandon the land when human hearts no longer blaze with desire for, and feel timidity in the face of, them—when human hearts have "settled down" in a skillful, almost professional interaction with the sacred. "For when it's over and Day's light gone out /"—as we find in Hölderlin's hymn "Germania"—"The priest is the first to be struck, but lovingly / The temple and the image and the cult / Follow him down into darkness, and none of them now may shine. / Only as from a funeral pyre henceforth / A golden smoke, the legend of it, drifts / And glimmers on around our doubting heads. . . ."[44] In the history of the human being there are perhaps no events more disturbing than the toppling of the beloved images of the gods. Nothing strikes the substance of our existence harder. If human empires pass away, states collapse, and buildings decay, human life affected by such ephemerality can always still, being anchored, have knowledge in the "non-ephemeral" and be grounded in the sacred; it still knows its place and is positioned by the relation to the divine on solid, reliable hinges. However, when cults collapse and lose their sheltering, retentive power, the human being is cast out into an uncanny confusion, where he knows neither path nor bridge, where he no longer knows what the proper life is, what good and what evil are, what honor and what glory are, what disgrace and what infamy are. The divine is that great star by which for millennia humanity "orients" its dangerous path and peoples commence their historical passage. When cults petrify, peter out into feeble habits, and ancient images of the gods topple, a new star is usually already ascendant from the night in such dark times. The question is only whether it is always so and must always be so. Who can say what is happening in our time? Have the great religions on earth become exhausted—does a new faith somewhere reveal itself, a new manifestation of divine power? Or is there only a profound renewal, a reformation of the old faith and its churches? Are not merely a few images of gods now toppled, but rather all such images? Does human freedom not take its most extreme risk when it renounces all superhuman commitments and, alone, proclaims the formative-creative power of the human will as the unconditioned ground of its terrestrial existence?

What is happening today and what the time has truly come for cannot be expressed validly by individuals, perhaps because individuals can no longer have a superhuman legitimation, are no longer prophets and mouthpieces of the deity, but rather small waves in the immense human surge. With an extreme skepticism we doubt every purported herald's office, whether one may believe[45] it to be speaking in the name of God or as the mouth[46] of Being itself. In the end, a residue of "theology" remains lodged in all philosophemes that are conceived as "mandates." Yet if one is mistrustful of such claims, then on the other hand the human being is not thus absolutized, not understood as an utterly self-ruling power on its own, to which nothing superhuman would be opposed. Our age probably stands at the furthest remove from the primordial state of early times, when everything was still full of gods—it is probably the time of the greatest emptiness of gods so far, of the greatest dwindling of religious substance, which one ordinarily characterizes as "nihilism." As long as one characterizes nihilism only from the perspective of the phenomenon of religion, thus describing and deploring it as the growing wasteland of modern godlessness, the *opportunity* concealed in it is not caught sight of. This consists not merely in the fact that for the first time in his history the human being can attempt to ground himself solely and exclusively in his productive power and to achieve the European Enlightenment in a free self-production not bound by any metaphysical models. The opportunity lies more[47] in a possible openness to the world that would no longer be "mediated" by a highest being and would also no longer be disguised by this mediation. The thinking through of human play leads to such an openness to the world when human play is entirely detached from its cultic origins and—this is especially important—when this detachment is not carried out as a profanation of cult-play. The worldliness of playing does not emerge gradually in the dismantling of its primeval-religious character. We do not at all attain the worldedness[48] of existence by mere "processes of secularization" that only sap a religious substance and a "spiritual" interpretation of life. For that reason we have emphatically turned against the idea that the concept of human play pertaining to the world could be assessed to a certain degree as an echo-phenomenon of the cult. Profanation is itself a historical possibility that belongs to the sacred as such and is the mode of its decomposition in the weathering of time. The "profane" is initially the forecourt of the temple where ordinary everyday life surges up to the walls of the sacred but is still strictly separated from it; the name of the forecourt becomes the term for the whole sphere of life from which the sacred precinct was demarcated, against which it is set apart and which it elevates in such a separation. The sacred *and* the profane realms together constitute for the first time the whole of the religious world; however, the dividing borders between the two zones belonging together are not irrevocably fixed. For the most part, they have a stable cohesiveness in early historical times; the actual passage of history pulls even the sacred orders into the unrest within it and the borders are breached in various ways. There is also already a breach of sacred order when the money-lenders and the exchangers of currency spread themselves out in the temple and defile its sacredness—and a human being of pure heart erupts in anger and drives out the defilers of the temple with a scourge made from cord in his hand. Much worse, however, is the profanation that occurs when the ones consecrated to the service of God "make a profession" out of it. Cult-play falls to ruin in manifold profanations—it falls to ruin in the rut of habit, falls to ruin in empty ceremony, falls to ruin, too, when the play of the festival is no longer sustained by the vividly felt presencing of the god in sacred awe or itself led by the intimation of the sameness of Dionysus and Hades in orgiastic debaucheries. Countless are the ways in which the play of the human being who is opened up to the deity become profane in the consuming passage of time. However, insofar as profanation belongs to the sacred like shadow to light, profane play cannot be the paradigm for the question concerning the worldliness of human play—rather, only a paradigm that is neither sacred nor profane, neither consecrated nor unconsecrated, can do so. The world itself is neither sacred like God nor profane like the sacrilegious human being; it is "beyond" such distinctions.

Chapter Four
The Worldliness of Human Play

18. Polysemy of the Concept "Worldly"

The worldliness of human play—this is the question at which we have arrived. It is an obscure, difficult, and intricate question that already appears to us to be perplexing and opaque in its character as a question. What, in general, is questionworthy about it? Toward what is thought's gaze thereby directed, whence does it proceed, and to what does it relate the theme it has seized upon? There is talk of "worldliness" in multiple and various senses. Worldliness can be an entirely empty general term, a hazy and dim representation; however, we can link more specific contents of thought with it, contents that have preserved an intellectual and emotional hue from the history of "worldviews," and we can ultimately understand the term "worldliness" as an indication of a radical philosophical problem. Initially, "worldly" is an almost meaningless determination, fading away into empty thoughtlessness, something that we indiscriminately assign to all beings. Everything that exists at all is worldly; every thing, every matter, every occurrence, and every relationship appears "in the world." Thus the world is considered to be the unquestioned, comprehensive concept [*Inbegriff*] for everything that turns up, for everything that exists at all. It is considered to be the all-embracing actuality of everything actual, to be what integrates and gathers all things and occurrences, to be the encompassing total ordering of all substances and processes. And yet it not only manifestly spans that which is in each case "actual," thus things and events that are current; it also contains in itself the horizons of the possibilities of all things. If things come into being and pass away, grow and diminish, exchange places and are transformed, then all this happens manifestly within the world. *In* it there is continual coming and going, emerging and disappearing, change of place and limited sojourn—*in* it there is the continual tumult of things asserting themselves against each other, where the increase of one is the loss of another, the rise of one the fall of another, the manifestation of one the expiration of another. *In* the world countless processes run their course; *in* it there is rest and movement of beings; *in* it everything is essentially one and yet in their unity all things are always together with other things that are one [*einshaften Dingen*]; *in* the world there is unity and multiplicity. And, furthermore, things are *in* it in such a way that they are thereby, respectively, stamped by universal "ways of seeing things" on the basis of which they are integrated into their particular domains, into regions of similar aspects; and yet, over and above such distinctions, they have, as things, the same structure. Thus within the world we discover things determined by *eidos* and *category*. *Eidos* and category are different modes of the universal determinateness of beings. Each being has a species—for example, something is not merely a mineral but rather granite, not merely a plant but rather an oak tree, not merely an animal but rather an elephant. But *what* they are respectively within a framework of species and genus, they are individually and as examples. And however variously things may be distinguished according to species and genus, they nevertheless coincide in having the structure of thinghood, which can be laid out in categorial determinations. Among all things we can distinguish formal and categorial universality and the moment of singular individuality. And, furthermore, we can say that it is not only things that exist *by nature* that are "worldly," but also all artificial things, all creations of human freedom belong to the world—that thus even what is not at all included within natural causality, which to a certain degree "novelly" and "as though from nothing" "bursts into" the context of beings already existent, does not at all transcend the world but rather comes to pass *in* it. That obviously means that innerworldly beings are by no means[1] a specific quantity of things, even if innumerable for us humans, that there is no firmly delimited quantum in them that is subject to continual alterations and transformations but on the whole cannot be increased or reduced. The relation of innerworldly things to the surrounding and inclusive world-whole perhaps does not at all lend itself to being validly oriented by the popular representation of the relation between a world-stuff that is fixed in its quantity and variable only in its formations and a world-container. Furthermore, innerworldly things in each case have a place and a while, have a space and possess a span of time, are somewhere and at some time. They have a figure and a duration; the figure as the proper space of a thing and duration as the proper time of a thing at rest or in motion are, respectively, placed in a position in space and are temporalized within the whole of time. Things can "exchange" location with each other, can change places, without thereby having to give up their own proper form, their peculiar shape. Things can never exchange their position in time, but, with their always-unique time frame, they remain set into a much greater simultaneity. While an individual process runs its course, at the same time innumerable processes run their courses with it. No individual process is alone; it is always in a far-reaching temporal proximity to other processes and periods of rest. Even if the present appears to contract into a punctual "now," it only has this punctuality vis-à-vis the past and the future—vis-à-vis what is no longer and what is not yet. But the now as such is "endless" in the dimension of simultaneity, is immeasurably vast and broad, is now "present" in the whole world; the now is worldwide. (The measurement of the now, to be sure, is another question, the question of physico-metric time-determination, which we exclude[2] here.) The enumerated features of the innerworldly—that it appears in a total-actuality, stands within horizons of possibility, arises and passes away, waxes and wanes, changes place, is at rest and in motion, is in each case one [*einshaft*] and yet always one among many, is in each case individual and universal, universal in the twofold manner of universality according to species and the structure of things, thus determined by *eidos* and category; that, furthermore, it can be a natural or artificial thing, that it has figure and duration, place and compresence—all of that is thought together and understood together in an unclear and vague manner when we call things "worldly." That does not mean, to be sure, that we can at any time bring into relief what is thought together opaquely, as we have just done; for the most part understanding gets by with a hazy approximation, in a dim twilight, in the dusk of what is half known. Nothing is more difficult to grasp and to express than that hovering sense *in* which one moves, which one ordinarily comprehends without any conceptual acuity at all. To form a concept of the concept-less and to thus express the "sense" that is operative in what is concept-less is almost impossible. We employ the expression "worldly," however, with a naïve and self-evident fluency—we operate in such a fashion but do not ordinarily think it through. What "worldly" signifies is evidently understood of its own accord, has an unquestioned sense that everyone is familiar with and uses. If we have brought into relief the features contained in this all-too-self-evident sense, then it has come about in a somewhat alienated manner, because in doing so we have used distinctions drawn from philosophical vocabulary. We have formulated in philosophical words the pre-philosophical knowledge of the worldliness of things.

Pre-philosophical knowledge that withdraws into the near inconceivability of what is "self-evident" is by no means only the human familiarity with the world and things, which we possess *before* philosophy, and thus in the condition of theoretical "innocence." The force of the "self-evident" repeatedly overpowers thinking, which strives against it, and extends precisely into thinking, into philosophy. One example of such intra-philosophical self-evidence is the common usage of the concept "worldly" when we apply it to all things in general. All things belong within the world, one says; it is the gathering, ordering, and articulating of all beings. Each thing is worldly. Is that a piece of wisdom or a triviality? What does one actually mean by such a statement? Wherein does it have its illuminating and elucidating character, assuming that it is not merely a self-evident platitude? One could reply: it makes a statement about beings as such. First philosophy, in the strict sense, what one later called "metaphysics"—according to Aristotle—treats of beings as such, of beings as beings and of that which belongs to them. Is it thus a metaphysical question if the worldliness of things is explored? One could rather say: it is a question that for the most part metaphysics forgets or relegates to the unquestioned status of what is "self-evident." Each being is worldly: that then only means that each being belongs within an all-encompassing unity. The being-a-being [*Seiendsein*] and the being-worldly of things are almost used "synonymously." "World" becomes the title of the universality of Being; each thing that is belongs within this universality, and nothing remains outside of it; it is always encompassed by the encompassing context, by universal integrations; it is always one thing among others, is one thing in the midst of all. But then how do the being-a-being and the being-worldly of things actually stand in relation to each other? Is the relation between these concepts sufficiently indicated when we say they are synonymous? By no means. To be sure, the concept of being-worldly in a certain respect appears to explicate the concept of being-a-being, insofar as the universal context of things is thus emphasized. But the concept of Being obviously has a richer manifoldness in itself; it is multidimensional, while the concept of world appears markedly uniform. We distinguish the being-a-being of things in multiple respects and analyze it according to what-being and that-being, according to true-being and contingent-being, actual-being and possible-being; furthermore, we distinguish modes of Being such as being-present, living-being, the constitution of the Being of the human being and the sort of Being of number and figure, of artificial things, natural things, and so forth. All such distinctions, which are developed from the most universal concept of Being, remain situated within the all-encompassing fundamental feature of worldliness. Being-worldly in itself does not appear to be further explicable—it even appears to concern only the aspect of totality in the thought of Being. We employ the concept of Being [*Sein*] in regard to existing [*seienden*] things at one point in time in an empty, still indeterminate "universality," and then, however, in such a way that we thus intend a manifold of respects: the "what," the "that," etc. "Worldly" is synonymous with existing when the concept of Being is used in its emptiest and most universal manner. In considering the worldly-being of things, we experience, so to speak, nothing in comparison to the question-rich unfolding of being-a-being in the multiplicity of different modes of Being. Being-worldly has the appearance of a rather impoverished concept when it is measured by the more multidimensional concept of being-a-being. The latter has its deeper basis in the long history of western ontology, in the millennia-long work of the concept on the problem of Being. To be sure, the all-encompassing totality of the world for all things was thus always known, yet it has itself never been adequately[3] exposed with the explicit acuity of a rigorously conceptual posing of the question as a problem.

Yet this thesis manifestly contradicts the history of philosophy. Already in the Presocratics we find the doctrine of a multiplicity of "worlds," of states of world order [*Weltordnungszuständen*]; we find in Parmenides the separation of *eōn* and *dokounta*, the separation of the sphere of *existing* [seiend] from the sphere of emerging and passing away. And we ultimately find in Plato the cleavage of the totality of what *is* into the region of the visible and the region of the thinkable; we find the fundamental dimensions of the *chōra,* the dark material of the world, and then that of sensible things, while next we find that of the *cosmos* as the structured total ordering of all sensible things, and then that of the ideas and finally and highest of all the idea of the good, which contains all other ideas in itself and which as the encompassing whole idea is related to individual ideas like the cosmos is to sensible things. The further development of Platonic motifs then leads to the well-known distinction between the *mundus sensibilis* and the *mundus intelligibilis.* The concept of "world" now emerges in the plural, initially in the dual form of that which is sensible and that which is intelligible and ultimately in conjecturing the possibility of many possible worlds, of which only one is actualized, one that must have a sufficient reason for this distinction. The theme of "world" becomes a special theme within the framework of the universal question of Being, becomes a special question of metaphysics—as in Kant, for instance, where "world" signifies only the whole of appearance that is to be universally thought, but not of beings in themselves. The world is here understood from the perspective of appearance, not appearance from the perspective of the world, which amounts to an[4] inversion of the world-problem. Nevertheless, Kant represents a decisive high point in the concealed and subterranean history of the problem of the world. The extent to which the center of the Kantian critique of reason, its most formidable impact, lies in the antinomy of pure reason, and thus in the dialectic of the cosmological ideas, cannot be further developed here.

However, if a fleeting glance over the history of Western metaphysics attests to a manifold treatment of the problem of the world, how and in what sense were we able to make the claim that the being-worldly of beings has not been a theme for the rigorous work of the concept? To this one should reply: precisely insofar as the concept of the world was transferred into a pluralistic usage, insofar as "world" degenerated into a title for realms of Being, for dimensions of different things, the possibility increasingly disappeared of experiencing the worldedness [*Welthaftigkeit*] of each being simply as an open and pressing problem. Wherein do beings first of all show themselves in general in their Being, whence do they arise, and to where do they pass away according to the duration of existence apportioned to them? We can determine, interrogate, and conceptually analyze beings with respect to their Being, if they have come forth from the expanses of the world into presence for us. But how must beings be thought in their Beingness [*Seinshaftigkeit*], if we thereby think at the same time more specifically the provenance of all things from the maternal womb of the world and the reversion of all things to their ground [*Grund*], their true running aground [*Zu-Grunde-Gehen*]? In the end, is not all ontology "grounded" in an obscure and inexplicable, concealed knowledge of the world? That question is not settled by the popular synonymity of being-a-being and being-worldly but rather first of all looks for the correspondence of both concepts.

Do we even understand simply and without further ado what "worldly" means? "Worldly" is the adjective of "world" and expresses in this manner the way the world is. "Divine [*Göttlich*]" expresses the way in which God [*Gott*] is in the first place and above all. The properties of God are "divine"; the deeds and works of God are "divine." But we already sense a certain difference there. To be sure, God's works bear the stamp of divine fabrication in themselves, but they themselves are for that reason not "divine" in the same sense as God himself is. One also uses the adjective "divine" for the increasing determination of beings that come near to God, who approximate him, approach him. In the human soul, the spark of spiritual light is divine; the homesickness for the supraterrestrial is divine. The human being counts as "divine" to the extent that and insofar as he lives in such a way that he becomes like God, exists in the *homoiōsis theōi.* We thus have a noteworthy double usage of the concept "divine": at one moment it characterizes the Being of God himself and then in an analogous way also the Being of that which lives beneath God but toward God. We occasionally predicate divinity of that which is not divine and mean by this that such non-divinity retains certain features of God, even if it is far removed at an enormous distance, that it shimmers in the reflected glory of the splendor of God. Mantic rapture is divine in such a sense, as is enthusiasm, as is erōs, as is sacrifice for the fatherland, if Heraclitus's dictum is true, that human beings and gods honor those fallen in war—and perhaps even philosophy is divine, is a *theion ti.* The predicate "divine" now characterizes something that remains beneath the actual Being of God. There is only "the divine" in this manner because God previously exists and can reflect his radiance onto lesser things. The double usage of the word "divine" is made possible by an incline from the distance of lower things to the highest being. Yet over and across the enormous gulf that separates mortals from immortals, both races manifestly come together in *being beings.* The incline is a hierarchy determined by greater and lesser intensities of Being. The most ontologically intense and powerful of all beings is God—the human being is far weaker. God is able to perpetually maintain himself in Being, to persist ceaselessly as a being; the human being has an inconstant, ephemeral, and exhaustible intensity of Being—and is already characterized by demise when he begins his course of life. To be sure, the fundamental manner in which God has attributes is in many ways abyssally different from the manner of the human being, yet he does have attributes—such as substance in general. God is divine [*Der Gott ist göttlich*]—that is at first an empty tautology that first becomes problematic when we ask whether divinity [*Göttlichkeit*] is determined by God or whether God is determined by divinity. The indicated double usage of the predicate "divine" now becomes for us the background for raising the question as to what we actually mean by the word "worldly." When we use it "synonymously" with the word "existing [*seiend*]," initially only the moment of unity, which is implicitly thought together in the Being [*Sein*] of existing things, is emphasized. Every being [*Seiende*] is worldly: this now amounts to saying that every being is *in* the world. With the characteristic of being-worldly, a *being-in* is thought, a being-in that thoroughly attunes and pervades all beings; one relates, with understanding, the Being of things back to an encompassing wherein. This all-encompassing totality [*All*] remains, however, for the moment, within the vague and indeterminate emptiness of a "universality [*Allgemeinheit*]" that we are not able to determine: it is not the universality of genus and species and it is not the universality of the categorial structure. It is a universal, all-embracing "Being," in which each thing is to a certain degree exchanged, in which it is delimited and attains contour, determination, and distinctness from other things. Unified Being is "broken" by the multiplicity of things, split up, cleaved and torn asunder, but yet not actually "dismembered"; rather the unity of Being subtends the multiplicity of separated things—as soil runs beneath the furrows of the cultivated field or as the sea runs beneath the crests of waves. If we search for and interrogate existing things with respect to the Being that is present in them, then Being itself appears to us in the character of empty universality. If, in contrast, we understand existing things as modes of fragmentation of the Being subtending them, then Being instead comes to have for us the character of a single, concrete, all-encompassing unity. The beginning of Western metaphysics vacillates between both perspectives in a strangely undecided way. If being-worldly is thought together with the Being of things, then this initially comes into view as a pervasive character of *being-in,* of the belonging of beings to the world—and Being itself lights up as the one-and-all [*All-Eine*] that precedes all individuation.

Can one now, in turn, say of this one-and-all Being [*all-einen Sein*] that it "is"—can we, without completely confusing ourselves, make a statement concerning the Being of being-a-being? Is it like a thing, like a substance, like something finite? If it were of such a sort and were at least comparable to such things, would it then not have to be understood for its part as again contained in an encompassing, higher Being? Or must we resign ourselves to the condition that we may only attribute "Being" to things and processes and can call them "beings" but that we may never render judgment at all on Being in a fixed predicative form? That which is understood in advance withdraws from being fixed in an understood manner. The profound ambiguity of the concept of Being, according to which it means individuated things' constitution of Being, but then also the one, one-and-all Being that "breaks" into individuals, which is not individuated but rather itself individuates—this ambiguity encumbers the whole problem of how and in what sense at all one might be able to speak philosophically of Being itself. Are we—to speak metaphorically—able to see the earth behind the furrows, the sea behind the waves? If, concerning Being, what is problematic to the highest degree is whether and how we may make statements concerning it—for example, that it is, that it is constituted in such and such a way, and so forth—if here it is questionable whether we may even predicate something of it (which does not merely present a semantic problem), then this also holds, though in an even stronger manner, for the world. Is the world worldly? This simple question is an abyssal problem. Are we dealing with something akin to the divinity of God [*Göttlichkeit des Gottes*]? One might initially be tempted to hypothesize a parallel and speak of a double usage of the adjective "worldly." Only the world is genuinely worldly, one might well say then. Things are worldly in a derivative sense, insofar as they essentially belong to the world, or better: *belong within* the world. Being-worldly, said of the thing, means being-within-the-totality [*In-sein-im-All*], fundamentally means *intraworldliness.* And intraworldliness includes within itself delimitation, individuation, and determination of an individual by manifold "universalities." Thus the "limit" is not the decisive and governing phenomenon in the intraworldly as such but rather being-in-the-all-together-whole [*das In-sein-im-allhaften-Ganzen*]. There are numerous forms of being-in, which are structured entirely differently: the relation of parts set within a self-enclosed whole, the relation of abstract moments within something concrete, the relation of a small thing within a larger thing (the lectern within a lecture hall, the lecture hall within the university, this university within the city and the city within the countryside, etc.)—every such relation would be completely incommensurate if it were taken as a model for the being-in of beings in the world. The manner and mode in which what is intraworldly encompasses something else that is intraworldly and contains it in itself, is, for its part, founded in the singular encompassing of all things by the world-whole. All beings are finite and are included in the in-finite world. One could attempt in thought to employ the term "worldly" in a way analogous to the double usage of the concept "divine"—and then say: if "worldly" is applied to things, it thus always means intraworldliness. Even if we still do not at all know precisely what sense lies hidden in the intraworldliness of beings, we nevertheless understand that this concept cannot be applied to the world itself: the world is not intraworldly. Intraworldliness is a fundamental feature of *beings as such*, which, to be sure, is for the most part concealed and also not grasped in thought's direct regard for beings. In the sense of the prevailing of the world itself, however, "worldly" is then no thing, not at all a being, neither a small one nor an enormous one. On first thought it appears as though there obtained here a relation analogous to the relation in the concept of the "divine," where we can distinguish the strict and the analogous usage. But between God, who is actually divine, and things beneath God, which can only be called "divine" in a figurative sense, to the extent that a reflection of the radiance in which God dwells shines down on them, a real separation obtains; there exists in general an ontic difference as a disparity between things distinct in kind and also in number.

Is there also a difference of this sort between the world and intraworldly beings? Obviously not. The world is not an external framework around things, not a container in which they occur—like potatoes in a sack or jewels in a safe. Nor is it a *kratēr*[5] in which all things are intermingled and blended, although this is one of the most ancient metaphors. It encompasses and envelops all things and is not itself separate and detached from things, but rather things belong to it, and the intraworldly as such is an essential aspect of the world. What constitutes the difficulty and severity of the problem for human understanding is that it is always tempted to think the difference between the whole and that which is intraworldly, a difference that belongs *to* the prevalence of the world itself, on the model of a difference between things, and thus must perpetually experience the failure of every approach of this sort. The world is not "in the world"; it is not something actual in a total field of actual and possible things. If it has in itself every actual and every possible being, then is it itself, taken as a whole, "actual" or "possible" or "contingent" or "necessary"? Or in the end do these words lose their well-known and common sense? Can the world arise and pass away, wax and wane, appear and disappear—or does it encompass all that arises and passes away? Does it conceal every emergence and demise of beings in itself? But if it does not know any emergence and, further, if annihilation is excluded—is it then without emergence and decay, always identical to itself, unchanged, but encompassing the exchange of things? This thought does occur in ancient speculation about the world—alongside other projections of thought. The world attains the features of divinity, is thought on the model of divine constancy; something that is intraworldly, even if it is of the highest order, is placed in front of the prevailing totality and conceals it, conceals it by means of a model for thought that is meant to explain. In the history of European philosophy this has had almost[6] incalculable, fateful consequences and has decisively determined the onto-theological style of metaphysics. Pantheism is the clearest form of this dubious intermingling of religion and world-wisdom—and is a distortion of faith and of thought. The world is not grasped in its status if one calls it "divine" and ascribes to it the attributes of the highest being. One would then above all always be led to think that a personally thought prevalence, similar to the governance of the gods, would be the right way in which the world prevails, in which the world *plays*. It then becomes falsified into a game of a player. Furthermore, the question remains open as to whether the world, which embraces and involves the incalculable multiplicity of things that are one [*einshafter Dinge*], is for its part something one can at all encounter through the distinction between the one and the many. The looks of things and the structure of thinghood are within it. Does it itself have an *eidos* and a categorial structure? Does it exist by nature or is it an enormous artificial thing—does it have a location and a period of persistence? Are not rather all locations within it and all periods included in it? Even when we are supposed to specify what we understand under the vague heading "worldly," we are cast into a labyrinth of questions. How then are we still[7] to ask about the *worldliness* of human play?

19. The Worldliness of Play—In Contrast to the Metaphysical and Mythological Interpretation

If one calls human play "worldly," one thereby expresses what is most self-evident and superficial, but also what is deepest about it and most rich in problems. We *never* fail to know about the world and worldliness and *never* know them fully. We move within a familiar acquaintance and at the same time wander in a serpentine labyrinth. The world is what is familiar and at the same time what is uncanny—it entangles[8] our existence with its unfathomable distances and is at the same time what is most near and most intimate, is *before* every self-knowing selfhood and *before* every known thing, insofar as it first of all opens up the space and time in which the self is able to distinguish itself from alien beings. Worldliness is not a fundamental feature in the Being of each being in the manner in which, for instance, thinghood and substantiality are—it cannot be taken up with regard to individuated, delimited, and at the same time gathered things. It first enables the perspective of metaphysical thinking, which interrogates, determines, and identifies innerworldly things with regard to their structures of Being. Metaphysics *touches* on the problematic of the worldedness of all individuated beings when it poses the question concerning the "transcendental" determinations of things, to the extent that the latter are in each case something that is one, true, and good, and, in the enigmatic imbrication of oneness, truth and goodness, are in each case beings. In the problem of the transcendentals, traditional metaphysics stands much[9] closer to the original question of the world than in its explicit[10] "cosmological" discipline. The finitude of everything that *is* in the mode of determinateness and contour as *on horismenon* and in the mode of denominative addressability as *on legomenon* signifies a coming to appearance in the space-time of the world, signifies intraworldliness. The metaphysical interpretation of Being no longer specifically thinks through the intraworldliness of all finite things and does not experience it as a pressing problem. It has settled down *in* the worldwide coming to appearance of beings; it has a standpoint therein, an approach and an implementation of its ways of thought. However, that within which and in the enduring of which the coming to appearance and presence of individuated things happens thus remains in the shadow of that which is unthought. A thinking back to what is unthought here is still without path or bridge—and perhaps will remain for a long way more of a stumble than a straight gait. We are attempting a few paltry stumbling steps with the question of the worldliness of human play.

We can use the concept "worldliness" in a fourfold sense. First of all, it means a concealed character in all finite beings per se, belonging-within the world-whole, intraworldliness. We have briefly discussed the fact that this intraworldliness is divided into a manifold of internal distinctions—into the difference between the actual and the possible, into a multiplicity of kinds of movement, into oneness and manyness, into *eidos* and category, on the one hand, and individuality and thisness, on the other hand, into the regions of natural and artificial things, into position and duration—and we have thereby indicated that all these structures of the intraworldly cannot be applied to the world itself, that it itself never exists in the same way as the finite thing coming to appearance *in* it. Nor should we distinguish between the world itself and the intraworldly thing *in the way* that we do between things, however. We ought not to put the world on one side like an empty container, as it were, and innerworldly things on the other side, as its "content." The world relates to the beings in it not like a thing to another thing, nor even like the human being to the dimension of his self-alienation. The cosmological difference between world and thing is incomprehensible with the resources for thought provided by conventional thing-ontology. It could be that, in the understanding of play, one can perhaps find approaches that would allow us to formulate the relation between world and thing as a more determinate question. We use the expression "worldly" in a second sense to characterize the prevailing of the world itself, that letting-emerge of all finite and individuated beings into the daylight of appearance *and* at the same time the annihilation of everything that appears, which is inconceivable to us. What "worldly" means here, for now, is an obscure and murky problem. We take the term "worldly" in a third sense, to denote a decisive basic feature of the essence of the human being. The human being has a world-position, a specific position in the cosmos. He does not appear alongside other things in a merely objective manner, alongside land and sea and the open brightness of the sky, alongside rocks, plants, and animals, alongside the products of his freedom and work activity, thus alongside institutions, tools, and machines, alongside his intellect's ideal creations of sense, alongside number and figure. The human being comports himself with understanding to that which surrounds him, addresses that which surrounds him as "beings" and interprets the latter in manifold ways according to understood structures; he thereby always also comports himself to himself, to his own Being and to the Being of all things—and he also opaquely comports himself, in such understanding of beings, to the all-encompassing whole in which beings are "given" at all. The human being is in the world by comporting himself with an understanding of Being to all fundamental regions of things and also to himself and by existing in a manner that is open to the world. He stands in the slipstream of the immense, is torn open by the supremacy of the universe that at once elevates and bears down on him, is attuned by the native and uncanny proximity and distance of the world-totality. The human being is more "worldly" than every other thing. The stone lies without feeling in its place; stars revolve disinterestedly on their immense course; the tree stands placidly in the wind; the animal moves about in enclosed rings according to schemata determined by its species. Stone, tree, and animal: they are intraworldly, but they do not comport themselves *to* their intraworldliness, they do not comport themselves to their own Being and to the Being of surrounding things. They are, as it were, still held within nature, still "inside." They are natural creatures, which do not yet comport themselves in a questioning manner to their Being and which do not yet catch sight of the creative power. The human being, too, certainly feels encompassed by the maternal power of nature, but he experiences it *as* the maternal ground of life from which he ascends and from which he is estranged in the course of his life, and to be sure he does so all the more, to the degree to which his carrying out of life is formed consciously, intellectually, and in a self-possessed manner [*selbsthafter*]. His own being-in-the-world is a miracle and enigma for the human being, before which he finds himself placed and which constitutes the unrest of his existence. Here originate all cares and worries, but also all joys and felicities of our precarious life, the curiosity of the sciences and the wonder of philosophy, the creative act of the statesman and art's transfiguration of the world. The human being is in the world in such a way that he comports himself to his being-in [*Insein*]. That separates him from all things that we are familiar with and gives him the unique position in the cosmos of being the world-dweller. We do not merely turn up; we comport ourselves to the appearing of all natural things and make the latter into material for our work; we take the earth as a stage for our acting and suffering, for our struggles and our love,[11] for our colonies and cities; the earth for us is the soil of the fatherland, the field and pasture, the space for settlement, the battlefield for wars and the Golgotha of human death. But it is also for us the playground for our games and the precinct of our festivals. This understanding world-openness of the human being, which is at work in manifold dimensions and regions of life, thus characterizes a third sense of "worldly." Thus understood, the human being is alone worldly among all phenomenal things. But the human being is not only situated among such things, which he surveys in their coming to appearance; he divines superhuman beings and forces "behind" the sphere of what is given and shows itself—and already in the most primeval times stands in a relation of belief[12] to daemons and gods. And such super-human beings are apparently much more powerful and closer to the omnipotent than the frail human being; they are more worlded and akin to cosmic[13] prevailing. We leave aside the question as to how things might stand with the ontological claim about daemons and gods that are thus believed in, whether and how they disguise the universe and draw the human being's gaze from the space-time of Being away to a highest being. But with religion a peculiar tension in human existence is at the same time also formed: the more non-sensuous God becomes, the more he repudiates graven images or forsakes the statue [*Standbild*] in which he once had his epiphany, the more non-terrestrial and spiritual, the more metaphysical the concept of God becomes—the more severely does an opposition break open in human life between that which is sensuous and that which is beyond the sensuous. And in the fateful joining of philosophy and theology this opposition of two modes of life, which in the strictest contrast are arranged into the *mundus sensibilis* and the *mundus intelligibilis*, is exacerbated. In a peculiar way the kind of life that tends toward what is sensuous [*dem Sinnlichen*] is then pejoratively characterized as a "worldly disposition [*Gesinnung*]" while the basic position that is turned toward the intelligible world is positively assessed as the attitude that is related to God, as pious and more valid. In the Western alliance of religion and metaphysics God attains the ontological status and permanence of the idea, and the idea attains the heavenly radiance of God. God and the idea are reciprocally determined. Hence the sphere of God as the realm of essence [*Wesens*] is contrasted with the non-essence [*Unwesen*] of that which comes to appearance on earth; the land of what is thinkable is elevated beyond the land of what is visible. He who devotes himself to what is visible loses himself in the phenomena, remains a servant of sensuousness and ultimately a slave of appetites, falls prey to the irrational—and thus betrays the human being's highest possibility and genuine purpose. Fallenness [*Verfallenheit*] into the sensuous world is the human being's half-animal mode of existence; the turn to the supersensible world, in contrast, is the mortal human being's almost divine mode of existence, near to god, the human being who is able to live in *theōria* for a while like the blessed gods and resembles the immortals. One would expect that the attitude to the *mundus intelligibilis* would be characterized as a "worldly" one; after all, in the language of metaphysics the realm of ideas is held to be the "true world," the "genuine world" in distinction to the world of sensuousness that is merely apparent, illusory, and laced with semblance [*scheinbaren, scheinhaften und scheindurchwirkten*]. Why, then, is the form of life that projects itself beyond to the "true world" not called the "worldly" one?

Specifically Christian motifs in Western metaphysics' use of language are strongly at work here. The sensuous is associated with what is pagan, that which pertains to the ideas with the divine. Paganism is then considered to be religiosity that is caught up in superficial semblance, mistaken in its images of the gods, a religiosity that is not elevated to the true supersensible[14] and is not able to discover the right concept of God, and thus a human affair that remains in the flesh (*sarx*) and in the weaknesses of the flesh and does not apprehend the breath of God, who is spirit (*pneuma*). On this background of the distinction between creator-god and created world, paganism is then interpreted as fallenness into the world—a fallenness that no longer recognizes the traces of the creator in the divine work of creation, that misses the *vestigia dei* and surrenders to the seduction of sensuous appearance. The expression "worldly" is used to denote a disposition that is turned away from God, an imprisonment within dark desires, a captivation by the fleeting radiance of transitory things. All trumpery, all frivolousness, all levity, all desire for amusement and every rapture of the senses is worldly. The word "worldly" becomes a frightening anathema—and is directed not only against the superficiality of human beings' everyday life but also against the deeper mysteries of our terrestrial existence that is rooted in the earth. Hence the word "worldly" is fraught, laden with curses and imprecations; it belongs to the "best-slandered things."[15] And wherever such world-slandering tendencies are at work, human play is scorned, is condemned as trumpery and frivolousness, as idleness and beguilement of the senses, as levity and boisterousness, as folly and madness. Play is taken to be a worldly, all-too-worldly activity, to be a masquerade and joyful tumult in which what matters is the one thing that[16] is forgotten, where the happiness of the hour endangers eternal salvation.[17]

We have thus distinguished four meanings of "worldly": 1. The being-intraworldly of all finite things as such and in general; 2. The prevailing of the world itself; 3. The self-comportment-to-the-world with understanding; 4. A defamed mode of human sojourn in the world, the "pagan fallenness into the sensuous."

How is human play worldly? Was it necessary to intricately keep the four meanings distinct? Do they all have a relation to the human being's play? If we attend to the first meaning we certainly have to say that intraworldliness, because it belongs to each being in general, also belongs to the human being and thereby determines *a priori* all his activities, his serious and non-serious affairs. Human play is fundamentally an innerworldly process. That is no great insight, one will say; we thereby push against an open door. *That* the human being is a being in the world and *that* all his doings and everything he leaves undone, his energetic self-actualization, have likewise been determined and stamped and participate in the universally finite character of all intraworldliness, is easily admitted, but to say *how* he is intraworldly and how he is finite may be a quite profound problem with stringent difficulties for thought. Playing appears among human activities and activities appear in the Being of the human. How does the Being of the human being encompass his activity? In the way that a substance encompasses its accidental processes? In the way that the rock is the bearer of the processes of decomposition in it? In the way that the plant preserves itself in its vegetative processes or the animal roams about in carrying out its life? Can the human being be understood at all on the model of a substance, if the latter is interpreted as a persistent bearer of properties that abide and ones that change? Or is the human being above all and in the first instance existent freedom—and thus no substantial Being from which his deeds follow, but rather perhaps at bottom a primal deed [*Urtat*], a primal activity [*Urhandlung*], a choice as to his life's lot—spoken in mythological terms, is he transposed into a pre-existent existence [*ein präexistentes Dasein*] but interpreted phenomenally as the fundamental will of a human being from which the particular activities of the will then proceed and are conducted? Is the human being the project of his freedom or is he only free in a restricted sense, on the subsoil of natural conditions not able to be chosen? How the problem of the human being's belonging within the world as universe is explicated would already have to depend on the clarification of this question. Is he intraworldly as a substance or as a fact/act [*Tathandlung*]? If even finitude is an essential basic feature of all intraworldly things, then presumably the finitude of freedom ought to be conceived otherwise than the finitude of a thing placidly persisting in its *eidos* and its categorial structure. We *cannot* call human play worldly in the second sense of the word; it does not prevail like the world itself. No thing at all, neither in heaven nor on earth, predominates like the predominance of the totality. Everything intraworldly is quite simply not worldly in the second sense of the word. Or, expressed positively: the movement of finite things, however else they may be distinguished among themselves, is more radically[18] distinguished from the movement of the world. Human play is the temporary innerworldly mode of activity of an innerworldly being. Such innerworldly activity is abyssally separate from the total occurrence of the universe. Hence it is especially necessary to emphasize the stringencies of this separation, because we repeatedly resort to innerworldly models in philosophy in order to express the prevailing of the world. The extraordinary tension of such an expression may not be mitigated by a blurring of the difference between world and thing, nor reduced to a relation of affinity or analogy. And precisely when we want ultimately to speak of a play of the world itself, the play of the human being, who is indeed an innerworldly being, must in all brusqueness be separated and marked off from the predominating of the omni-potent. Measured against the prevailing of the world, human play is *not* worldly. In contrast, with the third sense of the word we must grant that play has the character of an openness for the world-whole, an openness that possesses understanding. It is "worldly" insofar as in it and through it the opening up, with understanding, of human existence to the world is sounded and stamped in a special sense. In playing, we understand the prevailing totality in a different way than in work, struggle, love, and the cult of the dead—other sides, other dimensions open up for us. The human sojourn in the midst of things and in the world is indeed not falsely characterized if one declares understanding to be the feature unique to human beings: the human being is thus in the world in such a way that he thereby comports himself continually and unceasingly to the Being of his very self and of other things and to the entirety of all beings and cultivates this relation as an understanding, which never fully penetrates the Being of beings, but in each case opens them up still deeper in their enigmatic nature. The human being exists as understanding of Being, is the animal that has language: the *zōion logon echon.* When the human being's relation to the Being of all beings is first and foremost shifted to speech, when the human being is addressed as a being with language, the "logical" arrangement and ordering of the intraworldly content of actuality thrusts itself into the foreground and at the same time conceals and disguises the comprehensive totality from which the logically conceivable articulations of the sense of intraworldly beings come to light. And it does not change much if one reverses the formula and responds that it is not the human being who has language and the understanding of Being articulated in language, but rather language, as the preserved, structured, and gathered light of Being, that has the human being. There are not only countless relations in which the understanding of the world and Being does not speak, is mute and speechless—albeit in a manner that is different from the manner in which the animal is mute. There are fundamental, basic phenomena of our social Being, such as the relation of lovers and of the living to the departed, which are never exhausted in their utterance and are beyond everything effable. But an understanding of world lives in them, too. Or again it is different in the case of the preponderantly active modes of the human sojourn in the world, which do not belong to *theōria,* to contemplative tarrying and beholding. Work is an irreducibly[19] independent basic form of being-in with understanding, and likewise the struggle for dominance. *Technē* and *polemos* shape human things—on the basis of a knowledge about the world that is wholly proper to each. To be sure, they are always already linguistically interwoven, have their basic words and their own rhetoric; their speech is practical, determined for use in work activity and political struggle. The speech that governs work activity and struggle does not express its conversant understanding of Being "thematically." Here the relation between immediate use and mediated reflection on use is different from what is at issue, for instance, in the dimension of beholding and catching sight of, where reflection more clearly brings into relief that which is already implicitly understood in simple seeing. "Theory" (in the primitive as in the more reflected sense) apprehends beings in their existence and presence, in their being present among us, without "altering" them. However, work and struggle are different basic positions of the human being with regard to things and still more primordially with regard to the world. But work and struggle can be taken up as models and used to form "world-concepts." That holds, for example, for all demiurgic conceptions, according to which beings as a whole are a universal piece of work, a divine accomplishment of labor or the like. And from struggle are borrowed all those ideas that interpret the world as a "strife" of heaven and earth, of the day and night of Being, of *peras* and *apeiron,* of *philia kai neikos.* Such borrowings would perhaps not be possible were there no world-relations contained in these basic human phenomena of work and war. The human being's world-openness is neither merely bound to language nor only a respectively individual one; it is itself multifaceted, according to the sustaining basic phenomena of our existence, and hence it is always social, too. Precisely insofar as the human being exists socially, he exists open to the world. Human play is a particular and unique mode of a socially existent relation to the world. Admittedly that is not obvious. The play of the human being is worldly in the sense of a being-in within the totality with understanding, in the sense of a comprehending intimacy. The being-in of all things within the universe, including the human being, we call the intraworldliness of beings; the particular way in which the human being experiences and lives through his being-in within the whole as a thinking-speaking being and as a worker, fighter, lover, player, and mortal, we call the "intimacy [*Innigkeit*]" of existence. This is in no way meant sentimentally here. Intimacy reveals itself just as much in the implacable hardships of strife as it does in "famous passion."[20]

And, lastly, the fact that play is also "worldly" in the fourth sense hardly requires closer specification and demonstration. It is thoroughly attuned by an elementary passion for life [*Lebenslust*], a passion that is more than delight in what is delightful, useful, enjoyable, a passion for the exuberance of life that can still include in itself what is dire, evil, and horrible, as the pleasure in the play [*Spiellust*] of tragedy does. In fact, there prevails an almost "pagan" carelessness in play, a sensuous delight, a mysterious passion for appearance, for beguilement, for the radiance of colors and for the ruddy complexion of things. At any rate, it is a questionable matter as to whether the pagan-worldly character of play, again and again seducing one to take to sensuous appearance, has to be judged disparagingly, whether the assessments of traditional metaphysics and religion should be adopted. The play of the human being is worldly insofar as it is intraworldly—insofar as it is permeated by the radiance of an intimacy with understanding and brings the human being together with the cosmic power of "appearance" in an entirely peculiar superficial depth or deep superficiality—and it is worldly as a pagan-festive attunement of life. A fullness of individual features could be unfurled, and play could be described as a richly structured phenomenon in the pattern of many "games" that are in our own and foreign cultural spheres. Ethnology and cultural history place an immense amount of material at our disposal: sacred and profane kinds of play, simple and highly differentiated ones, diversionary play for the passing of time and kinds of play belonging to a primordial rapture [*Ergriffenheit*], everyday games and games of the festival. But for us it does not come down to a "phenomenological description" of the multifaceted phenomenon of play but rather only to the illumination of its *world-sense*.

For us, play is not an arbitrary theme of philosophy, which can occupy itself with anything and everything. Play has an extraordinary status in its being an existential basic phenomenon, just as primordial as mortality, love, work, and struggle. But in love, work, and struggle there is the appearance that the human being involves himself exclusively with another *being*—as though he were relating to a nature that is to be transformed, to his fellow human beings, whom he needs for mating as well as for ruling. The human realm appears "enclosed," autarchic in itself, nowhere pointing beyond itself. The human being who works, struggles, and loves in each case comports himself to another being: he labors over it, subjects it to his own power, joins himself to his erotic partner. The bit of "natural material" that the working technician reshapes, the enemy that the warrior opposes, the weapons of the enemy and one's own, the beloved partner and the eternal things connected with this, the domestic hearth, the bed, the house, and so forth: all this is together in the same all-encompassing actuality as the working, fighting, loving human being himself. The beings he deals with are just as actual as he is. In this comprehensive total actuality there are certainly distinctions of different modes of Being: the human being is other than his tool or his weapon or his bed. And yet this heterogeneity is together, appears in one encompassing sphere of actuality. It is otherwise with play. Play is not a human enactment of life in which he involves himself with the other beings in his surroundings. Certainly this happens, too. The one playing takes hold of certain things—whether they have been prepared artfully and specifically for this or not—as "playthings." The thing *with* which he plays and the fellow human beings *with* whom he enters into a game are just as actual as he is—and also belong to the same dimension of actuality. But in their playing together they attain [*erspielen*] an irreal playworld in which they have their roles and which contains playthings of an imaginary character. Thus with human play an "irreal" sphere of sense bursts into a total actuality of real things and processes, a sphere that is here and yet not here, now and yet not now. With the designation "irreal" nothing at all is yet conceived at first but, rather, one only expresses that the "playworld" balks at a simple assimilation into the context of the actual world—that its "illusoriness [*Scheinhaftigkeit*]" prevents it from being placed alongside other things and contexts of things and from being assessed as something "actual." And if we designate the playworld as an "appearance [*Schein*]," it thus comes down to expressly holding this playworld-appearance at a distance from the otherwise familiar appearance that belongs to the givenness of things as, for instance, "superficial," exterior, or rooted in a mistaken subjective conception.

How the playworld is an *appearance*—this is precisely the question, the problem that we have pursued. The metaphysical interpretation of play in the beginning of Western metaphysics gave us the first answer to the question of the nature of this appearance: the playworld-appearance has the character of a *reproduction,* indeed of even a mere mirroring, and is to be determined as mimesis. "Non-actuality" signifies a lesser degree of ontological power than befits simply actual things. Play is only the variation on and afterimaging of ordinary things and hence of no fundamental epistemological value for philosophy. Inter alia, philosophy's guardianship also consists in exposing pretentious appearance and putting the poets in their place, revealing their belatedness. We received the second answer in looking at archaic cult-play, at its enchantment of masks and its magical technique and the playful bringing of the gods to presence in mythical dramatic play or spectacle. Here the so-called non-actuality of the playworld attains an elevated ontological status, towering above the ordinariness of everyday things. Play is considered to be a distinguished association with divine powers, the player as that life-form that comes closest to the heavenly ones. In the first and second answers, human play has been interpreted as a relation to beings. And here we have advanced and sought to develop our doubts so as to prepare the third answer, which construes play as a *world-relation* of human existence, thus as a sense-suffused relation to something that is no thing and no thinglike occurrence—and what we most readily can still think of, despite the failure of all finite models and metaphors, as a *game without a player.*

20. Play as the Ecstase of the Human Being toward the World and as the Proof of the Shining Back of the World into the Being That Is Open to the World. The World as a Game without a Player

The third answer to the question concerning the essence of play—following the metaphysical and the cultic-mythic interpretation—can be summarized in a few words as a "thesis": human play is an especially distinctive way in which existence relates with understanding to the whole of that which is, and in which it lets the whole resonate through it. In human play the whole of the world is reflected back into itself, letting features of in-finity emerge and shimmer in and on something innerworldly and finite. Play is an existentiell enactment that leads out from a purely immanent consideration of human things; it cannot be comprehended at all if one approaches the human being as a living being enclosed within itself, if one regards him as a being that has fixed properties adhering to it, if one considers him according to the general model of a substance with accidental determinations. Precisely to the extent that the human being is essentially determined by the possibility of play, he is determined by that which is unfathomable and indeterminate, that which is not fixed, that which is open, the dimension of the possible that undulates within the prevailing world that is reflected in him. In human play an ecstase of existence toward the world takes place. Playing is, therefore, always more than merely some innerworldly human behavior, activity, or being-in-action. In play the human being "transcends" himself, surmounts the determinations with which he has surrounded himself and within which he has "actualized" himself, makes the irrevocable decisions of his freedom revocable, as it were, leaps free from himself, and plunges from every fixed situation into the possibilities that stream forth in the primordial ground of life—he can always begin anew and cast off the burden of his life history.

Such a characterization sounds ambivalent and immediately arouses protest—and yet everything hinges on this ambiguity. The human being realizes himself by choosing himself in the course of life in thousands of ways: in all his choosing of things and circumstances he always ultimately chooses only himself. In the decisions of his freedom he determines himself as this human being who is unique in each case. It need not be mentioned here that the action of human freedom presupposes a foundation of life that cannot be chosen and is subtended by a vital endowment of nature that we must take up. We cannot argue with the great or small "gifts" that maternal nature confers on us and endows us with on our life's journey; she abandons us to ourselves—but then it lies on us "to make use of the talent that has been confided to us."[21] Henceforth we choose ourselves in the activities that we do, but also in our omissions and lapses. We become more and more the work of our deeds and misdeeds. In the decisions of our own freedom we are decided, commit ourselves, and achieve one actuality from many possibilities open to us. We can certainly overturn decisions that have been made, change old commitments in new decisions, but only in such a way that we further determine ourselves, further commit ourselves. In each act of free choice we commit ourselves to a habitual formation of the will. In the actions of freedom we form the entire way in which we are responsible for conducting our lives. We cannot at any time *actually* relinquish the way in which we have freely brought about and configured this form of life. We cannot actually escape ourselves and rid ourselves of the burden of our own responsibility, cannot actually skip over our deeds—but we can actually do all this in a "non-actual way": in play. On occasion play also[22] releases us from the history of our deeds, liberates us from the work of freedom, and restores to us a freedom from responsibility that we experience with pleasure. We sense an openness for living, an unlimitedness, an oscillating within sheer possibilities; we sense what we "squander [*verspielen*]" in the act of decision, the playfulness [*das Spielhafte*] at the basis of freedom, the lack of responsibility at the root of all responsibility. And, within ourselves, we thereby touch on a depth of worlded Being in us, touch on the playing ground in the Being of all existing things. The "ambivalence" of such a characteristic lies in the here inevitable interweaving of the actual and non-actual. Play liberates us from freedom—but in a "non-actual way." And yet precisely this "non-actuality" of play is a particularly essential relation of the human being to the world. In the medium of "non-actuality" the whole that is at work in all comes to appear within itself. The symbolic representation of the whole of the world in the midst of things cannot be a solidly actual thing or a human being's solidly actual deed; rather, the world can only become illuminated in itself if it enters into the mysterious ambivalence of play, into its actual non-actuality.[23] The world comes to appear [*erscheint*] in the appearance [*Schein*] of play: it shines back into itself [*scheint in sich selbst zurück*] in taking on an intraworldly relation, even if in irreal form, taking on features of the prevailing whole. The proof of the shining back [*Rückschein*] of the world into itself, into a particular intraworldly thing, into the human being who emulates the world "as if"—as if "all-powerful," as if "without responsibility," as if within all possibilities at the same time—this shining back, seen from the cosmos, is the same as what we have called, seen from the human being, the ecstase toward the world-whole.

And it is perhaps most difficult to conceive that this *relation between the human being and the world,* as it is documented in human play, does not present a relation between two separate things, but rather, as a relation, precedes the differentiation of what is enclosed together within it. The human being is not initially, and does not then become in retrospect, occasionally open and related to the world, but rather it belongs to his singular and strange Being to be opened up to the totality of the world with understanding—even though he may for the most part lose himself in intraworldly things and no longer see the forest for the trees. We have for the most part forgotten the "forest" of Being when we engage with things in earnest. In play's exuberance, in its sense of lightness and its lack of responsibility, which treats beings as playthings and moves them about, we hold ourselves out into the expansive openness that resonates in everything—and in fact resemble the "fowls of the air."[24] Because the playful ecstase of the human being toward the world and the proof of the shining back of the whole of the world into the intraworldly symbol are the same relation, human play does not allow itself to be treated in an "enclosed" anthropological thematization, does not merely allow itself to be described as a "behaviour."[25] The philosophical problem of play is always and necessarily *worldly,* insofar as it pertains to the *human being.*[26] The most conspicuous indication of the worldedness of human play for us was the problematic entanglement of actuality and non-actuality in play. In play the realms that we otherwise carefully keep separate—and we must hold them apart if we want to survive—are mixed and blended. In all serious occupations of life we divide what is actual from mere appearance, what is tangible from the merely imagined, what is reliable and certain from what is questionable and merely surmised. In play, however, we mix Being and appearance together without inhibition; we take enigmatic delight in that which is apparent, which occasionally verifies for us a higher truth than the solidly actual things of our everyday environment. Hence, the interpretation of human play is concentrated for us in the question of what sense and what status is possessed by the "non-actuality" of the "playworld" belonging to every kind of play. What sense of Being does the imaginary scenery of play have? Both the metaphysical and the mythical interpretation of play emphasized the otherness of the playworld in comparison to ordinary things. The playworld is *less* than the ordinary sensuous thing, according to Plato's metaphysics; it is only a reproduction, only the reproductive mirroring of sensuous things, which for their part are reproductions of the truly existing ideas—it is thus a reproduction of a reproduction. The playworld is, notwithstanding its being bound to appearance, *more* than ordinary things—this was what we learned from myth. In the playworld-appearance the epiphany of the gods is carried out; the daemon is conjured in the mask. In the metaphysical degradation as in the mythical elevation of the playworld there are one-sided, and thus abstract, moments of truth. The playworld is neither "less" nor "more" in comparison to the rest of things; it is unique in that it is less and also more. It is a symbol of the world in the medium of appearance. That which is imaginary does not measure its status from its distance to things, neither to the ideas nor to the gods; it obtains its status and its significance from the human world-relation.

What we have said about the sacred precinct holds in another way for play. It is constituted by "demarcating exclusion." It is set apart from the other human activities of life; it is not interwoven with them in a common striving toward a goal. It "interrupts" the continuity of purposeful activities; it has its purposes entirely in itself, indeed in such a way that the internal purposes of play-activity are not put back into the general and otherwise thoroughgoing striving of life. The activity of play is separated off from other activities, is sealed off against them and, in its medium of appearance, has its "own realm" enclosed in itself. The "scenery" of play of course always needs actual space and actual time in order to be able to unfurl itself at all, but space *in* the playworld and time *in* the playworld never coincide with the surrounding space and time. On the substratum of spans of time and pieces of space functioning as mere bearers of the playworld, the imaginary scene elevates itself with its inner space, which is nowhere and yet here, with its inner time, which is never and yet now. And the player, too, through his role, is removed from the context of the life he otherwise lives. Through this demarcating exclusion an innerworldly part is determined for the representation of the world-whole: individual things and persons are clothed with the feature of being "proxies" for the power that is at work in all. It would be a question of great import as to whether the way in which play separates off its field was engendered by the archaic form of cult-play, and thus whether the structures of play are derived from the structure of the sacred, or whether, because cult is originally play, that which is sacred comes to appear within the human realm in the demarcated and strictly circumscribed temple grounds that inspire reverence. At any rate, the *temenos*-structure belongs essentially to human play, turns it into a cosmic metaphor.

The expression "cosmic metaphor" conceals within itself countless difficulties and is a veritable *crux rationis*. For what can "metaphor" possibly mean here? Aren't there only "metaphors [*Gleichnisse*]" where certain equivalences [*Gleichheiten*] exist? But what is less equivalent than the world and beings—than the in-finite and the finite thing? Can a more stark and rigid difference even be conceived? Perhaps the difference between Being and nothing? But does the difference between Being and nothing actually exceed the difference between world and thing? As long as we think of Being as the *Being of beings,* that is, of finite things, the nothing, too, still belongs within the world as a limit, excess, and demise of things. It only becomes different when we think Being itself on a world-wide scale and in its totality [*allheitlich*] and, likewise, the nothing as the negation of the totality of Being. Speculation concerning Being and nothing remains for the most part stuck within the perspective of the finite, limited Being of innerworldly, fragmentary things, even where it—in Hegel—conceives the nothing as nihilation, as "negativity." How and in what sense can one speak of a Being of the world at all? Does the concept of Being encompass even the concept of world—or must the world be understood as that which is more primordial, that which contains the Being and nothingness of things in itself? Does cosmology form a part of ontology, or does true philosophical wisdom concerning the world [*Weltweisheit*] surpass the ways that traditional metaphysics asks questions? These are open but highly significant questions that are first gradually beginning to be formulated and will come to stamp the modern confrontation with the history of philosophy.

To return to our theme[27]—we have posed the question as to whether there could even be a cosmic metaphor, since indeed there exist no structural affinities between finite things and the infinite world. How is the world supposed to be able to show itself in a thing? How does what pertains to the world reveal itself in what pertains to things? Certainly we must hold fast to the incommensurability between world and thing; we must above all avoid thinking of the world as some all-mighty, gigantic thing that would relate to ordinary things like the mountain to its stones or the sea to its drops of water. The stoniness of the whole mountain is in a stone; the wateriness of the whole sea is in a drop of water. The finite thing is not a particle of the world that would relate to the whole of the world like a part of a thing to the whole of a thing. The intraworldly thing is not a miniaturized world—as the stone is the miniaturized mountain and the drop is the miniaturized sea. Here it is never a matter of a quantitative relation of the small to the large or vice versa. The relation between the world and the thing cannot be reduced to something quantitative; however, the quantum in general can presumably be traced back to the spatiality and temporality of the world. World and thing are incommensurate [*unvergleichlich*]—above all so long as relations of equivalence [*Gleichheit*] and correspondence between *beings* determine the perspective of thinking. One might wish to object to this that we do not speak of "metaphors [*Gleichnissen*]" at all when homogenous [*gleichartige*] things are put together and brought into relation, but rather when "heterogeneous things" are compared with each other. That makes sense. But heterogeneous things, despite all their differences, nevertheless have in common the fact that each is a *being.* Whether we compare the human heart with an insensate stone or human beings with gods, each of the things we are comparing is in each case a being: despite the great extent of difference, what is held apart and what is held together concur in the sameness of being a being. However, this does not hold for thing and world. The world is not like things are, and things are not like the world. Can the finite[28] ever become the metaphor for the infinite?

This could never be the case if the finite as the intraworldly itself were not an aspect of the world itself. Our task is to conceive the possibility and the meaning of a cosmic metaphor proceeding not from intraworldly beings but from the world. The whole of the world, as the whole lying beyond all finitudes, cannot go back into an innerworldly thing, nor appear there on a miniature scale. But the prevailing whole can "shine back" into an intraworldly being, illuminate features there, and bring aspects to light that are distinctive of the movement of the totality. The world shines back into the human as into the being that is distinguished by an understanding openness to the world. And the proof of the shining back of the world into the human realm is documented in ever-different ways in the various basic phenomena of our finite existence: differently in work and in struggle than in love and funeral rites, and differently in play. Which features of the world determine the playful character of human play? To answer this in even an initial and preliminary manner remains extraordinarily difficult. Things find themselves *within* the world in multifarious motions that do not come to appearance at random and also do not disappear groundlessly. Their coming and going is determined by fixed, regular connections. The movement of innerworldly things has a reliably abiding *modus operandi.* However much every individual thing changes and however much nothing between heaven and earth is spared from consuming transformation, as each and every thing is ultimately exhausted and its power to be perishes, the total *modus operandi* of unceasing transformation nevertheless abides. The fabric of actuality persists, while things that are temporarily actual come and go, emerge and disappear, blossom and wither. This is an a priori insight, as one says in philosophical terms. Things are woven into a single, all-encompassing total contexture, have in it their place and their allotted time, their flourishing and their decline. And the regularity of this course of all things within the time-space of the world is known by us independently of all factual experience, yet is verified and confirmed continually in and through experience. Now, it could obviously be the case that we are not able to fix the regularity of all innerworldly occurrence reliably enough into a formula, a law; that our interpretations of regularity turn out to be too short-sighted. We ordinarily characterize as "causality" the regular determinateness of the course of all things: everything that occurs has a ground for its occurrence, is grounded in an antecedent cause, and follows as its effect. It is one-sided to take only *one* mode of causation into account and to illegitimately extend it to all regions of beings, when one claims, for instance, that "mechanistic causality" is the universal, fundamental law. Alongside mechanistic causation we are also familiar with teleological causation in the realm of that which lives and, finally, causation by means of the will in the field of human activity. Everything in the world has its ground. But does the world itself, too, have a "ground"—or is the question devoid of sense here?

The world is *groundless*—but in a quite unique sense. Its groundlessness encompasses the pervasive groundedness of all innerworldly processes and events. *In* the world many acts of striving have immanent goals; in the realm of plants and animals we find myriad instances of reaching out toward conditions that are being pursued, and in human life we are familiar with a variety of ends pursued and goals passionately desired, which suggest their integration in the highest end of existence, in *eudaimonia*. Human life appears to stand under a *single* final end, to which all particular ends and partial strivings are subordinated. Many ends are at work *in* the world: but does the world, too, as a whole, have an end, a goal, a *telos,* toward which it moves? Now, there are religious and even philosophical interpretations of the world in which a goal is attributed to the world. But the immense cosmological significance of modern "nihilism" lies in the fact that here a total end for the world is not merely unrecognizable but rather is dismissed as absurd, and the world comes to appear in a strange and enigmatic aimlessness. The world is no longer taken to be the temporal process for the revelation of a god, nor as the unfolding of reason contained in it, nor as the history of spirit comprehending itself, nor however else the eschatological conceptions may run. The world in itself is aimless, and it also has no value in itself and remains outside every moralistic assessment, is "beyond good and evil." Without ground and without aim, without sense and without goal, without value and without plan—but it holds within it all the grounds for thoroughly grounded intraworldly beings. It encompasses with its universal aimlessness the paths upon which aims and goals are striven after. It even embraces in value-free fashion the beings multifariously tiered according to levels of ontological strength. It holds spaces and times open for the grounded, purposive, meaningful, and value-laden Being of things. But we must make clear and distinct to ourselves that the groundlessness of the world, its aim-, goal-, value-, and planlessness, cannot be thought on the model of a thing that is without value in an innerworldly sense. The groundlessness of the world is not less than, not inferior to, the groundedness of beings; it is something much more primordial. The worldly prevailing of the omni-potent happens without ground and without goal, aimlessly and senselessly, without value and without plan. These are the basic features of the world that shine back into human play.

But the human being is a being *within* the world. He is worldly, insofar as he, like all things, belongs within the universe. And he is worldly insofar as he, in an understanding manner, stands out toward the whole. Nevertheless, he is not worldly in the same way as the one and only world itself. And yet features of the world's prevailing [*des welthaften Waltens*] shine back into the human being and into his play, which thereby attains a world-symbolic sense. To the extent, however, that all human activity is determined and grounded by meaningful motives that are represented by the will, the human activity of "play" is also naturally integrated within the total *modus operandi* of human action. Yet this is so in a remarkable and striking way. The senselessness of the world shines back into the intraworldly sphere of human sense [*Sinnhaftigkeit*] *in such a way* that the human being, within his purposively determined activity, keeps open, so to speak, a free space in which a certain action becomes possible, one without a motive that would propel one further and would project it onto the human being's final end. Play is subject to no end pointing beyond it; it has its ends solely within itself—and is on the whole, as one says, "aimless." Human playing is one way in which, in the midst of the pervasive groundedness of innerworldly things, a groundless oscillating-within-itself of the carrying out of life appears as a symbol of the prevailing world. However, insofar as the "groundlessness" of play takes up residence in the midst of the human being's purposive, meaningful, value-laden, and planned activities, it must first contain *in itself* "ends," "meaning," "value," and "plans" and, secondly, can only be a metaphor for the cosmos *in the medium of "appearance."* No innerworldly thing can *actually* be like the cosmos and its majesty; it can be a symbol only within the field of appearance [*Schein*], indeed of the proof of the shining back [*Rückscheins*] of the world into its own intraworldliness. In human play, aspects of the world light up, but in a refracted manner—refracted by the binary of actuality and non-actuality, which is concentrated in play. Human play is thus[29] a symbol of the world. The features of groundlessness, senselessness, and aimlessness that loom within human understanding disencumber it for the carefree and dreamlike levity that belongs to the enactment of play. It is because we are open to the world, and because in this openness to the world on the part of human existence there goes hand in hand a knowledge of the groundlessness of the prevailing whole—it is because of this that we play at all. Because he is "worldly," the human being is a player.[30]

The philosophical clarification of the anthropological problem of play essentially includes a discussion of the human world-relation. In connection with this question we have repeatedly been referred to an idea that belongs to ancient myth but also to early philosophical thought, namely: that the world itself is a kind of play. What can that mean now? Has our inquiry into play to this point sufficed for thinking a play of the world explicitly enough? To each human kind of play belongs a player who loses himself in the role of the imaginary playworld, cloaking, veiling himself in the role that is played and masking himself therein. Can we think the prevailing of the omnipotent—in the metaphor of a game played by a player? The play of the world cannot be the play of a personal power. As long as we still think something with the concept of a person and do not allow it to fade away into the mist of a merely indeterminate perception of thought, we must also think of a being relating to itself, a being that is distinguished from other beings by such a self-relation. No matter how great, how mighty and powerful, how knowing the person may be represented, the person cannot in the strict sense be thought of as omni-potent, powerful in the way in which the totality is, because self-relation is a demarcation from another. The omnipotent cannot be a person, and no person can be omnipotent. The world is no god, and no god is the whole world. Gods can perhaps play—in a similar but superior way—in comparison with the human being. The totality can never at all play like human or divine persons. Does the world-totality play differently than the intraworldly creatures near to the world: gods and human beings? The world-totality plays, but neither as a person nor in such a way that it thereby attains [*erspielt*] an "appearance," a "non-actuality," an imaginary scene. If we wish to speak of a play of the world, we must decisively transform our thinking of the play-structures of human play, try to think anew those features by which it presents itself as *derived* from the prevailing of the world. The world prevails by giving emergence to all individual things, bringing things to appearance, letting them light up in the brightness of the sky and setting them back into the sustaining earth, apportioning to every individuated thing appearance and shape, place and allotted time, flourishing and withering. The world prevails as the power of universal individuation. It stamps things with specific and generic and yet at the same time also individual characteristics. It bears from its womb everything individuated and is at the same time also the tomb of all things. It is the space-time of emergence and demise. The prevailing of the world [*Das welthafte Walten*] in myth and sublimated in philosophy is interpreted by way of modes of comprehension that are familiar in basic human phenomena. Does the emergence of things into and out of the world and their demise back into the shapeless ground occur analogously to the manner in which a craftsman produces his finished product, thus according to the model of human work? Or analogous to how human children are conceived from the intimate union of man and woman? Is the world the mythical wedding of Gaia and Ouranos? Is it a generative and birth-giving principle? Is the world the war of two world-powers, a relation of domination of the principle of reason over that which is without reason? Or is it comparable to play? A groundless prevailing that includes all grounds in itself, an aimless production that includes all aims?

But does anyone play at all there? The play-metaphor fails as a cosmic likeness if we fixate on the personality of a player and on the character of appearance belonging to the playworldly scene. Only in a decidedly distorted and thereby fragmented "likening" can we speak of a *play of the world*. The play of the world is no one's play, because only in it are there first someones, persons, human beings, and gods. And the playworld of the play of the world is not an "appearance" [*Schein*], but rather the *coming to appearance* [*die Erscheinung*]. Coming to appearance is the universal emergence of all beings, things, and events into a common presence that integrates everything individuated into a presence—in our midst. What we ordinarily already call the world is the world-dimension of presence, the dimension of coming to appearance wherein things are really separated from each other, but also still integrated in spatial and temporal vicinity and connected to each other by strict rules. But the world is also the nameless realm of absence, from which things come forth into appearance and into which they again vanish—assuming Hades and Dionysus are the same.[31] The play of the world, if it is to have a sense that can be thought at all, must be conceived as the relation of the world-night to the world-day. In the problem of individuation, the coming to appearance of beings is plumbed, thought back into absent depths, which the terrestrial day on the surface for the most part conceals from us. All beings are cosmic playthings but all players, too, are themselves only played. Coming to appearance is a mask, behind which "no one," behind which nothing, is—precisely as the nothing. To make the play of the world the theme of speculative thinking is a task that still remains to be accomplished, which perhaps can only be fully ventured when the metaphysical tradition, which conceals play and is hostile to it,[32] has been worked off. Does it not then also belong to this task that the human being transform himself—that he no longer seek his measure above the stars and mistake himself in the radiance of the gods? Yet[33] it would be questionable to say that the human being must henceforth "conform," not to the intraworldly gods, but to the prevailing, playing world and find his future measure in it. We conclude our course of thought[34] with a still completely unresolved problem.[35] The human being—as a player—exists open to the world most of all precisely when he dismisses all measures and holds himself out into that which is limitless. And thus, after long and arduous conceptual exercise, we shall let the dithyrambic thinker "Zarathustra" have the last word:

> If ever I spread tranquil skies over myself and soared on my own wings into my own skies; if I swam playfully[36] in the deep light-distances, and the bird-wisdom of my freedom came—but bird-wisdom speaks thus: "Behold, there is no above, no below! Throw yourself around, out, back, you who are light! Sing! Speak no more!"
>
> (*The Seven Seals*)[37]

Play and Celebration {1975}

Human play attains a heightened significance and symbolic brilliance during the weeks when the world celebrates the Olympic Games. It becomes a sign of humanity; described in myriad ways, marveled at and criticized, it occupies the attention of millions, unifies nations in peaceful competition, and allows a thrilling event to unfold in arenas and on screens. Play casts its spell on the players and the spectators: the competitors are compelled to achieve peak performance in strenuous martial discipline and the public to provide thunderous applause on account of millimeters and seconds. What kind of remarkable fascination is this that springs from games? We will seek an answer to this, a preliminary and incomplete one, in starting with cult-play and the display of the human body.

Every one is familiar with play from their own experience, from the days of childhood and the hours of free time; each has already played with others and watched unfamiliar games. It is easy to name a variety of games, to describe types and forms, yet difficult to bring the colorful abundance into conceptual formulation. Play in its transformative power withdraws again and again from a perspective that would fix it in place; it shuns firm contours and escapes the net of reflection's delimiting determinations. Its impulsive immediacy is far removed from the spirit of sober scientific knowledge and philosophy's speculative flight of thought. But nevertheless it does not take place in dull animality, nor in the unconsciousness of vegetative processes; it is illuminated by its own understanding, reaching from simple imitation to the projection of new possibilities for lived experience. It knows modes of deep absorption and the heightened alertness of symbolic representation. The players, taken in the broad sense of the word, which encompasses both the active participants and their spectators, move within an aura of sense and communicative contact; they understand the game that is played and its rules, as well as the playful activity in its motivations. Play as a common and manifold phenomenon of the human world, which occurs just as much in solitary dreamers as in groups or even masses, is not only in itself suffused with sense and sense-manifesting; it is always evaluated and estimated differently, too. Such appraisals run a long spectrum and end in extreme antitheses. Sometimes play is affirmed, marveled at, lauded, construed as an intact existence that is close to the origins, as a possible way in which human life can be whole—in Schiller's words, the human being only fully is when he plays. . . .[1] At other times, however, play is disparaged as idleness and dalliance, as a frivolous waste of time and lack of seriousness. Or one allows it to ultimately count as a factor in relaxation, as an occasional release from the harsh yoke of the labors and serious tasks that are necessary for life. The cultural critics of our day see in play a colorful social phenomenon with positive and negative features. The civilizing apparatus of a highly technological society weighs on the human beings who inhabit it. They enjoy comforts and benefits and yet are hemmed in by a thousand different practical constraints that the rational system imposes on each of them in production, consumption, traffic, and regulation of communication. However, in play, so it appears, we escape our predicaments and externally apportioned time. We reclaim a land of free impulses and imaginative fulfillment of dreams. We dispose over space and time at our own discretion, in the presence of external resistance as well as in our imagination. We create new powers and a singular feeling of freedom from the experience of play. Play has a therapeutic effect on the modern human beings of industrial society. However, it also brings dangers with it, dangers of a new kind. Because it seizes hold of the masses in huge events that resemble the ancient circus, because sports on Sunday provide conversational material for the drab workweek, an immense industry for entertainment and diversion has already emerged, a factory for the consumption of play—but more alarming still is the possibility of the exploitation of the drive to play, an encompassing manipulation that is in control precisely where individuals feel themselves to be free and enjoying their own free choice.

In the era of global technology and increased awareness, human play today exists under new and not yet sufficiently researched conditions. It wanders through the ages in shifting masks and characteristics but is at work in all its metamorphoses as a vital power of mysterious allure and seductive enticement. What is play? Can one ask about it in this manner at all—and provide an answer with definitions, descriptions, structural analyses—or does it present too many facets and confusing aspects?

A central basic phenomenon of existence indeed never lies opposite us like some foreign object, from which we stand at a distance. We are players—perhaps just as we are also workers, fighters, and mortals. The fascination that comes from play is due not only to its levity, its cheerful exhilaration, its relief from the seriousness of existence—it has obscure and concealed roots that reach back to the dawn of the human race—and still have a lingering influence today within the element of celebration. The cultic origin of human play is of the utmost significance for philosophical insight. As priestly activity, play is drawn into the inmost core of the life of early humanity; it is not a "marginal phenomenon," not a peripheral appearance, without which life would be able to be carried out in more serious occupations. Cult-play forms the center of the primitive lifeworld, the fundamental act of its self-understanding and self-interpretation. This early life does not yet speak for itself in concepts and logical syntaxes; it speaks in visionary images, in gestures, in elevated and stylized rituals. It must act and behold, "understand" with the eyes and in bodily movement how things stand with it, how it is admitted into powerful, overarching forces, exposed and abandoned to them, how it "depends" on what is beyond the human. Cult-play informs the cult community of that which is essential, and of the human being's position in the midst of cosmic forces, of the "invisible powers" who bestow blessings and send calamity, whose enigmatic and unsettling presence is felt and yet not directly seen, grasped, or conceived, which in their proximity remain inconceivable and mysterious and lurk around small human settlements in the midst of the wilderness as though concealed and lying in ambush.

Yet cult-play not only provides an orientation; it is above all an activity in the sense of a magical technique, as cooperation and counteraction in relation to daemonic forces. The most important deed in the primitive tribe's framework of life is the activity of those who understand how to correctly deal with daemons, who know most of all about their secrets, who understand how to distinguish between good and evil spirits, who know the correct incantatory formulas and in the enchanter's mask dare to oppose overwhelming forces and detain them. The deed of the medicine man, of the enchanter-priest, is a "salvational deed," on which the weal and woe of the entire social organization depends. For that reason he has a highly privileged status, is the administrator of consecration and sacramental sanctifications; he gives his blessing to weddings, birthdays, hunting expeditions, and military campaigns; he conducts the festivals in which the whole of life, which has been disintegrated and scattered into the everyday, gathers itself again in the coming to presence of the gods. The magical technique of the enchanter-priest is the most important *technē* in the diversely structured system of primeval activities: divination binds together heaven and earth, human beings and gods, and places human things collectively and explicitly within the horizon of the whole. And it is highly significant that the human being's historical trajectory does not merely begin with purely economic activities, through which he produces the means of life and thus "indirectly" preserves his existence, but rather, already in the earliest dawning of history's trajectory, the phenomenon of the cult emerges and in it the intellectual [*geistige*] activity of making sense of life appears, precisely as the praxis of the enchanter-priest with his secret knowledge and secret arts. The peculiar solemn [*feierliche*] seriousness of early play, its sacrosanct ceremoniousness, its priestly dignity, is grounded in the close connection that play has with the primeval cult. Such play does not provide a variation on serious life in the amusing acting-as-if; it is itself the most serious seriousness, insofar as it has to do with safeguarding the social community in relation to invisible powers.

Of particular philosophical relevance is the positivity of the play-worldly appearance that emerges in the cult-play of early history, which was not yet denounced as a nugatory cobweb of fantasy and dream. Every spectator knows that a human being is behind the mask, but this knowledge does not disillusion; for the point is not that a human being has disguised himself, but rather that within a human disguise the daemonic itself comes into view. The awareness of semblance [*Scheinhaften*] in a mask, play, or scene does not lead to the dissolution of the intention to portray or to a "rupture" of ontological belief. The awareness of semblance is rather just the presupposition for the symbol's ability to come to light. If an event is "only played," only "appears [*erscheint*]" in the imaginary circuit of the scenario before spectators, it is not thereby devalued or deemed to be less than the actual actors or to be less existent than the spectators' stone benches. On the contrary: the "non-actuality" of magical representation becomes the distinctive "breach" of a deeper and truer, genuine actuality, precisely the actuality of the powers and forces at work everywhere. The representation of actuality thus attains a deep dimensionality with many levels.

To be sure, the symbol, taken as a thing, does not, in its signification, have the solid actuality of everyday things. But by distancing itself from solidly actual things through the "non-actuality" of the play-appearance belonging to it, it can point back to a more primordial power of Being. The "non-actual" becomes the locus of the hyper-actual. In the cult, the hyper-actual or the actual to the highest degree for the most part has the character of the daemonic and the divine. The symbolism of cult-play remains in the human being's relation to the god. Cult-play brings to presence the regime of the gods, their ordering and steering activity, which masters without effort and without exertion the transformation and passage of all innerworldly things—and it interprets the prevailing of the gods not merely in human play but rather in many ways as a kind of play, too. Cult-play, as it were, lets the play of the world-governing gods "appear" in the visionary symbolism of the scene, that is, lets it emerge before weak, human eyes in a metaphorical visibility. The magical invocation of the highest actuality brings an actuality of the highest degree to appearance before human eyes.

Festival-play can assume a variety of forms: it can be the sacred activity of consecration, the solemn service to the god in the great ritual that affords all spectators the sight of a magical-technical interaction of the priest skilled in enchantment with daemons and gods, makes those spectators into witnesses of his heavenly contact. With a mixture of dread, anxiety, and hope, primitive human beings watch their medicine man venture to manipulate the invisible ones, to spellbind, to influence them with mystical formulas and magic spells, to ascertain the ordained future from the flight of birds, from the blood of sacrificial animals, from the convulsions of the torn-out heart of the human sacrificial victim. But festival-play can also be a trustful attempt to summon the gods for fellowship, to produce a community of mortals and immortals in the joy of the feast, amid the sound of musical instruments and songs that sing the glory and praise of the gods. Occasionally such festive-celebratory feasts pass into an orgiastic delirium, a bacchanalian frenzy: human beings become certain of the contact with daemonic supremacy when they lose control of themselves, when they fall into a trance and shed the daytime's sober consciousness. By no means is the orgy of such festivals merely degeneracy, a debauchery of inebriating drink and unbridled eroticism. Already in Heraclitus we find, "If it were not Dionysus for whom they march in procession and chant the hymn to the phallus, their action would be most shameless. But Hades and Dionysus are the same, him for whom they rave and celebrate Lenaia."[2] What may appear to the outside observer as "debauchery" is for the participants of the cult a rapture that lifts them out of the ordinariness of everyday life. And in an entirely different manner, in turn, cult-play can comprise the moment of the staged coming to presence of the divine sphere in itself; it then becomes ritual dramatic play, which narrates the mythos and lets it become visible.

Festival play determines that which is playful from the perspective of the festival, that is, from the presence of the gods that is believed in, intimated, felt. Play then has for the most part an obscure, cumbersome, gloomy character. The overwhelming power of the gods unsettles the human heart with sublime terror. Even the good news of heavenly succor and the favor of the most high, which is perhaps proclaimed in such festival play, is not entirely able to brighten up the gloomy seriousness. The distance that separates mortals from immortals is too great. Cultic dramatic play or spectacle becomes tragedy, and play in general becomes a root of high art. As long as festival-play is primarily characterized from the perspective of the festival as the mysterious presence of the gods and the playfulness of cult-play is thus overshadowed by the magic of the cult, a dark seriousness governs the stage. Yet the aspect of play can on occasion come to fruition so strongly that all at once the festival is stamped by the playful, is dominated by mirthful delight and lighthearted grace, by the jocular character of free, pure play, by its imaginative exuberance. The satyr-play follows the tragic formulation of the mythos—liberating laughter, the ironic distance to our very selves—comedy—follows the heavy, serious bringing to presence of human suffering and the demise of heroes.

If we summarize the connection of cult and play, we can say: the cult is the distinctive phenomenon of life, above all in the early era of human history, in which play had a serious anthropological significance far beyond the playful, blissful activity of children, and in which it was not encountered in the "superficial," all-too-popular and all-too-familiar character of what is merely a lack of seriousness and dalliance. In the cult, human play from early history has the urgent, uncanny, and spellbinding basic feature of enchantment, the rapture that removes the human being from his everyday straightforwardness and determinedness. The mask is here not so much concealment for the masked one as it is rather human access, the door to the realm of daemons. It not only enchants the spectators; it first enchants the wearer of the mask, turns him into an enchanter, a medicine man, a priest, a mediator between the uncanny and invisible realm of "spirits" and his fellow human beings. The mythological dramatic play or *spectacle* does not only make evident what the dominant, overpowering forces are to which the human being is abandoned; not only does it orient—it is also efficacious, in a practical manner: if the human being brings the powers to epiphany in the dramatic play or spectacle, powers to which he knows he is fully exposed and handed over, then he accomplishes at the same time an atonement and a purification, a catharsis of the soul. The entirety of the cult is certainly not playful, and play, too, in its entirety is not originally only cultic. Already in the earliest human horde there are the games of children, aspects of play in the meeting and courtship of the sexes; there are kinds of play with excessive power, of martial dances and contests and, finally, the manifold pranks of everyday life. Yet cult-play predominates in archaic times.

In this belief in gods and daemons, vanished and gone in our later age, is the only phenomenon of play still left one that can merely profile an elementary comportment of the human being in contrast to work, to struggle between human beings, to the memorializing of the dead, to the love of humankind torn into two halves? What can play still celebrate? For the technological giants of our era, all playful imitations are too small; for the fighter of brutal wars of extermination and genocides, play can provide no sense-transfiguring model. What can play celebrate, if it lets a world of sense appear in the interplay of competitors and before the eyes and screens of the world's populace?

To give a substantial answer to this is perhaps hardly possible. But a slight, insignificant answer may be attempted. The Olympic Games celebrate playing human beings themselves in their embodiment, in their embodied performative power and finely honed skill. Is that not an impoverished theme, a cult of nerves, muscles, and disciplined will? Such an objection itself thinks of the body in an impoverished way, a body in which human power and magnificence come to light. The embodiment of human existence forms a philosophical problem of lofty status and great difficulty. The human being actually exists on the earth only in his body. Our love blooms in flesh; work and struggle cost blood, sweat, and tears; human play oscillates in the rhythm of gestures in dance and mime, in sonorous word and song; and death changes us into the lifeless corpse. The human being is not only bodily insofar as he possesses a body, insofar as in a certain sense he is tethered to this constant companion; he is embodied insofar as he always relates to his body, even if in historically variable dispositions. The biological discovery that he is an exemplar of a higher kind of animal does not constitute the philosophical problem of incarnation, but rather what does is the odd situation of being a perceiving, mobile, and thinking midpoint of the appearing environment in a sensuous, sense-suffused way. The bodily relation signifies the psychical-intellectual and volitional-active manner in which the human being relates to the natural evidence of his animal existence [*Vorhandenheit*]. This sense-saturated relation is transformed in the course of history, not only in the way in which the human being "understands" his embodiment, but in the manner in which he puts it into practice. The human being does not only have, for better or worse, a body like a container for his psychical substance, and he also does not operate in it merely instinctively like an animal; he has experiences in it and with it. He knows that he "possesses" a body, is incarnated therein. He is alienated or delighted by his body, can feel it as a nagging burden or as the realm of action for free and unfettered movements. The Greek glorification of the body was a magnificent mode of the human relation to the body; another was the spiritual era's ascetic, world-fleeing hostility to the body.

What does incarnation signify for human self-understanding: a kind of contingent fact or an essential determination of the *condition humaine?* Is the body the murky, obscure vessel that hinders us from "mounting up with wings as eagles"[3] and overshadows the heavenly light of the realm of ideas, the lifelong prison from which death alone releases us, which thus must be called a "doctor" and for which according to the words of Socrates "a rooster is to be sacrificed"?[4] In Plato we find contradictory statements about the body. It is even emphatically elevated if it is beautiful. The shapeliness of the beautiful body is taken to be a sign that points in advance to the pure shapeliness of thought.

The body, the beautiful body of the ephebe, for which Greek pederasty was aflame, becomes a signpost to a higher beauty that is more suffused with light, to the beauty of the single form of the beautiful, which ultimately coincides with the good, the *kalon*. Pederasty and philosophy are intertwined in the Platonic perspective, because the true is first illuminated in the radiance of the beautiful. And the beautiful is not a predicate that among other things can also apply to the body—as it does in other ways to the sun sinking below the purple sea, the temple towering between silver olive trees. Beauty is first understood not as the enchanting character of nature or as the symmetry of artworks, but rather as the human being's bodily beauty. We first attain natural and artistic beauty through the body and through its sensuous perceptions. The radiant body is the golden trace that leads to philosophy. No artistic creation can ever fully free itself from what is sensuous and experienced bodily—dance cannot free itself from the supple, flexible body and the allure of sex; sculpture cannot free itself from marble or bronze; music cannot free itself from the resounding tone and the tangible instrument. We are only open to all sensuous things at all to the extent that and because we have a body. Being-sensuous is a mode of human existence that cannot be cast off.

The body is not an appendage of the human being, not an external natural finding, with which the person, finite human freedom, is unfortunately just afflicted and stricken. Certainly, the human being has already at times been ashamed of his embodiment, has suffered in the chains that bind him his whole life long to the space-time of the world. A long and harmful tradition has misinterpreted the terrestrial mode of existence belonging to the earth and made us lose sight of the ancient, indeed the most ancient mysteries of the human race, has obscured from us the world-profound significance of elementary, sensuous, and bodily processes of life. Do we know essentially what the sense of eating, drinking, and procreation is, however subtle our natural-scientific knowledge about them may be? These processes emerge in a clearer light when we celebrate festivals. We celebrate even the loftiest festivals with the symbolic gifts of "bread and wine" as communion of the earth's children with the Great Mother.

All essential moments of human existence are connected to the body and sensuousness. Our intellect [*Geist*] is sensuous, and its sensuousness is not a lower preliminary stage, with "seeing and hearing passing away"[5] when the human intellect is set in motion. Perhaps we never think as the bodiless "angel" does, removed from everything earthly. Our thinking happens as language and is documented by voice and writing, our reason needs images, and our activities [*Handlungen*] refer to the hand [*Hand*]. The struggle that founds positions of power and ruling orders, that erects cities and states, takes place as the most severe threat to the body. From beginning to end, labor involves the bodily activity of work. Only because the human being lives in an earthly, bodily manner and is not an immaterial intellectual being can he objectify and reify his activity, really intervene in the matter of the elements, invent tools and machines. And play, too, with all its real and imaginary features, is bound up with the body and exhilarated by it. Incarnation pervades all structures of our existence. There have doubtless been eras with a gloomy view of the body, which we like to call "idealistic," that dismissively condemned the body, denouncing it as a source of disturbance for the intellect that was resplendent with thoughts, as a confusion of reason, as a blurring of truth; that saw in it a principle of evil, the seat of lusts and wicked desires; that defamed it and yet have just not been able to ever "overcome" it.

For the sake of the body we need the necessities of life and even for the most part superficial things: nourishment, clothing, a house and village, tools, machines, weapons, all the myriad things of an artifact-culture, an immense technological apparatus. In the course of a long historical trajectory, the human being thereby surpasses in myriad ways the meager possibilities for action at the beginning, in which he transforms his immediate environment and utilizes the effectiveness of his body within still narrow limits. The body almost disappears in the manufactured suit of armor that the human being crafts. He advances with immense powers and technological modes of energy, with an artificial apparatus that he invents and controls, but which can no longer be understood as a bodily tool on a large scale.

The master of technology appears to have lost the body. And hence an odd reversal ensues—in the movement of modern gymnastics and sports. In the comportment of sports that is complementary with technology, the human body is not to be equipped more and more with contrived aids in order to multiply its powers, to accelerate its movements with machines, to expand the range of its actions in a million ways; rather, the task is to purely give prominence to the human body, to elevate it in its own performances, to cultivate delight in the body. The competitors who step up with their trained bodies and perform at a high level compete "naked" to a certain degree. They are not set inside an efficient apparatus. They perform a presentation of the human body in the possibilities that belong to it alone. The race, the toss, the blow, form exemplary basic models of a bodily action that is not technicized.

Yet that by no means excludes the fact that peaceful competitive play, which unifies nations, needs sporting sites of a technical perfection, an immense organization, which world play brings to world consciousness. A gigantic technology is deployed in order to present a primal phenomenon of human existence in its vital power, its beauty, and its capacity for performance, namely, embodiment. That is no contradiction. Technology serves, prepares the opportunity that in play and in the playworld of the Olympic tradition the human being plunges back, as it were, into a primal situation where bodies compete, where natural abilities and diligence in training are decisive, where the human being casts off his everyday armor like a bothersome garment—and ventures to find out what the body can be. Such competitive play is not a regression into pre-technological times, not an impoverishment of human possibilities; it is no antiquating idyll. In such play the playing human body in its free, creative self-actualization becomes the theme of play to be celebrated. While in other instances the body is the place from which activities proceed, whether they be those of war, labor, love, and the usual games, and while it for the most part remains that from which incarnated existence acts, in gymnastics and sports [*Turn-und Sportspiel*] the body itself comes into the shining light of appearance; it itself emerges into the celebratory circle, which takes place as a transfiguration of the body, as an apotheosis of our sensuous existence—which is not yet lost in the thunder of motors, not drowned in the global administration's deluge of papers, but is rather as old as the world and optimistic about the future.

Celebration encompasses the competitors and the enthusiastic spectators; it reaches its peak when the Olympic victor in the competition steps onto the rostrum to be crowned with an olive wreath.

Additional Texts

Child's Play {1959}

THE INTRODUCTORY LECTURE sought to make clear the fundamental significance of child's play as a distinctive key phenomenon for the existentiell self-understanding of human life. It thus proceeded from the methodological difficulty that child's play appears as a theoretical theme in the viewpoint of adults—and thus appears differently than it does to the living child who plays. The phenomenal character of this phenomenon is extremely problematic insofar as it is not fully accessible to the ways in which research is conducted by the positive sciences (for instance, psychological diagnosis, behavioral science, milieu sociology, ethnology, and so forth), but rather always requires an interpretation of objective observational findings through categories of life that the one who understands creates from his own inner biography after the fact, from the submerged memory of his own being a child. Access to the independent world of the child is difficult, is continually threatened by erroneous interpretations that assess the distance in life between childhood and the world of adults sometimes too slightly and sometimes too greatly. Then, with methodological caution, a provisional distinction was made between the "play of movement," which is a "testing-out" of the kinesthetic possibilities of one's own body, predominant in early childhood, and the "play of sense [*Sinn-Spiel*]" of the one just beginning to speak, in which the child already imaginatively forms a fictive "playworld" and gives itself a "role" in it. The play of sense gradually achieves a "portraying function" and is the child's first sense-imbued engagement with its environment, is the beginning of a self-relation and world-relation. It is thus by no means the case that, in playing, children only "reproduce" the adult world, that they only stand in an imitative relation to it. Each generation, each new surging wave of life brings a unique and original tone to the immemorial melody of human life, lives from an obscure and almost unconscious inner anticipation of life toward the future, to a certain degree as a vital project. The child anticipates its future in playful self-portrayal. (Reference to *Plato's* insight into this state of affairs in the *Laws*.)

What constitutes the peculiar enchantment of child's play is not merely its fresh and lively primordiality and cheerfulness, but above all the lack of concealment and disguise. The child still plays in a naturally innocent way, while the games of adults are "masked" in many ways, indeed even contain veiling and tabooing as moments of play. If child's play displays an affinity to the mentality of primitives, to a way of magically associating with things, if it bears archaic features in itself, then it still must be surprising that children in our time evince a particular interest precisely in technological things and prefer toys that are copies of technological gadgets. Can the technological world, the product of a late, rational culture, be "near and dear to childhood"? There are almost no purely natural things anymore in the environment of modern human beings—except for clouds in the sky and stars in the night. It would be wrong if one wanted to interpret the child's "archaic primordiality" as a particular closeness of life to wild-growing nature, not yet deformed by humans. In this regard, much "romanticism" is touted by pedagogues. It is not only the technologically perfected toy that is difficult to interpret, but also the fact that the child's toy often simulates technological gadgets.

* * *

Above all, the discussion hinged on two problems: on the question of an actually revelatory access to the world of the child (according to the criteria of understanding that is possible here) and then on the relation between the child and the modern technological world (exemplified in the problem of toys). The discussion was very lively and opened up a plethora of insights drawn from experience, exemplary observations, and questions aware of the problems. In the course of discussion the distinction between bodily games of movement and games of sense receded and human play's bond to the body was emphatically given prominence. The body is the earthly site of human existence; we exist "bodily." Only an ancient tradition in intellectual history, Western Platonism, overshadows this elementary truth—and once disparaged the body as the "soul's prison" and as a source of the sensuous blurring of our ability to behold the ideas. Our times affirm physical education. Certainly—but our times consider the latter all too much as a task that takes a backseat to the education of the intellect and of character. Yet it ought to be recognized that all essential phenomena of the human being's existence are bodily. Embodied, we are the children of the earth; we live, work, struggle, die—and play in a bodily manner. Only when the total embodiment of the human being is recognized and acknowledged will the current underappreciation of physical education in the pedagogic space of schools disappear.

Play and Philosophy {1966}

SINCE ANTIQUITY, since there was philosophy, the meaning and status of human play have formed an unsettling and confusing problem for thought. And at the same time it is precisely the unquestionability, the elated cheerfulness of play, its blessed repose in itself, that which is unproblematic in the performance of play, which has posed question after question to conceptual thought. How is it possible to live for a time as though there were no looming darkness around us, as though there were not the night of oblivion in which what is known to us is only a small island, a wretched isle where we know our way around to some extent and nevertheless actually figure nothing out and realize nothing until the end—how is it possible to live as though there were not the burdensome toil of labor that is imperative and compelled by necessity, as though there were not the frightful struggle for dominance among human beings, not the vanity of the loving heart and not the shadow of death over all human things? Play is obviously the most extreme counterpart to everything "serious," to all purposive activity that is planned, is related to the future, and has foresight; it is a cheerful exuberance that takes life lightly and withdraws from every care and responsibility, and more than anything from the strict conceptual sobriety of philosophy. In the gloom of our life's setting, human play appears as an illuminated scene, as a transfigured and transfiguring intermezzo, as an action that needs no motive and does not look ahead to an end, as an activity that is self-sufficient and lives out its impulses unhindered. In contrast, philosophy is perhaps the most acute form of the "unhappy consciousness," the persistent mistrust of everything that exists—even of its own self, a despairing doubt [*verzweifeltes Zweifeln*] about the "given," about what is accepted and traditional, the destruction of the rootedness of existence and indeed by means of an ice-cold conceptuality bereft of images and hostile to the senses, and in the medium of an unceasing, abstract reflection.

This is the usual way of portraying the antipodean relationship between "play" and "philosophy," assessing it as an opposed relationship between "immediacy" and "reflective mediation." However, it should perplex us that supposedly simple and immediate play goes around confidently with a broken, fragmented "understanding of Being"—and that, on the other hand, philosophy that problematizes strives for distinct clarity in the knowledge of beings. The player's existentiell immediacy moves pleasurably in the labyrinth of Being and appearance—the thinker's existentiell fragmentation attempts to force its way through everything apparent to the true essence. Philosophy wants to disenchant, to reveal, to unveil, wants to tear things from concealment into the light of reason, does not want the beautiful for its own sake but at best as a prefiguring trace of the true. It scorns the charm of veiling, does not dread the unmasking of the most revered secrets; it wants only sober clear-sightedness into that which truly is. That implies much more than a psychological typological difference between player and thinker—the opposition of antipodes lies in the character of the world: in it Being and appearance are unceasingly blended, "essence" and "manifestation" are distinguished, in it things have surface and depth, in it nature conceals itself and opens itself up, in it the emergence and demise of all beings occur. Playing and thinking are two opposed relations to the world exhibited by the human who has an understanding of Being. The one: swinging into the round dance of worlded things, enjoying the polysemy of beings in the colorful twilight, where essence becomes surface and appearance becomes the core, where the "ruddy complexion of things" enchants and dons the mask. The other: the reduction of the colorful and manifold phenomena to the outline of what is essential, the conceptual insight into the structure of things, dismissal of the contingent, the working out of the architecture of the universe. If {thought} nevertheless strives passionately for "essence," breaks and shatters concealments in order to advance toward what is genuinely and truly actual, then it has as its path precisely the appearances that it denies, the trumpery of what is without essence, which it wants to set to the side; it is fettered to that which it negates. What is suffused with appearance, whether it be the appearance of illusion, of error, of hasty, all-too-human opinion, or whether it be the appearance of things themselves, their external, veiling surfaces or their will-o'-the-wisp sheen of the beautiful, becomes productive irritation for thinking, which relates itself negatively to that wherein human play has its joys. Play and philosophy have more in common with each other than the usual demarcations suppose; they refer in their immanent understanding of Being to the same appearing and manifesting of beings in the world, even if, respectively, in different, indeed, converse ways—they are antipodes on the same globe.

1.

After this general preliminary explanation of the peculiar oppositional relationship between play and philosophy, we will now attempt a philosophizing view of the phenomenon of play. Everyone is familiar with play; it is universally well known as something that occurs in the human world. Here, too, Hegel's dictum holds, that what is familiar [*das Bekannte*] is not on that account already understood [*das Erkannte*]. What is completely trusted in and self-evident often most tenaciously eludes the reach of the concept. Everyone is familiar with play from their own life, has had experiences with and of it, is familiar with the relationship of play among fellows, is familiar with numerous forms that play takes, is familiar with public games, the spectacles of the masses resembling the ancient circus, games of diversion, games of sport, competitions, the games of children and the somewhat more labored, ponderous and uptight games of adults. Everyone is familiar with elements of play in almost all realms of culture. *Homo ludens* is not fenced off from *homo faber* and *homo politicus;* there are half-concealed elements of play in the field of work and of politics, enticing and tempting kinds of play in the interaction of the sexes. Play is a dimension of existence that is intertwined with all the other fields of life, that determines interpersonal communities as much as cult, love, work, and ruling do. We are all conversant with the fundamental possibility of playing, even if we are not playing at present or are of the opinion that we have already left behind the phase of life for play. Everyone is familiar with countless situations of play in the private, familial, and public realms. Play activities are found in abundance time and again, are everyday events and occurrences in the human world. Play is alien to no human being; everyone is familiar with it from the testimony of their own life. Yet the everyday familiarity often hinders a deeper, more pressing question concerning the essence, concerning the ontological sense and status of play, and entirely prevents a question as to whether and how the human understanding of Being is altogether determined and marked by human playfulness [*Spielertum*]. An everyday interpretation of human play for the most part corresponds to the everyday familiarity with it. This tends to exclude play as much as possible from the essential core of human existence, to de-essentialize it, to conceive it as a merely "marginal phenomenon," to take the weight of its genuine significance from it. To be sure, one sees how common play is, human beings' ardent interest in play, the intensity with which they pursue it, the increasing appreciation of play in connection with the problem of free time in a technologized society. The aspect of play that thereby predominates above all is "recovery," relaxation, pastime, and cheerful idleness, a refreshing pause that interrupts the workday or is an activity for holidays. Wherever play is interpreted exclusively from an opposition to work or to the serious carrying out of life in general, we have the shallowest yet still predominant, in an everyday sense, interpretation of play before us. Play is now principally taken to be a complementary phenomenon, an ingredient, a supplement for a lifestyle determined by serious business. That implies that play is not grasped in its very own positivity; it is misinterpreted as an interlude [*Zwischenspiel*] between the serious activities of life, misinterpreted as a "pause," as a way of filling up free time.[1]

In Plato, who established and founded Western metaphysics, we find a peculiarly varied, colorful relation of thought to play—of philosophy to poetry, of the truth of what genuinely is to sensuous appearance in the radiance of the beautiful. His "critique of the poets" in the *Republic*, that great text on the state, is of an incisive, unsurpassed sharpness. A connection between being beautiful and being true, between *kalon* and *alēthes,* presides over his thoughts on the ascent of the soul from the cave's twilight of our earthly sojourn into the ideas' realm of light, above all in the *Phaedrus* and in the *Symposium.* In the work of his later years, the *Nomoi,* the "Laws," Plato constructs the second-best state by way of a meditation on play. Play is elevated to a principle that structures the state. The polis is ordered into three ranks, no longer into the static classes of worker, warrior, and philosopher-king as in the *Republic,* but rather into degrees of seniority. The difference in the stages of life is seen in a tension, different in each stage, between a natural instinctual force and rational insight. As children relate to their parents and legitimate teachers, so too do human beings in general relate to the gods. The human race is subject to divine discipline; the means of discipline, whereby the gods educate and train human beings, is the choral round dance. The festivals, which are celebrated for the gods and are dedicated to them, are not merely interruptions of everyday pursuits—the gods themselves have established them in order to again and again keep human beings once more under divine discipline. Thus Plato places the work of education and the structure of the state under the guidance and blessing of the gods. Above all, the guests in the divine festivals are the Muses, Apollo, and Dionysus, and thus the choral round dance is ordered into three divisions: the chorus of youth under the guidance of the Muses, the chorus of adults who are at the peak of life under the leadership of Apollo, and the chorus of the elderly under the banner of Dionysus. Rhythm is moderately ordered movement, is dance. Harmony is moderately ordered voice, is song. Dance and song constitute the choral round dance. The human being's sense for rhythm and harmony is a gift of the gods. Thus they nurture us. When youths excitedly band together to play in a round dance, they do not then know what it is in this at bottom that delights them. They do not understand rhythm and harmony as a numeric relation; they do not know that in all the joys of play the gods already draw them in the direction of true insight. The beautiful in its true mathematical nature is still opaque to them. Yet he who organizes such a musical chorus for youth must have an understanding of how the true is heralded in the beautiful, how philosophy is already prefigured in play. The task of a lawgiver organizing the state consists in allowing the song of praise of right living to sound in all the choruses of the polis—for the sake of playful inculcation into what is right. The youth chorus of the Muses and then the Apollonian chorus, too, sing the canticle of virtue, and by means of this continual bringing to presence, their existence is formed into a correspondence to true humanity that is, to be sure, not discerned by them and yet is felt. In the youth and in those who are at the peak of their powers the fire of life blazes up high, they are filled with the Dionysian, the surge of enthusiasm carries them high. Hence they need the constraint of musical and Apollonian restriction. The elderly, however, who are matured by long experience, already proceed along the declining paths of life. It is an irremediable tragedy of human existence that insight and passion, reason and the primordiality of life do not coincide, but are rather related in such a way that they are opposed. The chorus of understanding, yet weary elderly men is supposed to sing the most proper enchanting song of virtue, fuelled by their apportioned wine, and thus attain the highest condition: cool wisdom and playful-cheerful delight in life in one, as the fitting reconciliation of desire and insight, of *hedonē* and *phronēsis.* In this context, Plato gives an odd designation for the human being—from the perspective of play, he calls the human being *paignion theou,* plaything of the god. The human being, the free, creative player, is thereby humbled, pressed down into a marionette, degraded by the philosopher's "evil eye" into a thing that is moved about—or is there a deeper sense in the human being as a plaything of the gods? Does divinity, least in need of all things that are to be attained by work and struggle, need the human freedom of play—like a higher[2] plaything, as it were, in order to dream its dreams, to reach beyond into the domain of fantastical possibilities and enchanting silhouettes that present a nothing in Being and a Being in nothing—the divinity that is omniscient reason and sees through everything that exists[3] all the way down to the bottom and knows no deception?

With this open question, in which an explosive problematic lies,[4] we conclude our train of thought on play and philosophy.

The World-Significance of Play {1973}

HUMAN PLAY, to which our present reflection aims to do justice,[1] has many forms of appearance and shows itself as open and masked; sometimes it disguises itself in the demeanor of serious life, of pompous solemnity and affected dignity and at the same time is a mischievous, cheerful, and delightful activity, a carrying out of life that is full of buoyancy and exuberance, far from care and concern for the future, removed from the harsh hours of service and work—it is by no means only the domain of children and the paradise of youthful happiness; it beautifies and lightens the lives of adults, too, banishes boredom and gloom, conjures an illusory dream world within the pallid everyday routine. It socially and joyfully brings human beings together in entertaining and short-lived communities. It binds and releases with a gentle hand. It fascinates and enchants, relaxes and carries us away for a while from our burdens, offices, duties. It frees us from our real situation and brings marvelous possibilities before us.

Everyone is familiar with play from their own experience, from the days of childhood and the hours of free time and recreation; each has already played with others and watched unfamiliar games. It is easy to name games, to describe types and forms, yet difficult to bring the colorful variety into conceptual formulation. Play in its vitality and transformative power withdraws again and again from a perspective that would fix it in place; it shuns firm contours and escapes the net of reflected determinations. Its impulsive immediacy is far removed from the spirit of sober scientific knowledge and philosophy's speculative flight of thought; play does not reason argumentatively and yet it is not thoughtless. Its immediacy does not imply a dull animality, nor the unconsciousness of vegetative processes; it is illuminated by an understanding, reaches from the simple[2] tendency to imitate to the projection of new possibilities for lived experience. It knows modes of deep absorption and the heightened alertness of *symbolic* representation. The players, taken in the broad sense, which encompasses both the active participants and their spectators, move within an *aura of sense;* they *understand* the game that is played and its rules, as well as the playful activity and its motivations.

Play as a common and manifold phenomenon of the human world, which occurs just as much in solitary dreamers as in groups or even masses, is not only *in itself* suffused with sense and sense-manifesting; it is evaluated and estimated in a variety of ways. Such appraisals run a long spectrum and end in extreme antitheses. Sometimes play is affirmed, marveled at, lauded, construed as an "intact" existence that is primordial and close to the origins, as the "being whole" of human life—in Schiller's words, the human being only fully is when he plays. . . .[3] At other times, however, play is disparaged as idleness and dalliance, as a frivolous waste of time and lack of seriousness. Or one allows it to count as a factor in relaxation, as a recovery and break, as an occasional release from the harsh yoke of the labors and serious tasks[4] that are necessary for life. Play ends up being viewed under the aspect of a pleasurable reward. The cultural critics of our day see in play a colorful social phenomenon with positive and negative features. The civilizing apparatus of a highly technological society weighs on the human beings who inhabit it. They enjoy the comfort and benefits and yet are hemmed in by a thousand different practical constraints that the rational system imposes on each of them in production, consumption, traffic, and regulation of communication. In play, we escape, it appears, the preplanned world and externally apportioned time. We reclaim a land of free impulses and imaginative fulfillment of dreams. We dispose over space and time at our own discretion, in the presence of external resistance as well as in our imagination. We create new powers and a singular feeling of freedom from the experience of play. Play becomes therapy for the modern human being of industrial society. However, it also brings dangers with it, dangers of a new kind. Because it seizes hold of the masses in huge events that resemble the ancient circus, because sports on Sunday offer conversational material for the drab workweek, an immense industry for entertainment and diversion has emerged, a factory for the consumption of play, but more alarming still is the possibility of the exploitation of the drive to play, an encompassing manipulation that is in control precisely where individuals feel themselves to be free and enjoying their own free choice. The need for play enormously increases in intensity and scope within the social body today.[5]

In earlier epochs the mass of human beings had little time for play, and even children did not remain undisturbed in paradise for long.[6] They learned much too early the burden of labor and knew days that ran their course according to an externally imposed calendar. A large extent of free time and the kinds of play possible within it were the privilege of a ruling class that possessed power and wealth. Today, abundant[7] free time has already become a social problem. It must be "organized and managed," must be taken into consideration in city planning, in the sites for sports fields, in theaters, in places for amusement with automated games, in children's playgrounds, and the like. If long ago in the feudal era the play of the privileged class was occasionally so bored with its own mode of life that it sought new, tantalizing material for games by imitating the class that was oppressed and encumbered by the drudgery of work, and in idyllic pastoral games was deaf to the approaching revolution's rumbling thunder, then today the masses within the modern apparatus of civilization live—one could say—almost like princes. They have prosperity and much free time; they are bored and they need pastimes. Programmed entertainment has become an important sector of industry. Everyday life is permeated by elements of play.

Among the culture-critical censors, judgments vary on the advantages and disadvantages of modernity for life. They see an advantage in the growth of play with its spontaneity and its vital freshness, a disadvantage in the big business of gigantic mass events, in their planned, technologically and economically arranged implementation. However, perhaps it is premature to denigrate present-day life according to the standards of past ages. Is it so certain that play in the small format of individuals and groups was "more essential" than play in the great format of the masses? Does human play still have more changes before it that we cannot foresee, primordial stances of the collective soul, too? Even the human history of play has not yet come to an end that would provide a complete overview. Even if we collect a substantial amount of ethnological material, research the customs of play belonging to primitive and civilized peoples, and attempt an anatomy of *homo ludens,* we will still scarcely[8] arrive at a conclusive result, because the human being always plays with play, too. In this remarkable human possibility of comportment there is a provocative theme for ceaseless attempts. That makes all utterances about play fragmentary and preliminary. Indeed, it may almost be desperate to strive for an assured total understanding that would not be tarnished by partisanship and prejudices, that would not be ensnared by the protean charm of playful metamorphoses, that would not be enticed by the gracefulness of the play of the dance, would not be enthused by the spectacle of contests or the blissfully playful activity of children. Can one muster a value-neutral indifference to a phenomenon that is so colorful, so dazzling and shimmering, that spans both the most elevated cheerfulness and tragic seriousness, that is lived with exhilaration and at the same time mirrors the dark sides of existence? Or is the perspective more valid that, inimical to all levity, does not banish the heavy shadows that are cast over the landscape of our life, does not gild them with dream figures, but rather keeps vision clear for the evil and terrible features of humanity, denouncing a deceitful gossamer and a concealing appearance, an illusory world of self-made delusion in play?

Contemplative reflection is already as such alien to play, has no nearness and kinship to that which it wants to grasp. Playing and thinking appear to exclude each other. The reflective human being all too easily goes astray in the labyrinthine phenomenon of play, in its grottoes and secret recesses, in its beguiling appearance, its con-artist world and its fantastical constructs. Play can be spoken of from the distance of the disinterested, who watch an unfamiliar game and then describe a strange human comportment—however, it can also be spoken of in the mode of testimony from experience, thus from the bright sense that play brings with it—and which still remains fully enigmatic despite all the light of understanding. After these reservations, play may now be inquired into according to its *anthropological status,* according to the *problematic of its mode of Being* and according to its *world significance.*

According to the popular view, play has no clear significance vis-à-vis the human manifestations of life. To be sure, the phenomenon is common. It governs the early phase of childhood, which soon transitions into the preparatory phase for adult life; when playtime grows smaller the seriousness of learning begins. Play is increasingly displaced from the center of existence, becomes peripheral, while other kinds of conduct occupy life's stage. What anthropological status, then, does human play have? Because it is fleeting and unstable, is it itself a transitory mode of human comportment that the human being forgets or sets aside when more essential tasks claim him? Is it itself rubbish and useless exuberance because in it exhilarated mirth and all manner of masquerades occur? Is the human being only a player occasionally and casually? Or does play belong precisely to the *fundamental phenomena* of our existence? That is a question for which there is no short answer ready, because the human being who poses the question never knows himself the way he knows his surrounding environment. The latter is filled with facts, things, and processes, which we also do not investigate all the way to their basis, but which are present and, as objective findings, can at least partly be pre-scientifically and scientifically grasped, known, determined, and conceived. The human being who wants to know is not a clear discovery for himself. He strives after self-knowledge, and the formulations of his self-understanding guide his historical trajectory like stars or will-o'-the-wisps. Because the human being exists relationally, in relation to encompassing nature, to inanimate matter and to the animate realm of plants and animals, his self-understanding always also includes a total interpretation of all things. However, this brings with it the danger that he seeks to understand himself from that to which he relates in praxis and theory.

Anthropology is situated in a Tantalus-like position. The human being can interpret himself as "material," as the "animal that has *logos,*" as made in the image of divinity or as the vessel of world spirit. Each respective anthropological conception makes a preliminary decision concerning the status of human phenomena. A biological lens thus sees in play something like the "cunning of life," which drills its vulnerable and endangered young in advance, awakens and cultivates their capacities, before they become involved in the merciless struggle for existence, or harmlessly works off the pent-up aggressive drives in the mature living being. A function useful to life is conferred on play. In a theologically determined anthropology the evaluation is more ambiguous: play can be viewed suspiciously as frivolity, which detracts from the care for the salvation of the soul, or even appreciated as a comportment that is rapturously drawn away from common need, which beautifies the celebration of divinity. One can even venture the attempt to determine the human being from his phenomenal relations without such preliminary decisions concerning the human being's "essence." Here we initially encounter the relation between the human being and nature. Certainly he is himself a natural creature, brought forth by nature and rolling along in its deluges, yet never calmly appearing in advanced growth; he is rather the founder of unrest who does not let things stand as they have for eons. He proceeds offensively against his surroundings. Driven by need and conscious of his creative power of freedom, he transforms the earth that bears and endures him; he transforms the wilderness into land inhabitable for human beings. Work brings him all the necessities of life. It becomes a power that permeates his life. The human being is a worker. That is not an arbitrarily contrived characterization; it is the way in which he communicates with nature and preserves himself. Yet work is not an isolated possibility of the individual; it happens within a community, it is an elementary social phenomenon. The togetherness of human beings in groups, peoples, is stirred by contradictory strivings, by the contention for power and rule. Indeed, struggle is just as elementary as work. The human being is a fighter. Human beings in each case belong to one of two sexes; they emerge from the loving union of both halves of life; they are born, grow up, spend a fairly long time in the light, then must go down again, pass away into death. That is not blind fate, which they suffer unwittingly; they know themselves to be involved in the round dance of love and death. They also seek to understand themselves as lovers and mortals. The anthropological conception of the human being that is oriented by labor today dominates half the globe. Perhaps that is a disastrous one-sidedness insofar as it makes *one* fundamental phenomenon, *one* human relation, absolute, and "interprets" the other features of equal status that belong to our polysemous existence on that basis. Can the struggling, raging "will to power" or the love of the sexes with its mysteries or the shadow of death over all human things be understood in a sensible manner and methodically derived from the active entwinement and imbrication of the human being in the economic production process? It can be doubted whether the human being in the discord of strife exists as "totally" as he does in the concord of erōs, in the tensions of the world of work or even in the bright happiness of play. Yet from doubt there is still a long way to a reliable human self-knowledge.

What status does play have? Is there a quick and concise answer to this question? Have not traditional customs and cultural conceptions in the changing course of history decided on the "meaning and value" of human play? Can the individual liberate himself from all collective judgments and prejudices concerning play and determine what and how it "is in itself"? What the human being can say about the human being indeed never has the straightforwardness of an objective collection of facts, and is for the most part clouded by a "partisanship" lurking in the background. One says of play that it belongs to children, that it is their sort of authentic life, the original way in which their environment and shared human world emerges, that it is a gentle kind of training for existence. However, among adults it appears in a reduced form—as a counterweight to the seriousness of life and its difficult decisions, as "recovery," a break, filling up of free time. Others in turn set play over activity that serves the extension of life and self-assertion, elevate it to creative existence. Play remains resistant to such classification and fixed determination of place in a hierarchy, balks at its relegation to social classes, biological stages of life, or gender [*Geschlechter*].

The human being plays—always from the core of his life, even when he is thereby hidden and veiled in a hundred masks. As an eruptive power of life, play prevails throughout the Being of the human [*durchwaltet . . . das menschliche Sein*] and cannot be specified as an unambiguous, goal-oriented carrying out of life. There is no work in which playing crystallizes and comes to an end. Its process is itself its work, it happens spontaneously[9] and ceases, it is an activity that happens for its own sake. Initially, a play activity appears to be not much different than any other activity of everyday life, thus like a message, like a sequence of steps in a labor process, like a business errand—just like an action that runs its course for a time within a sense-imbued framework and in a succession determined by the end. To be sure, everything humans do is underlain by a base of vegetative and animal ways of carrying out life, run through by an undercurrent of unconscious and obscure drives, steered and pulled in a manner alien to consciousness, but activity as such, which feels itself to be conscious and "free," pursues an intention, has a goal, and exists ahead of itself in the projection of the goal. That holds for all deeds that alter need [*Not-Wendung*] through labor or for the militant unfolding of powers, for the striving after love and for the gloomy futural horizon of death. Yet in playing, the time in the future that remains outstanding is submerged as a motive force of acting. The futural whip drops away that otherwise goads us, hounds us, drives us, uses up the moment as a means. An existence pacified in itself in its carrying out of activity pervades the player and bestows a pure, felicitous present. One can object that this is only possible because playing is not a serious carrying out of anything, not an actual struggling with the recalcitrance of nature that is opposed to the efficacy and works of human drudgery, not a life-and-death struggle for power and rule, not a sacrifice for the beloved other, and not mourning for what is irrevocably lost. Playing, one says, is something that happens "as if." It brings features of an odd non-actuality along with it, an imaginary *appearance* that is *more* than a mere subjective delusion, more than an illusory representation of consciousness. An "appearance" that stands there as a structure that allows the players and their audience to be in accord. This *irreal* feature in the real occurrence of play is a difficult problem, insofar as we understand talk of "appearance," irreality, and constructs of the imagination in an approximate manner and can clarify it for ourselves in view of the phenomenon of play, too, yet at once fall into perplexity with every attempt at a conceptual determination.

In playing, one says, we are transposed into a fantastical situation, as it were: we are not subject to the difficulties and pressures of our ordinary actual real condition; with unrestricted wishful thinking, vivid juggling of fantasies, we produce a dreamed-up condition that suits us. We act *as if* it existed; we act according to a fictive goal for activity. Yet in so doing we are not bound by our deeds; we reserve for ourselves the right to immediately break whole chains of experience in the dream-world of play, to declare that they never happened and to create new sequences of events right away. Played activities can begin *anew* at each moment and have different "pasts" in each case, according to whim. The temporal sequence of events in the sphere of play takes place to a certain degree on two temporal levels, as the time of playing and as the time of occurrences in a "non-actual realm" that is put into play [*erspielt*]. And something similar also holds for the space that is occupied by play activity—and on which the imaginary setting is erected.

Certainly, it would be a misunderstanding of play to want to write it off as a pure product of the imagination, as an immanent dream with vivid imagery, as engagement with mere "figments of thought" that run their course within the interiority of consciousness. Play happens "outside," as an activity of human beings, as solitary or cooperative activity, carried out in open, intersubjective space and proceeding within a commonly apportioned time. Nonetheless, human play is pervaded by irrealizing moments of sense, is run through by fantasy and dream. But it always has a sensuous hold in actually present things, a basis in everyday reality.

That holds for all kinds of play. One can quite roughly distinguish mere diversionary games that help us pass the time, and then more essential kinds of play: the games of children, competitive games, and kinds of play in which there is portrayal or the playing of roles. This is obviously not a complete catalog, but rather only an indication of three basic types with differing relevance. In each type we find that odd mixture of sheer actuality and imaginary appearance, which makes human play into a provocation for conceptual understanding. Card games have their exciting atmosphere in the mingling of sociable intimacy and rivalry, of individual skill and fortune's favor. Factors that generally[10] govern social life are here set in motion and consciously represented on an inconspicuously small scale, to the delight of the players.

In child's play an "imitation" of adults occurs, but from the perspective of a still undeveloped understanding of life. Indeed, the brisk animation springs from the young living being's drive to employ its motor skills, yet there are already sense-moments of conscious imitation at work therein. The dichotomous structure of human play, its mingling of what is actual and non-actual, emerges most clearly in role-playing and games in which there is portrayal. Even a preliminary glance can confirm this. Role-playing occurs as the production of sense of an imaginary playworld that does not lie before the one who created it like a finished product, but rather "involves" him, draws him in, and engulfs him—sometimes with such an intensity that the player "gets lost" in his role. And yet he never actually loses himself; he remains the actor who is presently portraying King Lear or Wallenstein. He does not even fool himself about the identity of his person in the great emotion caused by the drama's poetic power. However, he knows that his ego is taken in, "possessed" by a sense that he lets become present in a sensuous spectacle with the gestures and gesticulations, the mimicry of his body, the modulation of his voice. He lends his own figure, though in theatrical costume, to the "heroes on the stage," and animates them as an interpreter of the poet. The process on the stage takes up time. The time portrayed in the stage play belongs to an imaginary realm; it coincides with the play's length of time just as little as the space on the stage coincides with the Castle of Eger. But both spaces and both times are there with each other, exist "at the same time" and yet not like other simultaneous occurrences within the same spatial field. To a certain degree, a spatio-temporal clearing arises on the stage from out of an irreal play-"world" whose irreality is nevertheless created with real means, where sensuous spectacle and fantastically generated appearance are mixed. And the spectator in front of it belongs to a play-community that encompasses actors *and* the public. Thus, not only the people acting in roles, but also those for whom they portray and figuratively, pictorially bring to presence an imaginary sense are participants in the playworld, even if they do not appear in it.

To be a spectator has a double sense. We can watch an unfamiliar form of playing without interest, and we then see a more or less comic and useless kind of behavior. Or we take an active interest in the sense of the play, see in Oedipus's suffering the essential misfortune of human existence and fall under the play's spell. The playworld is a spellbinding circle, an odd sphere that enchants, entrances, ties us down, and temporarily transforms us. If one customarily opposes the conduct of play to serious activities and situations of life, lets playing be contrasted with work or struggle, then one overlooks how far the playful [*Verspieltes*] extends, even in the so-called serious life of professions, the relations of the sexes, the false pomp of the funeral procession—and one also overlooks the fact that human play privileges for its thematic content precisely the great, tragic, and fateful stories, that we "play" the panting exertion of labor, the spitting rage of battle, the grief of Electra, the wedding celebration of lovers—and occasionally we even again play non-serious playing itself. The non-playful mode of existence is a favorite theme of play. Children playfully imitate adults, and poets and actors playfully imitate the sufferings and joys of mortals. The spellbinding power proceeding from play is thus marvelous. How can a phenomenon of life that is so saturated by the non-actual and by fantasy touch us so much, move, enchant, and spellbind us so much that we become "entranced," as it were, and forget for a while the actual situation together with its events?

With critical awareness one can withdraw from the play's spellbinding and enchanting power; we can distance ourselves from the dream fabric of the play-world and realize that the "hero" becomes a citizen when he removes his makeup, when the mask drops away, that even the spectator who was just a moment ago a witness of incredible events reflects soberly on the performance of the mime and starts joking with his neighbors about it. One then distinguishes with some fluency the real aspects of the bearer from the illusory ones[11] in the playworldly scene. One distinguishes the wooden floor of the stage and the citadel of Thebes, as if the latter were an augmentation, the effects of lighting and the heavens blazing[12] above the battlefield. One distinguishes the props and the fake "deadly weapons." The great dramatic play enters into the aspect of a successful technique of illusion that does not merely use words in order to establish a world of sense in consciousness but rather uses real human beings, acting beings, in order to bring about an embodied, sensuous view of what happens.

That such distinctions are possible is incontestable. Yet whether something is thereby conceived is questionable. Does the simple difference between being actual and non-actuality suffice for ascribing to play its place and status? In order to defame it as a way of acting riddled by nullities, an acting "as if," an impotent, merely apparent occurrence? To be sure, no one will say that it is nothing, yet one is quick to assess it according to the standard of serious and weighty things, to take from it its bloom, which {is} "such stuff as dreams are made on,"[13] to denounce its significance as fluff and mischief, in the best case to let it count as a kind of embellishment of our otherwise difficult or boring days. Play, one says,[14] belongs to the realm of appearance, even if it may also contain serious and actual basic elements. From this perspective, the gaze of the contemplative observer is oriented on that which is comprehensible in human play, as present in simple and plain actuality, even on activity as such, on the ball game or theatrical acting [*Schauspielerei*], but not on the "playworld" thereby presencing along with it. The latter is at once localized in an impotent representation, far removed from actuality, and is considered to exist only in the imagination. The term "imagination [*Phantasie*]" becomes the catchall for a phenomenal moment which one doesn't get—or about which one has already made a negative decision.

Perceptions, corroborative memory, experience that is in agreement, rational processing of these for scientific, intersubjectively verified knowledge—all of this aims toward objects in the human environment, toward objects that exist, that are, that appear in subjective presentations and prove to be "actually" given in highly complex systems—even if only provisionally and until further notice.

They encounter us from out of more encompassing horizons, from out of *regions*, from out of the world's breadths of space and depths of time, *without* it being the case that the whole that encompasses us would ever become a defined, enclosed object. We do not face the universe as an external "subject." We are included within the totality. All epistemological comportments that secure an "actuality" of objects are fundamentally "intraworldly." In the imagination, however, we are not bound to the fixed orbit of actuality that can be experienced. We can rethink things, imagine their figures and properties in ways other than how they are; we can invent arbitrary combinations—we can also, however, swing out beyond what is present and given, leave it behind in an adventurous dream of thoughts and send ourselves to the ends of the world, fly beyond the limits of experience. We can even be "carried away" from the space-time continuum and the strict causal chain of events, certainly not "in actuality," yet in the imagination, which, in fairy tales all the way to speculative philosophy, lends us wings. Thus not only things in the environment, near and far, but also the totality of the world, which cannot be reached by experience, is able to become a theme of fantasy-inspired representation. Not, however, in such a way that we represent the universe as an object, but rather in such a way that we think it in an analogy to innerworldly models, an analogy that is at once posited and canceled. Thinking regarding the world, cosmological thinking, can never do without the imagination wandering in the nebulous realm of the non-actual. However, it is also not able to explain it as a legitimate instance of knowledge but can make use of it as an operative resource.

Assuming that human play is primordially not a pastime, but rather a gathering of time, the consolidation of all cosmic fragments, a symbolic representation of the world, thus magical cult-play that honors the gods, bestows a fleeting, fluttering manifestation on the universe's prevailing powers of sense, then there would certainly only be a faint, twilight glow, which one denies to the solid relation to actuality, in all kinds of play today. Perhaps human play is the human root of religion and art, of the elevated games of our soul.[15]

The world-significance of human play is never manifestly brought to light as an identifiable discovery in the phenomenon; it is always an addition of creative consciousness, which brings to presence for itself in the symbol the totality of everything that is. Play as a cosmic metaphor characterizes no mere anthropological occurrence. It also does not mean the manifold and various kinds of modes of play within the human realm, from simple flirting all the way to the profound sense of dramatic play or spectacle. The world itself is interpreted as play. That does not imply any denial of causality in the occurrence of intraworldly things, nor any proclamation of arbitrary freedom in the course of the world; play is used as a model for understanding the total process of the world's movement as the emergence and demise of all things, as the foreground of the coming into appearance and as the depth of the concealed essence, as the interpenetrated play of opposites, as the removal of temporal demarcations and of the boundaries between life and death, as the rendering nugatory of modalities, when everything possible becomes actual and everything actual becomes possible. The world's process, which rational understanding can only survey in intraworldly space-times and time-spaces and can only grasp and elucidate in strict categories, becomes, as a totality and all-encompassing unity [*Allheit und Alleinheit*], a challenge for the human intellect. And occasionally, when rational models break down, the human intellect resorts to the dreamlike power of playfully creative imagination and attains possibilities for understanding the totality in the structures of human play. What the status and truth-value is for such cosmological analogies, which want to force the whole into words as a roundelay of things in an "eternal return of the same," as a "divine roll of the dice," can only first be unfolded as a problem at all if the knowledge of intraworldly objects is no longer recognized as the only normative way of discovering truth. The masked god Dionysus perhaps then becomes a profoundly meaningful [*sinntiefen*] parable for Being and the world.[16]

The problem of the magical-mantic interpretation of play also surpasses the present phenomenological and positivist "epistemology." The mode of Being and world-significance of play will remain in the shadows for a long time still. Already in his essay, "On the Essence of Philosophical Critique," Hegel says: "although we must not mistake this passion for change and novelty for the indifference of play which, in its extreme insouciance, is at the same time the most exalted and only true seriousness."[17] Paradoxes of this sort are clues, not findings. As long as human play is judged from the superficial, though not untrue, perspective that holds that, as a specific embodied behavior, play is led and guided by ideas that only concern an imaginary play-world—that play thus remains in the contrasting shadow of serious life—then an ontological understanding prevails that too quickly only distinguishes being actual and non-actuality, demarcating the simply real aspects of play (embodied activity) from the fictive play-world. The *ontological problem* of what an *existent appearance* is, what shadows, mirroring, image, and what *symbolic representation* are, is not dealt with at all.

In the course of our thoughts up to now, we have perhaps placed too much emphasis on the *imaginary* aspect of human play, on that which is dreamed up in it, is invented by it, and represents a magical product. The *human body in play* is of equally fundamental importance. Is it only a real aspect, a simply actual organ for the carrying out of our activity—or does it, too, achieve an imaginary radiance? Is the body just the "prison of the soul," an instrument for the actualization of voluntary human action, an outer bastion of the intellect [*Geist*] that is itself without intellect—or is it the concrete, earthbound mode of human existence itself? One should be able to provide information about this, if it is true that, after the kind of play that involves roles, competitive play comes to the fore for discussion. It seems as though it were a pure doing and acting, exclusively a real enactment without moments of fantasy, without its own "play-world." One always outperforms the other in terms of strength, skill, stamina, vying with the other fairly, and following the rules in a playful semblance of combat [*Scheingefecht*], and finds the approval of a public. The human body's capacities and possibilities are given an impressive demonstration. Competitive play requires health, strength, beauty, discipline, and training of the self and the team, and has physical and psychical effects. By "gymnastics" the Greeks understood the trinity of the human body's health, strength, and beauty. To be sure, this word had different connotations depending on whether it was uttered in Attica or Sparta. Ancient gymnastics is not to be dissociated from the fundamental decisions of Hellenic life, from the relations to war and to play. In our way of life that is so different, the culture of the body is not to be understood from only the striving after health, strength, and beauty. The main goal is not the well-rounded, balanced harmony of human capabilities. The contemporary human being's awareness of his body is to a great degree determined by the life phenomenon of sports.[18] It has almost become its own "form of life." It belongs to the modern world of work as a complementary manifestation. Perhaps we are just as conceptually helpless in regard to sports as we are to rampant technology. In this century, sports and technology have advanced rapidly and vertiginously. Both point to a change in the basic position of human existence in relation to its sojourn in the world. The human being is not only bodily insofar as he possesses a body, insofar as in a certain sense he is tethered to this constant companion; he is embodied insofar as he always *relates to his body,* even if in historically variable dispositions. The biological discovery that he is an exemplar of a higher kind of animal does not constitute the *philosophical* problem of *incarnation;* it is rather the *existentiell situation of being a perceiving, mobile, and thinking midpoint of the appearing environment in a sensuous, sense-suffused way* that does. The bodily relation means the psychic-intellectual and concretely active manner in which the human being relates to the natural evidence of his animal existence [*Vorhandenheit*]. This sense-saturated relation is transformed in the course of history, not only in the way in which the human being "understands" his embodiment, but in the manner in which he "puts it into practice." The human being does not have, for better or worse, a body like a container for his psychic substance, and he also does not operate in it merely instinctively like an animal. He knows that he "possesses" a body, is incarnated therein. He is alienated or delighted by his body, can feel it as a nagging burden or in free and unfettered movement. The Greek glorification of the body was a magnificent mode of the human relation to the body; another was the spiritual era's ascetic, world-fleeing hostility to the body.

What does incarnation signify for human self-understanding? A contingent fact, an essential determination of the *condition humaine?* Is the body the murky, obscure vessel that overshadows the heavenly light of the realm of ideas, the lifelong prison from which death alone releases us, which thus must be called a "doctor" and for which a rooster is to be sacrificed? In Plato we find ambiguous, contradictory statements concerning the body. It is even emphatically elevated if it is beautiful. The shapeliness of the beautiful body is taken to be a sign that points to the pure shapeliness of thought; the body, the beautiful body of the ephebe, for which Greek pederasty was aflame, becomes a signpost to a higher beauty that is more suffused with light, to the beauty of the single form of the beautiful, the *monoeides-kalon,* which ultimately coincides with the *ontōs-on,* what truly is, and with the *agathon,* the good. Pederasty and philosophy are intertwined because the true is first illuminated in the radiance of the beautiful. And the beautiful is not a predicate that among other things can also apply to the body—as it does in other ways to the sun sinking below the purple sea, the towering temple under dark green oaks and silver olive trees. Beauty is first understood not as the enchanting character of nature or as the symmetry of artworks, but rather as the human being's bodily beauty. We first attain natural and artistic beauty through the body and through its sensuous perceptions. The radiant body is the golden trace that leads to philosophy. No artistic creation can ever fully free itself from the sphere of the sensuous—dance cannot free itself from the supple, flexible body; music cannot free itself from the resounding tone; sculpture cannot free itself from marble and bronze. Yet we are only open to all sensuous things at all because we have a body. *Being-sensuous* is the human mode of existence. The body is not an appendage of the human being, not an external natural condition, with which the person, finite human freedom, is unfortunately just afflicted and stricken. Certainly, the human being has already at times been ashamed of his embodiment, has suffered in the chains that bind him to the space-time of the world. A long and harmful tradition has misinterpreted the terrestrial mode of existence belonging to the earth and in many ways made us lose sight of the ancient, indeed the most ancient mysteries of the human race, and has obscured[19] from us the world-profound significance of elementary, sensuous, and bodily processes of life. We scarcely still know what eating, drinking, and procreating signify *in a sense-imbued manner,* even if we possess excellent natural-scientific knowledge about them. These processes emerge in a clearer light when we celebrate festivals. We celebrate even the loftiest festivals with the symbolic gifts of "bread and wine" as communion of the earth's offspring with the Great Mother.

All essential moments of human existence are connected to the body and sensuousness. Our intellect [*Geist*] is sensuous, and its sensuousness is not a lower preliminary stage, with "seeing and hearing passing away"[20] when the human intellect is set in motion. The intellect is not only[21] in the senses; the senses are in the intellect, too. We never think as the bodiless "angel" does, removed from everything earthly. Our thinking is language and is documented by voice and writing; our reason needs images, and our activities [*Handlungen*] refer to the hand [*Hand*]. Struggle, which founds ruling orders and relations of power and erects cities and states, is the most severe threat to the body. From the very beginning, labor involves the bodily activity of work; only because the human being lives in an earthly, bodily manner can he objectify and reify what he does, can he invent and use machines. And even play with its irreal and real components is bound to the body and exhilarates it. Incarnation pervades all of human existence's structures of co-existence: mortality and love, work, ruling, and play. There have doubtless been eras with a gloomy view of the body, which we like to call "idealistic," that dismissively condemned the body, denouncing it as a source of disturbance for the intellect that was resplendent with thoughts, as a confusion of reason, as a blurring of truth, that saw in it a principle of evil, the seat of lusts and wicked desires, that defamed it—and yet still could not discard it. For the sake of the body we need the necessities of life and even for the most part superficial things: food, clothing, a house and tools, appliances, machines, weapons, all the myriad things of an artifact-culture, an immense technological apparatus. The human being thereby surpasses the limited possibilities for embodied action in myriad ways; he installs himself within an apparatus of enormous proportions. He now acts setting out from his own body, with immense formative powers and uncanny energy. The powerful rivalry of economic competition that includes even war has vastly increased and continues to grow. Human beings compete with each other with the utmost brutality and technological perfection.

It is *entirely otherwise* when competition is to occur *as play*, when it springs from an accord, a shared sentiment for the joy of existence, when it observes rules that ensure the health and life of the other competitor. A characteristic feature of peaceful competition is the reduced equipment of means that render the competitors' vigorous struggle more efficient; to a certain degree they contend "naked." The race, the throw, the jump, the possibilities for enhancing human bodies that are unarmed and not technologically modified are paradigms. Of course, such sports cannot do without equipment, cannot do without the racetrack, the playing field, the swimming pool, and so forth.

Nowadays, people take part in competitive sporting activities that involve machines, such as Formula 1 and Formula 2 racecars, motorboats and fast planes, where psychological toughness, coolness, skill and courage, and quick reaction times are the decisive qualities, where technical struggles, intertwined in manifold ways with commercial interests, are fought out and have a large public, the masses of industrial culture. Playing has then become a technical occupation. *Of a completely different essence* is that competitive play where bodies contend, where natural abilities and diligent practice are decisive, where a tense, eager carrying out of existence constitutes and stamps the occurrence of play before any technologizing of it, where the human being plunges back, as it were, into a primal situation and casts off the civilized armor like a bothersome garment. Such competitive play is not an impoverishment of human possibilities, not a regression to an archaic form of society that is ignorant of motors, rockets, and computers; it is no antiquating idyll.

One is perhaps quite ready to denigrate a sports performance that is primarily[22] played out in an arc of suspense between the human body and free nature, for example, sailing on a stormy sea, climbing a sheer surface, or skiing beyond the ski run. Yet such competitive play is much more than an activity with merely real, simply actual aspects. It is illumined by a peculiar transparency: in such play the playing human body in its beauty, vital strength, and free creative self-actualization is precisely itself the theme of play. If the body is otherwise the place from which activities proceed, whether war, work, love, or even the many and diverse forms of human play, then it remains for the most part that from out of which incarnated existence acts. In competitive play that has cast off technical armament (save for a few pieces of equipment), the body comes into the shining light of appearance; it portrays itself. Even competitive play in this sense is a mixture of embodied reality and imaginary sense. It would be too facile a thought to equate this productive imaginative element with the spectator's amazement at the competitors. It is fame in a more genuine and primordial sense: the glorification of the body, the apotheosis of our sensuous existence—which has not been lost in the thunder of motors, which is not drowned in the flood of papers, which is not laid to waste in the interventions of a global administration, but rather, old as the world and optimistic about the future, conducts itself like the "playing child," the *pais paizōn* of the Ephesian thinker.[23] That always happens anew when the Olympic victor in the competition steps onto the rostrum to be crowned with an olive wreath.[24]

Play and Cult {1972–1973?}

Play and cult—these two concepts combine opposites in an almost unseemly manner: play with its cheerfulness, with its lively pleasure and buoyant levity, and the highest seriousness of human existence, the relation to the divinity. Presumption, trifling, a pastime on the one hand, awe, reverence, anxiety, and the most extreme intimacy of the heart on the other hand. Or does play have a connection with the cult that is more primordial than this well-established difference, even more primordial than the occasional endowment of cult activities and sanctuaries with elements of play that belong to art, to ornamentation, to the celebration of the festival? That is our question. What kind of a question? A philosophical question?

Every one of us is acquainted with play, is acquainted with it from the testimony of their own experience and from observation of the everyday human environment. Play is well known as a phenomenon, familiar and common to us. We do not need to discover it as we would something unfamiliar. Everyone has already been a player. As adults we marvel, perhaps with muted envy, at the play of children, the blissful devotion with which they engage in it, the wealth of imagination, the abundance of the forms and self-imposed rules. We marvel in this at the freely unencumbered élan for life. To be sure, even in adult life we are acquainted with manifold "games," practices for whiling away idle hours, events resembling the ancient circus that serve as entertainment and conversational material for the urban masses—we are acquainted with playful situations in the midst of life's serious business, when adventurous or fairy-tale-like features suddenly descend on human existence. We are acquainted with playful moments in "flirting," in sports, in all sorts of ventures and risks, and of course are also acquainted with explicitly delimited events involving play [*Spielveranstaltungen*] in the theater and cinema, and on the radio and television. Although familiarity with the phenomenon of play is incontestable and encompasses a wide-ranging abundance of forms and structures, we are {not} yet able to express this knowledge of our advance familiarity with play in a sufficient way and to formulate it with conceptual rigor. Our understanding of play has a customary use-character. As soon as we reflect on it, the customary immediacy of usage is disturbed and it loses its fluid self-evidence—and we do not even know how we should approach the problem. All serious thought initially makes our existence groundless. We lose every sure foothold—we no longer know who we are, what the human being is, what custom and justice, thing and world are. There is perhaps no more essential metaphor for this transformation of humanity than the fate of Laius's unfortunate son. Oedipus stands in radiant glory, the ruler of the city, who won Thebes and the hand of the queen because he knew how to solve the Sphinx's riddle and to her question gave the answer: the human being. Oedipus obviously knows who the human being is—this knowledge brought him into kingship. He is able to see better, is more clear-sighted than the others; he is the one who most of all understands, to the extent that such understanding comes from human cleverness. He takes his knowledge to be secure, takes his happiness to be abiding and firm. Oedipus lives with an undaunted trust in Being: his world is valid, his rule stands, sons and daughters are the assurance of the continuity of his family line. Then, as a sign of divine wrath, the pestilence breaks out across the city and with terror the citizens and Oedipus himself gain an intimation that, seen from the higher knowledge of the gods, things are not as good as human beings imagined. The intimation demands clarification [*Aufklärung*], radical truth. And gradually the uncanny unveiling is carried out. The seer, mouthpiece of the gods, is compelled by the king to reveal the horror little by little. Oedipus looks outside for the man who struck dead the former king of Thebes and finds him inside, in himself, revealed to be a parricide and defiler of his mother. It is a compelling symbol that he gouges out his eyes and thereby blots out the sensuous truth that kept him deluded. Only when he no longer sensuously sees and the light of day is extinguished for him does he see more truly what is. Bereft of his eyesight, shattered by the death of his mother-wife, deserted by his sons, void of power and driven from the city, he travels the long, bitter path to Colonus, in order, absolved, to be transported away by the gods. In the tragedy of Oedipus the most extreme and severe human will to truth is interpreted in a play. Philosophy can perhaps express what play is. But play, too, can provide an uncanny disclosure about philosophy. Play becomes a symbol. What does the term "symbol" mean?

Fink's Notes on Play

The Philosophical-Pedagogical Problem of Play, 1954

First Session

1. General considerations concerning the task of a proseminar:

Precursor to the scientific posing of questions, not the complete working out of such questions, and so forth.

2. Course—First stage: Taking up the phenomenon of everyday familiarity; Second stage: Attempt at a conceptual grasp; Third stage: Reflection on the operative categories: explicit exposition of the *problem*.

Second Session

1. Human phenomena are not simply given in advance, they are always already "interpreted"; a multiplicity of "interpretations" also belongs to the everyday familiarity of the phenomenon of play.

2. Delimitation of "play" from similar or opposed phenomena of life: in the first place, *who* plays? Human being, animal—gods, angels, God?? Is play an anthropological or a universally biological phenomenon?

Play and Work	Play and Seriousness?
Play and the Drudgery of Need	Play and Leisure
Play and the Creative Urge	Play and the Impulse to Portray
Play and Freedom	

3. Doing and letting alone, active and passive human comportments? Playing as "doing." General analysis of doing: doing as making (τέχνη), in which a fabricated work results as outcome—and doing as enactment, which is itself the goal in itself (πρᾶξις).

All human doing, whether τέχνη or πρᾶξις, is set in motion by the *final goal* of *eudaimonia*. Structure of the *final*-goal: ultimate that-for-the-sake-of-which. Example: a shoemaker makes shoes, in order to clothe, but why clothe? For the sake of health, but why health? = a good. In what relation to the highest good, to the purpose of life?

Eudaimonia is striven after by all human beings, but interpreted differently. Reference to Aristotle's three βίοι.

In a religious attitude the "sense of life" is interpreted by a wisdom that is beyond the human. In this, strictly speaking, there is no "problem." It is otherwise where the *human being* seeks out the sense.

4. Playing as doing? Playing as an "oasis" within the goal-oriented unrest and chase after *eudaimonia.* A "blessedness" [*Seligkeit*] (but not yet *the* blessedness of happiness [*Glückseligkeit*]).

Third Session

1. In the last session: Enactment character of play? Framework: a universally held description of doing and letting-alone. Play belongs to human activity, an intense expression of spontaneity. Doing—production (τέχνη) and enactment as end in itself [*Selbstzweck*] (πρᾶξις); work and deed. Both forms of doing happen "for-the-sake-of." Last or highest for-the-sake-of is not "life as such" (ζῆν), but rather εὖ ζῆν, εὖ πράττειν: εὐδαιμονία.

The human being *strives* for *eudaimonia,* is held taut, chases after happiness. Human enactment of life: permeated by *sense!* Estimation of life, worth or worthlessness of one's own existence and of human existence in general. Interpenetration of private and general judgments! Balance of happiness-unhappiness, optimism-pessimism; lack of differentiation: "senselessness" also an answer to the continual question of sense.—A prince who left his palace once saw a poor person, a sick person, a dead person.—All strive for happiness, but "no one is to be counted happy before death."[1] Frailty and questionworthiness of happiness.

Basic feature of our existence: burden, care, privation, unrest.—More than the necessity of needs.—Forgetting, relaxation, leisure—boredom—oasis of "relaxation": play. It is attuned by a joy, the pleasure of play, the bliss of play. Intensity? Or the unquestionability of this pleasure?

2. Essential feature in play is the deep pleasure of enactment. What kind of pleasure is this? A "sensuous" or an "intellectual" pleasure? Biological "interpretation": pleasure of movement, release of pent-up energy and so forth??—Essence of pleasure in general: human pleasure is always a saying-yes and a saying-amen!—Immediacy and reflectiveness possible, naïve joy in play and conscious, refined joy in play. Manifold modes. For instance, in sports and in the case of chess. The activity of playing is in itself pleasurably confirmed, "serves" no purpose.—But play "plays" goals!

Pleasure is not a simple activity's simple mode of enactment.—The pleasure of play opposed in itself: tragedy or played sorrow [*gespielte Trauer*] is pleasurable!?

Play-suffering, which is experienced as pleasure, is a κάθαρσις of the soul?? Convulsion—biological sense of this purification?? To live out "possibilities"?

The pleasure of play an "open question."

3. The aspect of sense in play: every kind of play has an immanent, internal play-sense.

4. The "as-if" aspect? Play an element of a unique "appearance." How is this "appearance" to be determined? Not a deception, an acknowledged appearance!

5. Refined description of kinds of play—players—roles—playworld. Self-concealment of the ones playing.—Aspect of portrayal.

Kinds of play in playing, iterative forms, and so forth.

6. Playing—in adults and children!?

7. Playing and the social component: socially formative function of play. Cultic kinds of play, dances. Communicative sense of play.

8. Paraphrases of play to this point.—Transition to a conceptual grasp.

Fourth Session

1. Recap of the context

First stage: Taking up the phenomenon from everyday familiarity and interpretation—initially in a contrasting delimitation from other phenomena of human life: seriousness, work, purposive action, from what is difficult, burdensome, and harsh in life.

Play: alleviation of life, elation. Oases of happiness. Spontaneity that is joyfully attuned.—Last time the pleasure of play was the theme, attempt to distinguish specific sensuous pleasures (where pleasure and aversion remain related). The pleasure of play more than a mere delight in movement, relaxation of pent-up energies, and so forth.—In all kinds of play there is an intellectual [*geistiges*] aspect (self-relation of existence).

The pleasure of play can include its opposite (sadness, suffering, terror can be components of the pleasure of play). If this is so, then how can a recollection of a past suffering make one glad?[2]

Play portrays: internal and external sense of play: internal = the sense-context of played things or data or relations; external: the sense that play has for those who have decided on it.—The aspect of portrayal obviously highly significant. Not equally strong in every kind of play.—Portrayal and "appearance." Brief structural distinction: play = first playing; second the played sense-context (the playworld).

The player is at some point the one playing, then the "role" in play. And it is a unique spontaneous activity. To be a player (the real human being who plays, and the role of the human in play). We said that the role "conceals" the players. But *how??* Possibility of self-forgetting? Is this analogous to the self-forgetting in delighting, in imagination? Playing is different from delusion. Delusion takes "appearance" for actuality. But the difficulty is that the play-appearance is a specific, special kind of "actuality." Paradoxical determination: "non-actual appearance."—Comparison to the actual object "image." For instance, mirroring on something that is gleaming, in water, or shadows: such a thing is actual and, to be sure, as reproductive. What is visible "in the image" is not actual.—The whole of Platonic ontology operates with this phenomenon of reproduction, without ontologically penetrating it.—With the image we have a specific phenomenon of actual appearance and a relation of the image to what is really actual. Even images in images.

2. The playworld: description!? Actual human beings play a role, portray, "themselves"? Or something that they are not, but might be? Imaginary fulfillment of the wish to be something else!?

The playworld: space of it and space in it; time of it and time in it. And yet it is "embedded" here and now!?? These structures most prominent in the "theatrical play [*Schauspiel*]." The stage: the playworld within the actual world, thus like an image in the frame. And yet "these boards signify the world"[3]—representation! The whole of the world and life is condensed [*verdichtet*] in an exemplary event. It is the human being who stands on the stage as Oedipus and Faust[4] or King Lear. The whole comes to appearance within itself in a manner that is suffused with sense!!

The playworld, to be sure, is here and now, but at the same time is everywhere and always.—The limits: real space and the space of the playworld do not cross over into each other. And yet each kind of play depends on a real setting and a real time.

3. The relation between actuality and appearance is so difficult because appearance is itself a kind of "actuality" and, furthermore, because it can only come to appearance *in* something real.

Elucidation: 1. There can be dismissal of subjective appearance, of sense-deception, hallucination, deceit. Considered thusly it has no objective significance. The "appearance" that is here in question is an "appearance" in itself. 2. This appearance *is,* is not nothing, but is not like beings otherwise are (like the tree, like water)—but the tree as mirroring in the water, the shadows of the tree in the sun: that *is*—and, in a certain way, is not. The mirrored tree is real as a mirroring, but irreal as a tree, yet it needs something real, for instance, water, in order to "appear" on it.

Analogously: play *is* as a phenomenon of life (and the playworld belongs to it), but it is not like the rest of human activity is. The playworld is not in the same sense in which the one playing is (not the role). And the playworld can only "appear" in a straightforward reality.

4. The difficulty increases: phenomenon of iterations—dream within a dream, and so forth, image within an image; play within different kinds of play.—One can say in general that the difference between simple actuality and actual appearance is not repeated at all, but rather is only repeated apparently and in the medium of "appearance."

Elucidation: play within an instance of play. The first playworld relates to the second as simple actuality to the playworld in general.—Considered more closely, this does not add up. All iterations of playworlds are played out in the same real space and the same real time. But the difference of real and apparent is now itself "played."—Playing is able to "represent" (with symbolic power) not only all simple things and relations of actuality but even itself.

Which forms of iteration? Play within play? For example, children play adults and have children who play. Or "Hamlet." Stages of iteration. But another tendency of iteration is also possible: a kind of play (first level) reveals itself as a game being played, thus as second-level play, and so forth. Reference back to the first. Previously it was progression from the first.

Analogies to an image within an image, or dream within a dream.

5. This is no sophistry. Adult games and children's games.

6. Communicative function of play: dance, festival.

7. Cult and magic of play: symbolic bringing to presence.

Fifth Session

1. Last time a series of seemingly fine-spun distinctions—a phenomenon of life lost from view in subtle hairsplitting!?! The phenomenon is subtle, although it is elementary. Indeed because it is elementary. Everyone understands something of love, of work, of death, of ruling, of play—and yet these elementary phenomena of existence are polysemous in themselves.

Drawn from play were the aspect of pleasure, the aspect of sense, the aspect of appearance, the aspect of portrayal, and the aspect of production: these aspects are intertwined, are not isolated. For instance, pleasure is—pleasure in self-created sense, pleasure in appearance, in the reality of what is imaginary.

The imaginary (not only as mental, psychical dimension), but as a special kind of actual Being, of things, configurations, and so forth.

Our reference to phenomena of light such as "image," "shadows," "mirroring." The iterative structures of play within play, of played play.

Appearance and actuality are nowhere interwoven in such an ambiguous way as in human life; we exist on the wavering limit between sober wakefulness and dream, between "actuality" and what is imaginary.

2. Through human playing and in playing imaginary worlds of sense, magical products emerge; playing: an original state of creative production belonging to the human soul:

Survey of what is factual and already existent, of the predominance of the creative capacity, the player as "lord" of his constructs, free relation to his creations; on the other hand, however, loss of self, too: being enraptured, release in the mask. The mask and its ambiguity as a profound characteristic of play.

Play can be the highest sovereignty of the self (Apollonian aspect) and the highest loss of the self (Dionysian aspect).

Play in magic, cult and rites of primitives, of mythology—but also in many elevated forms of culture.

3. Play and the stages of life: child's play and the play of adults. Among children play is "central," among adults a "marginal phenomenon" as a rule. Artist and child—the creative human being and magical atavism—play and "rationality" (even intellectual kinds of play). Child's play more than adult play reveals the magical features of the player.

4. The communicative function of playing (division of play like the division of labor?). Play-together—playing a distinctive mode of human being together.

Basic forms of co-existence: community of ancestry (which is based on blood) (family, tribe, nation)—community of wills (ruling, associations of men, and so forth) (freedom, struggle, war, will to power, and so forth)—community of labor.

Play: as more relaxed form of sociability, cf. Plato in the *Laws,* the "drinking bout" with its humorous, ephemeral forms of "joining together [*Gefüge*]."—Play originally: celebration of festival, dance, cult, presence of the gods: symbolic bringing to presence of existence in its ambiguity.

5. The regard for the difference between child's play and adult play leads to the question of whether play is *one* phenomenon of existence or the central

phenomenon of existence.—The fundamental difficulty of such interpretations of existence: the dialectic of basic phenomena, their respective usurpation.—What reveals a phenomenon to be a key phenomenon?

The phenomenal givenness of the phenomenon as "one among others" and its interpretation as the central phenomenon.

The assessment of a "key phenomenon" implies a speculative transformation of the naïve concept: certain features are retained, others are exaggerated and extended.

6. The speculative approach to a key phenomenon can be (a) anthropological or (b) cosmological (in which case the relation between the human being and the world thereby remains the problem).—"Play" can be taken up as "anthropological key," thus, for example, that play is supposed to be the essence of the human being—or as "cosmological key," such that play is supposed to be the essence of beings as a whole.

We have given both instances a philosophical interpretation that proceeds beyond the straightforward phenomenon.—Transition from the simple taking up of the phenomenon of play to its conceptual grasp! (Second stage of our reflections.)

Examples of the application of play as a key phenomenon and key concept.

"The human being is only fully a human being when he plays" (Schiller).[5] "I do not know any other way of handling great tasks than as *play*" (Nietzsche, *Ecce Homo*).[6] Hegel says of play that "it, in its indifference and its extreme insouciance, is at the same time the most exalted and only true seriousness."[7]

Sixth Session

1. Transition to the second stage of our reflection: conceptual grasp (with philosophical and pedagogical purpose). The first stage was the description of a phenomenon of life "in its familiarity" (to which there always also belongs a certain interpretation). Play as a remarkable phenomenon of life: iridescent and polysemous, mysterious and simple—escapes the strict teleology of human life, is released from the unrest of striving, is sometimes taken to be freely creative, sometimes activity without obligation, sometimes taken to be sovereign, sometimes an ecstatic mode of enactment—sometimes the center, sometimes a marginal phenomenon—an action of freedom and a marginal enchantment, association with the imaginary, ambiguous existence on the dividing line between actuality and possibility, a special phenomenon in a distinctive sense (communicative function), and so forth.

This phenomenon of life is thus not strictly "isolated" and "pure" in itself, it permeates the other phenomena of life in multiple and manifold ways, and therein lies a certain difficulty for grasping it.—In every theory of the human being play must appear, but, for the moment, it is questionable to what extent the human being is to be grasped and conceived essentially from the phenomenon of play. What is the status of play?

2. Life in its lived praxis has in each case already decided on a "status." Choice of existence.—This is not our concern now. The status that each human being or a people gives to play by its existentiell decision is not meant, but rather the status that "playing" has in itself. There is a great difficulty here. The human being is not a thing that is constituted by its constituent parts and "objectively" known by the human being. The human being is a theme unto himself. He is a "historical" living being. Place and status of a phenomenon of life are not ahistorically determinable, although there are "eternal phenomena of human existence" that merely change their costumes over the course of centuries. Perhaps history, its changing forms, its masks and possibilities, is even to be understood by way of play. Status-question of the degree of a phenomenon's primordiality, its peripheral or central significance!? Concept of the "key phenomenon" (anthropological and cosmological extension): a mode of analogical thinking.

Questions: Where do you see difficulties and problems? Does description suffice—no interpretation? And so forth.[8]

3. Structure of the key concept: symbolic representation, *pars pro toto, one* phenomenon stands in for a whole (whether it be human existence or the world). That presupposes not merely that we, the ones who know, choose a metaphor [*Gleichnis*], but that a likening [*Gleichung*] exists here. The possibility of such analogical thinking, if it is not supposed to be merely all-too-human, consists in the fact that the whole repeats, mirrors, represents itself in the part (macro-micro-cosmos-relation).

Are there such distinctive phenomena that stand in vicariously for the whole? Is there an inner mirroring of the whole in distinctive focal points? Since its beginning, Western philosophy has sought such correspondences, such symbols, such representing phenomena, which disclose the riddle of human being and world. Thales's water, Anaximenes's air, Heraclitus's fire, Plato's analogy of ἀγαθόν and ἥλιος, or "spirit" or "material" as what genuinely exists, and so forth.

Manifold forms and schemata of such "representations": appearance and essence, substance and accident, one and many, and so forth.

The "crux" of such interpretations forms the dividing line between "phenomenon" and "speculative interpretation." The "same in being other"! (up to absolute idealism).

Formal context: the key phenomenon (or the key concept) is based on a mirroring of the whole in a distinctive part (immanent repetition)—and the human being's achievement of knowledge consists in the insight into this symbolic representation of a specific individual phenomenon that is thereby taken to be a likeness [*Gleichnis*], an anthropological or even a cosmological metaphor [*Metapher*]. Such likenesses are based on an antecedent likening [*Gleichnung*] (*analogia entis, analogia mundi et rei*) (thing and world?).

The possibility of a speculative conceptual grasp of a specific individual phenomenon is grounded in a reflection, in a mirroring of the whole in the part. Manifold individual phenomena are positioned as cosmic (or even merely anthropological) metaphors.—The phenomenon of play is an individual phenomenon to whose phenomenal structure, however, symbolic representation belongs—which is perhaps significant here in an entirely particular and extremely distinctive sense.

4. Play's form of representation: for example, children play adults; adults play unlived possibilities, dramatic play or spectacle becomes the image of the world.

5. Critical thoughts: how far does such symbolic bringing to presence extend, which features are universal and representative and which are not??

6. Human life and play? Which analogies, which limits of analogies, and so forth.—Danger of violent reinterpretations.

7. World and play? Priority of an Aristotelian view? Ethics, physics? Work—τέχνη—play?[9]

8. Nietzsche as example of both.

Seventh Session

1. Formulation of the concept of play with philosophical intention! Philosophy and an individual phenomenon? The individual as likeness [*Gleichnis*] of the whole. Innerworldly symbol of the world. Symbol? Συμβάλλειν.

Formal difficulty: *which* features are "representative" and which are irrelevant?

2. "Play" as likeness and analogue: an important argument? An important argument: play as a phenomenon has the structure of mirroring in itself. Perhaps for this reason it is especially appropriate as a metaphor [*Metapher*] of correspondence!! Play is always essentially "likeness."

The magical character of play (rain magic, cult dances, festivals: what is played on a small scale must happen on a large scale). The creative aspect (analogous to nature's creativity). Cosmic processes' ability to be isolated, the imaginary is the symbolic space of the actual.

3. Play and mimesis: not mimesis of a "thing," but rather of "all of existence"! In play a "self-relation" of an extreme sort occurs. "Non-actuality" of play as "higher actuality" (devaluation and deepening).

4. Because play, in its phenomenal content, contains the element of representation, in a specific sense it is excellent for symbolic representation of the world (i.e., for a model of philosophical conceptualization).

First case of the metaphor of cosmic play in Heraclitus: αἰὼν παῖς ἐστι παίζων, πεττεύων; παιδὸς ἡ βασιλείη.[10] Interpretive possibilities:

Αἰών: Course of the world, time with its temporal contents; time the line of goals and purposes, it is, as a whole, a "playing child"? The whole [*Ganzheit*] has no time, no purpose . . . ?! Is rule (for the most part: plan, intention, purpose) the rule of the child? Primordiality, productivity, enchantment, and so forth.

At the end of Western metaphysics: play as formula for the world in Nietzsche. Innocence, beyond good and evil, productivity, etc.

5. Which features of the phenomenon of play must be bracketed out, however? Precisely symbolic representation! The feature on whose basis play is taken to be likeness of the whole must subsequently be factored out of the whole understood as play.

6. What is the understanding of the cosmos, in what way is the cosmos understood, in the metaphor of play??[11]

7. The struggle against play and its magical-mythic function of bringing the world to presence—in Plato.

Play revealed to be "mere reproduction"?!

Model of τέχνη gains the upper hand and even guides the Platonic destruction of play.

8. Play as model of the world? How is the whole to be thought then? *Who* plays? A person? Or "It"? The whole as an occurrence sufficient in itself (with immanent purposes [*Binnenzwecken*]), motion that is not "rational," does not work, does not strive. No goal for the world!? Productivity (in the doubling of freedom and ecstase)? The "imaginary" (in cosmic understanding)?? The world of things, "life a dream" that we do not dream but in which, rather, we are dreamed? The so-called actual would be the "imaginary"?? Exchange of "actuality" and "appearance"???

9. The *speculative world-theater:* dramatic play or spectacle: representation such that the *parousia* of essence comes to pass in the medium of the non-actual.

Play of "individuation."

10. "Aesthetic" and "ethical" view of the world.

Eighth Session

1. "Play" as speculative formula for the world?

a. Resistance to an interpretation of the entire occurrence under the guidance of a "goal," "final purpose," an ἔσχατον—not "work," "struggle," "striving," "seriousness"—"the soul's destiny," "progress": an ultimate lack of responsibility, a contingency, improvisation.

The process of the world has no goal, has no task, has no τέλος, neither as nature nor as history, it revolves within itself, autarchic.

b. "Motion" does not have the character of striving, of striving for something that remains outstanding, something in the future, but rather is sufficient in itself, the path is the goal of motion; the creative, the dance of chance.

c. Who plays: It, i.e., the whole, πᾶν.

d. "Actuality" = appearance. Variety of finite things = appearance of the playworld. The theater of the world, the play of the world and the finite characters [*Figuren*].

Play of individuation: entrance and exit of "characters," every hardship of individuation, antagonism and struggle, work and the like is only "appearance." Life is a dream in which we are dreamed.

e. The process of the world, interpreted as play, is pure productivity, creative activity, distinct from τέχνη.

f. With Plato's struggle against tragedy the world-model of τέχνη becomes primary. Structure of the cosmos as ἔργον of a demiurge, who "by laboring" brings a work about on the basis of planning and intention.

2. The human being's position in the cosmos, which is interpreted by way of play: the human being "beyond good and evil," beyond any salvation, and so forth, the player, the one creating, the child and the artist as prototypes.—An "aesthetic" interpretation of existence; cf. Nietzsche: existence only justified as an aesthetic phenomenon. "Around the hero everything turns into a tragedy; around the demi-god, into—what? perhaps into 'world.'" (*Beyond Good and Evil*)[12]

3. The priority of the playing human being, in such a play-interpretation of the cosmos, is to be understood from the correspondence of the human being: he is a co-player; is open to the character of movement that brings all things into play

and puts them at stake [*aufs Spiel*]. "Work," struggle, guilt, etc. as only intra-phenomena, as role-aspects of human existence.

4. A philosophical interpretation of the world from the concept of play can be a profound and perhaps "true" interpretation of beings as a whole. For example, Nietzsche's philosophy. But there are stark motifs of a speculative concept of play also in Hegel.

Play and the problem of individuation.—Here in the proseminar only an indication of the principal possibility of interpreting the prevailing of the world from out of "play," from a delimited human phenomenon of life.—However, if this particular phenomenon can become a cosmological key concept, then a higher status of the purely anthropological significance of human play is at the very least documented in it.

Transition to the pedagogical relevance of play.

5. Pedagogical "problem" of play? What does "problem" mean here? Educational praxis and theoretical penetration of the phenomenon of education. Methods of play, etc., here not of interest, but rather the theorems that found such methods.—Basic conception of educators concerning the essence and function of play?? Play as essential core of the human being or as merely a convenient vehicle for serious tendencies? Does play belong to the existence of children [*kindlichen Dasein*]? Or to the human being in general? Child and adult, play and seriousness??

6. Education? A "kind of play"? A "kind of work"? A mode of domination? Role-play of social functions? Education—a primal phenomenon of sociality? Rules of the game in social play!?—Education?? Two opposed fundamental tendencies: formation and nurturing. Traditional aspect and progressive aspect. Education as reformation—and education as letting-grow.

7. How are play and the playful manifestly regarded in "reformative education"? Precisely as means. Learning by playing! Guided striving. "Prescribed kinds of play": with insight into the situation of the respective stages of life according to developmental psychology. Kinds of play and toys suitable for children.

8. How is play manifestly regarded in "nurturing education"? As expression of the substantial core of the young human being, as inner anticipation of his future, as his self-portrayal, as document of unconscious depths, etc. But even such educators do not play along. They observe, furtively watching over child's play. Principle of self-activity, and so forth.

9. Pedagogically relevant: improvisational play without rules (extreme: playful flight of ideas)—or regulated play?!? That which is without rules is more revealing, that which is regulated more disciplinary.

Pedagogy has a specific content, if the human being's essence is "play" and a few other things, such as "work" or "ruling." And another content, if his essence is "service to God" (religion). Play and work in relation to freedom. Freedom and self-consciousness, or the unconscious (the creative depth)?[13]

10. Play: also rules of the game? What is a rule?—Play and plaything. Essence and nature of the plaything? = a symbolic formation (magical character).

11. Task of pedagogy: to penetrate kinds of play, to create an inner structure and yet not to channel productive imagination too strictly.

12. Limits of every anthropology that only proceeds from the playing human being, without seeing him in relation to cosmic play: reference to Rilke's poem:

> As long as you catch self-thrown things
> it's all dexterity and venial gain—;
> only when you've suddenly caught that ball
> which she, one of the eternal players,
> has tossed toward you, your center, with
> a throw precisely judged, one of those arches
> that exist in God's great bridge-system:
> only then is catching a proficiency,—
> not yours, a world's. And if you then had
> strength and courage to return the throw,
> no, more wonderful: forgot strength and courage
> and had *already* thrown . . . (as the year
> throws the birds, those migrating bird swarms,
> which an older to a younger warmth sends
> catapulting across oceans—) only
> in that venture would you truly join in.
> No longer making the throw easy; no longer making
> it hard. Out of your hands the meteor
> would launch itself and flame into its spaces . . .[14]

Ninth Session

1. Already transitioned to the pedagogical discussion of play. Not particular practices of play but rather a question of the principal, educational relevance of play. Play: *one* phenomenon of existence or the central one? In childhood, in middle age, in mature old age on the periphery. Child or adult closer to the essence of the human being? Every stage of life its own proper due! Developmental schema, ἀκμή-concept. Freedom and the unconscious depths of human life; in play both moments are intertwined, freedom and ecstase.—Danger of all enlightenment: loss of mythic substance. The human being = a light that blazes in and out of the night!

2. Basic anthropological tendency of play: productive (fulfillment in the imaginary), release (in the medium of appearance), portraying (as a self-interpretation that is not governed by caprice), social (insofar as "playing" unites; festival—celebration—cult).[15] Play unfetters from a factual bondage, allows the situation to appear to be not irremediable; eases the burden of existence, grants an imaginative happiness in the flight through possibilities that can be attained without the anguish of choice, i.e., of decision. Playing is a non-binding reaching out into the possible. Play is related to other essential phenomena of human life: to love, work, ruling, and in this sense is "social," "productive," "institutional."

3. Child's play pedagogically significant—but from the perspective of adults. It is not children who educate. The adult educators must accommodate themselves to child's play.—Already two extremes of pedagogy are distinguished: the formative, "authoritative," and the nurturing, indirect. These two "extremes" are not accidental positions. Rather, they are polar "primal forms" that belong together: the "paternal" and "maternal" element in the educational relationship. The triangle has precedence over the formal educator-pupil-relation.—In the two attitudes play is seen differently. In formative education play is a concealed prototype of seriousness. The sense-relation of child's play to adult life is utilized in order to practice, as battle is practiced in tournaments. Biological training for serious cases. Play as methodical vehicle, as educative means appropriate for children. It is otherwise in nurturing education: play is sense in itself. In order to live out its childhood with delight the child must play. Attentiveness to the unconscious, purposeless productive powers, to the anticipation of the future coming from the child's unconscious depths, an anticipation which the child itself carries out.

4. To what extent should the educator influence child's play? Guidance will always be necessary to a certain degree. "Improvised" play and play "with rules"? For the observer improvised play is obviously "more revealing"—conversely, play with rules is "more disciplinary" for the child.

5. The phenomenon of "rules of play"? One might believe that the charm of wholly free play in unrestricted improvisation is greatest. The pleasure of returning to the beginning, to the freedom before chaos. However, that is *not* the case. And yet that is a riddle.—"To invent games," the collective imagination greater and deeper. Symbolic content of kinds of play. Children's games, rudiments of the most ancient magical practices.

Precisely the child places the greatest value on the observation of and compliance with the rules of the game. The rules of the game are not the cancellation of creative imagination, but rather what is striven for in creative imagination. Pleasure of self-commitment!! Rituals of play! Setting and observing the rules is a coming-into-constitution. The human being is originally not composed, but strives toward "form," "constitution."

The rules of the game provide the possibility of communal playing. The rules have a social sense. Playing-together according to rules.

6. The pedagogical meaning of the rules of play? The rules order, establish, create a situation where children freely subordinate themselves, hold themselves to "self-imposed laws." A violation is punished by exclusion ("You can't play anymore!"). Right to dismissal.

7. A still further concept is relevant here: the plaything. Playing is playing-with others according to collective imagination with rules,[16] but also a playing with playthings.

The fundamental sense of the plaything is difficult to grasp. Of course, everyone can point out playthings. Abundantly in toy stores. The plaything belongs to the most everyday and common things. But the big problems lie in *those* things which we take for granted. The concept of the plaything? That with which one plays? It is a thing of the natural, actual environment and is a thing in the play-world. And those are not two sides. Rather, it has a meaning; certainly not like a sign for something else. Occasionally the contrast between the doll made of cloth and wire—and the baby doll. The plaything-character in the plaything is a magical characteristic (symbolic representation).

Is the human being himself the primary plaything? Or perhaps his body? There are theories of play that proceed on this basis. Thus, for example, it was Pestalozzi's view that the child first of all plays with itself. Discovery of the body is not already identical with play.

Just as the human being cannot remain purely in the anthropological realm, as he is reliant on primeval things (in work on the hammer and plow, in ruling on the sword, in love on the bed, in poetry on the lyre, in religion on the sacrificial altar), so in play he relies on the plaything. The plaything is a proxy of things in general, playing is a mode of confrontation with beings. In the plaything the whole of what is to be mastered is concentrated. Every kind of play is an attempt at life, is an attempt at a mastering of life, and, in the plaything, has hold of resistant beings in general.

8. The pedagogical signification of the plaything? To be sure, children can play with everything. Their magical power is still unexhausted. Yet it is mostly adults who produce and supply playthings for children. The primitive schema of the plaything: *diminutiva* of the things of the adult world, miniaturization and transformation into kitsch. Simple reproductions. To be sure, reproduction in general is something that appeals to the child because it still lives with a magical

understanding of the image.—A more essential form of the plaything is the "generic."—Still more essential is the turning out of "archetypes."

Elementary and pure design vocabulary of playthings, exemplary models, as it were. This, above all, {was} Fröbel's[17] ingenious thought. Playing is creative re-creation of reality from its pure elementary forms. Cf. his play-gifts [*Spielgaben*][18]: They are not supposed to be complex things that are difficult to see through, not reproductions, but rather pure basic forms, elementary shapes. The ball (the bouncing sphere), the rolling sphere, the cylinder, the cube and the decomposition of the cube into small plates (building blocks). The beginnings of human self-activity should be roused by simple geometrical shapes. In play the human child should learn to see into the fundamental structure of things. "Play reveals and unveils the laws of life, as of nature . . ."[19]

Fröbel's thought is fittingly a principle, but all-too-geometricizing with regards to his concept that the primordial = the spatial (influence of Pestalozzi's concept of intuition). The problem remains: to find the design vocabulary of elementary forms in playthings—but the elementary forms of things in the human environment (with attentiveness to the primal language of magical symbols).

Further theme: play-community, play as destructive social form.

Tenth Session

1. Pedagogical significance of play discussed from the perspective of adults, who speculate about child's play. Two extreme positions of responsible education: responsible to society, to culture, to the state—or to the child as a future free human being. Formative and nurturing education (in Fröbel's wording: prescriptive [*vorschreibend*] education and education that follows along [*nachgehende*]). Playing as "means" and playing as "documentation"—both instances: a "means"-lens!—Playing as a spontaneous enactment (what is the spontaneous: freedom or imagination?), play without rules and playing with rules. "Desire for bonds"—play-thing? The human being's relation to the "environment" as task. Diminutive reproductions or types—or "archetypes"? Primordial sense of the plaything is magical proxy. Plaything is neither the "I" with its body nor another. But "I," "body" and other or others together belong to play. Play is an elementary mode of community, of συνζῆν, not constant, to be sure, but yet for that very reason elementary. A field of free, impulsive, spontaneous communing. "Conviviality" as the essential feature of playing. Structure of this conviviality? Unstable, contingent, non-binding, and so forth.—Reference once again to Plato's model of a "drinking-club" as schema of the polis.—Playing-together: proper role and alien role? The communal sphere is *not* grasped in this way. Imaginative collective-production! Communicative relation in the communal interest in the mask, for disguise, for magical transformation. The players in a communal rapture.

Play and struggle and love and work are communicative primal phenomena of human existence. We leave open the question of whether they are the only primal phenomena (others: religion, philosophy, language, art, science, and so forth). Play-community, community-of-struggle, love-community and work-community. Here the "communal" does not lie in the fact that a number of people are doing the same thing or have in some way coordinated their activity. Rather, the communal precedes the activity of individuals.

2. Pedagogical meaning of the play-community? *Experimentum societatis??* Practice in the social virtues? Value of fair play, etc.—Different estimation of the play-community in the "formative" and in the "nurturing" kinds of education: on the one hand as prototype, then as spontaneous type. In both instances educators are "external": they do not play along.—Play is an "objective situation among the pupils"—for the educator, not an encompassing situation of educative being-with. The highest pedagogical possibilities for the play-community are obviously where what is educative has the pure form of being-with, does not have the technical relation to a prepared "material" nor the horticultural relation to what grows naturally, but rather co-existence with one's fellow human beings.—That does not mean that the educator should be childish with children; but another kind of inclusion: that of the spectators, who belong to the game and for whom it is played. The "openness" of the sphere of child's play for adults. (Cf. Rembrandt's painting *Saul and David.*[20])—The variety of exhibitions similar to the ancient circus is a remnant of magic, which is still there in play for the spectators. Play of the mysteries: epopts. Dramatic play or spectacle as age-old form, as inclusive relation.

3. In the essential feature of play, that of being portrayal for spectators, there is a *danger* in its origin: empty acting [*Schauspielern*]. The playful as loss of substance, a thousand skins and no core. Wavering lack of commitment, frivolousness, groundlessness, charm.

4. The pedagogical danger of play lies here in "play-acting [*Schauspielerei*]," posing, the façade, convention.

Many modern educational experiments founder because they are not able to distinguish "play" from the "playful."

5. In playing the human being has a great but also dangerous possibility; it is not entirely unclouded for him. Only the Greek god is able to really play without danger, to lose himself. Human being: παίγνιον θεοῦ.

Above all, human play is imbricated with other fundamental phenomena and exists in tension with them. Fundamental phenomena of human existence such as love, struggle, work, play. The "child" plays from the core of its being. In contrast, the adult plays in open tension with the life of work, of struggle and of love. Struggle and work are fundamental modes of self-assertion.

Love is experience of supra-individual meaning of life (immortality). And play, too, releases from the "I," to the extent that it is magically enchanting. In children's play other fundamental phenomena are present—in a *gentler* way (love, death, war, work, etc.). In the "plaything" the child has those dimensions, which it itself does not yet understand, in a magically abbreviated form. Children's games are games of mysteries, unconscious playful mirror-symbols of the mysteries of human existence. Of childhood we read in the fourth *Duino Elegy*:

> . . . Oh hours of childhood,
> when behind each shape more than the past appeared
> and what streamed out before us was not the future.
> We felt our bodies growing and were at times
> impatient to *be* grown up, half for the sake
> of those with nothing left but grownupness.
> Yet were, when playing by ourselves, enchanted
> with what alone endures; and we would stand there
> in the infinite, blissful space between world and toy,
> at a point which, from the earliest beginning,
> had been established for a pure event.[21]

The necessary dialectical disintegration and tension of the phenomena of existence. Play has genetic precedence, is the matrix for opposed aspects of human existence. To this extent something extraordinarily distinctive. It contains the other fundamental phenomena "in the manner of portrayal."

6. Review of the course of our reflections:

I.

a. Attempt to take up the phenomenon of play from its everyday familiarity and interpretation;
b. Differences from "work," leisure, seriousness, drudgery of need, creative impulse, artistic productivity, and so forth;
c. Analysis of human doing and letting-alone, insofar as they are guided by foresight into the final goal and the architecture of mediate goals grounded therein. Play drops out of this referential tendency; oasis of happiness;
d. Discussion of the delight in play (in contrast to sensuous and intellectual pleasure), self-conflicting pleasure in play, which can contain suffering as an ingredient;

e. The sense-aspect of play; internal and external sense;
f. The aspect of portrayal: question concerning the nature of "appearance" (playworld), a remarkable kind of "actuality" (image, shadow, mirroring). Iterative forms of appearance in general and of playing in particular;
g. Play's world of appearance as magical dimension of the imaginary;
h. The human being's ambiguous relation to the imaginary; in part, freedom that disposes over it, in part enchantment that enraptures us;
i. Play and the stages of life (children's play and adult play);
k. [sic] Communicative aspect of play: origin in the cult and primitive rites, bringing the whole of existence to presence.

II.

l. Play as phenomenon and as key phenomenon;
m. Status of play: in anthropological and ontological-cosmological purview;
n. Formal structure of a key concept: representation, *pars pro toto.* Presupposition is the mirroring of the whole in the part;
o. Play a single phenomenon to whose fundamental structure symbolic representation already belongs: perhaps especially suitable for that reason;
p. Play-metaphor at the beginning of Western philosophy in Heraclitus and at the end in Nietzsche (play of individuation, speculative world-theater).

III.

q. Transition to the pedagogical-anthropological status of play: always assessed differently in formative and in nurturing kinds of education: play as vehicle for the conveyance of knowledge—or as documentation;
u. {sic} Improvised play and play with rules, the phenomenon of the rules of play and their pedagogical significance;
v. Essence of the plaything: symbolic form of non-human beings;
w. The play-community—playing-together—spectating—the danger of what is "merely" playful;
x. Play and the other primordial phenomena of existence, which are "manifest mysteries."

7. Here we have taken a specific course—of questions, views, and partial insights into an enigmatic phenomenon of life that is well-known to us, have arrived at many confusing, manifold problems, have had the experience that here not only

do human opinions concerning the matter contradict each other, but that an unsettling ambiguity lies in the matter itself. That is a precursor to philosophical wonder. If we have attained that in our *working*-group on *play,* then that is somewhat fitting for the propaedeutic goal of a proseminar. I would now like to let you go on holiday with the wish that, after your term paper, you may experience something of the happy play of human life on your travels and journeys.

Sport Seminar on February 24, 1961

1. After the presentation on human embodiment there will be today only a sketch of open questions that should be discussed: embodiment and physical education [*Leibeserziehung*].

2. The human being's association with the body is very diverse, knows many possibilities, degrees of intensity, and degrees of awareness.

The body is the ground of existence, the life soil of our Being, which has nothing more behind or beneath it. It is operative throughout and thoroughly attunes what is pre-conscious and what we are highly conscious of.

One can neglect it or attend to it. Waking-sleep-rhythm—freshness-fatigue—health-sickness—"burden" or "delight"—young-old.

Metabolism, organism—assimilation—union of bodies and procreation, separation at birth—death and corpse.

The fundamental dimensions of life are related to the body: work, ruling, love, play, death—language.

We are embodied [*leiben*] in all realms of culture: words, writing, image . . .

Human culture inescapably a culture of the body—i.e., co-conditioned by the body as formative materialized power—thus culture *through,* not always *for* the body.

3. Culture of the body is pursued in every human society: gestures, rituals and so forth, temple dances.

Education begins as physical education, and this accompanies all other kinds of education.

Flourishing, health, good senses, power, dexterity, proficiency in fighting.

Archaic societies were far more oriented to bodily education.

Hunt, fighting, dance, cult—

the great necessities.

4. Human life, which is determined by the body to a great extent, for the most part has at its disposal a meager language for the self-understanding of bodily Being.

Sport = its own language.

Most bodily functions are only in the realm of language among doctors.

The categories of association with the body are lacking!

5. Task, to create knowledge about human embodiment, to deepen such knowledge.

A particular bodily praxis—and a knowledge of this bodily praxis.
Bodily praxis partially enactment, partially in pedagogical intent—
The latter is physical education.

Pedagogy = a. educational praxis
b. scientific knowing of the educational praxis
(= education sciences)

6. Physical education is not a "means" (that is used) for a "cultivated [*erzogenen*]" body.

= mediation. Cf. youth is not a means for adult life.
Bodily activity is worthwhile in itself.

7. The concepts are relatively easy to find for formulating the goals of physical education—it is difficult to determine the concepts for the bodily activity or Being of the "cultivated."

8. The human being (as existence) and things (of which he avails himself)—the body is not a thing in which a dimension of existence is objectified.

9. The human being "in" the body—the human body's own possibilities: running, jumping, throwing—movement, gymnastics

Running track, sites for jumping, jumping mat, throwing (ball, bat).
Gymnastics (vaulting horse, bars, rings, and so forth)
Dance, calisthenics.

10. Is "simple" equipment related to the body just like the tool?

Sphere of activity and "inclusion"?

11. Human sport with equipment

Human sport with animals (horses)
Human sport with machines
Astronautics (cf. Jünger, the "*Hunt* [Jagd]")

12. Provocative function of "reflection" → intellect,

Provocative function of sport → embodiment.

13. These are all open questions that will contribute to the question of how far physical education is a part of the exercise of educational praxis or education sciences.

Play and Sport {1962}

1. Surprising, a project group from the *Institut für Leibesübungen* [Institute for Physical Exercises] and *Studium Generale* [General Studies] on the theme "Play and Sport"—or, not surprising, insofar physical exercise concerns all students regardless of discipline and the Studium Generale applies to all students, too. In what does the general interest agree?

2. Play and sport appear to be human modes of comportment that flee the concept—modes of an intensive immediacy, not without consciousness of being carried out and tension, but without the tendency to reflection.

Is an undertaking that ventures to ponder play and sport thus contradictory with the immanent tendency of play and sport? Division of thought and Being?—in that which is human?

Socrates in the Athenian *palaestra*—in the baths and arenas in conversation with beautiful youths—even in *agōn*—reflexive understanding as a contest—"gymnasium"

3. Diversity of sciences that target aspects of play and sport. Examples: psychology, physiology, ethnology, sociology, political science (*panem et circensem*)

Twofold task of the tutorial:

a. Phenomenology of play and sport
b. Education sciences' statement concerning physical education in play and sport.

Both of these aspects explicate again and again!!

4. Play and sport—not to separate from each other through definition, not to create a vocabulary, to see in the first place the multiplicity and richness of the phenomena.

Play and kinds of play? Sport and kinds of sports? (being-human and human modes of comportment?)

Play — versus work, struggle, erōs, cult of the dead
versus seriousness
versus duties and services (social activity)

Elements of play — in work, struggle, erōs, cult
in seriousness (and in honors)
in duties and services

Kinds of play iterate other ways of carrying out existence

Kinds of play = Types of play? Principles of classification??
Kinds of play involving motion, play and dance, rhythms,
Playful fighting (tournaments, contests)
Kinds of cultic play
Kinds of play involving love (dance—)
Kinds of play involving portrayal—the "as if"—the "*appearance*"

Kinds of sport? Physiological classification. Running, throwing, jumping—wrestling, gymnastics, boxing—motor sports, sailing, rowing, skiing, climbing, cycling—cosmonautics

Sport and the body

?

Play and the body

The embodiment of human existence a fundamental problem—against the background of an anti-physical (metaphysical) tradition of the West

Play and sport—as symptoms of a positive relation to the body

The apologetic situation sometimes compels one to a false setting of standards.

5. The positivity of play and sport—for the embodiment of our carrying out of existence is expressed in unelaborated categories such as "health," "power," "beauty." Cf. Nietzsche's "great health"

Elevated embodiment, festival and celebration

Gestures, symbol

6. Objection: Kinds of play "without" body-relation: kinds of play that are diversions, "social games," chess, cards, games of dice, play as a pastime, games of dexterity

7. Kinds of play that portray (role-playing)
    Masquerade, masks—relation to possibilities
    Theater—film, television

8. Regarding kinds of play that portray—to pick out a few features
    a. Player and role (prop) (plaything)
    b. Player and co-players—in front of the community
    c. Playworld

9. Comparison to sport
    a. Team (a club)
    b. What resembles the ancient circus
    c. The "great sporting event" (for example, soccer)

10. Sport—often as the unforced continuance of colonizing activities, climbing, navigation, aviation and flying

For example, herdsmen and horse-riding
Maritime peoples and seafaring
Bellicose tribes' proficiency in fighting (maneuvers)
Sport takes on the character of play
Contest
Performance at a high level
Limits of human capacity
Sport and technique
Motor-sports—devices of a technical kind
All of these are the motifs that will be treated at length in the presentations.

Phenomenology of play and sport difficult, because they are extensive phenomena and because adequate categories are lacking.

11. Play and sport—as factors in education—courses of education—not as mere means for achieving a goal that lies outside the one playing and the sporting activity. One does not play, do gymnastics, engage in a sport in order to reach a state, to attain a condition where one *no longer* plays, does gymnastics, or engages in a sport.

Sport and play—can also be a pedagogical means to other goals, first of all must be intended for their own sakes. Concept of a play- and sport-culture.

Architectonic of the goals of existence and the variety of dimensions of existence?

12. Play-education, physical education, sport-education—and the *education sciences?* It must take up what is there as phenomena, secure these against misleading interpretations, elaborate new categories of the active, embodied carrying out of existence, grant physical education the status it merits—the status of the earthly human being's primordial educative power.

Notes on "Play and Philosophy" {1966}

{Text 1:} Disposition *Play and Philosophy*

I

1. Status, scope, meaning of play in human life

2. Abundance of kinds of play, modes of play, which are openly manifest, well-known phenomena, and masks of play (masks in masquerading [*Masken in Maskentreibens*])

3. Allurement of appearance, enchanting power of the beautiful, play as alienation.

4. Philosophy is disposed—obviously in opposition—to the ambiguity, variety, opacity of beings as a nuisance for the striving for truth, univocity, certainty and reliability of beings—the struggle with appearance which is more than error, deception, and making a mistake—beings themselves appear, the human being and the perturbation that is at play within beings themselves,—the enigmatic and appearance-laden character of the world as stimulus, impetus, and nuisance for philosophy—philosophy wants to disenchant, wants clarity and truth, does not want the charm of disguise, the dreadfulness of the mask, wants to expose, reveal, unveil, wants sober clear-sightedness—the contrast between philosophy and play is more than a psychological-typological one, is not to be grasped with "seriousness" and "joking"—is an opposition that is ontological and cosmological.

5. Philosophy must admit the "appearance," the imaginary, not cast them aside as unimportant and insubstantial—the human being is just as primordially a player as he is a fighter, worker, mortal, and lover—the world is just as much true Being, as it is a dream, appearance, "surface," and a ruddy complexion.

6. This tense relation of opposition is by no means that which philosophy posits as relation of foreground and background, of appearance and essence (in the epistemological sense), but rather a relation that Hegel formulates as: "Essence must appear."[1]

Immediacy and Reflection

Multidimensionality	and simplicity (even if endless iterations of reflexive movement evince themselves)
The dance of things	unrest of the concept

(cf. *Zarathustra*, "Roundelay")

Philosophy sees itself challenged by play (by the nothing in Being and Being in the nothing)—more than by work and struggle, perhaps like love and death—

But does play concern philosophy or is play blessed in itself?

Play—as cheerful pastime, as playful combat,

As *agōn* and contest,

As "play that involves portrayal" with representation and symbolism like the theater (*theatrum mundi*), tragedy.

Here play makes evident, teaches, even if not in tenets, conceptual constructs, and arguments, it teaches in the sign, in the image, in the gesture.

(Perhaps Hegel's reading of *Antigone*) "Of the human being in general there are nameless sufferings, which the unfortunate son of Laius experienced, vicariously for 'everyone and no one.'"

Sense, a profound sense, lives through play—to a certain degree like a communal intimation or even a kind of collective vision—ecstase—of cults, of kinds of play that belong to the mysteries, whose leveling-out reaches all the way to the everyday or into the play of children—magic!!

II

Play and philosophy permeate one another in still another way: as unification and reciprocal negation of freedom and creativity. Not every freedom is creative. Not every creativity is free.

In play—everything can be once more, the opportunity to begin is unlimited, but only in the dream-realm of fantasy—the power of revulsion, of neglect, of transformation "in thoughts" (which are mere representations, not rigorous thoughts).

Where the arbitrariness of capricious invention passes over into a compulsion, an inescapable guidance, play becomes "necessary [*notwendig*]"—turning need around [*wendend eine Not*], becomes art, project.

Play as the basic root of cult, art and festival.

III

The plaything: everyone is familiar with such things, everyone has played with them, as a child, as an adult—it need not be shown to anyone for the first time.

Plaything is older than the human being—it is a *primal device*, like a weapon, a hammer, a sickle, a plow[2]—(like a house, bed, jug and bowl, cradle, coffin).

Origin of jewelry, of a kind of adornment, the "playful [*verspielten*] forms" in useful things, tools, dwelling, and so forth.

Plaything—as imitation, as "miniatures" of adult things, doll = child, log = weapon of war, automated game [*Spielautomat*] = machine.

Yet what is important is not that playthings are miniatures and imitate [*nachahmen*] the "things" of the adult world (or better: prefigure [*vorahmen*])—the plaything is a self-contained site for the transposition of existence in the sites of things (cf. *Ausstattung* [Equipment] in the lecture-course, *Ontologie der Arbeit* [Ontology of work][3]). There are not means of play because we play, but it is also the case that human beings do not play because instruments of play are available—rather, reciprocal condition!!

Human beings are normally not playthings, they are partners in play, members or spectators of communal play. Exoteric and esoteric play-communities. Kinds of play resembling the ancient circus. Gladiatorial matches were a degradation of the human being into a human plaything{—}[4] human beings (the play of the sexes is more a metaphor—"amorous play" [*Liebesspiel*]).

Plaything = in its kind of Being extremely problematic. Its phenomenological analysis might be more difficult than other kinds of devices.

Natural thing or artifact? In the case of a weapon, bed, devices for work, burial: the element of removal.

The plaything can be a natural thing (with imaginative features) or an artificial thing specially fabricated. The artificial character is not as important as its imaginary enchantment.

Plaything-industry??

III. {sic} Play and Philosophy of the Festival—in Plato's Laws—
(Text taken from "Problem der Paideia bei Platon u. Aristoteles"
[Problem of paideia in Plato and Aristotle]).

IV. Conclusion: παίγνιον θεοῦ? Human Being as Plaything of the God, as Marionette with Three Wires.

Not the fellow player, not the play-companion of the god, not a relation like that between child and father in communal play—but rather plaything (something frail, but intelligent, free, daring, not foreseeable, and yet to be directed with "wires")?

The whole ambiguity that lies concealed in the philosophical proposition concerning the human being as plaything is concealed like an explosive charge: can the player (who depends on the plaything as site of his drive to play) be thoughtfully determined for a higher freedom by alienation into a plaything—or is this Platonic thesis an indication of the fact that our freedom is not embedded in nature and contains impulses from obscure sources, but rather lies still more in the hands of the divinity—like a plaything? I want to conclude with this open question.

{Text 2}

1. Play and Philosophy

Status and scope and significance of human play has been a theme of philosophical reflection for a long time, one of the inexhaustible objects for questioning. And yet play itself is what is unquestionable, unproblematic, to a certain extent the counterpart of philosophy's serious, deadly serious, rigorously sober comportment of thought. If human existence trembles in the care, the anxiety, and the sublime shudder of thought, if on the other hand the solution to and release from all earthly difficulties is found in child's play, and in the play of adults—an island of happiness in the geography of life—what do play and philosophy have to do with each other (to a certain degree two extremes, polar opposites)?

Play is blessed in itself—philosophy is not blessed and desires *eudaimonia* with longing, denies itself all illusions.

Play does not need a philosophy—and philosophy is not play. (Primordial forms of genuineness [*Urechtheitsformen*] are denounced as conceptual games [*Begriffsspiele*]—to a certain degree the most vexing insult, to attach what is nonbinding, arbitrary, and capricious to groundless philosophizing. A popular denunciation of positivist science against philosophy.)

To emerge from the rigidified classification of extreme comportments!!

1. {sic} Play is *multidimensional,* reaches from child's play all the way to tragedy, is the *exchange* of aspects, of the many into one, of the one into many, seriousness and joking, irony, satire and deeper meaning in one.

Philosophy—has a productive nuisance in the ambiguous, shimmering nature of the playful comportment, but must explain the *appearance* as such.

Life a dream and dream a life.

Notes on "The World-Significance of Play" {1973}

{Text 1} The *World-Significance* of Play

Disposition 1

1. Play in its anthropological status
2. Play in the context of the structures of existence
3. Manifestations of play in art, religion,[1] and so forth
4. Forms of play belonging to struggle, work, love, death—play
5. Play as biological preparation for serious situations—as practice for "times of peace"—as entertainment in a society where free time has become common—as valve for congested states of affairs, illusionary "liberation"—as modalization of decisions, retrieval of lost possibilities
6. Play—as play of *portrayal* and as *competitive* play—and both *entertainment*[2]
7. Play and body
8. Play and world[3]

Play—anthropological status
Play—as *ontological* problem
Play—in its *cosmological* significance[4]

1. Play—universal
2. Play and leisure (free-time for all) The ruling class's play with weapons
3. {breaks off}[5]

I.

1. Play in its manifold manifestations
2. Play in its manifold assessments
3. Play not easy to delimit, because it plays along everywhere
4. Leisure class (games with weapons)—free-time society
   Counterforce to the constraints of the civilizing apparatus[6]

II. Play a fundamental phenomenon (not reducible to labor, etc.)

1. Communal structure—
2. Variation on (discharge of) labor, etc. (imitation is not itself imitation)

3. Play and cult (religion), art, creativity, imagination, education as playful imitation, distancing from fixed, established life—
   Play not religion, but a human root of religion, ritual, liturgy and at the same time a destructive motive in life. Playing is building and breaking down, joining together and breaking apart, Dionysian happiness—play, appearance-building and appearance-dissolving—[7]
4. The anthropological status of play: shifty, antithetical nature, *full of enigmas*
5. Portrayal (imitation—and presentiment, sounding out of possibilities)
6. {breaks off}

{Text 2} Disposition:

1. I. Anthropological status, II. Mode of Being, III. World-significance

2. I. Play = an irreducible fundamental phenomenon, just as primordial as struggle, work, love, death

Playing: analysis of structures.—Playing: an exciting activity that does not proceed toward an end, but rather is enjoyed in being carried out. Playing is not a chaotic staggering around, but rather lit up by bringing sense to presence, which leaves familiarity with the rules behind—player: in roles, in functions of an insistent nature, exchange of roles, player and play-community, the playworld (a context of sense that does not rest on the serious world, neither forgets it nor is an "error." The player—play-community, "mere play," the irreal components??—"Playworld"—as central category of an understanding of play that is oriented on the model of play that involves portrayal.—Other kinds of play: Diversionary kinds of play, agonistic kinds of play, kinds of adult child's play, imitation—dice games, ways of filling up time, play for money, professional player (= actor), professionals who work on shows [*Schau-Professionals*], and so forth.

(Play interpreted with play-categories?)—(Imitation not "imitation")

Play not a variation, not a belatedness, not an epiphenomenon—rather equal in its anthropological status with work, love, death, and struggle. An anthropology that is not only oriented to the "human being in general" and his characteristics of reason, language, freedom, historicity, and embodiment, but turns to the fundamental features of coexistence (work, struggle, love, death—and play), becomes for the first time able to contrast play—but can then set its sights on our enigmatic existence's entwinement into an inextricable knot.

Play does not only engage in quasi-struggles, in the as-if, it sometimes is engaged in real struggle, etc.

Aspects of play within work (invention)—in struggle, in outdoing an adversary, not wanting his death

Play = an essential basic phenomenon of human existence—we play because we are temporally transient

Play and cult, religion, rituals, celebration, ceremonies, putting on shows of power, emblems of ruling, *representation, not reflection,* art

3. II. The problems of play:
    1. Motivation, nature, *Frh.* {*Freiheit*} [freedom]
    2. Play and freedom, creativity—play and embodiment
       Play and historicity, play and reason, and language
    3. Appearance and Being—the world of *appearance* not a "deception"
       Natural relation of play—
    4. Time, space, recurrences

4. III. Play, *body,* representation—*intuition* à la Bergson—intraworldly representation

Zarathustra: for one who thinks in this manner all things dance (The Convalescent)[8]

{Text 3} Disposition

Play-activity:

1. Not an animalistic-vegetative occurrence, not motorized movement—but rather sense-imbued activity—doing something, throwing, jumping, running
2. Not a mere process of consciousness. Objection: imagination and dream, active modes of remembrance, of delightfully thinking up possibilities—a bodily operation, self-enjoyment of movement, recurrence
3. Not a *simple,* purpose-driven activity (be it through instinct or intention) rather a *two*fold activity—a real doing and a play-meaning—

Playworld

4. Play involving portrayal or role-play
   Pleasure, which encompasses—play-rule, play-community, play-means, and plaything
5. Competitive play—competitive performance
6. Play as only pastime, diversion
7. Aspects—and themes
8. Play and time, space, possibility, recurrence, open "Being"
9. Play and symbolism: root of cult and art
10. World-significance of play

—as a path of understanding of the human being—in relation to things and the world
—as movement of the world (model and play-enactment of the world)

11. Divination of play: body as {breaks off}

{Text 4} Side-Disposition

1. The vague appearance-non-actuality-thesis—ontological characterization of play hardly possible, because we operate with the opposition of actual/non-actual and designate it as true or false.
2. Involving oneself in real space and real durations of time, here and everywhere, now and at all times.
3. Involving oneself in the basis of reality: stage, running time [*Spielzeit*]
4. Imaginative aspects and real aspects, equipment for play, devices and plaything
5. Human activities, real factors and mere representations.
6. Playing—as involving oneself in things, some of which are and some of which are not
7. The imaginary = imagination [*Phantasie*][9]
10. [sic] The playworld?
11. Play as originary access? To what?
12. Play and retrievable possibilities
13. Time as continuity of events or irreal occurrences?
14. Sphere of influence [*Bannkreis*] = imaginary sphere with real inclusions?—Imagination—Covering over simply actual things??
    Playworld
15. Sphere of influence—
    Celebration, glorification of the body[10]
    1. General characteristic
    2. Anthropology of play
       a. of {games of} diversion
       b. of child's play
       c. of role-playing
       d. of competitive play
    3. Cosmological significance
       a. as ways of understanding
       b. as world-movement (Eternal Recurrence)
    4. The *body* and play[11]

The *turn* in the understanding of Being of play
Not a combination of *actual* Being and *imagined* Being
Not perception—and—imagination

Rather, magical understanding that does not concern what is objectively real, but beings in the vacillating realm of possibilities—the correlate of invocations and of magic—symbol-understanding

Play's mode of Being is the counter-turning conception of being real and being possible—

the mode of Being is the inverted understanding of Being that attributes a higher cognitive status [*Erkenntnisrang*] to magical representation than to knowledge that apprehends [*feststellenden Wissen*]—and also sets imagination above perception.[12]

{Text 5} Disposition

1. Perceptions, experiences, rational processing, scientific knowledge express that which is, even if in a preliminary manner and in processes of verification that remain open—objects that persist, change according to rules, causally interwoven in the chain of occurrences, spatially and temporally determined—the one context of actuality—the experience that reveals objective beings is only had *once*—recurrence is in each case different.

This experience is accompanied by a consciousness that runs ahead—imagination, which only encounters what is not actual.—And to human activities that are guided by plans, anticipations, projects, projections—thus by imaginative ideas, too—is added the conception that they can be "realized." Imaginative actions without reference to future realizations have no value, are nugatory, empty possibilities—aspects of imagination in human activities—such as the playworld in an activity of play—are, according to the common view, "insubstantial," "nugatory," themselves form a region of that which is nugatory;

this prejudice is an understanding of Being (Being, nothing, the nugatory, "appearance" [which does not emerge in consciousness, which is outside like shadows, the mirror-image, acting as if, play][13]).

As long as play in its mode of Being is characterized by this perspective of its being nugatory, an understanding of Being predominates that is oriented toward innerworldly things, processes, occurrences, and causal structures. The ontological standard is the thing of experience and its lawfully determined motion—what is actualized is irrevocable.

S. u. N {*Sein und Nichts?*} [Being and Nothing?]

If *this* understanding of Being[14] is the vantage point from which play's status and mode of Being can be assigned then play's power ultimately remains underdetermined.—Appearance—! Dualistic categories of actuality. It might be the case that imagination and human play can be seen in other terms, too. No combination. But not an equal objectivity. Playing and imagining are related to existence's world-relation—to possibilities that are taken back again, to streaming time, to the roundelay of beings—archaic world-relationship!—This is not meant psychologically or according to depth psychology. Playing as magical invocation—to represent the whole through invocation from a situation within the universe. Divinatory feature of human play, practice of enchantment, cult play, root of religion and of art. That would require a critique of ontology—by way of play, a critique that dismantles the defamation of play, remembers world-relations, conceives of play as a unity of *WzM* {*Wille zur Macht*} [Will to Power] and *EW* {*Ewige Wiederkehr*} [Eternal Return], brings to language the Dionysian understanding of world and Being.

Citations of Hegel and Nietzsche. *Symbolism*

2. Do we not thereby presume a possibility of play in which neither the fresh, immediate phenomenon of life nor its practical significance is appreciated??

{Text 6} Disposition of I

1. Status of the phenomenon of play.—From where to determine it? From a *biological* viewpoint—certainly a multiplicity of positive aspects. Preparatory exercise for the struggle for existence—practice in capacities without danger, youthful playing with weapons among nations, release valve for aggressive and destructive drives—manifold destruction a Dionysian happiness.—From a religious viewpoint: play as ? From a philosophical viewpoint: human being between animal and god—or a *hermaphroditic* being: *in, with,* and *against* nature. Already in Plato a high estimation of play.

—The human being?? Anthropology? Many forms of self-understanding—the context of the structures of existence? Reason, *Frh.* {*Freiheit*} [freedom], language, historicity and embodiment—

Work, struggle, love, and death—and *play*

How else?

Like *in* the structures of existence, how?

Like the other themes of play, how?

2. Analysis of play oriented to play that portrays

3. Play in religion, art, festival, and celebration—elements of play in leisured culture

4. The human *mode of Being* and human play's mode of Being? Understanding of Being of play? Play and appearance, understanding of time, understanding of space, truth—lie—deception, appearance as the locality of the exemplary "essence"—passage from the lecture course (concerning play*world*)—

Model-limitation: everyday kinds of play. Card games, obviously no sense of portrayal—conversely, sports and gymnastics—the community more open, sport plays with the body. If we suppose the body is a fundamental, basic structure of our existence, then human play's embodiment is a significant problem (play of thoughts, sand table exercises [*Sandkastenspiele*] of strategists, simulation games of economic planners)

The *body*

{Text 7} Disposition

1. Play as activity that is illuminated with sense, not a vegetative-animalistic enactment—and a manifold yet welling delight in life, not merely a biological occurrence, although many impulses are discharged within the economy of human life. Delight in play, joyful attunement—that does not have to signify a plan, nor a program of play—there are kinds of play that take place without disciplined purposes, without the structure of a project.

No purposive guidance of play—it is just as primordial as loving, a pure carrying out and discharging of life, an intimacy of life [*Lebensinnigkeit*].

{Text 8}

Anthropological aspect

1. Analysis of the activity of play
2. Role-play and play as recreation
3. Imagination and dichotomy of *Being and appearance*
4. Playworld, real basis and imaginary aspect—
5. Understanding of Being, etc.
6. Root of religion and art
7. Anthropological status = multidimensional existence—in the context of co-existentials

{Text 9}

1. Introduction

I. 2. The *activity* of play (role-play)

3. The play*world* (understanding of Being)

4. *Status* of play

II. World-significance: symbolism (cult, art)

a. Ways of understanding

b. World-movement

III. *Embodiment* of play

Body as place, means for and medium of play. Gymnastics and sport—sport as disciplined play. Accomplishment of the human body, experience of situations of nature (sea, wind, climbing)

Play as cultic, artistic mode of world-sojourn, profoundly symbolic [*symbol-tiefer*] carrying out of life

{Text 10}

1. Activity of play

Bodily action, dream-plays, embodied dreams, impulses and programs, happiness of enactment, joy in the present—not a futural activity for the sake of something

—Goals of play, inner and outer, goals in play, with play—Play and process of education

{Text 11}

[15]Play—common phenomenon, not the domain of children, in every stage of life and social class, no longer the privilege of one class that devises cultivated forms, tournaments, for example, festivities, diversions, pastimes, and amusement—feudal society had the *power* and could play, dallying like the *ancien régime* before the French Revolution—play belongs to chivalrous culture, to courtly life, to the represented wealth of the bourgeois—then also in the folkloric form of simple folk, for its manners and customs. Play as adornment of existence, as enactment of impulsive and spontaneous joy in life—sparse time, superfluity of time—kinds of play as diversion and pastime—*ora et labora—carpe diem* = underclass and upper-class. Play vacillating in the appraisal and in the self-understanding of the classes.
Negative-aspects: levity, wasting of time, not being serious, uselessness
Positive valuation: preparatory exercise, maneuver, release valve. Ordering within free time:

Play, positive relation to *freedom, creativity.*

This mixing of positive and negative valuations, in its radiantly colorful, polysemous form, belongs to everyday life and {breaks off}[16]

1. Play has many forms of manifestation, manifold characteristics, multiple estimations

I. 2. The anthropological status = *one* essential aspect of human existence

3. Context: reason, language, freedom, sexuality, embodiment
Human being and coexistence: work, struggle, love, death, and play
Human being—*in* nature, *with* nature, *against* nature.

4.—as *problem*

II. 5.—in its cosmological significance (body and world)[17]

{Text 12}

Another consideration for the exposition of the problem than for the description the simple understanding of Being!??? actual/non-actual

Perception and imagination?? Truth and illusion??

So that magical production, creative intuition, the entrancement and play in things and in the ground of the world may be experienced, displaced into the *non-existent,* into the land of non-being

Magic—Symbol—*open* actuality.[18]

But is something understood by the critical capacity that divides human play into a real occurrence and an illusionary sense-aspect?[19]

actual

Simple understanding of Being—*doubt*

non-actual
{what is} accessible to imagination

Imagination and symbolism[20]

Competitive play, the body—apparently *without* playworld—only harder to grasp.

The celebration, the gloriole, the renown of the body, of the embodiment of existence—

the *body* and *play?*

{Text 13}

Play—Chance (dice game, "Zarathustra")

Suspension of univocally determinative causality.

Play and *arbitrary discretion* [Willkür] (freedom)

Play and creativity

Place in the universe, where the *new* bursts in as *Frh.* {*Freiheit*} [freedom], creativity, and play—the gaps in fixed Being—play not merely a way of understanding, but rather an ontological riddle.[21]

Play of the world?

{Text 14}

The essential world-significance of play does not lie in its possible character of being a *model* for a universal understanding of the world (as, for instance, in Heraclitus's παῖς παίζων—or in Nietzsche's hymnal encomium of chance, happenstance, and the divine game of dice), it lies in the position of *cosmic openness* that the playing human being *is.*[22]

{Text 15}

If *positivism* disqualifies metaphysics as a kind of play with concepts, it is justified in a sense, insofar as it does not know how and with what profundity play is an understanding of Being and world

{Text 16}

Experience—scientifically knowing relation to intraworldly-concrete beings, to a thematic[23] realm, where occurrences of action, illusionary "worlds of sense," means of play and playthings {exist} with material, sensuously experienceable constituent element{s} and an "appearance-laden" coating; a behavioral model that is partially given in a historical situation, and is partially "invented," dreamed up, made up, fabulated—and yet is not nothing, precisely an ontic appearance.

{Text 17}

At first, neglect of the *body* in play, then neglect of the "*playworld,*" which is imbued with symbols and *appearance,* in the discussion of the body.

Sport is cultivation, a training, an exercise, a cult, an elevation of bodily existence. Competition is measuring of bodies in a sporting *arena,* a celebration, an invocation—almost a kind of cult-play.

{Text 18}

[24]Reflection on play, understanding of play—concerning a phenomenon of our existence that is too familiar—and yet full of riddles. Reflection and play flee from one another—impulsive immediacy and thoughtful consideration! Does thought not simply spoil play—if it strives for clarity and truth, the univocity of the situation? Does what is veiled, delighting in masks, furtive, capricious, labyrinthine, polysemous, belong to play? Thinking is tedious, says Aristotle, is the work of the concept, struggle with the withdrawal of things, love for beings, relation to the nothing and is itself also play—and play takes up work, seriousness, struggle, *aspects* and such *themes* (sense-program).

Appendices

The Layout of the Volume and Description of the Texts

The Layout of the Volume

The present volume contains the texts that Eugen Fink devoted to the theme of play and that he did not integrate into other works that go beyond the theme of play, such as the extensive passage on play in *Grundphänomene des menschlichen Daseins* [Basic phenomena of human existence]. These texts are arranged into three parts, each chronologically ordered. In the process, both the writings published by Fink himself and the hitherto unpublished Nachlass materials were considered. Fink's scholarly Nachlass is archived at the Universitätsarchiv Freiburg under the call number E 11. The Eugen Fink-Archiv at the Pädagogische Hochschule Freiburg is in possession of a copy of the Nachlass; parts of the Nachlass can also be found in the newly established Eugen Fink-Forschungsstelle at the University of Mainz.

In the first part, the texts that Fink himself published are reprinted: "Oasis of Happiness" (1957), *Play as Symbol of the World* (1960), and "Play and Celebration" (1972). *Play as Symbol of the World* goes back to a lecture course that Fink held at the University of Freiburg and that, like all his lecture courses, is preserved in a typescript he prepared himself (see the following section). Fink worked out the material of his lecture courses prior to the individual sessions and typed the text—as he customarily did with the prototypes of his public lectures—on A4 paper himself on a typewriter, always with single line spacing and the same formatting with small margins, in order thereby to be better able to structure the lectures in a time-efficient manner.

The second part, titled "Additional Texts," comprises, also in chronological order, works that either were not published by Fink or possess a special publication status. This part is introduced by a summary of a lecture and the concomitant discussion that appeared in print under the title "Child's Play" and that Fink himself probably produced. There is no further textual basis in the Nachlass for this lecture, which was delivered at a pedagogically oriented conference that took place in Osnabrück in 1958. The second text, "Play and Philosophy," pertains to a lecture that Fink held in 1966 in Cologne. Like the text of "Play and Celebration," which is also related to it in terms of content, "The

World-Significance of Play" from 1973 was broadcast as a radio lecture on Südwestfunk Baden-Baden. The undated sketch "Play and Cult" seems to stem from this period as well.

The third part, "Fink's Notes on Play," reproduces notes on the theme of play that Fink took on various occasions. They appear here for the first time. They begin with Fink's preparation for his proseminar on "The Philosophical-Pedagogical Significance of Play," which he conducted in Summer Semester 1954 at the University of Freiburg. Fink used to prepare all the seminars he held by laying out the basic structure of each subsequent seminar session with a few keywords. From the 1950s on he recorded these notes in small notebooks; later he also had his assistants write protocols of the sessions. The notebook containing notes for the seminar on play presents Fink's first attempt to unfold the theme of play in a systematic way. Along with the publication of these notes, what is printed here includes two further preparatory sketches for the "Seminar on Sport" from the years 1961 and 1962. The "Seminar on Sport" was a result of seminar sessions that Fink had arranged for prospective teachers as a part of the general course of studies at the University of Freiburg. The individual sessions were led by representatives of various disciplines. The conclusion of this part contains notes that Fink wrote down for the two lectures "Play and Philosophy" and "The World-Significance of Play"; these are based on the most comprehensive handwritten materials considered for the present volume. The notes collected here consist predominantly of "dispositions" and reveal how Fink attempted to give structure to a theme when he was working out concepts that were being projected in ever-new ways. For his notes, Fink used paper of various formats; often, large pages are cut or folded into smaller ones, and notes also appear on already written pages. In contrast to the single-spaced character of the typescripts he prepared for his lecture courses and lectures, most of the handwritten notes are distinguished by their spacious structuring and clarity.

All of Fink's texts published in this volume were left in their original form, in which the orthography and punctuation follow the German spelling rules that were valid during Fink's time, prior to the spelling reform. Obvious slips of the pen, grammatical mistakes, mistakes in spelling as well as incorrect or missing punctuation were corrected or filled in without comment. Cases in which such emendations modify the sense have been indicated in the endnotes. Editorial interpolations were put in curly brackets. With regard to the somewhat numerous underlining that Fink did above all in his handwritten notes and that often simply aided him when reading, only the words that were especially emphasized have been indicated by italics. In Fink's publications, as for the most part also in his typescripts, terms of Greek philosophy are rendered with the letters of the Latin alphabet, often in capital letters; these terms have been consistently rendered here in lowercase letters and italics. However, when Fink uses the Greek alphabet, as he does above all in the handwritten texts, this practice has also been followed here.

Description of the Texts

Oasis of Happiness

In Fink's Nachlass, there are four typescript versions of this essay: (1) The oldest version seems to be a fourteen-page typescript abbreviated here as TS 1, the cover page of which bears the title "Eugen Fink *Ontology of Play* (Given as a lecture at the Evangelische Akademie, Herrenalb on October 2, 1955." The thirteen pages of the text proper are, in Fink's typical manner, delineated in a single-spaced format; they exhibit changes Fink made in ink and are paginated in ink from 1 to 13. Version (2a) is a twenty-four-page typescript with one-and-a-half-spaced formatting; the pages contain slight alterations that Fink made in ink and are paginated by him in ink from 1 to 22. Before these pages two cover pages can be found with the titles "Eugen Fink *Thoughts toward an Ontology of Play*" (cover page 1) and "(Given as a lecture on October 2, 1955 at the Evangelische Akademie Herrenalb)" (cover page 2). Identical with (2a) is a thirty-four-page typescript version (2b), which was broadcast by Südwestfunk and contains no handwritten additions. The cover page bears the title "*Kulturelles Wort* / date of transmission: January 27, 1957 / Time: 10:30–11:00 A.M. / *Die Aula* / Thoughts toward an Ontology of Play / 1st Part / by / Eugen Fink / (Given as a lecture on October 2, 1955 at the Evangelische Akademie Herrenalb)." Version (3) is the same typescript version as (2a), likewise paginated from 1 to 22 by Fink in ink, yet with several revisions and changes in ink and pencil (abbreviated here as TS 2). Version (3) may have been the basis for the first printed edition: *Oase des Glücks, Gedanken zu einer Ontologie des Spiels* (Freiburg/Munich: Alber, 1957), 52 pp. Version (2b) was published under the title "Gedanken zu einer Ontologie des Spiels" by Südwestfunk in an anthology: Horst Helmut Kaiser u. Jürgen-Eckardt Pleines, eds., *Gedanken aus der Zeit: Philosophie im Südwestfunk* (Würzburg: Königshausen & Neumann 1986), 11–34. As a comparison shows, there must have been at least one further, no longer extant version of the text between versions (1) and (2a). Decisive for what we have published in this volume is the printed version from 1957. The endnotes indicate the substantively relevant deviations in TS 1 (1) and TS 2 (3).—Versions (1) through (3) bear the call number E 11 / 177.

Play as Symbol of the World

The printing in this volume is based on the initial publication: *Spiel als Weltsymbol* (Stuttgart: Kohlhammer, 1960), 243 pp. Page 243 contains a "bibliography" and is undersigned "Stuttgart, April 11, 1960." The bibliography lists the following works, to which Fink does not refer in the main text itself:

Ausschuß Deutscher Leibeserzieher (ed.): *Das Spiel*, 1959.
G. Bally: *Vom Ursprung und von den Grenzen der Freiheit: Eine Deutung des Spiels bei Tier und Mensch*, 1945.
O. Becker: "Von der Hinfälligkeit des Schönen und der Abenteuerlichkeit des Künstlers," in *Festschrift für E. Husserl*, 1929.
——: "Von der Abenteuerlichkeit des Künstlers und der vorsichtigen Verwegenheit des Philosophen," in *Konkrete Vernunft: Festschrift zum 70. Geburtstag von Erich Rothacker*, 1958.
F. J. J. Buytendijk: *Wesen und Sinn des Spiels: Das Spiel der Menschen und der Tiere als Erscheinungsform der Lebenstriebe*, 1954.
R. Caillois: "Über das Wesen und Einteilung der Spiele," in *Diogenes*, 1955.
J. Chateau: *L'enfant en jeu*, 2nd ed., 1954.
——: *Le réel et l'imaginaire dans le jeu de l'enfant*, 2nd ed., 1955.
——: *Le jeu de l'enfant après trois ans, sa nature, sa discipline*, 2nd ed., 1955.
K. Gross: *Die Spiele des Menschen*, 1899.
J. Heidemann: "Philosophische Theorien des Spiels," in *Kant-Studien* 50 (1958/1959).
J. Huizinga: *Homo ludens: Vom Ursprung der Kultur im Spiel*, 1956.
G. v. Kujawa: *Ursprung und Sinn des Spiels*, 2nd ed., 1949.
J. Piaget: *La formation du symbole chez l'enfant: Imitation, jeu et rêve*, 1945.
H. Rahner: *Der spielende Mensch*, 2nd ed., 1955.
A. Rüssel: *Das Kinderspiel*, 1953.
H. Scheuerl: *Das Spiel: Untersuchungen über sein Wesen, seine pädagogischen Möglichkeiten und seine Grenzen*, 1954.
——: *Beiträge zur Theorie des Spiels* (*Kleine pädagogische Texte*, no. 23), n.d.
P. Slade: *Child Drama*, 1955.
H. Zullinger: *Heilende Kräfte im kindlichen Spiel*, 2nd ed., 1954.

The published volume reproduces the text of a lecture course that Fink gave under the title "Das menschliche und weltliche Problem des Spiels [The human and worldly problem of play]" in Summer Semester 1957 at the University of Freiburg. This text is preserved in a typewritten version produced by Fink. It is archived under the call number E 11/126. The cover page bears the title "Eugen Fink *Das menschliche und weltliche Problem des Spiels* S.S. 1957 [The human and worldly problem of play Summer Semester 1957]." The typescript displays a few handwritten changes made in ink or red pencil as well as (probably during the original stage of writing) in pencil, and is paginated in red pencil 1 to 140. It is divided simply by the individual sessions of the lecture course, in which each new session begins with a new page; a division into paragraphs, which essentially corresponds to the paragraph divisions in the book version, is made in red pencil. The typescript does not yet contain the division into four chapters (with 20 sections) including titles; the sections, however, correspond to the individual sessions of the lecture course, which are designated as such in the typescript. Deviations of the printed text (D) from the typescript (TS) are indicated in the endnotes [when this is relevant for the English reader]. Those instances in which it is clear that something was copied incorrectly during the transfer from the typescript to the book form were corrected by returning to the wording of the typescript and [when this is relevant for the English reader] are likewise designated in the endnotes.

Play and Celebration

This article appeared in 1975, the year of Fink's death, in the first volume of *Perspektiven der Philosophie* (Amsterdam: Rodopi) on pages 193–205. Fink delivered this text under the title "Olympische Sicht auf Spiel und Sport [The Olympic view of play and sport]" as a part of the "Aula"-series of Südwestfunk Baden-Baden. It was broadcast by the station on August 20, 1972, shortly before the opening of the Olympic Games in Munich. What has been preserved is a thirteen-page transcript made by the station. The cover page bears the title "Südwestfunk / Kultur / Sendung: 20.8.1972 / Zeit: 10.30–11.00 Uhr / Redaktion: Herbert Bahlinger / 2. Programm" (Eugen Fink-Archiv Freiburg). The publication from 1975 forms the basis for the imprint in this volume.

Child's Play

This sketch for a no-longer-extant lecture that Fink delivered in 1958 within the context of a conference on physical education held in Osnabrück from October 2 to October 5, 1958, was published with the title "Das kindliche Spiel [Child's play]" under Fink's name in 1959 in the collection *Das Spiel* [Play] (edited by the Ausschuß Deutscher Leibeserzieher, Frankfurt am Main: Wilhelm Limpert Verlag). With his lecture, Fink introduced the "6th Workgroup," which he himself led and which was devoted to child's play. The short text gives a summary of the lecture and an outline of the discussion; both were probably composed by Fink himself. The imprint in this volume is based on a special printing that can be found in the Eugen Fink-Archiv Freiburg and bears the title "Spiel-Kongress Osnabrück Oktober 1958 [Play-conference Osnabrück October 1958]," which was written in ink in Fink's hand.

Play and Philosophy

In Fink's Nachlass (call number E 11/486), there is the beginning and ending of a text titled "Spiel und Philosophie [Play and philosophy]," which Fink typed single-spaced. The four pages are paginated in pencil with the numbers 1 and 2 as well as 28 and 29. On the top right of page 1 there is an annotation written in ink: "*Vortrag in Köln am 25. Okt. 1966* [Lecture in Cologne on Oct. 25, 1966]."

Fink delivered the lecture in the Volkshochschule Köln. Upon the request of the organizer, Fink sent the following summary in a letter from July 22, 1966: "Play is a phenomenon of existence that, in its exhilarated cheerfulness, appears to contradict the gloomy seriousness of philosophy. And yet, throughout the history of Western thought, the sparkling gleam of play has enchanted and captivated philosophers—not much differently than the power of erōs. In the Platonic dialogue *The Symposium*, philosophy begins to contemplate erōs and thereby makes the astounding discovery that erōs is housed within the essential basis of philosophy itself. Perhaps it could be similar with play."

The middle part of the lecture (pages 3–27) comprises excerpts from the manuscript of Fink's lecture course "Grundphänomene des menschlichen Daseins [Basic phenomena of human existence]," which at the time was still unpublished. Fink held this course in Summer Semester 1955 at the University of Freiburg. The excerpts can be found on pages 307–12, 314–15, 317–21, 323–24, 329–33, 345–46, 348, and 350–51 (of a typed transcription of Fink's typescript; to these correspond pages 361–419 of the book version: Eugen Fink, *Grundphänomene des menschlichen Daseins*, ed. Egon Schütz and Franz-Anton Schwarz [Freiburg: Karl Alber, 1979]). In the Nachlass, there exist two further pages written with a black ballpoint pen that pertain to this compilation. The text of these two pages reads:

Page 1:
"Use of text: 2 pages on play and philosophy
(from the notion that play is an anthropological finding and thus an *object* of philosophy, transitioning to the thesis: play as a path of the understanding of Being and world—e.g., tragedy)
345 top"

Page 2:
"1. Everyday interpretation of play—as free-time activity
2. Everyday interpretation of play—as a phenomenon of childhood
3. Basic features of human play (307). Not a 'Futurism'
4. Play = not a preparatory exercise (308/309)
4. Pleasure in play and rules of play (309)
5. Means of play (310). Ambiguity of 'plaything'
6. Playworld (311/312)
7. The overly broad concept of play
    a. Play of animals
    b. Play of lights (317) (318)
8. Our discussion up to now has moments of enactment (319, 320)
9. Play-community (323, 324)

10. Foreignness or identity (330, 331)
11. Comedy (333)
12. Festival (345)
13. Festival—of the gods (347)
14. Plato: the keenest adversary of the poetic art [*Dichtertums*], rational iconoclast, in the *Republic,* takes a different attitude toward play in the late work."

In the present volume only the beginning and end of the typescript "Spiel und Philosophie" are reproduced. The typescript exhibits changes on p. 29 that were made with a blue ballpoint pen.

The World-Significance of Play

This text is transmitted in a version that Fink himself produced in a single-spaced typescript. It contains a cover page and ten paginated pages of text (call number E 11 / 492). The cover page bears the title, likewise typed: "Eugen Fink: *Die Weltbedeutung des Spiels.* Funkfassung. Aufnahme: 14. Mai 1973 [Eugen Fink: The world-significance of play. Radio version. Recorded: May 14, 1973]." The text features emendations and material crossed out with ink and pencil. This version of the text is the basis for the printing in this volume. The introductory passage and the second part of this version present a more detailed version of the corresponding portions of "Play and Celebration." There is also a transcription of the radio lecture of "The World-Significance of Play" on seventeen typed pages (Eugen Fink-Archiv Freiburg). The cover page provides the information "Südwestfunk / Kultur / Sendung: 27.5.1973 / Zeit: 10.30–11.00 Uhr / Redaktion: Herbert Bahlinger / 2. Programm," broadcast as a part of the series "Aula" of Südwestfunk Baden-Baden. This version is significantly shorter than the original text produced by Fink.

Play and Cult

This text is based on a two-page typescript produced by Fink (in E 11 / 126). The purpose and time of composition of the text cannot be determined with ultimate certainty. We can assume that it stems from the ambit of works on "Play and Celebration" (or the radio version "The Olympic View of Play and Sport") and on "The World-Significance of Play." At the end of the text, there is the specification "p. 67." This could be a reference to the typescript that served as the basis of the book version of *Play as Symbol of the World,* since "Play and Cult" concludes with the question "What does the term symbol mean?" and pages 67ff. of the typescript (Section 10 of the book version) treat of the "symbol-problem" and this makes reference to cult.

The Philosophical-Pedagogical Problem of Play

This text reproduces the content of a small notebook in which Fink noted in ink the planned progression of the seminar session prior to it taking place (call number E 11 / 474). On the front side, it bears the title "Eugen Fink: Das philosophische-pädagogische Problem des Spiels. S.S. 1954 [Eugen Fink: The philosophical-pedagogical problem of play. Summer Semester 1954]" and comprises on sixty-three written pages the plan for ten seminar sessions. The text contains only a few emendations.

Sport Seminar

The text for this seminar session held by Fink on February 24, 1961, reproduces a manuscript that was composed on two pages written with ink on both sides and paginated 1 and 2 (in the bundle E 11 / 464). On the side, one finds a marginal remark: "Prior to this session there was another seminar session in which I read the lecture 'Das Schicksal leibhafter Existenz [The fate of embodied existence].'" This lecture, which does not refer to the theme of play, appeared in Hans Hoske, ed., *Gesundheit als Schicksal? Tagungsbericht: 5. wissenschaftliche Arbeitswoche über Fragen der Jugendgesundheit. 25.–31. Januar 1960 in Freudenstadt / Schwarzwald* (Wiesbaden: Jörg, 1960), pp. 181–89.

Play and Sport

This text is based on a five-page manuscript that was written in ink and features much underlining in red pen (in bundle E 11/ 463). Next to the title one finds a note that provides the occasion for and date of this text: "Referat am 19.XI.62 im Sport-Seminar [Presentation on November 19, 1962 in the Sport Seminar]."

Notes on "Play and Philosophy"

Reproduced are two manuscripts composed with black ballpoint pen (in E 11 / 486). The first text is written double-sided on two pages that are paginated 1–2; the second text is recorded on a single, double-sided page.

Notes on "The World-Significance of Play"

For the preparation of his text "The World-Significance of Play," Fink composed a series of sketches, developed his chains of thought, and noted sudden ideas (in E 11 / 492). Since much is repeated in these text fragments, which comprise forty-one pages, a selection was made for the printing in this volume. About half of the material has been reproduced: after what Fink himself calls "dispositions"—first conceptual inquiries into the theme to be worked out—there follow texts with aphoristic remarks on specific aspects. The notes printed here are written with ballpoint pen on paper of various formats. The pages are not numbered.

German Editors' Afterword

Eugen Fink's *Play as Symbol of the World,* which appeared for the first time in 1960, is rightly considered to be the key work of its author. It brings together much of what Fink had previously worked out in the 1930s, and sheds light on research that Fink was still to present until his death in 1975. Since, with the theme of play, Fink connects the philosophical directions of his gaze—the anthropological and the ontological, the pedagogical and social-theoretical, but also the aesthetic—to his proper concern with the cosmological, this theme is interwoven into many of his works. Since the present volume gathers together only those texts in which play forms the primary reference point, we shall connect what is worked out in them above all to those works of Fink's in which play is also discussed substantially.

Play as Symbol of the World does not, however, merely bring together a multitude of individual facets that are characteristic of Fink's work. Much more essential is the fact that here the decisive, fundamental feature of Fink's thought, his *cosmological formula,* is explicitly expressed and unfolded. "Play as Symbol of the World" itself already has a formulaic ring to it; what is essential is to make the sense of that formula known through this formulation. The formulation says simply: "play" is related to "the world" (thus neither identical with the world nor fully different from it) in the mode of the "symbol." Play—world—symbol are initially the three unknowns in a relation that comprises the core of the formula as such.

Beginnings

The genesis of the meaning of this formula originated with Fink's dissertation, which he composed in 1929 under Edmund Husserl's direction and which was published for the first time the following year in Husserl's *Jahrbuch für Philosophie und phänomenologische Forschung* [Annual for philosophy and phenomenological research].[1] On the final pages of this work, titled "Vergegenwärtigung und Bild: Beiträge zur Phänomenologie der Unwirklichkeit" [Bringing-to-presence and image: Contributions to the phenomenology of non-actuality], in the context of an analysis of the spatial image, the reader is confronted with the concept of a relation between the intraworld and the world, or, in the wording of the investigation itself, between an actual non-actual thing (the spatial image) and the actual thing in which it is included. If the image, measured against the actuality of space, presents a specific non-actuality, then the perception of the image, insofar as it embraces the image as its content, is, as a "*medial act*,"[2] related to both, to the image itself and to the image in its emplacement within space: the real bearer of the image is then also still in view when one's interest is turned toward the image itself. The relation to the bearer is not thereby attenuated or "neutralized," as Husserl thought, but rather appears in a unique way, which Fink characterizes as "transparency": Only in the mode of such transparency is the bearer there for the apprehension of the image and is it capable of "shining [*scheinen*]" *through* the image, although it does not itself thereby come to appear [*erscheint*].[3] Moreover, the special co-presence of the bearer in the manner of transparency prevents it from being grasped within the unity of a horizonal system of relation—from being, not indeed neutralized, but transposed into the background of a world of perception consistently unfolding in horizons; on the other hand, this co-presence guarantees the unity of the perception of the image as an act that brings together the apprehension of the image and the co-givenness of the bearer in the mode of transparency. Here for the first time, Fink develops that complex and in itself paradoxical structure that says that, *within* an intra-situation, what likewise *fully* surpasses it becomes illuminated in its withdrawal—this is the nucleus for his world-formula. And already in his dissertation, Fink remarks that this structure of medial acts holds manifestly for all apprehending of a non-actuality with the structure of the spatial image, and he mentions, next to consciousness of the image and presentation, "the apperception of play."[4]

The edition of Fink's folders of handwritten notes stored in large cardboard boxes from when he was Husserl's assistant, which has been prepared by Ronald Bruzina,[5] shows how Fink time and again refers to the structure of such non-actuality and in doing so also mentions play. Thus one reads already in a note from around 1929: "World as the whole of beings is itself not a being, but rather the play-space of beings. World 'given' in play-space-consciousness, a consciousness which is not an objective consciousness (consciousness-of), but an unthematic, horizon-forming consciousness."[6] An early indication of this play-space-consciousness shows up for Fink "in egological temporality as de-presentings,"[7] whereby "*time constitution*" is itself "*in play*."[8] As Fink records in a late review of his drafts for the edition of Husserl's Bernau manuscripts on time: already in the confrontation of these years (1932–1935), the time-constituting subject began to recede in favor of time as *world*-time, insofar as the latter proved to be an "encompassing, supraobjective and suprasubjective *primordial happening* [Urgeschehen]." In this "leap away from 'transcendentalism,'"[9] the theme of "life" comes to have more and more significance. Thus, the concept of the "great play of life," which Heidegger took from Kant's 1792 Anthropology Lecture Course and adduced to characterize the existential concept of world, quite probably gave Fink the first impetus for his anthropo-cosmological conception of play, which would then stand at the center point of *Play as Symbol of the World* and other works.[10]

The notes and shorter studies further attest to what extent Nietzsche increasingly comes to the foreground in these considerations.[11] The first more detailed text to interpret play cosmologically with explicit reference to Nietzsche is a lecture Fink delivered under the title "Nietzsches Metaphysik des Spiels" [Nietzsche's metaphysics of play] in March 1946 within the framework of the *Habilitation* procedures in the philosophy department at the University of Freiburg.[12] Fink's work anticipates not only the result of his interpretations of Nietzsche that he would compose in the coming years, but also in particular his own conception, to think of play as a symbol of the world. In his lecture, Fink brings into relief the systematic approach of Nietzsche's thinking. For him, this systematic approach is an "ontology of becoming," and he grasps it as an ontology of play, of which he likewise says that Nietzsche unfolded it merely as a "metaphysical intuition." In doing so, Fink translates the relation of the Apollonian to the Dionysian into a cosmological dimension: if the Dionysian is conceived as the "playing of temporalizing time" and the Apollonian as "what is temporalized in the temporalization," the connection between them is interpreted in such a way that the Dionysian, as the comprehensive concept for becoming, for the processual, for creative production, drives the Apollonian forth from out of itself and therein makes itself finite. With that, not only is a differentiation within the concept of play anticipated, to which Fink will return time and again: the play of the world, on the one hand, whose movement, on the other hand, drives the play of the intraworldly forth from out of itself. Insofar as the Apollonian stands for what is available and visible, what is arranged into the historicality of a world that is specific in each case, and the Dionysian, from the perspective of the Apollonian, is what is unavailable, that which sets the latter into appearance, a paradoxical relational determination on the path to Fink's world-formula is likewise indicated: it is a matter of thinking, from out of the visible, from out of the phenomenalized, and from out of the temporalized, that which exceeds them: that which itself phenomenalizes, temporalizes.

Anthropology, Ontology, Cosmology

In the second half of the 1950s, Fink developed this relational determination, whose sustaining moment is the concept of play. Three aspects are relevant in this determination: not only the difference between the intraworldly, on the one hand, and the world itself, on the other hand, but also the problem of to how to gain access to the world by philosophical means, since the world withdraws when the intraworldly advances. Fink implements this program with respect to the theme of play above all in three steps: within the framework of an "existential anthropology," his Summer Semester 1955 lecture course *Grundphänomene des menschlichen Daseins* [Basic phenomena of human existence][13] is devoted to the demonstration of fundamental structures of phenomenality—one could say, to a description of the human being within the tension of his intraworldly situation. Fink breaks this phenomenality down into five "fundamental phenomena," into work, ruling, love, death—and play. The subtitle of the writing that opens this volume, "Oasis of Happiness,"[14] published in 1957, is announced as "Thoughts toward an Ontology of Play." Lastly, the book *Play as Symbol of the World*—which arose on the basis of a lecture course delivered in 1957—follows in 1960, again taking up points touched on in both previous writings and placing them within a cosmological perspective.[15]

Human Play

In *Grundphänomene des menschlichen Daseins,* Fink proceeds on the basis of the *phenomenon* of play. Although he does not connect horizons of everyday understanding or horizons of the philosophical tradition's understanding to what is to be discovered in the phenomenon of play, he approaches his analysis of human play by looking at how it shows itself to everyday understanding, as he did in his seminar from the year before, "The Philosophical-Pedagogical Problem of Play."[16] However, this approach is undertaken with the aim of bringing out precisely what remains covered up for common understanding. "Phenomenon" here does not yet mean fundamental phenomenon, but rather the way in which play is commonly experienced, the closest access to the way in which "play" shows itself to everybody. Insofar as the everyday interpretation of play places it in a one-sided opposition to work, to the "seriousness of life," and thus conceives it as a "marginal phenomenon" in the carrying out of life, it distorts it.[17] This demarcation between what is serious and what is not is incongruent with the distinction between play and non-playful comportments of existence. For, play as the kind of play that involves portrayal, for example, can indeed unveil a more profound seriousness than would be opened up in the everyday immersion in life. Thus the phenomenon of play that possesses its mode of Being in the everyday understanding of play covers up the "more profound sense," the fundamental phenomenon of play, how the everyday understanding of play at the same time points toward the latter—a problematic that Fink will take up again in 1966 in "Play and Philosophy."[18]

In fact, there is a moment that is constitutive of play that is opposed, not indeed to a factual stance of life called "serious life," but rather to a particular fundamental tendency of life. With Aristotle, Fink catches sight of this fundamental tendency of life in the universal *striving* for happiness, for *eudaimonia,* correlatively in life's universal concern with the attainment of this goal that is constantly pursued.[19] Despite partial fulfillments, this goal remains unreachable in life; striving toward it is therefore constantly in progress. In play, this tendency of life to be driven out beyond itself comes to a standstill for a certain time and in a certain space—in imaginary time and imaginary space. Play is not happiness, not the fulfillment of the universal intention; yet by interrupting this intention, it temporarily liberates one from this directedness and precisely thereby presents, in a spatially delimited way, happiness, an "oasis of happiness." Play fulfills, even if in its own delimited way, the universal intention of serious life; it does not stand opposed to the latter but first becomes understandable through the universal tendency of care belonging to human existence itself: "Only a being determined essentially by 'care' also has the possibility of 'carelessness.'"[20]

That, therefore, play stands precisely in a particular relation to the tendency of care belonging to life, indeed in such a way that, in it, the goal-directedness of caring life is suspended in a determinate way, grounds its "carelessness." Even play sets goals, which are goals in its playworld; yet these goals that are immanent to play are not "projected out toward the highest ultimate purpose."[21] These immanent goals of play can, however, be related to the highest goal of life, insofar as these immanent goals, which are not at all immediately subordinate to the highest goal of life itself, make the latter first of all visible. Fink expresses this as follows: Insofar as play "appears to *es*cape [ent*ziehen*] the standard flow of life, it *re*lates [be*zieht*] to it in a manner that is particularly imbued with sense, namely, in the mode of portrayal [*Darstellung*]."[22]

This peculiar interpenetration of the playful and the serious, the goal-related and the careless, withdrawn from real time and real space and yet integrated into them, characterizes play in what Fink determines to be its peculiarly "ambiguous nature."[23] The analysis of this ambiguous nature is able to indicate the structural constitution of the *basic* phenomenon "play." Fink attempts to clarify this ambiguity of play, its vacillation between actuality and non-actuality, by analyzing play as *appearance* [Schein] and *symbol*. This path compels a confrontation with the metaphysical tradition, which, beginning with Plato, interpreted play as an *image*. Thus it is not only in his early work, where he treats of the image, that Fink mentions play. He also, conversely, makes reference to the image in his later analyses of play. He shows how, through the interpretation of play as imitation, of imitation as copying and of copying as mirroring, play was indeed associated with a higher Being, yet in the concomitantly accomplished reduction of it to a mere reflection was fully robbed of its independence. Even this metaphysical interpretation of the concept of play, its interpretation as copying and mirroring, its directedness toward a divine Being, is, according to Fink, to be cast off. This is accomplished in a comparison Fink undertakes between the image and play, whereby the character of the non-actual is here to be clarified anew.

The essential character of the image comes forth only when the image is interrogated in its original ontological constitution, thus not when it is thought in advance as the mere derivative of a more primordial original. The image is original not as a copy, but rather only as the image itself. And Fink adds to this: "The less 'reproductive,' the more strongly 'symbolic' an image is."[24] This shows that Fink does not employ the concept of symbol in the sense of a representation that has recourse to reproductivity. The image is not a symbol for something else, it is a symbol in itself. It is a symbol not, for instance, because it is non-actual, but because it presents an actual non-actuality, something imaginary within real space-time. As Fink establishes, every kind of image is an "*independent* sort of being,"[25] an "objective or ontic appearance."[26] It "contains as a constitutive aspect of its actuality something that is in itself specifically 'non-actual'—and, furthermore, in this way rests on another, simply actual being."[27] The poplar mirrored in the water does not cover up the piece of the water surface on which it appears; the mirroring of the poplar is as such actual and comprises within itself simultaneously the non-actual poplar of the mirror-world. In just this way, playing is an actual comportment that comprises within itself the imaginary playworldly comportment according to roles.[28]

In what sense, then, are we to speak of this imaginary thing in the image- or playworld, of this objective or actual appearance, even of a *symbol?* The image [*Bild*] and play are not first symbol-forming [*symbolbildend*] in such a way that they point to this or that, thus to beings; rather, they proceed by symbolizing because they, as Fink established already in his dissertation, are themselves of a *medial* constitution. Insofar as the emergence of imagistic or playful non-actuality marks a rupture in reality, however thin; insofar as it leads to a rejection of actuality, so to speak—it opens up a space in which the imaginary can move. In this opening up of space, the imaginary is medial in a primordial sense: play "has the structure of 'mediation.'"[29] The fact of this mediating role, this being-medial, designates the sense of "symbol" meant here. It is only because this space of mediality is opened up within the imaginary that the image- and playworld can indicate manifold relations that are opened up in existence. Still more, play reflects the fundamental feature of existence, the universal concern of life, for it is precisely where existence is liberated from this fundamental feature that play lets the latter "come to appear [*erscheinen*]" in its momentary absence. Something intraworldly (a particular instance of play) can in this way mirror the intraworldly aspect of human existence as such.

Fink connects the symbol back to its etymology, to the Greek *symballein,* and interprets this as a "a coming together of a fragment with what completes it."[30] It is, however, not to human existence alone that the symbol-mediality of play points; rather both form only one half, insofar as existence is mirrored already in the playworld. If, however, existence is the *symbolon* in the mode of the playworld—then what corresponds to it as the other half? Fink's answer: the *world*. "The world comes to appear [*erscheint*] in the appearance [*Schein*] of play."[31] What "completes" human-play is the non-phenomenal, and thus not to be phenomenalized, character of the world. Seen structurally, this is the way in which Fink attempted thirty years prior to determine the transparency of the image and the peculiar co-having of actuality in being related to the image. Fink characterizes the mediality of existence in many places as a "relation," as the way in which existence is admitted into world-space and world-time. Consequently, in the mediality of the symbol, the mediality of existence lights up [*scheint . . . auf*] in the manner in which existence relates to the world; this "testament" of the world in the mediality of the playworld thereby points to the authentic counterpart, the other *symbolon,* on the basis of which the togetherness of both halves first becomes intelligible—as if it were as phenomenologically accessible as human existence itself.

The Transition: Speculation

For Fink, the phenomenal is what shows itself and is visible; however, insofar as it is not exhausted by its visibility, it is for Fink a *symbolon*. Its visibility cannot interpret itself; there remains an undissolved remainder, whose problematic can be expressed by the question: *In relation to what* is the symbol a fragment? If one does not wish to refer the answer to the subject or existence, which appear within the intraworldly, one is compelled to inquire beyond the realm of the phenomenal. How, though, does understanding the visible fragment reach its self-withdrawing counterpart?

For Fink there are no bridges that extend over the abyss rent open with this question, but there are springboards. Lifeworldly knowledge of the encompassing character of the world presents such a springboard. Fink emphasizes that there is a knowledge of the world that is not attested to in the objectivity of experience.[32] This knowledge of the encompassing character of the world determines the world mostly as a sum total of individuals, for the whole is hereby likewise represented as a being. In contrast, all experiential knowledge of beings is pervaded by an implicit, unthematic knowledge of the conjuncture of these beings, which is itself no longer of the ontological mode of beings, since it is not nameable and slips from conceptual grasp; this knowing is not to be confirmed through experience, insofar as experience is always related to a being that shows itself. Yet in what does the proof for this thesis consist, insofar as the "totality [*All*]," which is also known, albeit unthematically, in lifeworldly experience and cannot be measured against beings, can at best be an indication? Fink catches sight of a more viable springboard than this unthematic knowledge precisely in play, more clearly said, in its aporetic structure, which consists in play's inability to be clarified within the realm of the phenomenal without remainder, in its "transparency."

Herein lies the decisive aspect of Fink's cosmological approach. The aporetic structure of play means that the playworld "balks at a simple assimilation into the context of the actual world."[33] Insofar as the playworld posits an objective appearance and thus inscribes a rift in reality—since with it a distinctive time-space-field is opened up, in whose mediality the fundamental mode of human existence is mirrored—it provides an index for something that it itself *is,* but that is neither identical with it nor capable of grounding it. Thus both—the interruption that follows from the enactment of play in actuality, and the mirroring of the fundamental feature of human existence in the mediality of play unfolded through the interruption—announce in a peculiar way something that itself remains concealed, that does not show itself. The factual, ontic interruption points *ex negativo* to a legitimate possibility of rupture; the opened space of movement belonging to mediality points to what extends this space to the whole of human existence, to its ecstatic outreach.

In this way, Fink catches sight of a point of departure in the structure of play for philosophical speculation, which asks about the world itself. Fink therefore speaks of a "speculative concept of play," which becomes stark where "the sense of being" is to be grasped "from out of play"; he defines such speculation as a "characterization of the essence of being *in the metaphor of a being,*" as "a conceptual *world formula* that springs from an *innerworldly* model," whereby play itself "is already distinguished by the fundamental feature of symbolic representation."[34] Such speculation no longer traverses the positive arrangements of sense that lead from a first to a second philosophy, as is still the case in the philosophical tradition. Yet the fundamental model of such speculation also proves that Fink's attempt at a speculative determination of the world can no longer be measured in terms of the traditional schema of the Being-in-itself versus the subject-relative Being of the world—it announces another world-relation. In 1934, Fink strictly demarcates what he calls the cosmological concept of the world even from Heidegger's existential concept of the world: "This 'existential concept of the world' is, however, in no way the authentic *cosmological* concept of the world, nor is it *more primordial. . . .* It is not because *existence* [Dasein] as *transcendence* is 'ecstatic' beyond all beings that there is *world,* but it is because the world as the cosmic container also includes existence that the *ecstatic structure of existence* is *first possible.*" The "infinity of the world as the metaphysical constitution of the human being" does not thereby contradict "the latter's *finitude,* since this is the antonym of *speculative infinity.*"[35]

The Play of the World

Since human play points to the world in a special way, insofar as the breach of the world into the intraworldly only just lights up, play is also for cosmological thinking the decisive, Archimedean point, the eye of the needle that only just connects speculation with the givenness of experience. On this basis, speculation attempts to think the "world-position" of the human being, the human's relation to what is not a being yet "pervades [*durchmachtet*]" every being.[36] Fink conceives the carrying out of this "pervading" also as play, indeed as play that remains withdrawn from human access, as play of the world itself.

Yet do we not find here an all too casual and ultimately impermissible transference of the human concept of play to a cosmic happening? If human play points to the world, in what sense then can the world itself still be play? However, an intraworldly concept of play and existence mirroring itself in it would not be applicable to something other than it, to the world itself; rather, the sense of human play points, in itself, even if negatively, to its necessary complement in something wholly other. It is in precisely this that its specific symbolic function consists. Consequently, human play can be interpreted as the prominent, visible end of a total happening, which is itself concealed. The symbol-structure of human play points to the fact that all finite things are "fragments," "rubble of Being," which are "subtended" "by the omnipresence of the one, world-wide Being." Since, for cosmological speculation, the finite no longer signifies a falling away from the idea or a nugatory semblance, but rather "essentially *that which is intraworldly*," which "can flare up in the light of the world," human play, like things, are those *symbola*, understood not as signs for something else, but symbols "as themselves, inasmuch as they exhibit their finitude as intraworldliness"[37] and at the same time—like play—point to completion.

The world, which is never visible as such, appears in play as in a field within itself [*Binnenfeld ihrer selbst*]; it is "reflected back [*reluzent*] into itself":[38] "The whole, which is never visible as a whole," says Fink, "appears in a field within itself."[39] In a similar sense, Fink also speaks of a "proof of the shining back [*Rückschein*] of the world"[40] in human play. Play reflects, consequently, not only the ecstatic openness of human existence toward the world; it also reflects the prevailing of the world itself, or—expressed speculatively—the world itself reflects itself in play and thus evinces human play as a happening within world-play itself. The investigation of human play, in which the world appears, thus ultimately opens onto the speculative demonstration that this appearing of the world in play is itself an event of the enactment of the world; thus while the prevailing of the world was initially to become graspable from out of intraworldly play, it is now the prevailing of the world from out of which every factical enactment of play is illuminated.[41]

The concept of the "proof of shining back [*Rückschein*]" in Fink displaces the model of a gradation of horizons, with which Husserl attempts to conceive the world. If horizons are thereby read in a, so to speak, inverted direction—no longer as external relations constituted in the immanence of a subjectivity, but as an announcement, ensuing within the immanence of a life's ambit, of that which surpasses this ambit—the sense of horizon is itself ultimately surpassed. For a system of horizons is not only connected to a (subjective) bearer but correlates with a particular direction, inasmuch as the openness of such a system consists in the fact that its bearer stands outside it. With the inversion of the system, in the standing-within of the world, the bearer finds itself placed into something that, on the basis of the changed sense of direction, can no longer actually be characterized as an interpenetration of horizons. Accordingly, for Fink, it is insufficient to bind the sense of the world to the relation of horizons, as Husserl does when he defines the world as the harmonious total horizon of all experience; precisely for this reason, Fink emphasizes that Husserl's analyses of horizonal and unthematic background consciousness are of "high and inestimable" worth for the endeavor to bring Husserl's analyses of consciousness "onto a path to the problem of the world."[42]

Is there not, however, a phenomenological demonstration for the peculiarly negative character of the standing-within of the world, for its "relucence [*Reluzenz*]"? Such a demonstration may be contained in the fact of human existence itself: For, as demonstrated by the experience of being finite, human existence is a fragment; it exists, without itself being able to determine its own existence. To be a fragment also means, however, to itself possess a sort of transparency: in the discovery of being "not everything," that which is, the fragment, is open to that "whole" that is itself open insofar as it, as a whole, precisely cannot be de-fined. The "whole" can only be determined negatively: through the limit that is drawn between it and existence. If in this way the world, as something that is encompassing and that is thought in the negative, becomes graspable only from out of something inner, something intraworldly, then, along with this, something else is nevertheless also grasped: that the inner is not in the position to bear itself of its own accord. If, however, existence does not itself occasion its fragmentation, its transparency is also indebted to another, to the "world." If human existence as a *symbolon* is the visible medium in which the invisibility of world "presents" itself, then the fragment "points" to a "whole" whose "part" it is. "To present" or "to point," along with "whole" and "part," should be in quotation marks here, since there is no experiential foundation and thus no direct presentation for which a whole or part, *as* part of a whole, could be caught sight of. And yet, insofar as it demonstrates in itself *that* it is a fragment, the fragment shows this as well: that it belongs in a context that does not show itself.

In what way, however, does that prevailing of world, the play of the world, become determinable? When Fink formulates that the world, in shining back into itself, *comes to appear* in the appearance of play [*daß die Welt im Schein des Spiels in sich rückscheinend* erscheint], the appearing of world is on the one hand thought as an event of an enactment, is on the other hand withdrawn from the visibility of everything phenomenal, from everything that appears within the world. The appearance, then, is rather the cosmic happening that in each case lets an individual, intraworldly thing appear. Therefore, Fink understands the appearing of the world to be "the universal emergence of all beings," which releases from itself that which is customarily called the "world," the "world-dimension of presence," intraworldliness, and thereby at the same time withdraws, remains hidden in the "nameless realm of absence."[43] This cosmic movement of the appearance of the world as the process of the extension of intraworldliness, of individuatedness, this movement from "the world-night to the world-day"[44]—Fink also refers to this as *play.*

The ultimate justification for the employment of the concept of play in this context lies in the fact that speculation thinks the appearing of the world in such a way that this appearing becomes comprehensible on the basis of the formal senses exhibited by the basic phenomenon "play." These senses are first the exclusivity and, connected with this, the form of movement belonging to play: play is an autarchic system; its foundational, imaginative structure closes play off and lets it run its course within itself; with this a direction of movement is sketched out that is not a linear progression, but rather accomplishes itself in the form of a circle. Accomplisher and accomplishment become one; regarding world-play, consequently, there is no longer a divine person, a creator God, who paves the way. World-play is therefore for Fink, on the one hand, groundless,[45] driving all grounds forth from out of itself; on the other hand, it exhibits no personal features.[46] World-play is a game without a player.[47] When Fink notes that human play becomes a world-symbol because in it "a groundless oscillating-within-itself of the carrying out of life" takes place,[48] because in it "the lack of responsibility at the root of all responsibility"[49] is to be felt, this is not a refusal to acknowledge responsibility and obligation for human action; it means rather the space of human play, in which the players are liberated from the work of freedom, from the goal-directed and goal-positing structure of care belonging to existence, and which consequently indicates the "free-space" in the play of the world itself, which precedes and opens up both the realm of possibilities of human freedom as well as the factually "free" activities of the human being.

Fink already remarks in notes from the 1930s that "*Play* as metaphysical essence of the human being . . . has the mode of the *play of Being.*"[50] "Ontogonic metaphysics" proves to be "the path of life to the truth of itself, the completion of its worldly-fragmentary existence," the "*empowering of the power of the play of Being* occurring in the liberation of freedom."[51] A continuation of these considerations—renewed in view of Nietzsche—is found in the 1947 lecture course *Vom Wesen der menschlichen Freiheit* [On the essence of human freedom].[52] Here, too, taking the words of Zarathustra as the point of departure—"The child is innocence and forgetting, a new beginning, a game, a wheel rolling out of itself, a first movement, a sacred yes-saying"[53]—the essence of freedom is determined as a game. Play is thereby not only the positive essence of human freedom, but also the fundamental constitution of Being as such. Fink thereby points again and again to the fact that at issue in this determination is not a simple, paradigmatic reference, but a cosmic correspondence of the "player of worlds," the human being: "The essential world-significance of play does not lie in its possible character of being a *model* for a universal understanding of the world (as, for instance, in Heraclitus's παῖς παίζων—or in Nietzsche's hymnal encomium of chance, happenstance, and the divine game of dice), it lies in the position of *cosmic openness* that the playing human being *is*."[54]

The fundamental significance of Heraclitus should therefore not be overlooked. Not only is Heraclitus and in particular Fragment 52—*aion pais esti paizōn, pesseuōn; paidos hē basilēiē* / "Lifetime is a child at play, moving pieces in a game. Kingship belongs to the child"[55]—of decisive significance for Fink's interpretation of Nietzsche's metaphysics of play.[56] Fink himself also develops his cosmological concept of the world with recourse to Heraclitus's fragments, especially in view of the sameness of individuating generation and decay expressed in Fragment 15,[57] whereby the tragedy of the "moved unity of dismembered and dissected Dionysos Zagreus and simple, undifferentiated Hades" is to point beyond the fate of the finite individual to the "primordial character of the world itself."[58] The world prevails as play, as what makes finite and lets appear from out of the womb of the earth and from the sinking back of every shape into the tomb of the earth. And: "The play of the world is no one's play, because only in it are there first someones, persons, human beings and gods. And the playworld of the play of the world is not an 'appearance' [*Schein*], but rather the *coming to appearance* [*die* Erscheinung]. Coming to appearance is the universal emergence of all beings, things and events into a common presence that integrates everything individuated, into a presence—in our midst. What we ordinarily already call the world is the world-dimension of presence, the dimension of coming to appearance wherein things are really separated from each other, but also still integrated in spatial and temporal vicinity and connected to each other by strict rules. But the world is also the nameless realm of absence, from which things come forth into appearance and into which they again vanish—assuming Hades and Dionysus are the same."[59]

When Fink speaks of the human existing in a manner that is most open to the world "when he dismisses all measures and holds himself out into that which is limitless,"[60] he is not thereby making an appeal for a noncommittal way of life. The freedom from measures recommended here is meant not in an anthropological but in a cosmological sense. It says that the determination of the world-relation of the human being should not be made from something delimited and intraworldly, nor by means of something measurable, in other words, a being or something innerworldly. Play, too, should not be misunderstood as such a merely innerworldly occurrence.

Yet if the play of the world knows no player and is such that it encompasses everything, where, then, is the human being, what do his ability-to-be-free and his practical, free comportment still mean? If the human being becomes a co-player in the play of the world, which itself possesses no player that plays it—then, considered from the standpoint of cosmological speculation, do not both realms, the play of the human being and the play of the world, ultimately collapse into one? The relation of the human being and the world is, according to Fink, not "a relation between two separate things," but as a relation it precedes "the differentiation of what is enclosed together within it."[61] In a similar sense Fink formulates that "The proof of the shining back of the world into itself, into a particular intraworldly thing," is, "seen from the cosmos," "the same" as what the ecstase of the human being "toward the world-whole" is.[62] The human being is accordingly a player in the distinctive sense that with him, who is himself already a relation, a space is opened up that allows him to be free. Human play announces in an especially emphatic way the rift that opens up this space. Formulated speculatively, one could say that the world passes [*zuspielt*] to the human being the space in which he constitutes himself as a relation and consequently becomes a co-player in the play of the world.

Social Philosophy and Pedagogy

Fink presented further determinations of this middle-Being of the human in relation to the world itself within the context of his social-philosophical and pedagogical considerations, indeed where he speaks of a *sharing and dividing* [Teilen] of and in the world as well as attempts to determine anew the traditional concept of the *ideal*. The relevant texts likewise stem originally from the 1950s. With them, the systematic architecture of the entire approach of Fink's thinking is strikingly illuminated, how it is focalized in the theme of play.

In his lecture course *Existenz und Coexistenz* [Existence and coexistence],[63] Fink analyses division according to those two aspects that were distinguished here, namely how in the accompaniment of the human being in the play of the world the world "appears" paradoxically in a non-phenomenal way, insofar as it withdraws in the intraworldly, and how the world in itself plays and lets appear. On the one hand, the world apportions itself [*teilt sich . . . zu*] and thereby brings forth the symbol-character of itself: in the rift through the halves of the *symbolon*, the day and night as cosmic powers, the sayable and unsayable, Being and nothing. This primal division [*Ur-Teilung*] lets Being be, insofar as it founds Being. On the other hand, the human being divides the world by dividing himself into it. Division into the world in this way likewise founds the fact that the human being is a relation. He stands within this participation [*Teilnahme*], insofar as he is individuated. Such division of the world, in which every horizonal-perspectival sense of participation in the world is grounded, is, according to Fink, not a dis-memberment or dis-section of world; on the contrary: the way in which the world itself appears is a "unifying," a "gathering" of the world. The experience of the world takes place primordially not in an individuated subject, not above all in the synthesis of a transcendental subject, but rather is grounded in the happening of a unification. This unification is a *unification,* because in it something other than Being, a *nothing,* shows itself in a unique, united way, and it shows itself as other, as nothing, only insofar as it likewise withdraws.[64]

The "co-division [*Mit-Teilung*]" of the world accordingly has a threefold significance: First, the world apportions itself to us in each case, yet, second, only in such a way that what we gain a share [*Anteil*] in is of such a nature that it is, even if perspectivally broken, *the same whole* in which all possible others can gain a share, so that, third, world-dividing as the sharing-with-one-another [*Mit-einander-Teilen*] of the world primordially founds community. Only because we divide ourselves into the world in such a manner, is communication [*Mitteilung*] in the customary sense possible.

With his determination of the ideal, Fink even more clearly indicates how the human being takes part in the world in his relation to it, assumes and takes on the space of his ability to be free that is opened up to him. Fink determines the ideal, therefore, as the particular material formation of the universal care-structure of existence; the ideal itself comprises the being-stretched of human transcendence, of ecstasis. Now, the figure of movement belonging to the ideal is precisely, according to Fink, play. Fink's statement that the human being is a "*co-player in the play of the world*"[65] suggests that, in a reciprocally uniform process of the letting appear of the world, the projecting and discovering of states of sense meld together into and for human comportment. The human being, as the co-player in the play of the world, inscribes himself, as it were, into a circle that, under the visible script of his dealings, lets a circling that is withdrawn from visibility be intimated.

The emergence of what shows itself from out of the world is the process, the game, in which the human being is a co-player. The co-play of the human being is, as Fink formulates it in his lecture course *Grundfragen der systematischen Pädagogik* [Basic questions of systematic pedagogy], "the human being's accompanying the creative movement of Being; it is a self-insertion into cosmic correspondence."[66] Fink calls this accompaniment "formative education [*Bildung*]." The co-play of the human being in the play of the world is "accompaniment in ideal formative education [*Idealbildung*]."[67] Fink operates here with the double meaning of the word *Bildung:* "Accompaniment in ideal formative education" points on the one hand to the endowment of the ideal with sense [*Sinnstiftung von Idealen*] (*Bilden* as bringing-forth), on the other hand to the educational formation of the human being, whereby ideals function as guiding *images* [Leitbilder]. Fink thinks both concrete aspects back into a *single* ground. This single ground possesses two "sides": corresponding to the difference between what shows itself and self-showing there is on the one hand the facing visage of the *one* "world-ideal,"[68] the epitome of the "totality." This world-ideal is constitutive for the ontological mode of human existence, insofar as it first of all holds open, in its extension, in its lying-out-beyond, the space of movement for the self-relation of the human being, which is likewise a world-relation, enabling his co-play in the play of the world. However, the world-ideal possesses on the other hand its "side," which faces the world itself and its play and is invisible to the human being. Here in the invisible self-showing of world, which itself does not come to appearance, all formation [*Bilden*] is also grounded. As the self-showing of the world is itself invisible, so this last formation is formless: "It is the formless, because it is what as such forms."[69] The twofold unity of the world-ideal and the formless is the fulcrum on which the uniform-twofold process of the play of the world and the co-play of the human being pivots. In the world-ideal in the play of what forms as such, the circle is opened up in which the human being in his accompaniment forms ideals—the manifold of ideals, as they appear within the horizon of his historical existence. These are the images [*Bilder*], since, although they point to an infinite distance, they are nevertheless made finite in the visible formation [*Gebilde*].

Aesthetics and Embodiment

In his late work, Fink integrates play into considerations of aesthetics and embodiment. The results of this are his essay on *Mode* [Fashion] commissioned by the Spengler Modehaus in Basel and published in 1969, whose subtitle reads . . . *ein verführerisches Spiel* [. . . A seductive game]; moreover, there are investigations into drama and theater, which he gathered together with further contributions in the short volume *Epiloge zur Dichtung* [Epilogue to poetry] and published in 1971;[70] finally, there are several scattered texts on play as athletic competition.[71] In these texts he discovers, in various facets, the human living body as a new theme. As he develops in "The World Significance of Play" (1973)[72] and also expresses similarly in other writings from this time,[73] the human being is "not only bodily insofar as he possesses a body, insofar as in a certain sense he is tethered to this constant companion; he is embodied insofar as he always *relates to his body*, even if in historically variable dispositions. The biological discovery that he is an exemplar of a higher kind of animal does not constitute the *philosophical* problem of *incarnation*; it is rather the *existentiell situation of being a perceiving, mobile, and thinking midpoint of the appearing environment in a sensuous, sense-suffused way* that does."[74] The fundamental phenomena of existence—work, struggle, love, and death—are related to the body, and play, too, as the phenomenon encompassing even these fundamental phenomena, is, in its cosmological dimension, tied back to the embodiment of the human being.

The "fundamental problem"[75] of the embodiment of human existence, emerging against the backdrop of a meta-physical tradition, is treated by the late Fink in, for example, a session of his "Sport Seminar" (1961),[76] which is devoted to the questions of embodiment and physical education. Both in looking back to Greek *gymnastikē* and in view of the not merely pedagogic significance of sport in the age of the dominance of science, technology, and bureaucracy, Fink emphasizes in what way athletic competition enables the human being to stand out in an exemplary way both "in" his body and in his own capacities.[77] In this, categories like "power" or "beauty" remain undeveloped, since they, as it is put in "Play and Sport," must necessarily remain provisional against the background of the metaphysical tradition.[78] While Fink thus on the one hand indicates the traditional forgetting of the body, which is always likewise a forgetting of the "nightly" dimension of the world, to which the human being comports himself insofar as he belongs bodily to the earth—Fink speaks of "incarnated" freedom—he emphasizes on the other hand that the human being, precisely *in* this embodiment, remains related to playworldly appearance, and that means that he remains related to the freedom that makes room for and is granted to him. This comes to light in a special way in athletic competition: while the body ordinarily is the place from which incarnated existence carries out concrete actions, in athletic competition the body in itself, like the "playing child," the *pais paizōn* of Heraclitus, comes into a free, unencumbered movement and thereby into a "shining light of appearance"—an "apotheosis of our sensuous existence."[79]

The "shining light of appearance" overlaying the dark ground of the earth stands moreover in a specific relation to the "mask," as the 1968 lecture "Maske und Kothurn" [Mask and buskin] makes clear. The play of ancient tragedy with its delight in the mixture of actuality and non-actuality points to the fundamental rift of human existence that is stretched between two poles, and consequently to the cosmic difference between the dimension of appearing and the dimension of absence. Mask and buskin, those unavoidable requisites of archaic tragedy, raise the question as to how it is at all possible for the human being to live for a certain time, "as if there were not great obscurities around us, as if there were not the night of concealment."[80] In the mask, which transposes him first of all into the possibility of "*appearing* [scheinen] ambiguously and polysemously,"[81] the human being is able to disguise for a certain period his nature that belongs to the placeless and timeless dimension of absence and to raise it to the brightness of appearing, without however thereby forgetting the obscure ground, let alone overcoming it without remainder. "Human freedom is and remains," as it is also put in Fink's book on fashion, "submerged in the natural ground of our existence"; "the body is our earthly, terrestrial actuality, where nature and freedom interpenetrate."[82] Like the mask, the dress, which "takes incessant part in the language of symbols and signs belonging to the body,"[83] can also "transfigure, adorn, expose while concealing" the body "and increase its expressive possibilities."[84] Fashion thereby "exists in a dress-like medium of incessant seduction and temptation. Its Being is precisely seductive appearing."[85]

Manifestations of such a "shining light of appearance" let the temporary shape of the human being—if one turns back to Fink's dissertation from 1929 and the beginnings of Fink's thought on play found therein—become "transparent" with respect to his obscure ground—in that paradoxical structure which says that, *within* an intra-situation, what likewise *completely* surpasses it lights up in its withdrawal. As it is put in *Play as Symbol of the World:* "Coming to appearance [*Erscheinung*] is a mask, behind which 'no one,' behind which nothing, is—precisely as the nothing."[86] In summarizing the primary features of play—the production of playworldly appearance, the self-intuition of human existence in play as the mirror of life, the freedom and revocability of its shapes, its capacity to encompass all other fundamental phenomena of human existence (work, struggle, love, and death), as well as to play itself even as play—one final feature comes to light, according to Fink: the *festive* character of play. "The human being plays when he celebrates existence."[87]

Bibliography of Fink's Works Available in English[1]

Prepared by Ian Alexander Moore and Christopher Turner

"Eugen Fink's Editorial Remarks." In Edmund Husserl, *Introduction to the Logical Investigations: A Draft of a* Preface *to the* Logical Investigations (1913), edited by Eugen Fink, translated by Philip J. Bossert and Curtis H. Peters, 13–15. The Hague: Nijhoff, 1975.

Nietzsche's Philosophy. Translated by Goetz Richter. London: Continuum, 2003.

"Oasis of Happiness: Thoughts toward an Ontology of Play." Translated by Ian Alexander Moore and Christopher Turner. *Purlieu: A Philosophical Journal* 1, no. 4 (2012), pp. 20–42. Also published as "The Ontology of Play," trans. Sister M. Delphine, *Philosophy Today* 4 (Summer 1960): 95–110; republished in *Sport and the Body: A Philosophical Symposium,* 2nd ed., edited by Ellen W. Gerber and William J. Morgan (Philadelphia: Lea & Febiger, 1979), 73–83; republished in *Philosophic Inquiry in Sport,* 2nd ed., edited by William J. Morgan and Klaus V. Meier (Champaign, IL: Human Kinetics, 1995), 100–109. Further published in part as "The Oasis of Happiness: Toward an Ontology of Play," trans. Ute Saine and Thomas Saine, *Yale French Studies* 41 (1968): 19–30.

"Ontological Problems of Community." Translated by Michael R. Heim. In *Contemporary German Philosophy,* vol. 2, pp. 1–19. University Park: Pennsylvania State University Press, 1983.

"Operative Concepts in Husserl's Phenomenology." Translated by William McKenna. In *The Human Being in Action: The Irreducible Element in Man, Part II: Investigations at the Intersection of Philosophy and Psychiatry,* edited by Anna-Teresa Tymieniecka, 56–70. Dordrecht: Reidel, 1978. Republished in *Apriori and World,* edited by William McKenna, Robert M. Harlan, and Laurence E. Winters, 56–70. The Hague: Nijhoff, 1981.

"The Phenomenological Philosophy of Edmund Husserl and Contemporary Criticism." With a preface by Edmund Husserl. In *The Phenomenology of Husserl: Selected Critical Readings,* edited by R. O. Elveton, 73–147. Chicago: Quadrangle, 1970. Second edition published in Seattle: Noesis, 2000, pp. 70–139.

"The Problem of the Phenomenology of Edmund Husserl." Translated by Robert M. Harlan. In *Apriori and World,* edited by William McKenna, Robert M. Harlan, and Laurence E. Winters, 21–55. The Hague: Nijhoff, 1981.

Sixth Cartesian Meditation: The Idea of a Transcendental Theory of Method, with Textual Notations by Edmund Husserl. Translated with an introduction by Ronald Bruzina. Bloomington: Indiana University Press, 1995.

"What Does the Phenomenology of Edmund Husserl Want to Accomplish? (The Phenomenological Idea of Laying-a-Ground)." Translated by Arthur Grugan. *Research in Phenomenology* 7 (1972): 5–27.

With Martin Heidegger. *Heraclitus Seminar.* Translated by Charles H. Seibert. Evanston, IL: Northwestern University Press, 1993. Earlier published in University: University of Alabama Press, 1979.

Schutz, Alfred. "The Problem of Transcendental Intersubjectivity in Husserl (With Comments of Dorian Cairns and Eugen Fink)." Translated by Fred Kersten. *Schutzian Research* 2 (2010): 9–51.

Cairns, Dorian. *Conversations with Husserl and Fink.* The Hague: Nijhoff, 1976.

Secondary Literature on Fink in English

Prepared by Ian Alexander Moore and Christopher Turner

Bertolini, Simona. "The Forces of the Cosmos before Genesis and before Life: Some Remarks on Eugen Fink's Philosophy of the World." *Analecta Husserliana* 116 (2014): 37–46.

Bruzina, Ronald. "[Reception of Fink in the] Anglo-American World." In *Eugen Fink: Sozialphilosophie–Anthropologie–Kosmologie–Pädagogik–Methodik*, edited by Anselm Böhmer, 294–301. Würzburg: Königshausen & Neumann, 2006.

——. *Edmund Husserl and Eugen Fink: Beginnings and Ends in Phenomenology*. New Haven, CT: Yale University Press, 2004.

——. "The Enworlding (*Verweltlichung*) of Transcendental Phenomenological Reflection: A Study of Eugen Fink's '6th Cartesian Meditation.'" *Husserl Studies* 3 (1986): 3–29.

——. "Eugen Fink and Maurice Merleau-Ponty: The Philosophical Lineage in Phenomenology." In *Merleau-Ponty's Reading of Husserl*, edited by Lester Embree and Ted Toadvine, 173–200. Dordrecht: Kluwer, 2002.

——. "Ideas for Raising the Question of the World *within* Transcendental Phenomenology: Freiburg, 1930." In *Japanese and Western Phenomenology*, edited by Philip Blosser, Eiichi Shimomissé, Lester Embree, and Hiroshi Kojima, 93–114. Dordrecht: Kluwer, 1993.

——. "Solitude and Community in the Work of Philosophy: Husserl and Fink, 1928–1938." *Man and World* 22 (1989): 287–314.

——. "Translator's Introduction." In Eugen Fink, *Sixth Cartesian Meditation: The Idea of a Transcendental Theory of Method, with Textual Notations by Edmund Husserl*, vii–xcii. Bloomington: Indiana University Press, 1995.

Cairns, Dorion. "[Review of] '*Die Frage nach dem Ursprung der Geometrie als intentional-historisches Problem*' ('Inquiry Concerning the Origin of Geometry: A Problem of Intentional History'), by Edmund Husserl. . . . (Preface by Eugen Fink . . .)." *Philosophy and Phenomenological Research* 1, no. 1 (1940): 98–109.

——. "Review of Eugen Fink's 'The Problem of Edmund Husserl's Phenomenology,'" edited by Lester Embree, Fred Kersten, and Richard Zaner. *New Yearbook for Phenomenology and Phenomenological Philosophy* 4 (2004): 323–39.

Chida, Yoshiteru. "Phenomenological Self-Reflection in Husserl and Fink." In *Japanese and Western Phenomenology*, edited by Philip Blosser, Eiichi Shimomissé, Lester Embree, and Hiroshi Kojima, 81–92. Dordrecht: Kluwer, 1993.

Crowell, Steven Galt. "Fink's Untimely Nietzsche: Between Heidegger and Derrida." *International Studies in Philosophy* 38, no. 3 (2006): 15–31.
——. "Gnostic Phenomenology: Eugen Fink and the Critique of Transcendental Reason." *New Yearbook for Phenomenology and Phenomenological Philosophy* 1 (2001): 257–77.
Dronsfield, Jonathan Lahey. "The Resistance of the Question to Phenomenological Reduction: Husserl, Fink and Adequacy of the *Sixth Cartesian Meditation* as a Response to Heidegger." In *Logos of Phenomenology and Phenomenology of the Logos,* vol. 1: *Phenomenology as the Critique of Reason in Contemporary Criticism and Interpretation,* edited by Anna-Teresa Tymieniecka, 293–305. Dordrecht: Springer, 2005.
Elden, Stuart. "Eugen Fink and the Question of the World." *Parrhesia* 5 (2008): 48–59.
Embree, Lester. "Introduction: Dorian Cairn's Review of Eugen Fink's 'The Problem of E. Husserl's Phenomenology.'" *New Yearbook for Phenomenology and Phenomenological Philosophy* 4 (2004): 319–22.
Grugan, Arthur. "Metaphysics and the Problem of Death: [Review of] Eugen Fink. *Metaphysik und Tod.*" *Research in Phenomenology* 1 (1971): 147–56.
Hart, James G. "Parts of the Fink-Husserl Conversation." *New Yearbook for Phenomenology and Phenomenological Philosophy* 1 (2001): 279–99.
Homan, Catherine. "The Play of Ethics in Eugen Fink." *Journal of Speculative Philosophy* 27, no. 3 (2013): 287–96.
——. "What's at Play in Ethics." Dissertation, Emory University. 2014. http://pid.emory.edu/ark:/25593/fszvc.
Hyland, Drew A. *The Question of Play.* Lanham, MD: University Press of America, 1984.
Krell, David Farrell. "The Heraclitus Seminar: [Review of] M. Heidegger and E. Fink. *Heraclit* [sic]." *Research in Phenomenology* 1 (1971): 137–46.
——. "Towards an Ontology of Play: Eugen Fink's Notion of Spiel." *Research in Phenomenology* 2 (1972): 63–93.
Leichtle, Sean. "Husserl and Fink: *Two* Phenomenologies." *New Yearbook for Phenomenology and Phenomenological Philosophy* 1 (2001): 301–17.
Mickunas, Algis. "Philosophical Anthropology of E. Fink." *Problemos* 73 (2008): 167–78.
Miller, David L. *Gods and Games: Toward a Theology of Play.* New York: World, 1970.
Moore, Ian Alexander. "Fink's (Heideggerean) Nietzsche, or the Possibility of a *Verwindung* of Metaphysics." *Purlieu Journal* 1, no. 1 (2010): 53–72.
Moran, Dermot. "Fink's Speculative Phenomenology: Between Constitution and Transcendence." *Research in Phenomenology* 37 (2007): 3–31.
Sallis, John, and Kenneth Maly, eds. *Heraclitean Fragments: A Companion Volume to the Heidegger/Fink Seminar on Heraclitus.* University: University of Alabama Press, 1980.
Sepp, Hans Rainer. "Eugen Fink (1905–1975)." In *Handbook of Phenomenological Aesthetics,* edited by Hans Rainer Sepp and Lester E. Embree, 119–21. Dordrecht: Springer, 2010.
Wilkerson, Dale. "A 'Dictatorship of Relativism' and the Specter of Nietzsche: Between Heidegger and Fink." *American Catholic Philosophical Quarterly* 84, no. 2 (2010): 257–81.

Wolf-Gazo, Ernest. "[Review of] Eugen Fink. The Basic Phenomena of Human Existence [Eugen Fink. Grundphänomene des menschlichen Daseins]." *Philosophy and History* 15, no. 1 (1982): 32–33.
Zahavi, Dan. "The Self-Pluralisation of the Primal Life: A Problem in Fink's Husserl-Interpretation," *Recherches Husserliennes* 2 (1994): 3–18.

Notes

Translators' Introduction

1. As recorded by Husserl's daughter Elisabeth Husserl Rosenberg on February 3, 1938. Quote and reference found in Ronald Bruzina, *Edmund Husserl and Eugen Fink: Beginnings and Ends in Phenomenology* (New Haven, CT: Yale University Press, 2004), 69. Other laudatory statements made by Husserl about Fink can be found throughout Bruzina's book as well as in Bruzina's "Translator's Introduction" to Eugen Fink, *Sixth Cartesian Meditation: The Idea of a Transcendental Theory of Method, with Textual Notations by Edmund Husserl* (Bloomington: Indiana University Press, 1995), vii–xcii.

2. *Eugen Fink Gesamtausgabe*, vol. 7: *Spiel als Weltsymbol*, ed. Hans Rainer Sepp and Cathrin Nielsen (Freiburg: Alber, 2010).

3. Lawrence Vogel has made this same point with regard to a work by another student of Heidegger's, namely, Hans Jonas's 1966 *The Phenomenon of Life: Toward a Philosophical Biology* (Evanston, IL: Northwestern University Press, 2001), xi and xxn1.

4. Gadamer cites Fink's works, including *Play as Symbol of the World*, several times throughout *Truth and Method*, 2nd rev. ed., trans. Joel Weinsheimer and Donald G. Marshall (London: Continuum, 2004), 99n163, 167n39, 265n153, 493n137. He also wrote reviews of *Play as Symbol of the World* and the book version of Fink's "Oasis of Happiness." See H. G. Gadamer, "[Review of] *Eugen Fink: Oase des Glücks, Gedanken zu einer Ontologie des Spiels*," *Philosophische Rundschau* 6 (1958): 141; and H.-G. Gadamer, "[Review of] *Spiel als Weltsymbol*," *Philosophische Rundschau* 9 (1961): 1–8.

5. See p. 206.

6. Even if they may be familiar with his book on Nietzsche (*Nietzsche's Philosophy*, trans. Goetz Richter [London: Continuum, 2003]) or his collaborations with Husserl (*Sixth Cartesian Meditation*) or with Heidegger (*Heraclitus Seminar*, trans. Charles H. Seibert [Evanston, IL: Northwestern University Press, 1993]).

7. Unless otherwise indicated, the following biographical information has been drawn from Susanne Fink, "Die Biographie Eugen Finks," in *Eugen Fink: Sozialphilosophie–Anthropologie–Kosmologie–Pädagogik–Methodik*, ed. Anselm Böhmer (Würzburg: Königshausen & Neumann, 2006), 267–76. For Fink's connection to figures like José Ortega y Gasset and Jan Patočka, which we will be unable to address here, see the reports on Fink's reception in Spain and in the Czech Republic in ibid., 341–49.

8. Martin Heidegger, "For Eugen Fink on His Sixtieth Birthday," in Heidegger, *The Fundamental Concepts of Metaphysics: World, Finitude, Solitude*, trans. William McNeill and Nicholas Walker (Bloomington: Indiana University Press, 1995), 367.

9. Bruzina, *Edmund Husserl and Eugen Fink*, 3.

10. Quotes found in ibid., 5.

11. Bruzina, "Translator's Introduction," xxiv.

12. Bruzina, *Edmund Husserl and Eugen Fink*, 7–10.

13. Ibid., 10.

14. Such as Heidegger's Winter Semester 1935–1936 lecture course *Basic Problems of Metaphysics,* published in German as Heidegger, *Gesamtausgabe,* vol. 41: *Die Frage nach dem Ding: Zu Kants Lehre von den transzendentalen Grundsätzen,* ed. Petra Jaeger (Frankfurt am Main: Klostermann, 1984) and in English as *What Is a Thing?* trans. W. B. Barton Jr. and Vera Deutsch (Chicago: H. Regnery, 1967); as well as Heidegger's Winter Semester 1956–1957 seminar "Zu Hegel: Logik des Wesens," in Heidegger, *Gesamtausgabe,* vol. 86: *Seminare: Hegel–Schelling,* ed. Peter Trawny (Frankfurt am Main: Klostermann, 2011), 444, 809, 814. Bruzina, "Translator's Introduction," lxxixn87; Bruzina, *Edmund Husserl and Eugen Fink,* 550n177. For other such courses and events in which Heidegger and Fink participated, see our discussion below, as well as Cathrin Nielsen and Hans Rainer Sepp, "Nachlass Eugen Fink," esp. pp. 89–90. Available online at https://www.blogs.uni-mainz.de/fb05philosophie/files/2014/07/Bestand-Nachlass-Eugen-Fink1.pdf.

15. The dedication continues: "Presumably this is where we must look for the reason why, over the past decades, he repeatedly expressed the wish that this lecture should be published before all others." See Heidegger, *The Fundamental Concepts of Metaphysics,* 367; and Martin Heidegger, *Gesamtausgabe,* vol. 27: *Einleitung in die Philosophie,* 2nd rev. ed., ed. Otto Saame and Ina Saame-Speidel (Frankfurt am Main: Klostermann, 2001), esp. §§34–36. The latter has yet to be translated into English, although William McNeill is preparing a translation for Indiana University Press. Fink's notes on this course can be found in the Eugen-Fink-Archiv. For more details, see Bruzina, *Edmund Husserl and Eugen Fink,* 12–13.

16. Heidegger later recalled, for instance, the fact that Fink helped Heidegger move in to his new home in Zähringen. Heidegger, "For Eugen Fink on His Sixtieth Birthday," 367.

17. Ibid.

18. Bruzina, *Edmund Husserl and Eugen Fink,* 18.

19. Ibid., 13n53. Bruzina refers to Fink's now published *Phänomenologische Werkstatt,* vol. 1: *Die Doktorarbeit und erste Assistenzjahre bei Husserl,* ed. Ronald Bruzina (Freiburg: Alber, 2006).

20. Quote found in Bruzina, *Edmund Husserl and Eugen Fink,* 23.

21. Ibid., 10.

22. "Fink richtig erzogen—hat Heidegger immer gehört, aber hat 'Affinität' für Husserl. Alles mitgemacht. Der einzige Student, der treu geblieben ist." Dorian Cairns, *Conversations with Husserl and Fink* (The Hague: Nijhoff, 1976), 106. Conversation from June 27, 1931.

23. Bruzina, "Translator's Introduction," vii; Eugen Fink, *VI. Cartesianische Meditation,* vol. 1: *Die Idee einer transzendentalen Methodenlehre,* and vol. 2: *Ergänzungsband: Texte aus dem Nachlass Eugen Finks (1932) mit Anmerkungen und Beilagen aus dem Nachlass Edmund Husserls (1933/34),* ed. Hans Ebeling, Jann Holl, and Guy van Kerckhoven (Dordrecht: Nijhoff, 1987–1988).

24. Bruzina, "Translator's Introduction," ix.

25. Husserl in a letter to Roman Ingarden from March 19, 1930. Quote found in Bruzina, "Translator's Introduction," xii. On the uncertainty as to whether Fink's revisions would supplement or replace the relevant selections of the older version, cf. ibid., xvii and lxxivn48. It should perhaps be noted that other scholars downplay the extent to which Fink's contributions mark a *collaborative* development of Husserl's thought, rather than an external importation of other philosophers' ideas. J. H. Mohanty, for example, writes: "[Fink] was seeking to incorporate into a Husserlian thinking Heidegger's problematic and results, as well as, through Heidegger, Hegel's phenomenology. These are laudable efforts that deserve serious consideration on their own, but we must be aware of not ascribing the resulting positions as constituting the goal of Husserl's thinking." Mohanty, *Edmund Husserl's Freiburg Years 1916–1938* (New Haven, CT: Yale University Press, 2011), 430–34; quote on p. 430.

26. Cf. Bruzina, "Translator's Introduction," ix.

27. Cf. ibid., lxxvn63.

28. Bruzina, *Edmund Husserl and Eugen Fink,* 43–44, lists three reasons for Fink's unwillingness to leave Husserl for Heidegger: (1) Heidegger's behavior toward Husserl, (2) Heidegger's and Fink's different approaches to addressing the question of world, and (3) Heidegger's assumption of the rectorate in 1933 and reorganization of the university along Nazi lines.

29. In *The Phenomenology of Husserl, Selected Critical Writings,* ed. R. O. Elveton (Chicago: Quadrangle, 1970), 73–147. The German first appeared as "Die phänomenologische Philosophie Edmund Husserls in der gegenwärtigen Kritik I," *Kant-Studien* 38 (1933): 321–83. The Roman numeral of the German title suggests more to come—and thus further work on and with Husserl. Although such work did not appear in *Kant-Studien* in the coming years, Fink did publish another article in 1934 on Husserl in the journal *Tatwelt,* later translated into English as "What Does the Phenomenology of Edmund Husserl Want to Accomplish?"

30. Eugen Fink, "The Phenomenological Philosophy of Edmund Husserl and Contemporary Criticism," with a preface by Edmund Husserl, in *The Phenomenology of Husserl: Selected Critical Readings,* 2nd ed., ed. R. O. Elveton (Seattle: Noesis, 2000), 71. For a discussion of the motivations behind Husserl's statement, see Bruzina, "Translator's Introduction," xx–xxi.

31. Bruzina, "Translator's Introduction," lxxviiin78.

32. Bruzina, *Edmund Husserl and Eugen Fink,* 40–42, 47–48, 57–67, 70.

33. Ibid., 522, 525.

34. Ibid., 523.

35. Ibid., 526–33; quotes found on p. 530. For more on the pernicious rumor, see Bruzina, "[Reception of Fink in the] Anglo-American World," in Böhmer, ed., *Eugen Fink: Sozialphilosophie-Anthropologie-Kosmologie-Pädagogik-Methodik,* 295. Fink's lecture was recently published in German as "Nietzsches Metaphysik des Spiels," in *Welt Denken: Annäherungen an die Kosmologie Eugen Finks,* ed. Cathrin Nielsen and Hans Rainer Sepp (Freiburg: Alber, 2011): 25–37. As Bruzina records in *Edmund Husserl and Eugen Fink,* 532: "'My thesis,' Fink writes [in June 1946], 'is this: That play is the *central metaphysical concept in Nietzsche* and also in modern philosophy insofar as modern philosophy conceives being as *creative.*' . . . Play is 'the unitary phenomenology of the *double visage*—Apollo and Dionysos,' Fink notes. 'Antecedent to the *religion of art* in the modern period, the essence of play has to be grasped at its most profound level.'"

36. Susanne Fink, "Die Biographie Eugen Finks," 272.

37. See the reports on the reception of Fink in *Eugen Fink: Sozialphilosophie-Anthropologie-Kosmologie-Pädagogik-Methodik,* 331–33, 337–41.

38. A link to a recording of Fink's "The World-Significance of Play" can be found at http://www.ub.uni-freiburg.de/?id=148.

39. Martin Heidegger, *Letters to His Wife, 1915–1970,* ed. Gertrud Heidegger, trans. R. D. V. Glasgow (Cambridge: Polity, 2008), 243; Martin Heidegger, "Wiederbesetzung des Lehrstuhls für Philosophie," in Heidegger, *Gesamtausgabe,* vol. 16: *Reden und andere Zeugnisse eines Lebensweges 1910–1976,* ed. Hermann Heidegger (Frankfurt am Main: Klostermann, 2000), 550; and Martin Heidegger, "Dankansprache von Professor Martin Heidegger," in *Martin Heidegger 26. September 1969: Ansprachen zum 80. Geburtstag* (Messkirch: Stadt Messkirch, 1969), 35. The last text reproduces a speech Heidegger gave on the occasion of his eightieth birthday in Messkirch. Fink was one of two the main speakers. See his "Dank an den Denker," in *Martin Heidegger 26. September 1969,* 21–32.

40. Hannah Arendt/Martin Heidegger, *Briefe 1925 bis 1975 und andere Zeugnisse,* 2nd ed., ed. Ursula Ludz (Frankfurt am Main: Klostermann, 1999), 296.

41. Max Müller, *Auseinandersetzung als Versöhnung:* polemos kai eirēnē; *Ein Gespräch über ein Leben mit der Philosophie,* ed. Wilhelm Vossenkuhl (Berlin: Akademie-Verlag, 1994), 115. Heidegger mentions the "Graeca," as well as his attendance at some of them, in Martin Heidegger, *Briefe an Max Müller und andere Dokumente,* ed. Holger Zaborowski and Anton Bösel (Freiburg: Alber, 2003), 30–35, 39, 41.

42. This information can be found in Martin Heidegger, "Colloquium über Dialektik (Eugen Fink, Max Müller, Karl-Heinz Volkmann-Schluck, Marly Biemel, Walter Biemel, Henri Birault)," *Hegel-Studien* 25 (1990): 37–38; and Müller, *Auseinandersetzung als Versöhnung,* 258–65. Heidegger's lecture does not appear to have ever been published, though a transcript by Rudolf Alexander Mayer is available in the Martin-Heidegger-Archiv in Messkirch. For details, see Hans-Jürgen Blenskens, "Gottfried Benn und Martin Heidegger: Respekt und kritischer Bezug," *Benn-Forum* 4 (2014/2015): 196.

43. Martin Heidegger, "Colloquium über Dialektik," 9–40. Republished in Martin Heidegger, *Gesamtausgabe,* vol. 86: *Seminare: Hegel–Schelling,* 745–63.

44. Martin Heidegger, *Gesamtausgabe,* vol. 76: *Leitgedanken zur Entstehung der Metaphysik, der neuzeitlichen Wissenschaft und der modernen Technik,* ed. Claudius Strube (Frankfurt am Main: Klostermann), 400. Andrew J. Mitchell and Christopher Merwin are preparing a translation of this volume for Indiana University Press. Heidegger's text and notes for the discussion can be found in ibid., 239–61. Fink's lecture is available as Eugen Fink, "Exposition des Problems der Einheit der Wissenschaften," *Studium Generale: Zeitschrift für die Einheit der Wissenschaften im Zusammenhang ihrer Begriffsbildungen und Forschungsmethoden* 9, no. 8 (1956): 424–53. "Science and Reflection" is available in Martin Heidegger, *The Question Concerning Technology,* trans. William Lovitt (New York: Harper & Row, 1970), 155–82.

45. Martin Heidegger, *Gesamtausgabe,* vol. 14: *Zur Sache des Denkens* (Frankfurt am Main: Klostermann, 2007), 103, 151, 154.

46. Martin Heidegger and Eugen Fink, *Heraklit: Seminar Wintersemester 1966/1967* (Frankfurt am Main: Klostermann, 1970); *Heraclitus Seminar.* See also Martin Heidegger, "Aus den Aufzeichnungen zu dem mit Eugen Fink veranstalteten Heraklit-Seminar," *Heidegger Studies* 13 (1997): 9–14. For the reception of the seminar in English, and for more information about the history of its emergence, see David Farrell Krell, "The Heraclitus Seminar: [Review of] M. Heidegger and E. Fink. *Heraclit* [sic]." *Research in Phenomenology* 1 (1971): 137–46; and *Heraclitean Fragments: A Companion Volume to the Heidegger/Fink Seminar on Heraclitus,* ed. John Sallis and Kenneth Maly (University: University of Alabama Press, 1980).

47. Edmund Husserl, "Die Frage nach dem Ursprung der Geometrie als intentional-historisches Problem," ed. Eugen Fink, *Revue Internationale de Philosophie* 1, no. 2 (1939): 203–25. Fink's foreword can be found on pp. 203–6.

48. Leonard Lawlor, *Derrida and Husserl: The Basic Problem of Phenomenology* (Bloomington: Indiana University Press, 2002), 236nn1–2. Cf. Edward Baring, *The Young Derrida and French Philosophy, 1945–1968* (Cambridge: Cambridge University Press, 2011), 122–24, 143–44.

49. Maurice Merleau-Ponty, *Phenomenology of Perception,* trans. Colin Smith (London: Routledge, 2002), xv. On Fink's importance for Merleau-Ponty, see Bruzina, *Edmund Husserl and Eugen Fink,* 541–42; and Ronald Bruzina, "Eugen Fink and Maurice Merleau-Ponty: The Philosophical Lineage in Phenomenology," in *Merleau-Ponty's Reading of Husserl,* ed. Lester Embree and Ted Toadvine (Dordrecht: Kluwer, 2002), 173–200.

50. Jacques Derrida, *Edmund Husserl's* Origin of Geometry: *An Introduction,* trans. John P. Leavey (Lincoln: University of Nebraska Press, 1989). For Derrida's praise of Fink in this text, see pp. 69n66, 141n168, and especially p. 89: "What Fink writes about speech in his excellent transcript of the *Origin* is *a fortiori* true for writing." See also Jacques Derrida, *Of*

Grammatology, corr. ed., trans. Gayatri Chakravorty Spivak (Baltimore: Johns Hopkins University Press, 1997), 19–20.

51. Jacques Derrida, "[Review of] Eugen Fink, *Studien zur Phänomenologie, 1930–1939,*" *Les Études Philosophiques* 21, no. 4 (October–December 1966): 549–50; quote on p. 549. Derrida's review is immediately followed by Théodore Quoniam's review of the 1966 French translation of *Play as Symbol of the World* (pp. 550–51).

52. Lawlor, *Derrida and Husserl,* 7, 11, 238n10. See the entirety of his discussion in chapter 1 ("Genesis as the Basic Problem of Phenomenology"), pp. 11–23.

53. Derrida, "[Review of] Eugen Fink, *Studien zur Phänomenologie,*" 549.

54. Derrida, *Of Grammatology,* 326n14. On the importance of play in Derrida, see, for example, Derrida, "Structure, Sign and Play in the Discourse of the Human Sciences," in *Writing and Difference,* trans. Alan Bass (Chicago: University of Chicago Press, 1978), 278–93; as well as Françoise Dastur, "Axelos et Fink," *Rue Descartes* 18 (November 1997): 29; H. Hillis Miller, "Jeu," and Sean Gaston, "Writing and World," in *Reading Derrida's* Of Grammatology, ed. Sean Gaston and Ian Maclachlan (London: Continuum, 2011), 43–46, 68–70; and Bernhard Waldenfels, *Phänomenologie in Frankreich* (Frankfurt am Main: Suhrkamp, 1983), 543.

55. See especially the final chapter of Fink's *Nietzsche's Philosophy.* For Derrida, see, for example, "The Ends of Man," in Derrida, *Margins of Philosophy,* trans. Alan Bass (Chicago: University of Chicago Press, 1982), 109–36.

56. *Nietzsche aujourd'hui?* 2 vols. (Paris: Union Générale d'Éditions, 1973); Fink's contribution and the ensuing discussion can be found in vol. 2 under the title "Nouvelle expérience du monde chez Nietzsche," pp. 345–69. The information on the Royaumont conference can be found in François Dosse, *Gilles Deleuze and Félix Guattari: Intersecting Lives,* trans. Deborah Glassman (New York: Columbia University Press, 2010), 132 and 544n13.

57. See, for example, Jean Wahl, "Le Nietzsche de Fink," *Revue de Métaphysique et de Morale* 67, no. 4 (October–December 1962): 475–89.

58. Kostas Axelos, *Vers la pensée planétaire: Le devenir-pensée du monde et le devenir-monde de la pensée* (Paris: Minuit, 1964); Axelos, *Le jeu du monde* (Paris: Minuit, 1969); Axelos, *Horizons du monde* (Paris: Minuit, 1974).

59. See the section titled "Kostas Axelos, Henri Lefebvre and *Mondialisation*" in Stuart Elden, "Eugen Fink and the Question of the World," *Parrhesia* 5 (2008): 53–54, as well as the works cited therein. See also Dastur, "Axelos et Fink," 25–38.

60. Christian Kerslake, *Immanence and the Vertigo of Philosophy: From Kant to Deleuze* (Edinburgh: Edinburgh University Press, 2009), 250. For an essay that brings Fink and Deleuze into dialogue, see Dai Takeuchi, "Zweideutigkeit des Meon und Kosmologie als Phänomenologie der Immanenz: Fink und Deleuze," in Nielsen and Sepp, eds., *Welt Denken,* 237–49.

61. There is a picture of Fink standing with Levinas in Davos in the photo section of Marie-Anne Lescourret, *Emmanuel Levinas* (Paris: Flammarion, 1994).

62. Eugen Fink, *Metaphysik und Tod* (Stuttgart: Kohlhammer, 1969); Emmanuel Levinas, *God, Death, and Time,* trans. Bettina Bergo (Stanford, CA: Stanford University Press, 2000).

63. Levinas, *God, Death and Time,* 174–75; Levinas, *Otherwise Than Being, or Beyond Essence,* trans. Alphonso Lingis (Pittsburgh: Duquesne University Press, 1988), 116; Levinas, *Proper Names,* trans. Michael B. Smith (Stanford, CA: Stanford University Press, 1996), 53.

64. See Herman Leo Van Breda's speech "Laudatio für Ludwig Landgrebe und Eugen Fink," delivered on the occasion of the conferral of the honorary doctorate, in *Phänomenologie Heute: Festschrift für Ludwig Landgrebe* (The Hague: Nijhoff, 1972), 1–13.

65. *Eugen-Fink-Symposion, Freiburg 1985,* ed. Ferdinand Graf (Freiburg: Pädagogische Hochschule Freiburg, 1987).

66. *Eugen Fink: Actes du Colloque de Cerisy-la-Salle, 23–30 juillet 1994*, organized and edited by Natalie Depraz and Marc Richir (Amsterdam: Rodopi, 1997).

67. See, for example, *Bildung im technischen Zeitalter: Sein, Mensch und Welt nach Eugen Fink*, ed. Annette Hilt and Cathrin Nielsen (Freiburg: Alber, 2005); *Lebenswelten: Ludwig Landgrebe–Eugen Fink–Jan Patočka; Wiener Tagungen zur Phänomenologie 2002*, ed. Helmuth Vetter (Frankfurt am Main: Lang, 2003); Böhmer, ed., *Eugen Fink: Sozialphilosophie–Anthropologie–Kosmologie–Pädagogik–Methodik;* and Nielsen and Sepp, eds., *Welt Denken.*

68. For a description of the project, see Cathrin Nielsen and Hans Rainer Sepp, "Das Projekt einer Gesamtausgabe der Werke Eugen Finks," in Böhmer, ed., *Eugen Fink: Sozialphilosophie–Anthropologie–Kosmologie–Pädagogik–Methodik*, 286–93.

69. For more on this term, see Stefan Deines, "Formen und Funktionen des Spielbegriffs in der Philosophie," in *Spielformen des Selbst: Das Spiel zwischen Subjektivität, Kunst und Alltagspraxis*, ed. Regine Strätling (Bielefeld: transcript, 2012), 27.

Oasis of Happiness

1. TS 1: instead of "structure," "total sense [*Sinnganzen*]" is written.
2. TS 1: after "its," "categorial" is crossed out with ink.
3. TS 1: after "Plato," "or Nietzsche" is crossed out with ink.
4. TS 1: after "salt," "the subtleness of Zarathustra's masks" is crossed out with ink.
5. Instead of "One" up to "activity," in TS 1 is found: "Insofar as it is a possibility of the human being that one is acquainted with firsthand, we are much more familiar with play firsthand than with any phenomenon of the external environment or with the findings researchable by natural science regarding our own embodiment, {crossed out in ink: 'inasmuch as these are withdrawn from the immediate testimony of our experience'}. Playing does not primarily signify processes that we become aware of, let alone first discover, but rather an activity that we engage in, that we enact spontaneously."
6. Instead of "especially," in TS 1 is found "obviously."
7. TS 1: after "not," "definitively" is crossed out with ink.
8. Before "in contrast," in TS 1 and 2 is found "as a counter-phenomenon."
9. Cf. Friedrich Schiller, *On the Aesthetic Education of Man: In a Series of Letters*, ed. and trans. Elizabeth M. Wilkinson and L. A. Willoughby (Oxford: Clarendon, 1967), Fifteenth Letter, 107: "For, to mince matters no longer, man only plays when he is in the fullest sense of the word a human being, and *he is only fully a human being when he plays.*"
10. Cf. Martin Heidegger, *Being and Time*, trans. John Macquarrie and Edward Robinson (New York: Harper & Row, 1962), 68 passim.
11. TS 2: "threefold" is interpolated.
12. Instead of "an utter," in TS 1 and 2 is found "the Babylonian."
13. TS 1: "whole," written in ink, is a substitution for "otherwise."
14. *The Selected Poetry of Rainer Maria Rilke*, ed. and trans. Stephen Mitchell (New York: Vintage, 1989), 171–73.
15. TS 2: Instead of the paragraph that begins section 2, there is written, "This warrants being grasped more precisely. In order to at all attain the approach to a sufficient concept of play, insight into the structure and the structural context of play as such is required. Initially we can characterize as an essential aspect the fact that play is 'attuned.' To be sure, every human activity and omission is attuned in some way, be it cheerfully or sorrowfully or submerged in the gray mist of indifference. Play, however, is pleasurably attuned on a fundamental level. The joy of play pervades and holds sway over the whole instance of play in each case, sustaining

and animating it. If the joy of play is extinguished, the activity of play dwindles straightaway. That does not mean, however, that, in playing, we are always cheerful and glad. The pleasure of play is a remarkable pleasure that is difficult to figure out. It does not resemble ordinary sensuous pleasure, which, for instance, accompanies unhindered corporeal movement, the bodily thrill of speed and the like; and it is also not a purely cerebral pleasure, a merely intellectual joy. It is a pleasure that belongs to a creative process of an entirely special sort, and is in itself polysemous: namely, it can precisely contain within itself profound sorrow and abyssal grief. It has such a breadth that it takes on its evident {TS 1: 'apparent'} opposite as one of its aspects."

16. TS 2: after "what is terrible," there is written, "The portrayal of what is horrible excites in a pleasurable way."

17. TS 2: "which is in and of itself" to "heartache" is an emendation in ink of "which so mixes and blends, so shoves the otherwise separated oppositions into one another."

18. [This is an untranslatable word-play in which Fink is referring to German *Trauerspiel,* a form of tragic drama.]

19. TS 2: After "playful," the following lines have been crossed out with ink: "But it is able to do that only as an ingredient of the encompassing pleasure of play. The pleasure of play belongs in a distinctive way to the enactment of play. It cannot be compared with other well-known ways of taking pleasure in performing a function. To be sure, everywhere that we do not accept our own lives passively, everywhere that we exist spontaneously therein, carry out our lives of our own accord and shape it through creative processes, we also always feel a pleasurable joy that need not at all be joy about something. The productive form of existence is in itself an 'upsurge [*Aufschwung*].' But playing production is pervaded by a pleasure that is incomparable with other joys of enactment and psychical upsurges."

20. TS 2: "The pleasure of play is grounded not only in the aspect of productive spontaneity—it" was replaced in ink by "This pleasure of play."

21. TS 2: "imaginary" is an emendation in ink of "objective."

22. [*Zirzensischen . . . Spielen.* See n. 4, p. 334.]

23. TS 2: "or cultic kinds of play" is added in pencil.

24. "and constituted" is not found in TS 1.

25. [This phrase can be found in Friedrich Nietzsche's *Also Sprach Zarathustra,* II, "Auf den glückseligen Inseln," in *Kritische Studienausgabe* (KSA) 4, new ed., ed. Giorgio Colli and Mazzino Montinari (Munich: Deutscher Taschenbuch, 1999), 110: "Schaffen—das ist die grosse Erlösung vom Leiden, und des Lebens Leichtwerden. Aber dass der Schaffende sei, dazu selber thut Leid noth und viel Verwandlung"; *Thus Spoke Zarathustra: A Book for All and None,* Second Part, "On the Blessed Isles," ed. Adrian Del Caro and Robert B. Pippin, trans. Adrian Del Caro (Cambridge: Cambridge University Press, 2006), 66: "Creating—that is the great redemption from suffering, and life's becoming light. But in order for the creator to be, suffering is needed and much transformation."]

26. TS 1: "imaginary" is a replacement for "magical."

27. Friedrich Nietzsche, *The Anti-Christ, Ecce Homo, Twilight of the Idols: And Other Writings,* ed. Aaron Ridley and Judith Norman, trans. Judith Norman (Cambridge: Cambridge University Press, 2005), "Why I Am So Clever," §10, p. 99.

28. [See n. 10, p. 335.]

29. After "playing," in TS 1 and 2 is found: "as a dimension."

30. Instead of "ascertainment [*Erfassung*]," in TS 1 and 2 is found: "conception [*Auffassung*]."

31. Instead of "demarcated," in TS 1 is found: "enclosed."

32. Fragment 52 (in Diels/Kranz's enumeration). Cf. Charles H. Kahn, *The Art and Thought of Heraclitus: An Edition of the Fragments with Translation and Commentary* (Cambridge:

Cambridge University Press, 1979), 71: "Lifetime is a child at play, moving pieces in a game. Kingship belongs to the child."

33. Friedrich Nietzsche, *Philosophy in the Tragic Age of the Greeks,* trans. Marianne Cowan (Washington, DC: Regnery, 1962), 62; Fink's emphasis.

34. Ibid., 58; trans. modified. Fink emphasizes "is," rather than "play."

35. [A more literal translation would be "put into play."]

36. *Uncollected Poems: Rainer Maria Rilke,* trans. Edward Snow (New York: North Point, 1966), 139.

1. Play as a Philosophical Problem

1. Shakespeare, *Hamlet,* act 3, scene 1.

2. ["You will be like God."] Genesis 3:5.

3. Instead of "primordially," TS has "more primordially."

4. [*Zirzensische Veranstaltungen.* Fink probably means something broader than "circus" in its contemporary sense and intends something closer to the Roman circus as catchall for every manner of public spectacle and diversion, from musical and theatrical performance to sport and carnival. Context suggests that Fink is also pointing to attempts to organize, channel, and control the open and creative possibilities of play that public festivals such as the Olympics and circus represent.]

5. After "substance," TS has "an event, what 'inanimate' and 'living' are, what artificial things are."

6. Immanuel Kant, *Critique of Practical Reason,* ed. Mary Gregor (Cambridge: Cambridge University Press, 1997), 133: "Two things fill the mind with ever new and increasing admiration and reverence, the more often and more steadily one reflects on them: *the starry heavens above me and the moral law within me.*"

7. Fragment 30 (in Diels/Kranz's enumeration). Cf. Charles H. Kahn, *The Art and Thought of Heraclitus: An Edition of the Fragments with Translation and Commentary* (Cambridge: Cambridge University Press, 1979), 45: "The ordering, the same for all, no god nor man has made, but it ever was and will be: fire everliving, kindled in measures and in measures going out."

8. After "saying," in TS is found "But there is also frequently a cheap modesty that relieves itself of making any effort on its own."

9. Fragment 52 (in Diels/Kranz's enumeration). Cf. Kahn, *The Art and Thought of Heraclitus,* 71: "Lifetime is a child at play, moving pieces in a game. Kingship belongs to the child."

10. Instead of "brings all beings to pass," TS has "lets all beings be."

11. In Diels/Kranz's enumeration. Cf. Kahn, *The Art and Thought of Heraclitus,* 71: "Immortals are immortal, mortals immortal, living the others' death, dead in the others' life."

12. *Laws* II 644d, VII 803c.

13. From Fragment 90 (in Diels/Kranz's enumeration). Cf. Kahn, *The Art and Thought of Heraclitus,* 47: "All things are requital for fire, and fire for all things, as goods for gold and gold for goods."

14. From Fragment 32 (in Diels/Kranz's enumeration). Cf. Kahn, *The Art and Thought of Heraclitus,* 83: "The wise is one alone, unwilling and willing to be spoken of by the name of Zeus."

15. "above all" is not in TS.

16. [This rare term can also mean "thoroughly gives power to."]

17. TS: "at most" is an interpolation in ink.

18. Martin Heidegger, "On the Essence of Ground," trans. William McNeill, in Heidegger, *Pathmarks*, ed. William McNeill (Cambridge: Cambridge University Press, 1998), 123. [Fink does not italicize *occasion*.]

19. After "been," "grasped and" is found in TS.

20. *Goethe's Faust*, trans. Walter Kaufmann (New York: Anchor, 1990), First Part, l. 1339–40.

21. *The Selected Poetry of Rainer Maria Rilke*, ed. and trans. Stephen Mitchell (New York: Vintage, 1989), 169.

22. Fragment 52 (in Diels/Kranz's enumeration). Cf. Kahn, *The Art and Thought of Heraclitus*, 71: "Lifetime is a child at play, moving pieces in a game. Kingship belongs to the child."

23. Instead of "brings forth," TS has "lets be."

24. Fragment 15 (in Diels/Kranz's enumeration). Cf. Kahn, *The Art and Thought of Heraclitus*, 81: "If it were not Dionysus for whom they march in procession and chant the hymn to the phallus, their action would be most shameless. But Hades and Dionysus are the same, him for whom they rave and celebrate Lenaia."

25. After "questions," TS has "In what way there is a problem lying behind these questions is still to emerge for us."

2. The Metaphysical Interpretation of Play

1. Instead of "restorative play," TS has "a means of restoration."

2. D: "scene of non-actuality" (corrected in accordance with TS).

3. D: "Being" (corrected in accordance with TS).

4. Rainer Maria Rilke, *Sonnets to Orpheus*, trans. Willis Barnstone (Boston: Shambhala, 2004), Part Two, Sonnet III, p. 161.

5. Instead of "must," in TS is found "can."

6. Friedrich Nietzsche, *Thus Spoke Zarathustra: A Book for All and None*, ed. Adrian Del Caro and Robert B. Pippin, trans. Adrian Del Caro (Cambridge: Cambridge University Press, 2006), 185. [Our interpolation.]

7. D: "new objective impressions" instead of "objective impressions to us" (corrected in accordance with TS).

8. TS: "seems to be" is an emendation in ink of "is."

9. TS: "privileged" is an interpolation in ink.

10. [An epopt is someone who has been initiated into the highest level of the Eleusinian Mysteries, or into a secret society or mystery of some kind more generally. It is an Anglicization of the Greek *epoptēs*, literally "someone who looks on/upon."]

11. "Awkward" is not in TS.

12. After "keeping alive," in TS is found "a hesitation."

13. Fragment 52 (in Diels/Kranz's enumeration). Cf. Charles H. Kahn, *The Art and Thought of Heraclitus: An Edition of the Fragments with Translation and Commentary* (Cambridge: Cambridge University Press, 1979), 71: "Lifetime is a child at play, moving pieces in a game. Kingship belongs to the child."

14. TS: "Yet, measured by actual Being, the semblance is a derivation."

15. TS: "more abstract."

16. Cf. *Goethe's Faust*, trans. Walter Kaufmann (New York: Anchor, 1990), Second Part, l. 12104ff.: "What is destructible / Is but a parable; / What fails ineluctably, / The undeclarable, / Here it was seen, / Here it was action; / The Eternal-Feminine / Lures to perfection."

17. "Strange" is not in TS.
18. TS: "that encompasses him" is an emendation in ink of "of the whole."
19. TS: after "is," there is crossed out in ink: "nothing other than."

3. The Interpretation of Play in Myth

1. TS: "basis" is an emendation in ink of "background."
2. Friedrich Hölderlin, *Hyperion,* trans. Ross Benjamin (Brooklyn, NY: Archipelago, 2008), 215.
3. Instead of "however," one reads in TS "in my opinion."
4. Georg Wilhelm Friedrich Hegel, *Science of Logic,* trans. George di Giovanni (Cambridge: Cambridge University Press, 2010), 8; trans. mod.
5. "Perhaps" is not found in TS.
6. TS: "rational science" is an emendation in ink of "the disenchanted."
7. [Immanuel Kant, *Critique of Practical Reason,* ed. Mary Gregor (Cambridge: Cambridge University Press, 1997), 133; unitalicized following Fink.]
8. Instead of "primordial," TS has "primordially."
9. Instead of "one may declare as a free-thinking opinion," in TS is found "I wish to declare as a subjective opinion."
10. Instead of "It follows from this," in TS is found "I mean."
11. Matthew 26:52.
12. Friedrich Nietzsche, *Ecce Homo,* in *The Anti-Christ, Ecce Homo, Twilight of the Idols: And Other Writings,* ed. Aaron Ridley and Judith Norman, trans. Judith Norman (Cambridge: Cambridge University Press, 2005), 151.
13. "Alone" is not in TS.
14. Instead of "counts as foremost," in TS is found "is the foremost."
15. After "dead," in TS is found "Yet a relation might well prevail between them both, even if we are incapable of formulating it."
16. TS: "empires [*Reiche*]" is an emendation of "states [*Staaten*]."
17. "Often" is not found in TS.
18. *Laws* II 644d; VII 803c.
19. TS: "house" is an emendation of "thing."
20. "Yet" is not in TS.
21. After "so to speak," in TS is found "which one produces together with the manufacturing of the mask."
22. Instead of "not so much from a freer," TS has "not from."
23. From Goethe's *Lila:* "Cowardly thoughts' / Fearful wavering, / Womanish hesitancy / Anxious complaining / Turns away no misery, / Makes you not free. // (Against) all forces / To defiance maintain, / Never yielding, / Strong one's self to show, / (This) calls the arms / Of the gods to one's side." Translation found in Deborah Stein and Robert Spillman, *Poetry into Song: Performance and Analysis of Lieder* (Oxford: Oxford University Press, 2010), 271.
24. [The sense of the German *initial* in Fink's term *Initialzauber* (translated here as "initiatory enchantment") is very close to the Latin *initium* and its three senses of (1) constituent parts/elements; (2) beginning/origin; and (3) sacred rites/mysteries. In Fink's example, the medicine man pours water on (1) a *part* of the dry land, and in doing so (2) *initiates* a process that Fink characterizes as a reversal of symbolism (the symbol reflects the whole into a part), in which what happens in a part "shines back" into the whole—in pouring water on a small part of dry land the medicine man begins an enchantment that will see water pouring onto the

"whole" of the dry land. Finally, the medicine man's practice is (3) a *sacred rite*, a cultic/mythic practice, something one must first be "initiated" into.]

25. TS: "throughout" is an emendation in ink of "as."

26. Instead of "between" to "single events," in TS is found "between a somehow causal consideration of the single events and a conception of the comprehensive connection of all events, which is 'groundless' as such."

27. TS: "Breach [*Durchbrechung*]" is an emendation in ink of "breakthrough [*Durchbruch*]."

28. Instead of "Hierophantic," in TS is found "Priestly [*hieratisch*]."

29. Instead of "hierophantic," in TS is found "priestly."

30. Hebrews 10:31.

31. Friedrich Nietzsche, *Thus Spoke Zarathustra: A Book for All and None*, ed. Adrian Del Caro and Robert B. Pippin, trans. Adrian Del Caro (Cambridge: Cambridge University Press, 2006), 31.

32. Fragment 52 (in Diels/Kranz's enumeration). Cf. Charles H. Kahn, *The Art and Thought of Heraclitus: An Edition of the Fragments with Translation and Commentary*, 71: "Lifetime is a child at play, moving pieces in a game. Kingship belongs to the child."

33. "Astounding" is not in TS.

34. Instead of this sentence, TS has: "Yet we will still have to deal with the fact that kinds of play can generally, however, be included in each other in manifold ways."

35. "Precisely" is not in TS.

36. "perhaps" is not in TS.

37. TS: "derive" is an emendation of "explain."

38. "To pit this single insight, that in the Absolute everything is the same, against the full body of articulated cognition, which at least seeks and demands such fulfillment, to palm off its Absolute as the night in which, as the saying goes, all cows are black—this is cognition naïvely reduced to vacuity." Georg Wilhelm Friedrich Hegel, *Phenomenology of Spirit*, trans. A. V. Miller (Oxford: Oxford University Press, 1977), ¶16.

39. "still" is not in TS.

40. TS: "Hegel turns against" to "within his majesty" is struck out with a diagonal arrow.

41. Instead of "its own," in TS is found "a."

42. TS: After "spirit," "to the concept conceiving itself" is crossed out.

43. Instead of "is movement," in TS is found "is in movement."

44. Friedrich Hölderlin, "Germanien/Germania," trans. Michael Hamburger, in *Hyperion and Selected Poems*, ed. Eric Santer (New York: Continuum, 1990), 211.

45. Instead of "believe," in TS is found "profess."

46. Instead of "as the mouth," in TS is found "by proxy [*im Auftrage*]."

47. "more" is not in TS.

48. Instead of "worldedness [*Welthaftigkeit*]," in TS is found "world-sustaining character [*Welthaltigkeit*]."

4. The Worldliness of Human Play

1. TS: "by no means" is an emendation in ink of "not."
2. Instead of "exclude," in TS is found "disregard."
3. "adequately" is not in TS.
4. Instead of "an," in TS is found "—so we would like to believe—the complete."
5. [Greek for "mixing bowl."]
6. TS: "almost" is an interpolation in pencil.

7. TS: "still" is an interpolation in pencil.
8. Instead of "entangles [*umschlingt*]," in TS is found "oscillates around [*umschwingt*]."
9. TS: "much" is an interpolation in pencil.
10. TS: "explicit" is an emendation in pencil of "particular."
11. TS: "our love" is an emendation of "festivals."
12. Instead of "relation of belief," in TS is found "believed relation."
13. TS: "cosmic" is an emendation in pencil of "its."
14. TS: "supersensible" is an emendation in ink of "spirit."
15. [Friedrich Nietzsche, *Human, All-Too-Human: A Book for Free Spirits,* trans. Marion Faber and Stephen Lehmann (Lincoln: University of Nebraska Press, 1984), 4.]
16. TS: "is the one thing that" is an interpolation in pencil.
17. From "where" to "salvation" is not in TS.
18. D: "radically" instead of "more radically" (corrected in accordance with TS).
19. TS: "irreducibly" is an emendation of "entirely."
20. [*Berühmten Gefühl.* From Rilke's first "Duino Elegy." See *The Selected Poetry of Rainer Maria Rilke,* trans. Stephen Mitchell (New York: Vintage, 1989), 152–53.]
21. [Cf. Matthew 25:14–21.]
22. "also" is not in TS.
23. After "actual non-actuality," in TS is found "or non-actual actuality."
24. [Matthew 6:26.]
25. [In English in the original.]
26. D: "human being" is not italicized (corrected in accordance with TS).
27. TS: "theme [*Sache*]" is an emendation of "interrogation [*Fragestellung*]."
28. After "finite," in TS is found "in general."
29. Instead of "thus," in TS is found "as."
30. TS: "Because the human being {'human being' is an emendation in pencil of 'he'} is 'worldly,' he is essentially {'he is essentially' is an emendation in pencil of 'the human being is a'} player."
31. "—assuming" to "same" is an emendation in ink of "Hades and Dionysus are the same."
32. TS: "and is hostile to it" is an interpolation in ink.
33. "yet" is not in TS.
34. Instead of "conclude our course of thought," in TS is found "close the lecture course."
35. TS: "still completely unresolved problem" is an emendation in ink of "problem that has been completely left open."
36. "playfully" is italicized in TS.
37. Friedrich Nietzsche, *Thus Spoke Zarathustra,* in *The Portable Nietzsche,* trans. Walter Kaufmann (New York: Viking, 1954), 343.

Play and Celebration

1. Friedrich Schiller, *On the Aesthetic Education of Man: In a Series of Letters,* ed. and trans. Elizabeth M. Wilkinson and L. A. Willoughby (Oxford: Clarendon, 1967), Fifteenth Letter, 107: "For, to mince matters no longer, man only plays when he is in the fullest sense of the word a human being, and *he is only fully a human being when he plays.*"
2. Fragment 15 (in Diels/Kranz's enumeration). Cf. Charles H. Kahn, *The Art and Thought of Heraclitus: An Edition of the Fragments with Translation and Commentary,* 81: "If it were not

Dionysus for whom they march in procession and chant the hymn to the phallus, their action would be most shameless. But Hades and Dionysus are the same, him for whom they rave and celebrate Lenaia."

3. [Isaiah 40:31.]

4. Plato, *Phaedo,* 118a.

5. Georg Wilhelm Friedrich Hegel, *Phenomenology of Spirit,* trans. A. V. Miller (Oxford: Oxford University Press, 1977), ¶132: "In the dialectic of sense-certainty, Seeing and Hearing have been lost to consciousness. . . ."

Play and Philosophy

1. Here follow parts of a text that Fink took from his lecture course *Grundphänomene des menschlichen Daseins;* cf. the description in appendix 1.
2. "higher" is an interpolation in ballpoint.
3. "exists [*besteht*]" is an emendation in ballpoint of "is."
4. "in which" to "lies" is an interpolation in ballpoint.

The World-Significance of Play

1. "to which" to "justice" is an interpolation in ink.
2. "simple" is an interpolation in ink.
3. Friedrich Schiller, *On the Aesthetic Education of Man: In a Series of Letters,* ed. and trans. Elizabeth M. Wilkinson and L. A. Willoughby (Oxford: Clarendon, 1967), Fifteenth Letter, 107: "For, to mince matters no longer, man only plays when he is in the fullest sense of the word a human being, and *he is only fully a human being when he plays.*"
4. After "serious tasks," "and duties" is crossed out in ink.
5. "today" is an interpolation in ink.
6. "for long" is an interpolation in ink.
7. "abundant" " is an interpolation in ink.
8. "scarcely" is an emendation in ink of "never."
9. "spontaneously" is an interpolation in ink.
10. "generally" is an interpolation in ink.
11. "from the illusory ones" is an interpolation in ink.
12. "blazing" is an interpolation in ink.
13. [Shakespeare, *The Tempest,* act 4, scene 1.]
14. "one says" is an interpolation in pencil.
15. Marked in the margin and provided with a cross.
16. This paragraph, beginning with "The world-significance" and ending with "Being and the world," is found on a separate page. It was inserted here according to the arrangement provided in the transcript of the Südwestfunk.
17. Georg Wilhelm Friedrich Hegel, "Introduction for the *Critical Journal of Philosophy:* On the Essence of Philosophical Criticism Generally, and Its Relationship to the Present State of Philosophy in Particular," trans. H. S. Harris, in *Miscellaneous Writings of G.W.F. Hegel,* ed. Jon Stewart (Evanston, IL: Northwestern University Press, 2002), 217.
18. Before "life phenomenon," "modern" is crossed out in ink.
19. "obscured" is an emendation in ink of "put into the shadows."

20. [Georg Wilhelm Friedrich Hegel, *Phenomenology of Spirit*, trans. A. V. Miller (Oxford: Oxford University Press, 1977), ¶132: "In the dialectic of sense-certainty, Seeing and Hearing have been lost to consciousness. . . ."]

21. "only" is an interpolation in ink.

22. "primarily" is an interpolation in ink.

23. Heraclitus Fragment 52 (in Diels/Kranz's enumeration). Cf. Charles H. Kahn, *The Art and Thought of Heraclitus: An Edition of the Fragments with Translation and Commentary*, 71: "Lifetime is a child at play, moving pieces in a game. Kingship belongs to the child."

24. "the olive wreath" is an emendation in pencil of "laurel."

The Philosophical-Pedagogical Problem of Play

1. Cf. Ovid, *Metamorphoses*, 3136–37. [As the reference to the universal human striving for happiness makes clear, Fink has in mind the passage in Aristotle's *Nicomachean Ethics* I.10, 1100a10–11, with its Herodotean antecedent in the famous story of Solon and Croesus (*Hist.* I.32), of which the Ovid passage is a later echo.]

2. In MS: "like a memory {. . .} can make one glad."

3. [See Schiller's *An die Freude* ("Ode to Joy").]

4. "Faust" is an emendation of "Hamlet."

5. Friedrich Schiller, *On the Aesthetic Education of Man: In a Series of Letters*, ed. and trans. Elizabeth M. Wilkinson and L. A. Willoughby (Oxford: Clarendon, 1967), Fifteenth Letter, 107: "For, to mince matters no longer, man only plays when he is in the fullest sense of the word a human being, and *he is only fully a human being when he plays.*"

6. Friedrich Nietzsche, *Ecce Homo*, in *The Anti-Christ, Ecce Homo, Twilight of the Idols: And Other Writings*, ed. Aaron Ridley and Judith Norman, trans. Judith Norman (Cambridge: Cambridge University Press, 2005), 99.

7. Georg Wilhelm Friedrich Hegel, "Introduction for the *Critical Journal of Philosophy:* On the Essence of Philosophical Criticism Generally, and Its Relationship to the Present State of Philosophy in Particular," trans. H. S. Harris, in *Miscellaneous Writings of G.W.F. Hegel*, ed. Jon Stewart (Evanston, IL: Northwestern University Press, 2002), 217: "although we must not mistake this passion for change and novelty for the indifference of play which, in its extreme insouciance, is at the same time the most exalted and only true seriousness."

8. "Questions" to "and so forth" is an addition in pencil.

9. "Priority" to "play" is an addition.

10. Fragment 52 (in Diels/Kranz's enumeration). Cf. Charles H. Kahn, *The Art and Thought of Heraclitus: An Edition of the Fragments with Translation and Commentary* (Cambridge: Cambridge University Press, 1979), 71: "Lifetime is a child at play, moving pieces in a game. Kingship belongs to the child."

11. Between square brackets and crossed out: "Play of individuation?!! Symbolism of the dramatic play or spectacle (of tragedy)."

12. [In full, aphorism 150 from Nietzsche's *Beyond Good and Evil* reads: "Around the hero everything turns into a tragedy; around the demi-god, into a satyr play; and around God—what? perhaps into 'world'?—" Trans. Walter Kaufmann (New York: Vintage, 1989).]

13. "Pedagogy" to "depth" is an interpolation.

14. *Uncollected Poems: Rainer Maria Rilke*, trans. Edward Snow (New York: North Point, 1966), 139.

15. "festival—celebration—cult" is an interpolation.

16. "with rules" is an interpolation.

17. Friedrich Wilhelm August Fröbel (1782–1852) was a German pedagogue and student of Pestalozzi.

18. [Fröbel's works on *Spielgaben* are available in Friedrich Fröbel, *Ausgewählte Schriften,* vol. 4: *Die Spielgaben,* ed. Erika Hoffmann (Stuttgart: Klett-Cotta, 1982).]

19. Cf. Fröbel, "Vorschulerziehung und Spieltheorie."

20. [Referred to by Fink in German as *David spielt vor Saul* or "David Plays for Saul."]

21. *The Selected Poetry of Rainer Maria Rilke,* ed. and trans. Stephen Mitchell (New York: Vintage, 1989), 171–73.

Notes on "Play and Philosophy"

1. [Georg Wilhelm Friedrich Hegel, *Science of Logic,* trans. George di Giovanni (Cambridge: Cambridge University Press, 2010), 418.]

2. "like a sword" is crossed out.

3. [Fink's lecture-course has not yet been published in German, though it is planned for the fourth division of his *Gesamtausgabe.*]

4. "for" is crossed out.

Notes on "The World-Significance of Play"

1. After "religion," "eroticism" is crossed out.

2. "1" through "6" are marked in the margin.

3. After "world" there is a horizontal line over the entire page.

4. The last three lines are marked in the left and right margins.

5. After "3" there are horizontal lines.

6. "I" to "II, 3" is marked in the margin.

7. "2" and "3" are marked in the margin.

8. [Friedrich Nietzsche, *Thus Spoke Zarathustra,* trans. R. J. Hollingdale (London: Penguin, 1969), 234: "'O Zarathustra,' said the animals then, 'all things themselves dance for such as think as we: they come and offer their hand and laugh and flee—and return."]

9. After "imagination," the following is crossed out: "-construct and concrete real things. 8. Image of imitation, appearance of imitation [*Nachahmungsbild, Imitationsschein*]?—role-playing—competitive play. 9. Aspects and themes."

10. After "body," there is a horizontal line across the whole page.

11. "General characteristics" to "play" is in the margin.

12. "The *turn*" to "perception" is marked in the margin.

13. [The brackets here are Fink's.]

14. In MS: "understanding of Being, which."

15. Before "Play," the following is crossed out: "Re (1) Human play—once a seldom manifestation in the serious, obscure landscape of life, pressed to the margin, denied, assigned to children as their activity before harsh struggle begins—is *known* [erkannt] in its powerfulness and *recognized* [anerkannt] as a legitimate, fully valid behavior. The *anthropological* rank = no longer contested by cultural critics and behavioral scientists—a significant phenomenon in the human being's carrying out of life."

16. The note is marked in the margin.

17. The entire note is marked in the margin.

18. "Magical production" to "actuality" is marked in the margin. After "actuality," the following is crossed out: "With some practice, we distinguish between the playworld and the actual world, in which playing as an imaginary [*phantastisches*] activity appears, between the player and his role, between his body and the prop, between the man and the costume."—after which there is a horizontal line across the whole page.

19. "But" to "sense-aspect" is partly crossed out.

20. Provided in the margin and after which there is a horizontal line across the whole page.

21. "Place" to "riddle" is marked in the margin.

22. This note is marked in the margin.

23. MS: "a thematic" instead of "to a thematic."

24. Crossed out: "the passage written in ink an interpretation of the activity through the categories of play??"—after which there is a horizontal line across the whole page.

German Editors' Afterword

1. It appeared for the second time in Eugen Fink, *Studien zur Phänomenologie 1930–1939* (*Phaenomenologica*, vol. 21) (The Hague: Springer, 1966), 1–78. This study will be published in Volume 1 of the *Eugen Fink Gesamtausgabe* (henceforth EFGA).

2. "Vergegenwärtigung und Bild," in Fink, *Studien zur Phänomenologie* 72.

3. Ibid., 76.

4. Ibid., 71.

5. The edition of these various notes is arranged within the EFGA in four volumes under the title *Phänomenologische Werkstatt* (EFGA 3.1–4), of which the first two appeared in 2006 and 2008. [The third should appear in 2016. We thank Ronald Bruzina for this update, as well as for providing more specific information about his edition and about notes 50 and 51.]

6. *Phänomenologische Werkstatt: Die Doktorarbeit und erste Assistenzjahre bei Husserl* (EFGA 3.1), ed. Ronald Bruzina (Freiburg: Alber, 2006), 117–18.

7. *Phänomenologische Werkstatt: Die Bernauer Zeitmanuskripte, Cartesianische Meditationen und System der phänomenologischen Philosophie* (EFGA 3.2), ed. Ronald Bruzina (Freiburg: Alber, 2006), 118.

8. Ibid., 376.

9. Ibid., 440 (Loose sheets [1968/1969]).

10. Cf. Ronald Bruzina, *Edmund Husserl and Eugen Fink: Beginnings and Ends in Phenomenology 1928–1938* (New Haven, CT: Yale University Press, 2004), 136.

11. Cf. EFGA 3.3 (Text OH VII—forthcoming).

12. This text will be published in EFGA 15, which will contain Fink's works on Nietzsche. A preprint of this early study can be found in Cathrin Nielsen and Hans Rainer Sepp, eds., *Welt Denken: Annäherungen an die Kosmologie Eugen Finks* (Freiburg: Alber, 2011): 25–37.

13. First edited under this title in 1977 by E. Schütz and F.-A. Schwarz. [Eugen Fink, *Grundphänomene des menschlichen Daseins*, ed. Egon Schütz and Franz-Anton Schwarz (Freiburg: Alber, 1979).] The edition of this lecture course within the EFGA is planned for Volume 8.

14. See pp. 14–31.

15. See pp. 33–215.

16. See pp. 253–72.

17. Cf. *Grundphänomene*, 358, and "Oasis of Happiness," 16–17.

18. See pp. 229–33.

19. *Grundphänomene,* 361, and "Oasis of Happiness," 19.
20. *Grundphänomene,* 374.
21. "Oasis of Happiness," 20; cf. *Play as Symbol of the World,* 86–87.
22. "Oasis of Happiness," 21.
23. Ibid., 18.
24. *Play as Symbol of the World,* 119.
25. "Oasis of Happiness," 29.
26. Ibid., 28; cf. *Play as Symbol of the World,* 87–88.
27. "Oasis of Happiness," 29.
28. Cf. ibid.
29. *Grundphänomene,* 406.
30. Ibid.
31. *Play as Symbol of the World,* 207–8.
32. Cf. ibid., 47–48.
33. Ibid., 205.
34. "Oasis of Happiness," 30.
35. EFGA 3.2, p. 253.
36. *Play as Symbol of the World,* 61. [*Durchmachten* can also mean "thoroughly gives power to."]
37. Ibid., 121.
38. Ibid., 123.
39. Ibid.
40. Ibid., 208.
41. Cf. ibid., 76–77.
42. Eugen Fink, "Bewußtseinsanalytik und Weltproblem" (1968), in idem, *Nähe und Distanz: Phänomenologische Vorträge und Aufsätze,* ed. Franz-Anton Schwarz (Freiburg: Alber, 1976), 280–98; here p. 294. [A new edition is forthcoming in EFGA 1 as *Nähe und Distanz. Studien zur Phänomenologie,* ed. Hans Rainer Sepp (Freiburg: Alber).]
43. *Play as Symbol of the World,* 215. The conclusion of Fink's *Welt und Endlichkeit* [World and finitude] contains the approach to a speculative-cosmological theory of the world. Cf. Eugen Fink, *Welt und Endlichkeit,* ed. Franz-Anton Schwarz (Würzburg: Königshausen & Neumann, 1990), chaps. 22 and 23.
44. *Play as Symbol of the World,* 215.
45. Cf. ibid., 212–13.
46. Cf. ibid., 214.
47. Cf. ibid., 206.
48. *Play as Symbol of the World,* 213.
49. Ibid., 207.
50. EFGA 3.3, OH-V/27, p. 411.
51. Ibid., OH-V/47, p. 416.
52. This still unpublished lecture course will appear in EFGA 5.2.
53. Friedrich Nietzsche, *Thus Spoke Zarathustra: A Book for All and None,* ed. Adrian del Caro and Robert B. Pippin, trans. Adrian del Caro (Cambridge: Cambridge University Press, 2006), 17 ("On the Three Metamorphoses").
54. Note within the ambit of the text "The World-Significance of Play" (1973), 291.
55. [Trans. as Fragment XCIV by Charles H. Kahn, *The Art and Thought of Heraclitus: An Edition of the Fragments with Translation and Commentary* (Cambridge: Cambridge University Press, 1979), 71.]

56. Cf. Eugen Fink, *Nietzsche's Philosophy,* trans. Goetz Richter (London: Continuum, 2003), 31–33; "Oasis of Happiness," 30; *Play as Symbol of the World,* 52.

57. "If it were not Dionysus for whom they march in procession and chant the hymn to the phallus, their action would be most shameless. But Hades and Dionysus are the same, him for whom they rave and celebrate Lenaia." Diels/Kranz Fragment 15. Translated as Fragment CXVI in Kahn, *The Art and Thought of Heraclitus,* 81; cf. *Play as Symbol of the World,* 77 and 215.

58. Eugen Fink, *Metaphysik der Erziehung im Weltverhältnis von Platon und Aristoteles* (Frankfurt am Main: Klostermann, 1970), 112–13.

59. *Play as Symbol of the World,* 214–15. Cf. Eugen Fink, *Grundfragen der antiken Philosophie,* ed. Franz-Anton Schwarz (Würzburg: Königshausen & Neumann, 1985), 130ff.

60. *Play as Symbol of the World,* 215.

61. Ibid., 208.

62. Ibid.

63. Fink held this lecture course for the first time in 1952/53 under the title *Grundprobleme der menschlichen Gemeinschaft* [Basic problems of human community]; he repeated it in an altered and expanded form in Winter Semester 1968/69 under the title *Existenz und Coexistenz:* First published as *Existenz und Coexistenz. Grundprobleme der menschlichen Gemeinschaft,* ed. Franz-Anton Schwarz (Würzburg: Königshausen & Neumann, 1987).

64. Cf. ibid., chap. 12.

65. Eugen Fink, *Natur, Freiheit, Welt: Philosophie der Erziehung,* ed. Franz-Anton Schwarz (Würzburg: Königshausen & Neumann, 1992), 193.

66. Eugen Fink, *Grundfragen der systematischen Pädagogik,* ed. Egon Schütz and Franz-Anton Schwarz (Freiburg: Rombach, 1978), 180.

67. Ibid., 184.

68. Ibid., 179.

69. Ibid., 180.

70. Eugen Fink, *Mode . . . ein verführerisches Spiel* (Basel: Birkhäuser, 1969) (to be published as EFGA 11); idem, *Epiloge zur Dichtung* (Frankfurt am Main: Klostermann, 1971) (scheduled to be published in EFGA 10).

71. See pp. 216–24, 253–78.

72. See pp. 234–48.

73. Eugen Fink, "Phänomenologische Probleme der Verfremdung" (1967), in *Nähe und Distanz,* 250–67; Martin Heidegger and Eugen Fink, *Heraclitus Seminar,* trans. Charles H. Seibert (Evanston, IL: Northwestern University Press, 1993), 146–49; Fink, *Existenz und Coexistenz,* 157.

74. "The World-Significance of Play," 245.

75. "Play and Sport" (1962), 275–78; here p. 276.

76. "Sport Seminar on February 24, 1961"; see pp. 273–74.

77. Ibid., 274.

78. "Play and Sport," 275–78; here p. 276.

79. "Play and Celebration" (1975), 216–24; here p. 224.

80. Eugen Fink, "Maske und Kothurn," in *Epiloge zur Dichtung,* 1–18; quote on p. 3. Cf. the notes on "Play and Sport," 277: "Mask: Relation to Possibilities"; "Play and Philosophy" (1966), 279–82; "The Philosophical-Pedagogical Problem of Play," 257–58.

81. *Play as Symbol of the World,* 150.

82. *Mode,* 25–26.

83. Ibid., 50.

84. Ibid., 77.
85. Ibid., 101.
86. *Play as Symbol of the World*, 215.
87. "Maske und Kothurn," 17.

Bibliography of Fink's Works Available in English

1. For a bibliography of Fink's works in German, see "Bibliographie: Eugen Fink," in *Eugen Fink: Sozialphilosophie-Anthropologie-Kosmologie-Pädagogik-Methodik*, ed. Anselm Böhmer (Würzburg: Königshausen & Neumann, 2006), 277–85; as well as Friedrich-Wilhelm von Herrmann, *Bibliographie Eugen Fink* (The Hague: Nijhoff, 1970). The latter also includes secondary literature on Fink. For more secondary literature, see the entries under the section "Rezeptionsberichte" in Böhmer, ed., *Eugen Fink: Sozialphilosophie-Anthropologie-Kosmologie-Pädagogik-Methodik*, 294–349.

Name Index

Eugen Fink (1905–1975) was a student and colleague of Edmund Husserl and Martin Heidegger. *Spiel als Weltsymbol* was published in 1960. This is the first English translation of his work.

Ian Alexander Moore is a Ph.D. candidate in philosophy at DePaul University and associate editor of *Philosophy Today*. With Alan D. Schrift, he is the editor of *Transcendence and the Concrete: Selected Writings of Jean Wahl* (Fordham University Press, forthcoming).

Christopher Turner recently earned his Ph.D. in philosophy from DePaul. In addition to Fink's *Play as Symbol of the World,* Moore and Turner have also translated Peter Trawny's *Freedom to Fail: Heidegger's Anarchy* (Polity, 2015) and Peter Sloterdijk's *Not Saved: Essays after Heidegger* (Polity, forthcoming).

www.ingramcontent.com/pod-product-compliance
Lightning Source LLC
LaVergne TN
LVHW040201080826
844660LV00001B/64
* 9 7 8 0 2 5 3 0 2 1 0 5 2 *